A ROYAL AFFAIR

Stella Tillyard's award-winning *Aristocrats*, which started the vogue for eighteenth-century women's lives, was followed by *Citizen Lord*, her biography of the Irish rebel Edward Fitzgerald. She is Senior Research Fellow at the Centre for Editing Lives and Letters, Queen Mary, London, writes regularly for the *Sunday Times* and *Prospect* and is a frequent contributor to Radio 4. She lives in Oxford.

ALSO BY STELLA TILLYARD

The Impact of Modernism

Aristocrats: Caroline, Emily, Louisa and
Sarah Lennox 1740–1832

Citizen Lord: Edward Fitzgerald 1763–1798

STELLA TILLYARD

A Royal Affair

George III and his
Troublesome Siblings

VINTAGE BOOKS
London

Published by Vintage 2007

2 4 6 8 10 9 7 5 3 1

Copyright © Stella Tillyard 2006

Stella Tillyard has asserted her right under the Copyright,
Designs and Patents Act, 1988 to be identified as the author
of this work

First published in Great Britain in 2006 by
Chatto & Windus

Vintage
Random House, 20 Vauxhall Bridge Road,
London SW1V 2SA

www.randomhouse.co.uk

Addresses for companies within The Random House Group Limited
can be found at: www.randomhouse.co.uk/offices.htm

The Random House Group Limited Reg. No. 954009

A CIP catalogue record for this book
is available from the British Library

ISBN 9780099428565

The Random House Group Limited makes every effort to
ensure that the papers used in its books are made from
trees that have been legally sourced from well-managed
and credibly certified forests. Our paper procurement policy
can be found at: www.randomhouse.co.uk/paper.htm

Printed and bound in Great Britain by
Cox & Wyman Limited, Reading, Berkshire

Contents

List of Illustrations

Prince William, Duke of Gloucester, Pompeo Girolamo Batoni, 1772 (Private Collection: Bridgeman)

Maria Walpole, Duchess of Gloucester, by Purcell after Sir Joshua Reynolds (National Portrait Gallery, London)

George III in his Coronation Robes, 1760, Allan Ramsay (Guildhall Art Gallery, Corporation of London)

Plate section 2

Dronning Caroline Mathilde, engraving after a pastel by Francis Cotes, 1766 (Nationalhistoriske Museum, Hillerod)

Christansborg (Det Kongelige Bibliotek, Copenhagen)

Caroline Mathilde in her regimental uniform, Peder Als, 1770 (Graf Rantzau, Gut Rastorf, Germany)

Christian VII, by Jens Juel, 1771 (Bomann-Museum, Celle, Germany)

Struensee, Jens Juel, 1771 (Bomann-Museum, Celle, Germany)

Caroline Mathilde, Jens Juel, 1771 (Bomann-Museum, Celle, Germany)

Voltaire, *Epitre à sa majesté le Roi de Dannemark*, 1771 (Dan Andersen)

Caroline Mathilde with Crown Prince Frederik, watercolour sketch by Peder Als, 1771. (Statens Museum for Kunst, Copenhagen)

Kronborg (Det Kongelige Bibliotek, Copenhagen)

'sentiments strompfenbänder' – Caroline Mathilde's garters, 1770 (Rosenborg Slot, Copenhagen)

The execution of Struensee and Brandt, 1772 (Det Kongelige Bibliotek, Copenhagen)

Princess Louise Augusta, Jens Juel, 1785. (Bomann-Museum, Celle, Germany)

George III, c.1775 by unknown artist. (Bomann-Museum, Celle, Germany)

To Nick Cavanagh and Claire L'Enfant;
a doctor and his queen.

Acknowledgements

My first thanks must go to my Danish teacher, Anna Grete Olesen, under whose enthusiastic guidance I advanced through the intricacies of her ferociously difficult language in weekly increments until I had learned at least enough to read slowly through printed texts and open the door to her happy country a tiny crack. In Copenhagen Niklas Jensen and Dan Andersen pushed it wider and supplied me with books, articles and transcripts that I hope gave me enough knowledge to tell the story of Caroline Mathilde and Johann Struensee from this side of the North Sea, looking out from Britain. Without Dan's patient reading of the manuscript I would have let stand a few misunderstandings of the chronology and import of crucial events between 1770 and 1772; so any mistakes I have made with so famous and notorious an episode in Danish history are very much my own. Niklas Jensen introduced me to Jakob Seerup who showed me the beautiful scale models of eighteenth-century Copenhagen and its warships in the Naval Museum, and to Asser Amdisen, whose knowledge of Johann Struensee puts mine to shame.

From Funen, Ivan Hill helped with names, titles and biographical details, and put me in touch with Denmark's Historiographer Royal, Knut Jespersen, whose new history of Denmark gave me valuable insights into the country's long history. In Ebeltoft, another immigrant and Danophile, my old friend Sally Laird, cheerfully shared her understanding of modern Denmark with me. She also introduced me to Kjeld Vierup, whose own researches into Caroline Mathilde made me understand the way in which, in her lifetime and for centuries afterwards, she has held such mysterious and mythic power in her adopted country.

In Germany, Britain and the United States, many other friends and colleagues were patient and generous with their time and knowledge. First thanks to Holger Hoock, whose wrestlings with German gothic uncovered much material that helped my understanding of Caroline Mathilde's later life. Apologies that so much of his work in the Hannoverian archive is more under the surface of my story than on top. I am very grateful also to Mattias Hattendorf, Lawrence Brockliss, Marius Kwint, Simon Schaffer, Patricia Fara, Angela Rosenthal, Nicholas Phillipson, Maggie Powell and Roy Ritchie, whose knowledge and advice were at different times invaluable. Special thanks are due to my supportive friends Valeria Frighi, Jamie McKendrick, Xon de Ros, Peter Mandler, Juliet Gardiner, Deborah Colvin, David Crane, Honor Clerk, Romilly Saumarez-Smith, Dorothy Porter and Simon Schama, and to John Brewer for living through my black moods. Without the support and advice of my agent Gill Coleridge and my editor Jenny Uglow this book could never have been written; to both, and to my publisher Alison Samuel, and her staff at Random House, my heartfelt gratitude.

Finally I gratefully acknowledge the permission of Her Majesty Queen Elizabeth II to publish material from the Royal Archives, and of Prince Ernst August of Hannover for permission to publish material from the Königliches Hausarchiv, Niedersächsisches Hauptstaatsarchiv, Hannover. I would also like to thank the staff of the following museums and libraries: The Bomann-Museum, Celle; Frederiksborg Museum, Hillerød; the Paul Mellon Centre for British Art; the National Portrait Gallery; the Yale Centre for British Art; The Bodleian Library; the British Library; the London Library, the National Archives of Scotland, Edinburgh; The National Archives, Kew; the Royal Archives, Windsor; the Kongehusarkivet, the Royal Library, Copenhagen; the Niedersächsisches Hauptstaatsarchiv, Hannover; the Huntington Library, San Marino, California and the Lewis Walpole Library, Yale University. For permission to reproduce illustrative material I am most grateful to the individuals and institutions credited in the list of illustrations.

Northern Germany and Denmark
in the later eighteenth century

0 10 20 30 40 500 miles
0   25   50   75 km

The Skaw · Göteborg

Aalborg

K I N G D O M   O F   S W E D E N

Kattegat

NORTH

K I N G D O M

O F Aarhus

JUTLAND

The Sound

Kronborg
·Elsinore
Hillerød·

·Hørsholm

Copenhagen·
Røskilde·

SEA

D E N M A R K

FUNEN

ZEELAND

Malmö

LANGELAND

*Baltic
Sea*

Sylt·

North
Frisian
Islands

DUCHY OF
SCHLESWIG

LOLLAND

MON

FALSTER

FEHMARN

RÜGEN

*SWEDISH
POMERANIA*

DUCHY OF
HOLSTEIN

Lübeck·

DUCHIES OF
MECKLENBURG

Stade·

Altona
·
Hamburg·

Lüneborg·

R. Elbe

OLDENBURG

ELECTORATE
OF HANOVER

·Celle

BISHOPRIC

R. Weser

Hanover·

E L E C T O R A T E
OF BRANDENBURG

OF

·Brunswick

MÜNSTER

R. Ems

Wolfenbüttel·

Introduction

'I have no other hope, I repeat it again, but in your friendship for me, and am persuaded that with the principles you have you will never abandon so near a relation, and one who is so sincerely attached to you, as is your most affectionate sister, Caroline M.' Thus, at the end of 1774, in a desperate moment, wrote Caroline Mathilde, Queen of Denmark, to her brother George III of Great Britain. Her emotional appeal to George III as her brother and as head of her family was necessarily political as well as personal, and laid bare a complex dilemma at the heart of all constitutional monarchies. The King was both the head of a state and a private man, but nowhere was the dividing line explicitly drawn between his private life and his public one. What rights, for instance, did the monarch have by virtue of his public position to defend his private honour? To what extent, too, was the royal family not a private entity at all, but an extension of the state, living out defined roles within it? How far might Parliament's reach extend into the family now that it paid for its upkeep, and need there be any control of what the press could investigate, speculate upon and report?

All through the eighteenth century the exact relationships between the monarch's private life, his public duties and his particular powers or prerogatives were a matter for heated debate and continual testing both in and out of Parliament. In the first twenty years of the reign of George III these issues dominated public life because the King himself seemed, especially to newly confident journalists and the opposition in Parliament, to be trying to push the boundaries of his powers outwards as forcefully as they were trying to squeeze them in. In the contest between the King, the press, Parliament and an eager audience of readers who had woken up to the scandal and entertainment in stories about the private lives of famous individuals, the King's brothers and sisters were swept up in the political drama and dragged into the public gaze. Putting their lives back into the story of the first twenty years of George III's reign allows us to understand and explain in a new way the King's reactions to the series of political upheavals that culminated in the traumatic loss of the American colonies at the end of the American War of Independence in 1783.

It was not often in Britain, after the establishment of the constitutional monarchy, that the private life and character of the monarch could influence public affairs. But in the long reign of George III it did, and when it did it was almost always because the King's notion of his duty as the head of his family extended into affairs of state which Parliament watched with a jealous eye. The Royal Marriage Act of 1772, whose consequences continue to bedevil Britain in the twenty-first century, was drafted under the King's personal supervision and pushed by his ministers through a reluctant Parliament when he had failed to control his errant brothers' behaviour. More importantly, George III thought of the American war as the rebellion of ungrateful children against their father, and it was undoubtedly prolonged by his desperate desire to preserve what he saw as his family entire and together.

Although they were public figures, George III's siblings were private individuals too, even if for those brought up in courts the boundaries between public and private were porous and one seeped constantly into the other. But George's brothers and sisters came to maturity at a time when domestic life was becoming fashionable and marriages arranged solely for dynastic reasons were becoming less commonplace among the aristocracy in which they moved. Royal marriages, though, were still diplomatic and dynastic contracts, so George's siblings Edward, William and Henry, and Augusta and Caroline Mathilde were among the first European princes and princesses who demanded, and struggled to find, married lives in which affection and love could find a place.

George III's two sisters, Augusta and Caroline Mathilde, were parcelled off as consorts for Europe's Protestant rulers, and were almost bound to be unhappy. His brothers Edward, William and Henry, allowed to stay at home but with no public roles allotted to them, were destined for idle lives and loveless unions with the daughters of allied monarchs. None submitted quietly, and this book tells the stories of their attempts, for better or for worse, to forge their own lives, and of the public consequences of their behaviour. Despite the crevasse of understanding and time that separates us from them, love, anger, joy and betrayal can leap across those barriers raw and unchanged, and I have tried to recapture and retell them.

George III was always bitterly angry when his role as father figure to his siblings was flouted, which may explain why much of the written material that could touch upon such failures has not survived. Windsor Castle, where his archive is stored, is a very incomplete repository of his private life. Pruning began in his lifetime and may have continued after his death. Much material about his siblings is lost and much of what remains is stored in far-flung collections over which the King could have no control. Much, too, is written in French or in Danish and German whose Gothic scripts defy the most persistent of researchers. This was especially true in the case of George's youngest sister Caroline Mathilde, whose tumultuous and angry life forms the centre of this book. Years before she died almost everything compromising about her had vanished from the archives, and only thirty-seven of her letters, together with some copied correspondence from spies, remain at Windsor.

George's brothers were poor letter writers and left no independent collections. Most of the material for their lives comes from the letters and diaries of those who knew them, and from the newspapers whose greedy editors gathered everything they could find about the royal family and published it with almost complete impunity. Almost everyone with access to the newspapers must have read or listened to Prince Henry's letters to his mistress when he was sued for 'criminal conversation' in 1770, and reports of the case and evidence from all sides were reported and reprinted everywhere. Prince Edward's activities are recorded in the memoirs of his friends, the gossip of associates and most of all in the letters and journals of the woman who believed herself to be his wife. Besides what remains in The Royal Archives at Windsor in letters between the King and his brothers, and the National Archives at Kew, where the reports of hapless diplomats who had to entertain the wandering princes are stored, collections in Scotland and in the United States hold caches of invaluable material.

So it was in foreign collections that I began my search; first stop Hannover in northern Germany. Hannover – or Hanover as it was known in the eighteenth century and as I have kept it throughout this book – was both the birthplace and the site of remembered tranquillity for the monarchs who came to Britain when the Act of Settlement came into force in 1714. George III never himself went further from British shores than the waves of Weymouth and the occasional admiral's cutter took him, but he and his brothers and sisters must have been told about Hanover by their father Prince Frederick who had grown up there. When, broken in spirit by conflict at home and abroad, George planned a dramatic abdication in 1783, it was to Hanover, 'the original patrimony of my ancestors', as he called it, that he planned to retire.

To the first British Hanoverian, George I, the Electorate was home, his new kingdom its polar opposite. Where, in his Electorate, there was order and regularity, in London there was murky chaos; where in Hanover everything appeared at least to run for his benefit, at St James's Palace he was quickly made to feel that he was the instrument of a wider plan. 'The first morning after my arrival at St James's', he said, 'I looked out of my window and saw a park with walls and a canal which they told me was mine. The next day, Lord Chetwynd, manager of my park, sent me a fine brace of carp out of my canal, and I was told I must give five pounds to Lord Chetwynd's servant for bringing me my own carp out of my own canal in my own park.' Everything in Britain, from the crown to the palaces and the money in his pocket, seemed to be conditional. No wonder, then, that the Elector was determined that he would try to go home as often and for as long as he possibly could. He belonged to Britain, but Hanover, just as surely, belonged to him.

Hanover, in the eighteenth century, as now in its newer clothes as the Lände of Lower Saxony, was a low-lying, sober slice of land, sloping down northwards to the Baltic and the North Sea in green waves of heath and pasture and bulging up to the south in the ore-rich Hartz mountains. It was pressed in upon to the east by the muscular power of Prussia and nudged to the west by the softer neighbourliness of the small state of Munster. The Electorate was a place of large Lutheran churches and thickset half-timbered houses, tall in the towns, two- or three-storeyed in the villages, their fronts patterned by rows of cruciform windows and announcing their dates of construction and their owners' names in bold black across white stucco under the eaves. Their occupants – farmers, brewers, tanners, craftsmen, small-time officials – had a reputation in the region for loyalty, stolidity and stubborn reserve. Every village had its pastor and its schoolmaster and almost every man and woman could read and write. Many, one way or another, worked for the Elector.

The capital was also a company town. With an income in Hanover of £700,000 a year, Georg Ludwig was much richer as Elector than as King of Great Britain. He was also in the satisfactory position of being much the wealthiest man in his kingdom and of having most of his nobility working for him as court officials. They had, indeed, fine houses clustered round the Leineschloss in town, and wide timber-framed palladian villas dotted through the green meadows near the summer palace of Herrenhausen. But none had the means to rival the Elector. And if the officials in the four executive councils that ran the state took much of the executive burden and some of the power away from him, Georg Ludwig retained and enjoyed the pomp and the trappings. He had his own standing army, twenty thousand strong, shouldering muskets made from local Herzberg iron; he had his estates, forests and hunting lodges, music, ceremony and women. Although Hanover had an executive that functioned independently, a civil service with its own source of funds, patterns of promotion and rewards for excellence, the relationship between the Elector, his court servants and his people seemed simply and satisfyingly hierarchical.

It was above all at Herrenhausen, so much grander than the dark medieval spaces of St James's, that Georg Ludwig insisted that court life be maintained. Mindful of his own pleasures when he returned for summer visits, and convinced of the importance of maintaining for his subjects the illusion of his presence, he continued to pour money into the sumptuous house and especially into its great garden, where the ordinary people of Hanover took the air on Sundays and saw their prosperity reflected, with their images, in its shallow lakes.

In sinuous vegetable calligraphy, in verdant sentences punctuated by statues and fountains, the Grosser Garten wrote for the Elector and many of his subjects a story of the world as he liked it to be. Dull flat land reclaimed from the water meadows behind the palace had been transformed by his mother and her gardeners into a great painted parade ground, its blocks of squares and oblongs intersected by paths, joined by water and bounded by a glassy drainage canal. Box and linden, expertly clipped at top and sides, lined each division, and led the eye and the visitor to the garden's focal point, the Great Fountain, where underground machinery threw a powerful cannonade of bubbling water thirty-five metres into the sky. Rising high above the palace and the trees, the white column, massive and solid-looking, challenged the empyrean and invited as much wonder as the most powerful ruler could wish. In its company and all around it in the garden subservient fountains played, rising and falling in synchronised and obedient symmetry.

Order, precision and contained caprice: that was how the Elector liked it and how his son George II liked it too on his frequent long visits home. Each Hanoverian monarch took something out of Hanover along with a sense of identity, place and connectedness to the great web of northern Protestant royal families that stretched along the North Sea and right round the Baltic to the edge of Russia. George I took civil servants; George II took his mistresses and musicians. Prince Frederick took the money of Hanover's richest citizens to supplement his inadequate annual allowance, and George III took troops and the services of the Hanoverian Minister in London when he conducted negotiations he wanted to hide from Parliament. All but the last grew up there and left in its archive exhaustive records of their life in its court.

Determined to miss nothing important about George III's parents Prince Frederick and Princess Augusta of Saxe-Gotha, who came from the neighbouring duchy of Weimar to the south, my researcher and I had trawled carefully through the archive's catalogue and ordered everything we thought might be relevant. At Windsor, the documents about George III's parents fill a few slender files; in Hanover we found something different. The first morning there, coming into the cool from the blanket-like heat of August on the north German plain, we were conducted into the reading room by a pained and solemn archivist. There in one corner, was our request, looking like the crowded hinterland of a container port. Metal boxes stood one on top of the other in a great wall, too many to be tackled, too high to be reached. Across the faces of other researchers, as we passed, flitted expressions that mixed polite astonishment with just a hint of disdain.

The Hanoverian archive is beautiful in its thoroughness, in its sense of life ordered and contained, filed and written down. Every court employee in Hanover had his employment logged, salary recorded, pension paid and tabulated, his life made out for posterity in letters and numbers. No detail of royal life was too small to order, document and file. Every time George II travelled through his Electorate, uniformed and tasselled trumpeters stood tall on the verges, cleared the roads and sped him on his way. In the archives, in hundreds of single sheets, are their instructions for each journey, telling them where to station themselves and when to expect the Elector. When his son Prince Frederick was inoculated for smallpox in 1724, his English doctor wrote a daily report on his condition, recording the Prince's mood and temperature and the number of his spots. Every one is there, filed, boxed, awaiting its historian. Later, when Frederick's father was searching for a bride for him, his envoy von Schrader sent detailed descriptions of every princess he secretly observed back to the ministers in Hanover: the Princesses of Wolfenbüttel were still children and besides had 'poorly shaped legs'; the Princesses of Plessen had no education; the Princess of Saxe-Gotha, who would eventually be chosen, had uneven teeth and a poor complexion, but she seemed fertile, had had her first period at eleven, and looked 'like the women who deliver robust children'. Mastering the complexities of the German Gothic script in record time, my partner in crime, Holger Hoock, indefatigably tackled the mountain of boxes, doggedly transcribing and translating day after day, while I worked at the documents in English and in French.

Travelling north from Hanover up through Schleswig Holstein and into Denmark, inclines fall away and the air and atmosphere become maritime. Despite the huge continental landmass to the south of Denmark, water is the nation's element and the wind, salty from the west, chilly from the east, chases all its citizens through its fields and streets. But when George III's sister Caroline Mathilde became its queen, Denmark was still a nation tied to its German neighbours. Court life and court business were conducted in German, and sometimes French, but both were often written up in Danish; monarchs and diplomats corresponded and negotiated in French. The last, again, I had reason to be grateful for; my Danish, learned week by week over eighteen months, was never going to be equal to the task of reading the Danish of three centuries ago. Two researchers, Niklas Jensen and Dan Andersen, helped me to negotiate the mass of Danish documents about Caroline Mathilde, and this book could not have been written without them.

Breaking up the niceties of eighteenth-century diplomatic French and the task of ploughing slowly through modern secondary literature about Caroline Mathilde's extraordinary life, I used my visits to Denmark to follow in her footsteps. I walked the streets of Copenhagen, as she had famously done, travelled north to where her summer palace stood, tracked inland to Roskilde where the Danish kings are buried, to Frederiksborg where the royal portraits hang, and looked as she did from the fortress of Kronborg across to the tree-fringed shores of Sweden across the sound. Although some modern historians argue that Denmark's history is one of slow and gradual reform, its castles and its countryside tell another story. Denmark was an absolute monarchy in Caroline Mathilde's time. Its great royal fortresses, rising above the flat landscape like ocean-going liners, with sparkling lead-framed windows and spire-topped, cloud-piercing turrets, were absolutism's embodiment; splendid, dominant and untrammelled, paid for by peasant labour and by the sea. Caroline Mathilde was both absolutism's beneficiary and its creature. She took advantage of the King's authority and his madness to forge a new way of life, but in the end fell victim to the same absolute power that had allowed her such freedom. It was from the castles she lived in and the streets she walked, as much as the archive where her voice is preserved, that I was able to tell the story of her life.

When I began this book I meant to make George III not so much a central character, as the string onto which I would thread the beads of his siblings' stories, making a necklace held together by the life of the King himself. But all work changes as it takes shape, and as I went on I realised that if George had necessarily a profound influence on his brothers and sisters, their lives made a huge impact on his. That impact was not just personal, it was political as well and it was also part of my story. So George III became one of the book's subjects in his own right. He will be seen, I hope, in a new light, not just as sovereign, or the father of many children, or the king who lost America, but as one of many siblings himself, a profoundly emotional man whose personal and political lives were never as separate as the framers of the constitutional monarchy had hoped.

Biography tends to be a vertical genre, going from parents to children, explaining its subjects by virtue of their childhoods and their relationships with their mothers and fathers. It rarely dwells for very long on brothers and sisters and the importance they can have in one another's lives. Perhaps because I am from a large family myself, my work has tended to go the other way, to be horizontal, seeking in the tangled web of brotherly and sisterly relations other clues to what makes us who we are.

1

Fritz ist Dode

Death came suddenly for Prince Frederick, ambushing him as he recovered from a temporary sickness, grabbing him by the throat, squeezing his life away. '*Je sens la mort*', he cried out in his third language and with accurate finality. Convulsed with spasms the Prince of Wales wrestled with the spectre, wordlessly and in vain, watched by his helpless wife and doctors. In minutes he was gone, a man who a little while before had been sitting up in bed listening to his dancing master Dunoyer play tunes on the fiddle, cheerfully demanding to see his friends. With him went the future and the hopes of his wife Augusta, the safety and bustle of a happy family home, and the childhood of his eldest son and heir. It was 21 March 1751, a little after nine o'clock on a black sharp evening in London, silent round the bed.

Eventually, someone whispered that the King must be told. Lord North, a courtier who had been idling away the evening in another part of the house, was summoned by the Princess of Wales and dispatched to St James's. Walking as fast as his dignity and fifty-year-old legs would allow him, North crossed the courtyard of Leicester House into the open space of the square in front, where the new, brightly gilded equestrian statue of Frederick's grandfather, George I, winked in the smoky darkness. Along by the royal mews at the bottom of Haymarket, acid fumes from scores of horses floated on the air. Lord North wove his way through servants out for the evening and chairmen carrying the rich home above the litter and dirt of the street. At the palace he found George II downstairs in the rooms of his mistress Lady

Yarmouth, playing cards after supper as he liked to do every day.

Accounts had it that when Lord North delivered his message, the King showed no trace of emotion or shock. 'Why, they told me he was better,' he said, and put down his cards. Walking across to Lady Yarmouth he leaned over her chair and whispered loudly, '*Fritz ist dode*', before leaving the room and breaking up the company. A few months later he declared without remorse or shame, 'This has been a fatal year to my family. I lost my eldest son, but was glad of it.' Thereafter he seldom mentioned Frederick's name.

At Leicester House, in the morning, surgeons began cutting up the Prince's body, looking into his organs for a way of explaining their failure to predict his death. The Prince's friend and creditor, George Bubb Dodington, upset at the cavalier way the doctors were flinging royal body-parts about, ordered that his discarded bowels 'be put in a box covered with red velvet and carried in one of his coaches, by such attendants as his Groom of the Stole should appoint, and buried in Henry VII's chapel in Westminster Abbey'. Soon afterwards, the rest of Frederick's corpse, emptied out, embalmed and re-dressed, was taken to a black-draped room in the House of Lords. His friends and relatives filed past in the muffled half-darkness and later the Prince's servants kept a vigil, standing by the waxy grey face from which all life had gone. On the morning of 13 April, the coffin was closed for its journey to Westminster Abbey. Four peers held a black pall taut over the top of the coffin and Frederick's servants walked behind it, called and following according to rank.

It was a muted procession and a short way to go. With the deep tenor of the abbey bell sounding its mournful toll over the bustle of the river and the streets, the coffin bearers left the House of Lords, crossed Palace Yard and filed between lines of stiff and silent soldiers to the grey sheer bulk of the abbey. Instead of using the main west door and processing down the long, monument-cluttered nave, they went discreetly through the abbey's side entrance into the south-east transept. Passing the tightly crowded area where the nation commemorated its writers and musicians, the party 'turned short into Henry VII's chapel', as Dodington put it. The funeral service was perfunctory and bald, 'performed without either anthem or organ', he wrote, and added in dejection, 'so ended the sad day'.

Frederick's coffin was added to the rest of his remains in the vault under the veiny white and black marble chequered floor, in cold proximity to his mother, Queen Caroline, who had been there nearly fourteen years. In decades to come the melancholy catalogue would lengthen and a warring family would be brought together again. Silent and unable to quarrel, they would crumble to dust while the busy air worked holes in their coffins. King George II and Queen Caroline, Frederick and his wife Augusta, his brother William and sisters Amelia and Caroline, his daughters Elizabeth and Louisa and his sons Edward and Frederick: they lie forgotten, their lives squeezed into inscriptions on the slabs above them, walked over by back-packed wanderers unaware of the hatreds and the loves boxed up beneath.

When Prince Frederick's eldest son Prince George was told that his father had died, he said nothing, though an observer noticed that he swayed and 'nearly fainted'. Then, with the odd, dislocated emotion he would always show in public until he went mad thirty-eight years later, he put his hand on his heart and said, 'I feel here as I did when I saw the workman fall from the scaffold at Kew.' Shock rather than grief was what the new heir to the throne expressed. Afterwards he did his best to hide his feelings, though in the months to come he was lethargic, as if grief was working its way through him slowly, tiring him out.

Until that March morning in 1751, Frederick's children had had happy childhoods, brought up in the country at Kew and in London at Leicester House, well away from the suffocating gloom of St James's and undisturbed by the quarrels which blighted both generations of Hanoverians that had come before them. Prince George and his seven siblings were British, nourished on Anglicanism and the sweet new mythology of Britannia. But their father and mother were German and all their four grandparents were German too. English may have been spoken at Leicester House but George II preferred his native tongue and his grandchildren were all good German speakers whose roots, snaking beneath British topsoil, were sunk deep into the bedrock that ran right under the North Sea to their ancestral land of Hanover. British-born, German-bred, Frederick's children never lost a sense of their connectedness to northern Europe and to its constellation of Protestant rulers. Joined by geography, custom, religion and the history of their own family to the Continent, their own lives were shaped by it invisibly, irrevocably and in ways that Britons sometimes never saw and often preferred to forget.

Prince Frederick, just to begin with, was not Frederick until he was twenty-one.

Until then he was Friedrich Louis, born in Hanover in 1707, grandson of its Elector, Kurfürst Georg Ludwig, son of the Elector's heir Prince Georg and his wife Wilhelmine Caroline. Friedrich's contented nursery happiness with his sisters at the Leineschloss in Hanover and especially at Herrenhausen outside the town, was shattered when, in 1714, the Elector Georg became George I of Great Britain. First the Elector grumpily left for his new country. Then in October, the new Prince and Princess of Wales followed, carting their possessions across the North Sea in a flotilla of twenty-two warships, four frigates, six transports for personnel and the royal yacht *Peregrine*, where the Princesses Anne and Amelia played as the autumn wind sped them across the channel.

Friedrich was left alone in Hanover, pale and small, his family's representative in a court that the Elector decreed must lose none of its order and magnificence. Much of the time he was allowed to be a little boy with dogs, pages and even a surrogate princess, Magot Veltsen, to play with. But he had adult duties too. The court was open every day, and each Sunday, and on other occasions when foreign diplomats or aristocrats passed through, a levée was held. Then, Elector Georg Ludwig in his long white wig with its rows of curls like waves on the sea, was propped up, in portrait form, on a ceremonial chair, while little Friedrich, beside him on another, received his guests. Visitors bowed first to the Elector's image, and then to the Prince, and spoke throughout in the hushed tones habitually used when Georg Ludwig was actually present. Meals and chapel services on these days were similarly conducted. The preacher addressed the Elector's empty pew, and the guests praised his table and his hospitality.

Friedrich, who would be elector one day, was more than happy to act his part, even though he was small for his age and his own straight pale hair was no match for Georg Ludwig's billowing wig. As time went on, study supplemented play. By the age of fourteen, Friedrich had two tutors, von Neubauer and Meinhardt Kunel, as well as an English teacher, Jean Hanet. Two army lieutenants taught him mathematics, 'artillerie' and fortification. He learned the histories and memorised the genealogies of the princely houses of Braunschweig-Lüneborg, Bavaria, the Palatinate, Brandenburg, and, of course, his own. He was now reading Latin prose, 'almost entirely on his own', studying philosophy in French and theology in German. Never a particularly scholarly or attentive pupil, he did learn to glance through a text, gut its contents and pass muster as a reasonably cultivated young man.

Hanet, Friedrich's English teacher, both taught him the language and gave him a picture of his future kingdom by taking him through Addison's *Spectator*, which had first appeared a decade before. The Prince was captivated by the vision of life Joseph Addison offered him and began to model himself upon Addison's protagonist, Mr Spectator himself, the ideal of urban politeness. In the journal's pages, comportment, politics, conflict and intellectual enquiry were removed from the court, the pulpit and the battlefield, transformed by the alchemy of good manners and conversation and put into the secular, self-consciously modern environments of the drawing room, the coffee house and the parlour. Addison declared that knowledge would be 'exposed upon every table', promoted with 'merriment' and embellished with the kind of light irony that came to be seen as quintessentially English. His ideal reader was, to be sure, a gentleman, but one who bore little relation to his uncouth forebears. Neither Restoration court wit nor rapacious military hero, he was an urban family man, cultiv-ated, educated, moderate and amused. In the *Spectator*, Addison was drawing the faint outline of the new age that was dawning. He had seen the changes in his city and he had read new philosophical work that advocated tolerance and described man as self-made rather than a creature at the mercy of forces beyond his control. He realised that the interlocking forces of religion, war and hunger would soon no longer drive events and dominate thought and feeling either in Britain or on the Continent. Subscribers to the *Spectator* were offered the chance to participate in a new world both as readers and actors. Friedrich was set fair to become its inheritor, a gentleman prince and an honorary member of Mr Spectator's club.

London, when Friedrich arrived there in 1728 – becoming Frederick on the way – was everything he hoped for. As Prince of Wales since his father ascended the throne as George II a year earlier, he could expect a sumptuous income, a household of his own and the delights of both court and city to be his. But the welcome he wanted from his own family never came. In fourteen years his mother and father had forgotten him. Besides, seven years before, Queen Caroline had given birth to another boy, William Augustus, the future Duke of Cumberland. As the Prince grew into a child whose cleverness matched the Queen's own, her lack of interest in Frederick turned into blank indifference and then into fixed dislike. Thwarted by the principle of primogeniture, which not even the most devoted mother could overturn, she came to see William as the worthy heir and Frederick as a frustrating obstacle. When her eldest son actually arrived in London dislike turned to hatred.

Queen Caroline was a difficult, clever, restless woman. As the orphaned child of minor Bavarian princelings, moved from court to court at the whim of her extended family, she was treated as a burden and starved of affection. At thirteen she went to live with the King and Queen of Prussia outside Berlin, and there she quickly seized her chance to act upon a wider stage, impressing a host of visitors with her intellect and fine figure. In the wealthy, cosmopolitan Prussian court, Caroline developed a love of dispute and a yearning for power that were fuelled by years of insecurity and neglect. These qualities, which became more exaggerated as the years went by, defined her far more than any of her personal relationships, particularly those with her children.

Becoming Queen of England and first lady at the court of St James's did not improve Caroline's narrow and domineering character. Courts often brought out the worst in their denizens, making the humble servile and the exalted self-indulgent. Gossip and scheming followed those close to the royal family, and whispers ran round every corner. Courtiers vied for the monarchs' approbation and Caroline liked to demand extravagant gestures of loyalty before she gave it. But the Bill of Rights and the Act of Settlement had severely limited the powers of the monarch, and, besides, Caroline was outsmarted by the long-serving Sir Robert Walpole who was kept on by George II despite the fact that he had been his father's minister. Caroline had urged her husband to retain Walpole as First Lord of the Treasury and effective Prime Minister, but her support of him did her no good, and Walpole described his dominance over the monarchs with one of his famous barnyard flourishes, saying, 'I have the right sow by the ear.' Unable to exercise much more than her personal power over the King, Caroline diverted her immense emotional and intellectual dissatisfaction into thwarting those whom she believed opposed her and nurturing those who shared her growing bitterness.

The first of these was the Prince of Wales. It could not have taken Frederick long to realise not only that his brother William had thoroughly supplanted him in his mother's affections, but that the Queen had nothing left to give him but her scorn. George II, always influenced by his wife's opinion of others, took little notice of him. 'I think this is not a son I need be much afraid of,' the King was said to have announced to Walpole with evident relief some time after Frederick's arrival. Thereafter he relapsed into indifference and seemed unconcerned when visitors at drawing rooms noticed his evident coolness.

George II publicly demonstrated his disdain for his eager and inoffensive heir by refusing to hand over the money Parliament had intended for him. Instead of the £70,000 a year that he himself had lived on as Prince of Wales, George gave his son £24,000, challenging him to a rebellion that would prove him disloyal. Frederick soon obliged, taking up opposition politics and borrowing money from aspirant politicians who hoped to reap the benefit when he came to the throne. Despite his family's contempt, he made a favourable impression on those he met. He was small but not ugly, lively and inclined to frivolity, but capable of stabs of attention and liberal with his charm. One of Queen Caroline's own Ladies of the Bedchamber, Lady Bristol, described him as 'the most agreeable young man it is possible to imagine', with 'the most obliging address that can be conceived'. The courtier and politician Lord Egmont, who was determined to work his way into the Prince's confidence and inner circle, tried his hand at the Prince's 'character', a short essay that anatomised his personality. "The character of the Prince is this', he wrote, 'He has no reigning passion; if it be, it is to pass the evening with six or seven others over a glass of wine and hear them talk of a variety of things, but he does not drink. He loves play, and plays to win, that he may supply his pleasures and his generosity, which last is great, but so ill-placed that he often wants the wherewithal to do a well-placed kindness, by giving to unworthy objects . . . He can talk gravely according to his company, but is sometimes more childish than becomes his age. He thinks he knows business, but attends to none. . . . He is extremely dutiful to his parents, who do not return it in love, and seem to neglect him by letting him do as he will, but they keep him short of money.'

With nothing to keep him at court, Frederick followed Mr Spectator into the teeming city, to the newly opened pleasure gardens at Vauxhall on the south bank of the Thames, to the Opera and to the playhouse. He found women and debts there, and picked up plenty of both. But what he really wanted was a wife, especially as the 1730s wore on and he found himself no role either at St James's, or with any symbolic appointment in the army. Queen Caroline, whose hatred of her son now extended to an obsessive hope that he would prove impotent or infertile, ignored or ridiculed him, egged on by Frederick's erstwhile friend Lord Hervey who had become her closest confidant.

Reluctantly, however, George II accepted the need for his heir to marry. In March 1734 an official from Hanover was dispatched to report secretly on the princesses of Saxe-Gotha, Wolfenbüttel, Holstein-Glucksburg and any other Protestants who might do. By July he had fixed on fifteen-year-old Auguste, Princess of Saxe-Gotha. She was neither beautiful nor especially well educated, but Frederick was not fussy. Anywhere from the court to the stage he could find female exquisiteness. What he wanted now was a family, a home where he would not be ignored and a focus for his life. His father, though, saw no need for speed. It was nine months before he reluctantly dispatched Lord de la War, a court official and Privy Counsellor, to ask the Duke for his daughter's hand.

Sitting in his castle in Weimar, surrounded by forest, the Duke of Saxe-Gotha was never likely to refuse. Sixteen-year-old Auguste, still a child and unable to speak any English, was packed off to London in March 1736, accompanied by her governess and a favourite doll. Arriving at St James's, with the e in her name changed to an English a, she was overcome by her loneliness and the court's magnificence, and threw herself abjectly at Queen Caroline's feet. During the wedding ceremony that followed, Caroline compounded Augusta's humiliation and sense of inadequacy, translating the marriage oath from English into German in a stage whisper clearly audible by the packed and perspiring crowd. The couple were then put to bed in front of a swarm of curious onlookers and the Queen ended a satisfactorily absurd day laughing over her son's nightcap.

By the spring of 1737, Queen Caroline's worst fears were realised. Augusta was pregnant. Frederick was too frightened to tell his parents, preferring to nurse his victory and his wife alone. It was not until the end of June, when the future royal infant could no longer be hidden even in the billowing silken folds of the widest and most fashionable sack, that Frederick confessed Augusta's condition to his parents, saying that her baby was due in September. Even then, Queen Caroline would not believe it. She declared her intention of being at the delivery because she was sure Frederick was lying and was planning to smuggle a changeling into his wife's bed, like the infamous 'warming-pan baby' that anti-Jacobites claimed James II had produced from under the bedclothes and declared his heir.

On 31 July 1737, a few hours after the young couple had dined in state at Hampton Court with the King and Queen, Augusta's waters broke. It was probably sooner than she had calculated, and Frederick panicked. He had wanted Augusta to be away from his mother when his child was born, perhaps because Caroline's campaign of disdain had worked and he was afraid that the baby might be a monster or stillborn. So, although it was ten at night, and the Princess was already in labour, Frederick ordered his coaches and set off on the sixteen-mile trip to St James's. Augusta, crying in the contractions, leaned unsteadily against her husband. As the coach tipped to the horses' gallop and bumped against the uneven road, she began to bleed. Despite this urgent warning, spreading in red across the white of the pillows, they hurtled on, clattering past Kensington Palace, up the Mall and into the palace stable yard, arriving just before midnight. The palace was shuttered and in darkness, and the maids could find no sheets in the gloom. Augusta was carried upstairs, where, lying on two folded tablecloths, she gave birth to a baby girl while they laid the fires and lit the candles around her.

All this time, Queen Caroline was sound asleep at Hampton Court. Woken at one o'clock by a lady-in-waiting with a letter from the Prince's Lords of the Bedchamber which blandly informed her of his departure, she summoned Lord Hervey and a Privy Counsellor the Duke of Grafton, and set off helter-skelter after him in pantomime fashion. She arrived too late of course, but she had some satisfaction in reporting to Hervey that the baby was 'a little rat of a girl about the size of a good, large toothpick case'. To her daughter Anne she wrote with witty malice in her execrable French, 'je suis tres sure quelle ne poura vives et ausy sure quelle est de luy': she was quite sure the baby couldn't live but also sure she was her son's.

Frederick's tiny daughter did not die, however, but flourished in a most provoking way. A few days after the birth, Lord Essex, the King's chamberlain, arrived at Frederick's door with a message ostensibly from his father, actually from his mother and composed, gossips had it, by none other than Lord Hervey. Essex stood and delivered the message, speaking it out loud like a king's herald from an earlier age. It was a single-sentence denunciation of Frederick that ended with the assertion that the Prince's flight from Hampton Court 'is looked upon by the King to be such a deliberate indignity offered to himself and the Queen, that he has commanded me to acquaint your Royal Highness that he resents it to the highest degree'.

Frederick had no wish to take up this parental challenge. 'I am extremely grieved', he wrote back, 'that a case should happen where my tenderness for the princess should remove for a moment what is otherwise first in my thoughts, my devotion to your Majesty.' King George replied that he declined to answer his son's letter. Frederick tried again, sending across the palace another humble note, in which, as his equerry George Lyttelton wrote, 'he asked pardon in the most submissive manner and expressed the greatest affliction at lying under His Majesty's displeasure'. Letters flew back and forth – from Princess Augusta to the King, declaring herself an object of pity and expressing a desire to explain the Prince's conduct; from the King in gruff reply, from both the Prince and the Princess to the Queen and back again, all delivered the few yards across the courtyards and corridors of St James's by messengers and emissaries while the aggrieved parties kept out of one another's sight.

Before long the quarrel had flown the walls of the palace and was making its way merrily round the town and the court. On 10 September, Lord Egmont picked up the story, noting in his diary that Lord Grafton had been to the Prince's lodging with another diatribe, again written by Lord Hervey. Headed 'Georgius Rex', and written in the voice of the King himself, it began: 'The professions you have lately made in your letters, of your particular regard for me, are so contradictory to your actions, that I cannot suffer myself to be imposed upon by them.' After rehearsing again the Prince's disgraceful actions on leaving Hampton Court, the King went on: 'the whole tenor of your conduct for a considerable time has been so entirely devoid of real duty to Me, that I have long had reason to be highly offended with you.' Blaming the Prince's advisers for fomenting 'the division you have made in my family', the letter ended by giving Frederick and his family forty-eight hours to get out of St James's.

When the Prince, his six-week-old daughter Augusta, his seventeen-year-old wife and his entire household left the palace, a sympathetic crowd gathered to watch, and noticed that the family's clothes, instead of being packed in sturdy and secure trunks, had been bundled ignominiously into open wicker washing baskets. In the coffee houses and parlours, on the street corners and on public coaches the details of the Prince's retreat were passed around.

The Earl of Bolingbroke, a veteran Tory politician who was fast becoming the prince's closest political adviser, was disgusted. Public appetite for the minutiae of the scandal went quite against his exalted idea of kingship and offended his old-fashioned belief that the monarch should be above faction, above party and above the everyday. 'I am at a loss to find the plausibility or the popularity of the present occasion of rupture', he wrote to another of the Prince's advisers, Lord Lyttelton. 'He hurries his wife from court when she is upon the point of being delivered of her first child. His father swells, struts and storms. He confesses his rashness and asks pardon in the terms of one who owns himself in the wrong. Besides all that seems to be boyish, it is purely domestic and there is nothing, as far as I can discern, to interest the public in the cause of His Royal Highness.'

Bolingbroke could not have been more wrong. As his own alliterative rendition showed, it had made a great story. More, it cemented mundane domestic drama to the most exalted family in the land, and public appetite for that combination, once excited, was never to wane. There had been any number of 'secret histories' of court life published before, mostly about the rakish gallantry of Stuart courts, and Frederick was no stranger to scandal himself, having, a few years earlier, been the subject of numerous squibs, poems and prints when his mistress Harriet Vane had given birth to a short-lived son. But this was a new and verifiable story, told in the words of the protagonists themselves as it happened and as the people of London watched and read. Royal scandal, and the embrace between press, public and royal family, was to fuel a huge appetite for publications about famous or notorious individuals in the years to come. Private life had become a tradeable public commodity and a culture of celebrity was being born. Though it was not to mature for another two decades, when a change in stamp duty suddenly meant that newspapers had space to fill and looked to scandal to fill it, the royal family were neither immune from its attentions nor aloof from its concerns. The story of Princess Augusta's birth showed that they were its protagonists from the very beginning.

As soon as the public began to take a close interest in the domestic concerns of the royal family, it became obvious that both parties to the quarrel had an interest in winning the good opinion of those outside the palace gates. Queen Caroline was certain both that right was on her side and that she had emerged victorious from the fray. Seconded by an eager Lord Hervey, she urged the publication of all the messages and letters exchanged between Frederick and his father. Eschewing their own licensed printers who published all the business of the court and government, they used the well-established system of mercuries, or wholesalers, who took papers from the printers and distributed them to hundreds of different outlets from booksellers' shops to street hawkers. One broadside contained the bulk of the story, a second, priced at twopence, the King's final, dramatic letter of dismissal.

The results of the internecine struggle were inconclusive, but the Queen was delighted not to see her son any more. She told Hervey that she would happily sign a declaration that Frederick was 'the greatest ass, the greatest liar, and the greatest [mongrel] and the greatest beast in the whole world', and added, as if emphasis were needed, 'I heartily wish he was out of it.' It was, however, Queen Caroline herself who would be first to go. A few weeks later she fell ill, poisoned by an infected umbilical hernia ruptured during the birth of her last child thirteen years before. Caroline had kept the injury secret and it was anyway untreatable. After three weeks of agony borne with the greatest bravery and ironic stoicism, she died on 20 November 1737.

For Caroline and her generation, growing up in the bellicose, under-nourished and insecure 1680s and 1690s, the world seemed a callous and unsparing place. But its shape was changing. On the Continent two hundred years of religious wars had come to an end. New ideas which were slowly shifting the focus of thought and enquiry from heaven to earth and from God to man were circulating widely in a plethora of books and periodical publications. Walpole's long administration, which promoted peace abroad and stability at home, was producing rapid bureaucratic and economic expansion that laid the foundations for the rapid growth of the British Empire in the next twenty years. This forward-looking world, commercially vibrant and cruel, but more open, rounded and generous than the fearful age that preceded it, would come too late for Queen Caroline and her husband. It was Prince Frederick and his children who would be its beneficiaries. All he had to do was set himself to learn its contours and its ways, produce heirs to shore up his position and wait for his fifty-four-year-old father to die.

The first proved supremely easy. Even as the Queen lay dying, Augusta's next child was growing in her womb, the prince that Caroline had convinced herself Frederick would never father. He was born on 24 May 1738 and christened with the name George amid muted celebrations. The Earl of Egmont recorded in his diary simply that 'The Princess of Wales was brought to bed of a boy, which the same night received private baptism, there being a doubt if he could live.'

After George's birth, Frederick's family grew at the rate of a baby every year and a half. Edward was born in 1739, Elizabeth in 1741, William in 1743, Henry in 1745, Louisa in 1749 and Frederick in 1750. Eventually the Prince ran out of space in his London bases of Norfolk House and Carlton

House in the Mall and, in 1743, he rented Leicester House, on the north side of Leicester Fields. It became his family's principal home, where George and his brothers and sisters grew up.

Moving the children to Leicester House took them to the heart of the new metropolis, away from the court world of St James's into the mixed bustle of a growing cosmopolitan city. A visitor could walk from Carlton House to Leicester Fields – or Leicester Square as it was soon known – in a few minutes, either by stepping with careful feet through the Royal Mews and across the dust and chaff of the Haymarket, or by going further along Pall Mall towards Charing Cross and then walking up the east side of the square. But he would notice during his stroll a change of tone from park to square and from noble houses to the flat-fronted modernity of the new urban terraces.

Until 1720, Leicester Square had been an open space, criss-crossed by paths, traversed by people taking short cuts and dotted with groups of boys playing ball games. Leicester House stood back from the road on the north side with a courtyard in front of the main house and a gatehouse and gates onto the street, where the gatekeeper, Thomas Paine, kept a constant lookout. It was flanked on its western side by another grand residence, Savile House, and it had a small shady garden at the back. Frederick employed a host of carvers, painters and paper hangers to make the house gilt-laden and princely inside, but outside it was neither modern nor imposing. Indeed, until the 1740s, a small gallery of lock-up shops sat in a row at the courtyard entrance, announcing that in London getting by and making money would always sit cheek-by-jowl with aristocratic splendour.

In the same way, a mixture of the well-to-do and the indigent lived in the square itself and in the streets beyond it, and Frederick was just one of the thousands of immigrants who made the area their home. Prosperous impresarios and merchants mingled with transient Italians working at the Opera in the Haymarket and with the French refugees who had arrived in the last decades of the seventeenth century. In 1732 the painter and engraver William Hogarth confidently announced his success by taking a four-storeyed house in the south-east corner of the square, but then defiantly undercut his respectability by hanging from the façade a shop sign decorated with a gilded head of the painter Van Dyck that whispered 'trade', every time it creaked in the wind.

As the 1740s progressed, Frederick and Augusta leased several other houses to temper the compromised grandeur of Leicester House: Cliveden by the banks of the Thames in Buckinghamshire, Park Place near Henley and Durdans near the racecourse at Epsom. But none of them was more than a rural retreat where they entertained, put on music and plays and escaped the summer stench of the city streets. No longer the bachelor Mr Spectator, Frederick now came to emulate 'Sylvanus Urban', the pen-name of the publisher of the *Gentleman's Magazine* which, since 1731, had been advertising and explaining each month new ideas, books, scientific advances, fashion and habits of thought. As his name suggested, Sylvanus Urban put himself forward as a man both of wooded glades and crowded streets, a cultivated metropolitan gentleman whose country park and estate would be at once experiment and retreat and who was equally at home in the drawing room and the field.

So the Spectator Prince became the gentleman father, improving his houses and gardens, collecting art and playing music, receiving opposition politicians at his small alternative court, visiting the nursery and the theatre alike. Three decades before the man of feeling became both a pattern of behaviour and an established cliché, Frederick was proud to reveal himself as an emotional and concerned father. Visitors noticed that while Augusta was an undemonstrative mother, aloof and nervously obsessed with protocol, Frederick, in pointed and obvious reversal of his parents' behaviour, liked to have all his children by him. 'He played the father and husband well,' a contemporary noted, 'always most happy in the bosom of his family, left them with regret and met them again with smiles, kisses and tears.' The children were allowed plenty of frolicking in the nursery and the garden. About 1744 a visitor, perhaps one of the Prince's friends who was an artist, perhaps an amateur, sketched one of the Princes playing war. The year before, George II had been the last British monarch to fight, leading his cavalry at the Battle of Dettingen in the long-running War of the Austrian Succession. In the drawing, one of his grandsons imitates him, reading a book sitting on straw in a tent made from two broomsticks and two chair-backs draped with fabric. A child-sized gun and sword lie on the floor and a standard, marked 'GR', stands guard outside. Although usually taken to be a portrait of Prince George, who was six years old at the time, the sketch may show Prince Edward, who was more theatrical, more bellicose and considerably more literate than his older brother.

Prince George and his brothers and sisters, away from the suffocating gloom of St James's, had a happy early childhood. They knew nothing of the failure of their father's political ambitions in the early 1740s and not much more of his partial reconciliation with the King after the fall of Robert Walpole in 1742. If they picked up the distant rumour of war in 1745, they had no understanding of the way in which their father was sidelined by his brother William, the Duke of Cumberland, when the Young Pretender landed at Glenfinnan in Scotland and began to gather Stuart loyalists to his standard. Safe in London, they must have heard the bells peal out a Protestant, Hanoverian and English victory, not knowing how Frederick had been ridiculed for his inaction in the press and the Duke of Cumberland hailed as the conquering hero.

Defeated in his worldly ambitions, the Prince of Wales retreated into his family. His growing band of English princes and princesses, the first royal family being brought up in England for over a century, were both his best way to popularity and his hope for the future. The children, sometimes as a group, sometimes just the two or three eldest, were taken on the river, brought out at performances of operas and plays, and paraded round the rotunda of the respectable new pleasure garden at Ranelagh in 1744. By then there were five of them, a descending golden-haired, blue-eyed line of Augusta, George, Edward, Elizabeth and William. George was a serious boy who had grown out of his earlier puniness into healthy, if stolid, good looks. It was not he, but Edward, however, who was his father's favourite. Named after the Black Prince, Edward was a thin, plain boy, strikingly blond with pale eyes like swimming fried eggs. But he was also witty and lively. Horace Walpole, son of the late Prime Minister and lifelong epicure of gossip, who brought his characteristically acidic blend of disgust and fascination to bear with special force on the royal family, described Edward as a 'sayer of things', a coiner of witty phrases that delighted his father, and made him the centre of family attention.

The two boys lived with their sisters in the nursery until 1744, when Frederick's Clerk of the Closet, Francis Ayscough, was promoted to be their tutor. When Ayscough was painted with the two princes by Richard Wilson, he appeared thin, alert and bent at the neck like an attentive crow. He was related by marriage to Frederick's equerry George Lyttelton, and described by his enemies as a man of 'low extraction' who had secured his post by paying particular attention to Prince Edward and winning Frederick's favour. Once appointed, he encouraged Prince Edward's taste and talent for performance and badinage, but almost completely neglected the boys' formal education. No matter; Frederick remained happily convinced of Edward's intelligence and good qualities, even if George's lack of progress did give enough cause for concern for one-to-one teaching to be considered. After receiving a flattering report of his sons' progress one day, Frederick wrote to the younger, 'My dear Edward. I rejoice to find you have been so good both. Pray God it may continue, Nothing gives a father who loves his children so well as I do so much satisfaction as to hear they improve or are likely to make a figure in this world.' As a father he was easily pleased, and far more relaxed than his wife, who worried continually about her children and feared for their moral strength as much as their intellectual progress.

Early in January 1749, after a bout of ill-health, perhaps feeling the weight of his seven children and forty-two years, his father's long life and his brother's popularity, Frederick sat down in Leicester House and wrote out an imposing title, 'Instructions for my son George, drawn by myself, for his good, and that of my family, and for that of his people, according to the ideas of my grandfather, and best friend, George I'.

Having just written his will, which disposed of his worldly goods, Frederick wanted to dispense something more intangible: his opinion and advice. The memorandum would be left in Augusta's hands, Frederick wrote to George, 'who will read it to you from time to time and will give it to you when you come of age or get the crown'. Frederick intended ten-year-old George to be impressed with what he wrote, and he was. He preserved the memorandum amongst his papers, and its solemn admonitions, and most of all its linking of families and nations, engendered a way of thinking about those in his charge that profoundly affected his personal and political conduct, determining not only the way he behaved towards his family but also a good part of his relationship with his subjects as well.

'My design', Frederick began, 'is not to leave You a sermon as is undoubtedly done by persons of my rank. 'Tis not out of vanity that I write this; it is out of love to You, and to the public. It is for your good, and for that of my family, and of the good people you are to govern, that I leave this to you.' The document that followed had three interwoven themes. First, George's duties as king, head of the family and father to his peoples; second, the importance of a financial system which would serve landed and commercial interests but would lift the nation out of the pockets of bankers and keep the national debt low enough to enable Britain to wage war without their help; and, last, the need to honour the will of George I and separate the Electorate of Hanover in perpetuity from the kingdom of Great Britain.

George I's will, suppressed by his son George II, was popularly believed to have asked for the separation of Britain and Hanover as soon as the existence of two male heirs in one generation made it possible. Had this been the case, Frederick would have inherited the British Crown on his father's death, and the Duke of Cumberland the Electorate, something Queen Caroline would never have accepted.

Frederick, who had boys in abundance, was quite ready to reverse his father's policy. He believed that if Hanover was a separate state, the continental powers whose real enemy was Britain, would have no particular interest in attacking it, and with greater stability on the Continent, would also lose interest in supporting Jacobites who still wanted to restore the Stuarts to the British throne. From the moment of separation, he told George, 'Jacobitism will be in a manner rooted out, and you will not be forced then, to court your Ministers'. The fear of Jacobitism, Frederick was telling his son, was what lay behind the long parliamentary supremacy of the great Whig families which had supported the Glorious Revolution and the Act of Settlement. Despite his reconciliation with his father and the failure of his own political opposition, Frederick still longed to see a monarch who could govern without dependence on any party. Once Jacobitism had faded away, and the taint of it had gone from the Tory opposition, the monarch would have greater flexibility in picking his ministers, and thus more influence generally.

If George III did not effect the separation of Britain and Hanover during his reign, it may in part have been because he took the first part of his father's instructions with the utmost seriousness and believed he could find no suitable candidate for the electorship of Hanover amongst his brothers. For Frederick impressed upon his son that he must regard family, dynastic and national interests as inextricably bound together, and that as king he was both head of the family and father to the nation and to its colonies. 'Convince the nation', he wrote, 'that you are not only an Englishman born and bred, but that you are also this by inclination, and that as you will love your younger children next to the older born, so you will love your other countries, next to England.'

As if this didn't give George enough potentially difficult children to look after, Frederick also gave him the care of his brothers and sisters, saying,

'You must not reckon yourself only their brother, but I hope you will be a kind father to them.' George took this advice very much to heart. Family affairs became in his mind national ones, and he would react to signs of unrest amongst any of his subjects and colonies with all the force of an angry father who feels his identity threatened by a rebellious child. Seemingly emotionally detached, even as a child, George became a man of trembling inflexibility, apparently undemonstrative but profoundly disturbed by the poor behaviour of siblings, sons and unruly subjects.

One defence against misrule was a trusted adviser and friend, a man whose integrity could be measured by his willingness to give good advice even when the monarch did not want to listen. 'Flatterers, Courtiers or Ministers are easy to be got', Frederick wrote, 'but a true friend is difficult to be found. The only rule I can give you to try them by is, if they will tell you the truth, and will venture for your sake, that of your family or that of your people (which three things I hope you will never separate, nor ought they ever to be separated) to risk some moments of disagreeable contradictions to your passions.' It made sense that a man who could give tough advice was a man who might be trusted. But it would be easy too for an uncertain and self-lacerating personality to turn the formulation around, and to feel that the man who told the king what he did not wish to hear must, because of it, be that trustworthy friend. Prince George, who continued to be shy and stubborn, uncertain and yet complacent, would be easy prey for someone who could divine how his mind worked and the directions in which it had been encouraged.

Unbeknownst to him, Prince Frederick had already met the man who would be for his son exactly the 'true friend' whom he described in such glowing colours. Eighteen months before he wrote his instructions, the Prince and members of his household had been marooned in a picnic tent on the Epsom racecourse in a downpour, bored and unable to escape. An equerry was sent out into the rain to find someone who could liven up the party and make up the last hand in a four at whist. He returned with the tall, elegant figure of John Stuart, the thirty-four-year-old Earl of Bute.

Bute's stagey entrance was corrected by his preoccupied demeanour and the grave manner with which he dispensed his small talk. He was a man who appealed to Augusta's rigid sense of propriety by making gossip seem like advice and opinion like a sermon. Frederick, who enjoyed banter and valued frivolity, summed Bute up as 'a fine, showy man', who 'would make an excellent ambassador in a court where there is no business'. But he under-estimated the tenacity and ambition of his new companion. As the jealously anxious Dodington noted in his diary in early 1750, Bute was a frequent visitor in London and at Kew, and soon became a Lord of the Bedchamber in the Prince's household.

Frederick tolerated Lord Bute partly because they shared an interest in botany and gardening. Bute had spent a decade in domestic seclusion at Mount Stuart on the Isle of Bute, bringing up a large family on a straitened income and developing the gardens rather than pursuing the political ambi-tions which he harboured. So when, in 1749, Frederick decided on a major programme of horticultural work at Kew, Lord Bute was on hand to advise and help direct the planting.

Two years later the plants at Kew were flourishing. It was Frederick who was dead, killed not as some declared by the bursting of an abscess formed when he was struck by a cricket ball, but more likely by lung failure compli-cated by pleurisy. The Princess of Wales, still only thirty-one years old, was left five months pregnant, with eight children, a sharply reduced income and a pile of debts. Worried as she was by money matters, her first concern was the King. If he wanted, George II, as head of the family and as King, could now assert his right to control the new Prince of Wales's education and upbringing. Augusta was terrified that she might have to give her son up to live in St James's away from his brothers and sisters. Hastily she decided that the only way of keeping him was to present to her father-in-law a public demeanour that displayed nothing but absolute submission.

In fact George II had no profound interest either in his twelve-year-old heir or in any of the vagaries and whimsy of childhood life. At sixty-eight, he was set in his ways, a martinet, and not inclined to be generous with his time. He had his cards, his mistress, his visits to Hanover; he had no wish for another family too. After a visit of condolence to Leicester House, when he plumped himself down on the sofa and lachrymosely hugged his eldest granddaughter, he left the Princess of Wales in charge, and allowed her to become Prince George's official guardian.

Augusta took care to thank the King effusively. 'Sir', she wrote, on hearing that the King was not going to take her eldest son into his care, 'I beg leave to lay myself at Your Majesty's feet, humbly hoping that Your Majesty will suffer me to return my most humble thanks for Your Majesty's great good-ness in permitting my son to continue his residence with me. This precious mark of Your Majesty's favour makes me unspeakably happy and fills my breast with the warmest gratitude.' When her baby was born in July, slipping out in an easy labour of just two hours, Augusta prudently decided to give her a name that would please the King.

Frederick, had he been alive to insist, would surely have added another old English name to the list he had been compiling in his family. But Augusta, keeping to his choice in her daughter's second name, prefixed it with that of the late Queen. Her last child was christened Caroline Matilda. She commemorated two queens, one a German, the other a French Plantagenet. It was an expedient choice, but, as it turned out, an apt one too. Caroline Mathilde was to become a formidable mixture of Plantagenet passion and her grandmother's wilfulness, and she would bring her brother King George more heartache than any other of his siblings.

2

A Sayer of Things

At the end of 1751, tiny Caroline Mathilde and little Frederick were still not much more than bundles of needs looked after by wet-nurses and nurse-maids But Augusta's older children had distinctive characters and allotted roles in the family. Prince George, though tall for his age, and a handsome boy with light brown hair and full lips, worried those who met him. The future king was shy and backward for his age, happy to sit in the shadow of his younger brother and showing no inclination to study or to shine. Edward, conscious of having been his father's favourite, was used to being the centre of attention. With his unfashionably pale hair and thick white eyelashes fringing bulbous and watery eyes, Edward was never going to be praised for his looks. But he wanted, and practised, to amuse. He told jokes, acted the fool and, like his father, was an excellent mimic. When his older brother showed his fear of his tutors, Edward mocked them, deflating his brother's anxiety. He stood guard over his mother, too, making sure that anyone who tried to gain her confidence was brought to earth by his sarcasm and mimicry.

Augusta, or Lady Augusta, as she was called in the old English way of giving titles to princesses, also swam in Prince Edward's orbit. She was a boisterous child, happy to make her opinions known and good at nursing a grievance, scornful of the Prince of Wales's timidity, and as fond as Edward was of music, acting and dancing. Her younger sister Elizabeth, over-plump and often unwell, usually kept her company. Prince William, fair like Edward but quiet, stolid and careful like George, was the last of the children out of the nursery. Together or in little groups, they might be seen walking with their mother at Kew, or at the pantomime in town.

Overnight Augusta herself had moved from being the future queen and become simply the mother of the future king, with half a lifetime of widowhood ahead of her. But, having been granted guardianship of the new Prince of Wales, she had to emerge from the shadows and, at least nominally, take care of the education and bringing up of her children. She had been a happy enough wife, dutiful and quiet, displaying all the lack of interest in influence and court politics that Frederick had so much insisted upon. Rarely recorded as having said anything, she had been memorialised in paint as the still, fecund centre of a new royal generation, her children grouped around her, the littlest at her knee or in her arms. The woman who emerged to stand alone in her widow's weeds was fearful, severe and suspicious. Even Dodington, who became the Princess's adviser in the years immediately following Frederick's death, described her in 1752 as having 'established a character for prudence, in not opening herself much to anybody'. Painted by the Scottish portraitist Allan Ramsay a few years later when she was in her late thirties, she chose to be enveloped in a thick winter brocade, topped with a black lace shawl. She stood for him clasping her hands tightly together, in contrast to most popular poses in portraits, in which the sitter's open hands, often offered out towards the viewer, suggested invitation or generosity of spirit. Ramsay caught the Princess of Wales walking in a dourly bleak landscape that seemed to mirror her mind, only turning her head to look out, tight-lipped and aloof.

Augusta knew she had too little money and too many leaseholds and freeholds. To bring the two more closely in line she quickly let go the largest houses they had rented, Cliveden and Park Place near Henley. Durdans, Frederick's lodge near the Epsom racecourse, was also abandoned, leaving only Kew House as a summer retreat. Kew sat among the villas that dotted the countryside on both banks of the Thames to the west of London all the way to Hampton Court, but it was only half a day's drive from town and felt more countrified for sitting in its own large park, walled off from Kew Green and the houses that fringed it. In town, Augusta hung on to Carlton House, partly because she was convinced that the King wanted to annex its pretty gardens, partly because it was convenient for riding in Green Park and Kensington Gardens. But the family still spent most of its time, as it had before Frederick's death, at Leicester House, which for Augusta was far too close for comfort to the bustle and clamour of London's streets.

Knowing nothing of the world outside St James's, the Princess of Wales soon became convinced that it was corrupt and that her children must be shielded from it at all costs. But the court itself was just as dangerous, and harboured enemies and vice. Faithful to Frederick's memory, she kept away from St James's and from the King as much as she could, and she maintained the family feud with the Duke of Cumberland until the day he died in 1765. No one was safe from her strictures. She admitted to Dodington in 1752 that she disliked Princess Amelia, Frederick's unmarried sister, saying that her heavy gambling at Bath was 'highly improper'. As for 'the young people of quality', she added, 'they were so ill educated, and so very vicious, that they frightened her'. Years later, Prince William told an acquaintance that no children 'were ever brought up in a greater ignorance of evil', than those at Leicester House.

The frivolity, the bustle of political machination and the daily tenderness that Frederick had brought to his family drained out of the household with his death. Prince Edward may have tried to take on his father's role, but the tone of the family changed. It became dour and inward-looking. The coming and going of pamphleteers and writers, of actors, singers and place seekers and even the occasional mistress; the excitement of aspiration and failure; the sense of the bustling commercial world pressing in and its explosive expansion beyond their gates; the travelling and parties; the incessant buying of paintings and furniture, silver and houses: all this was abruptly lost. London got bigger, the machinery of government grew and Britain looked for the new markets and imperial conquests that would nourish its economy. In 1756 a new war began that would deliver great tracts of India, the Caribbean and North America to the Crown, but the new Prince of Wales was only ever able to follow its progress from the schoolroom. Even as the Seven Years War expanded Britain's empire, the world of its future king shrivelled and shrank.

When excess and extravagance had been banished, music still remained. The royal children were talented musicians and numerous enough to make up their own ensemble. The princesses sang and played on the harpsichord. Prince Edward was a competent violinist and an occasional composer of dances and songs, and both Prince George and Prince William played plangent modern German flutes. Music, once the spicy and suspect accompaniment of opera and its singers had been sieved out, was decorous and genteel, and the Princess of Wales always encouraged it.

Plants, which could neither whisper nor conspire, were the Princess's other passion. Every year the family spent a long summer at Kew. The children played and rode, secluded from the world and even from the other families in the village by the high wall that ran round the estate. Augusta, with the advice of Lord Bute, continued the building and planting that Frederick had begun. Kew was the only place where Augusta displayed any extravagance and perhaps the only place where she was happy. She hinted to Dodington in 1752 that the burden of her husband's debts cast a pall over her conscience, but her economy was not merely the desire to show his creditors that she had little money. Lavish spending was something the Princess of Wales equated with vice; modesty in dress, in demeanour and in manner of living, she came to see as virtuous. Even at Kew, she waited nearly a decade before she began a botanic garden and added an orangery and a pagoda to the temples and follies Frederick had built there.

Gradually the royal children who were left closely in Augusta's care began to live as she wished rather than as their station demanded. The trappings of royalty fell away and modesty took their place. When she commissioned portraits of all her children in 1754, she turned away from the rococo grandeur, all fur and lace and drapery, that had been the hallmark of the painting of herself and her children painted by Jean-Baptiste van Loo in 1739. Instead she asked for simple pastel half-lengths from the French artist François Liotard that were deliberate and beguiling in their simplicity.

From the line of pictures that Liotard produced it would have been hard to identify more than a couple of the children as royal or even nobly born. Prince Edward, perhaps at his own insistence, and to satisfy his histrionic streak, wears the Garter sash and star that he had been given two years before. But nothing in Prince George's portrait hints at his royal birth. At fifteen or sixteen years old, the Prince of Wales, in a silver-embroidered white frock-coat and white cravat, powdered hair tied with a wide black ribbon at the back, looks more like a nervous young nobleman up in Paris for the first time than the future king of England. The girls' portraits were intended to show openness, purity and feminine sweetness. Seventeen-year-old Augusta has a face turned half-away and her light brown hair drawn tightly back. She wears no jewellery in her hair, no earrings and no necklace. Looped rows of pearls are sewn across the top of her stomacher, and the plain lace borders of all her garments give an impression of modesty and restraint. Little Caroline Matilda, just three years old, looks out with phlegmatic calm, dressed to play a milkmaid in bob-cap and frock. Only her arms, held stiffly away from her body, suggest that she is posing at all, sat on a bench or stool and told to keep still while Liotard worked.

Although Augusta withdrew immediately from any active political interests or intervention after the death of her husband, staying aloof was difficult. Real detachment was harder because she was tenderly nurturing her husband's old hatreds for the King and the Duke of Cumberland. She solved the conundrum of both wanting to know what was going on and believing that knowledge was corrupting by finding confidants who could move between her household and the vicious world beyond it. George Bubb Dodington was flattered, surprised, but not altogether delighted to find himself cast in this role after Frederick's death. Summoned to Kew one Sunday in October 1752, he stayed talking to the Princess until late one evening. The Princess was much more frank than he had expected. Dodington was flustered by her attention, and later wrote in his diary, 'I got home between ten and eleven, and have been the more particular in [recording] this conversation, because it carries an air of friendship and openness, which I, no way, expected from a great lady.'

Dodington was well aware of the need for discretion. The Princess had other informants. Lord Egmont, whose righteous austerity suited her, was one, and the Earl of Bute another. Moreover there were some titbits of news that even Dodington, who liked nothing better than to give the seething pot of jealousies and gossip a gentle stir, thought it best to withhold. He had no wish for the Princess to know, for instance, that he had already decided to throw in his hand with the government in a bid for political office. Nor did he want to be the bearer of bad news from the grubby world. Thus, when rumours began to circulate about the kind and quality of the education the Prince of Wales was being given, Dodington noted in his diary that he was careful not to tell the Princess what he had heard.

Prince George had never shone intellectually and his education atrophied after his father's death. The Princess of Wales was more concerned that her son should be good than learned, and she admitted to Dodington that 'She really did not well know' what his tutors taught him, 'but she was afraid not much'. What Dodington did not pass on were the allegations that by the autumn of 1752, the Princes were being trained in 'arbitrary principles', a shorthand for the kind of despotism associated with the Stuart kings.

That the rumours were given any credence was a measure less of alarm about the corruption of the future king, than of the isolation in which he was growing up. Although the Prince of Wales attended the weekly Drawing Rooms when his grandfather was in Hanover, the royal children were seldom seen around St James's and rarely discussed at court. Their mother seemed to have little fixed plan for their futures. By 1752, for instance, Augusta was fifteen, an age when most royal princesses were discreetly being made available to Europe's Protestant princes. But Augusta was still at Leicester House, continuing her desultory education in languages, music and dancing and history. Her discontent was fed by visits to the theatre and the pleasure garden, which gave her tantalising views of the world outside, and by the sallies and mockery of her favourite brother Edward. But nothing was done to remove her from the nursery atmosphere or offer her a prospect of change. Modest informality reigned. On 17 November 1753, Dodington wrote in his diary, 'The Princess sent to me to attend her between 8 and 9 o'clock. ... I went to Leicester House expecting a small company, and a little music, but found nobody but Her Royal Highness. She made me draw a stool, and sit by the fire with her. Soon after came the Prince of Wales, and Prince Edward and then the Lady Augusta, all quite undressed, and took their stools round the fire with us. We sat talking of familiar occurrences of all kinds, till between 10 and 11, with the ease and unreservedness and unconstraint, as if one had dropped into a sister's house that had a family, to pass the evening. It was much to be wish'd that the Princess conversed familiarly with more people of a certain knowledge of the world.'

Perhaps partly to open the door of Leicester House a little wider and partly to broaden and deepen the Prince of Wales's education, he was given a new governor, James, Earl Waldegrave, the next month. Waldegrave's task was less to instruct than to supervise the Prince's education and to reassure the world beyond Leicester House that the Prince of Wales was being taught to respect the Bill of Rights and the Act of Succession. George and Edward did their lessons together, and besides their main tutor George Scott, had language masters, a bishop to teach them Anglican doctrine, and teachers of music and dance. Waldegrave was there to remedy any deficiencies in the programme and to make sure that the Prince of Wales made steady progress.

At first glance, Lord Waldegrave seemed an eminently suitable choice. He was thirty-eight years old in 1753, a man of the world, shrewd, even-tempered and disinclined to burden himself or others with a passionate commitment to any cause. But these Walpolean attributes were not calculated to make for an easy relationship with the nervously insistent Princess of Wales, and to make matters worse, Waldegrave had a long pedigree as a Lord of the Bedchamber and friend to George II. Augusta viewed him with disapproving suspicion, and soon the Prince of Wales did too. Waldegrave's pragmatic attempt to bring Leicester House and St James's closer together by representing to each the best of the other was a failure in both households, and his idea of educating the Prince of Wales by rational conversation was misguided. Neither the Prince nor his mother was interested in compromise or reason. Augusta had no desire to be persuaded of the King's good intention. George, for his part, was seeking not so much the pleasure of rational instruction as the love and approbation of a father figure whom he could adore in return.

His new governor found the Prince of Wales in a fog of melancholy. Prince Edward accused his brother of 'want of spirit' in the face of their tutor's disapproval, but George was more miserable than idle, unable to concentrate, sleeping his days away when he could, and feeling ashamed that he did so. Waldegrave could make no headway with such a sullen, self-lacerating pupil, although he understood the Prince's temperament well enough, and summed it up a few years later, writing: 'He has great command of his passions, and will seldom do wrong, except when he mistakes wrong for right.' When he arrived, he found the Prince 'uncommonly full of princely prejudices contracted in the nursery', he wrote. He complained that these ideas proved impossible to shift and behind the Prince's recalcitrance he discerned the hostility of the Princess of Wales. Waldegrave had no interest in a struggle for the Prince's soul and after three years and little progress, he resigned his post.

Waldegrave was convinced that Augusta would not have opposed him alone. He suspected that one of her advisers in particular had set her against him, and identified the culprit as Lord Bute, who by now held pride of place in the Princess's confidence and closet. Bute's influence was easy to explain, Waldegrave believed. With his 'good person, fine legs, and ... theatrical air of the greatest importance', the Scotsman had seduced the Princess. Waldegrave was sure that by the time he resigned they had been lovers for years. But he underestimated the complexity of the relationship between them. Augusta, with her fear and hatred of vice, would never give in to, or even allow herself to feel, unbridled passion. The Earl of Bute was himself too chilly a personality to find much satisfaction in either physical or corporeal possession. Nonetheless, Waldegrave realised that Bute had some sort of power over the Prince and his mother, and that he was much more than an occasional companion and adviser, as Dodington and Egmont had been.

Lord Bute had only become intimate with the Prince and Princess of Wales six months before Frederick died, and thereafter had no official position at Leicester House. But he quickly made himself indispensable to Augusta, and he did so because he pursued his goal with a single-mindedness lacking in his rivals. Unlike Dodington, Egmont and Waldegrave, Bute had no immediate political aspirations and did not seem to look beyond Leicester House to a wider stage. His mentality, in a political world that was fast becoming professionalised, was that of an old-fashioned royal favourite. First and foremost he sought personal control over the Princess of Wales and her son. His great talents were for demanding unconditional affection while offering his own heart only partially and at intervals, and for convincing himself and his royal confidants that he acted from the most disinterested sense of duty.

By the mid-1750s, Bute's influence over the young Prince was almost complete. Yet despite its inequality and sinister as it may have been that Bute felt most alive when he could feel the effects of his personal dominance, there were benefits for the Prince of Wales in the relationship. Wanting Bute to approve of and love him pulled George out of his stupor. Bute worked hard to establish his hold over the Prince and George worked equally hard to maintain his own servitude. By 1755 he was convinced that he had had the amazing good fortune to find just that 'true friend' his father had recommended. Bute's tight-lipped severity and his habit of handing out home truths without any softening qualification were only confirmation of his fitness for the job. 'My dear Lord', George wrote to Bute in June 1756 a few weeks after his eighteenth birthday, 'I have had the pleasure of your friendship during the space of a year, by which I have reap'd great advantage, but not the improvement I should if I had follow'd your advice; but you shall find me make such a progress this summer, that shall give you hopes that with the continuation of your advice, I may turn out as you wish.' To keep himself worthy of Bute's attention and friendship, the Prince declared, 'I will throw off that indolence which if I don't soon get the better of will be my ruin.'

The Prince was as good as his word. In October, Waldegrave, seeing himself usurped by a man more desirous than he of the affection of his charge, walked gracefully away, and Bute took over as unofficial governor. Now, the boy who had written on his Latin translation, in bad French, 'Monsieur Caesar, je vous soite [souhaite] au diable', endured not only hours of essay-writing, but Bute's critical marginalia as well. He learned his lessons in carefulness so well that as king he initialled every page of every official document that was put on his desk. Bute gave the Prince a reason to hurry out of bed in the morning and fixed his quotidian timetable, which from that time forward the Prince never varied. Following a regime that gained in virtue what it lost in pleasure, he got up very early, sat at his desk for hours, ate the plainest of food very sparingly, and kept his figure trim with long and arduous sessions in the saddle. 'I beg you to be persuaded', he wrote to Bute in early 1757, 'that I will constantly reflect whether what I am doing is worthy of one who is to mount the throne, and who owes everything to his Friend.'

It was not surprising that, as the needs of both the Prince of Wales and his friend were so neatly sustained by their relationship, and as the Princess of Wales had herself fallen under Bute's cold spell, all of them should seek to solidify the Earl's position in the household even before the resignation of Lord Waldegrave. In July 1756, when George was eighteen, the King and his ministers decided that he should leave Leicester House and establish a separate household at St James's Palace. After consulting with both his mother and his friend, George accepted the offer of a household, but asked if he could set it up not at St James's, but at Savile House, next door to Leicester House, which his mother already leased and used as offices and occasional sleeping quarters for her staff. He could not be 'separated' from his mother, he wrote to the King, adding a further request that Lord Bute be made head of the new establishment.

Neither the King nor the Prime Minister the Duke of Newcastle wished to see an inexperienced peer in such a position of influence, and they would have heard the rumours that Bute was the Princess of Wales's lover. So the Duke of Newcastle tried to pre-empt a quarrel over the appointment by pushing in Bute's way a generous pension offer. But nothing, in Bute's case, could have been less effective. Though later he may have benefited from his former pupil's generosity when he came to buy his sumptuous country house at Luton Hoo, Bute was not greedy for money. Besides, he had anticipated Newcastle's reaction and prepared the Prince to ride out the administration's displeasure by writing to him. 'It will sooner or later be whispered in your ear, "don't you know that Lord Bute was your father's friend and is strongly attached to the Princess. He only means to bring you under your mother's government." Sure, you are too much of a man to bear that.' So when the objection to Bute was made clear to George, he reacted with predictable self-centred extremity, convinced that the King and the government meant to attack him personally rather than pragmatically remove a man who might become a problem to them, and he wrote to Bute, 'My friend is . . . attacked in the most cruel and horrid manner, not for anything he has done against them, but because he is my friend.' In the face of Bute's high-minded incorruptibility and the Prince's wild emotion, Newcastle gave in.

So, in the autumn of 1756, the Prince of Wales moved into Savile House with Lord Bute, a household of about fifty servants and office-holders, and his younger brother Prince Edward as a companion. George was delighted, but Edward was not. He carried within himself the memory of his father's special love and, having no need of a substitute, he resented Lord Bute. Refusing to bow to his will, he mimicked his Scottish accent and mocked his air of portentous gravity. While the Prince of Wales stayed within the confines of the household, working doggedly at his spelling and history, riding with Lord Bute along the new road through Hyde Park to Kensington and sending him notes when they were parted, Prince Edward slipped out of Savile House into a world he had up till then only seen through his coach window or from the velvet-padded seclusion of the royal box at the Opera House.

With an equerry mounted by his side or sitting with him in a carriage, five minutes' trot up the east side of Leicester House, across St Martin's Lane, along Long Acre and down James Street brought Prince Edward into Covent Garden. The Piazza, with the vegetable and flower market in the middle, the Covent Garden theatre at the north-east corner and coffee houses and 'bagnios' dotted all around, was described in the contemporary *Connoisseur Magazine* as 'the acknowledged region of gallantry and wit'. Prince Edward knew it as the home of his father's visitors from the Opera and the playhouse, a world away from Leicester House now, but still only a stone's throw, bustling and seductive, beckoning and waiting.

That autumn in the taverns round the Piazza – the Shakespeare and the Queen's Head, the Piazza and the Bedford where actors gathered bleary in the morning or late at night after performances – words were being slung to and fro across the tables with more energy than usual. Port Mahon, Bohemia, Silesia and St Kitts; the new war in Europe, India and the Americas was making their unfamiliar cadences commonplace. Maps and etchings were giving them site and substance, none more so than the star-shaped earthworks of Fort St Philip on the island of Minorca. The fortress looked as delicate as a snowflake on the pages of a periodical, but its loss broke the spirit of the British Marines on the island and led eventually to the execution of their commanding officer, Admiral Byng. The war started badly, but in the years that followed, new words with huge territorial implications were added to the lexicon – Quebec and the Heights of Abraham, Pondicherry and Plassey, St Vincent and the Grenadines – battles and lands that consolidated Britain's imperial power.

When war talk palled, Covent Garden offered plenty of other entertainments. There were shops and brothels, street-sellers and entertainers, and, at the Bedford Coffee House, Samuel Foote held forth. Foote was a comedian who mimicked his fellow actors and actresses with unmistakable precision and a hint of cruel exaggeration. When he had skewered them, he turned to well-known politicians and newly fashionable London professionals, like the Scottish doctor William Hunter, who ran a popular anatomy school stocked with wax cadavers and bottled specimens only a few doors away.

Foote's brilliance and veiled malice entranced Prince Edward, and he was delighted to take his place amongst the actors, rakish aristocrats and men on the make who clustered round him. If, on his first forays to Covent Garden from Savile House the Prince watched from a distance, it would not be long before he determined to join the fun. He was a younger son with a fleet of younger brothers and no obvious or defined role. With his mother worrying about Prince George and caught like him in Lord Bute's sticky web, no one was keeping an eye on his behaviour, and Prince Edward was fully determined to make the most of their inattention.

It was a cool summer and a cold autumn, noteworthy to rural weather watchers carefully tabulating temperatures and rainfall, but trouble-some for revellers who wanted to make the most of the capital's outdoor attractions. Wrapping up warm in a thick frock-coat or close-pulled cloak, Prince Edward might have gone eastwards to West Smithfield, where, amongst the condemned cattle awaiting slaughter and hanging sides of beef, 'eminent performers lately arrived from Italy' were singing, dancing and tumbling at Bartholomew Fair. At Vauxhall Gardens, not far from his father's boat-house at Lambeth, he could have heard Miss Stephenson and Mr Lowe belt out for the last of the summer visitors their season's sensation, 'Tell me

Lasses', which had already been printed up and sung in parlours and drawing rooms across the country.

But if he wanted to stay warm, the Prince had only to make use of the royal boxes at the theatres, to which he now had access with his gentlemen and friends and without the company of his mother or siblings. Garrick's company, ninety-five strong, opened at Covent Garden at the end of September, and with Rich's company at Drury Lane, was offering an enticing mixed bill of old favourites like *The Beggar's Opera*, classics like *Hamlet*, with Garrick himself in the title role, and new farces such as *The Funeral, or Grief à la Mode*.

While Prince Edward was making the most of his new-found independence, Prince George was becoming more bound up than ever with Lord Bute. Because he inclined to the extreme, and because Lord Bute had convinced him that their enemies lay waiting like wolves, stealthily encircling them and ready to strike, his reaction to political events was swiftly becoming apocalyptic. Believing in the spring of 1757 that his uncle the Duke of Cumberland was about to form a government with the fast-rising parliamentarian Henry Fox, a man he regarded as larcenous and depraved, he wrote to Bute from the safety of Savile House: 'If the government should remain two or three years in the hands of these mirmidons of the blackest kind, I imagine any invader with a handful of men might place himself on the throne and establish despotism here.' The most horrible scenes presented themselves to his pent-up imagination. In November 1757, when the war on the Continent was at last swinging away from the French and towards Britain and her German allies, he convinced himself that invasion was imminent, and wrote to Bute: 'I begin now to think that you and I, my Friend, shall see the end of this once great and glorious country.'

The Prince of Wales was only just nineteen. Sometimes he withered under his self-imposed task of making Britain 'again famous for being the residence of true piety and virtue', as he put it, and declared his desire of 'retiring to some uninhabited cavern', without even his mentor to keep him company. Bute, though, was unlikely to spring the Prince from Savile House life. Indeed, all through 1757 and the following year he kept George on a tightrope of anxiety, convinced that only his friend could save him from falling into the pit of lethargy and self-hatred that had made him little better than those he so despised. In September 1758 Bute upbraided the Prince for his laziness and reluctance to tackle his studies, threatened to leave his service and drew from him the usual abject response. 'If you should resolve to remain a little longer', the Prince wrote, 'and see whether these wholesome conversations have alter'd my ways of acting, I would with the greatest vigour attempt by my conduct to convince you that they have made a lasting effect.' Promising again 'to throw off that incomprehensible indolence, inattention and heedlessness that reigns within me', the Prince signed himself, in touching imitation of his own father, 'most entirely yours, George P'.

George was spending less and less time with the brother who had been his closest companion and his protector. Edward's dislike of Lord Bute and his desire for novelty and excitement drove him to make new friends, young men from outside the court who were riding the waves of each new fashion that rolled through the capital. They were as different as possible from the virtuous and anxious company he found at home: fast-living, fast-talking and seriously committed to folly. Principal among them was Francis Blake Delaval, whose life conformed so much to a rakish template that it was almost inevitable that by 1771 a part of it had already been turned into a novel with the alluringly romantic title, *The Genuine Distress of Damon and Celia*. Delaval was a decade older than Prince Edward, born in 1727. His life even before he met the Prince had been prompted in part by a search for the sort of sensation that might not have been out of place in a Restoration court, in part by a concentrated and even scholarly interest in invention and novelty that connected him to the experiments and discoveries of some of the best-known scientists of the day. He was both a rake interested in experiments and an aficionado of science who turned discovery into novelty. At a time when the commercial application of scientific discovery and mechanical invention was transforming attitudes to the physical world and at the same time harnessing these changes for the purposes of manufacturing, Delaval showed himself a man who both understood the newest discoveries and cheerfully stood aside from them, turning them into fun while others turned a profit.

Such fascination with and disdain for the union between science and commerce was a product of Delaval's childhood. For generations, the Delaval family of Northumberland had been gentlemen above the ground and merchants below it. They mined the rich coal deposits that lay beneath their sheep-cropped seaside estate, sending it out from their harbour at Seaton to warm the homes of Londoners and provide power for manufactures up and down the coast. Fortunate in the meeting of coast and coal, the Delavals had used their own fuel for four hundred years to heat sea water and extract the sparkling white sea-salt which was used to preserve fish in Hull and Yarmouth. Francis Delaval escaped from salt and carbon heritage as soon as he could, abandoning the huge gaunt mansion designed by Vanbrugh on the estate, and setting himself up in the family's town house in Downing Street in Westminster. Once installed he threw enough money about to get himself elected as MP for Hinden in 1751, but his tall, dark and commanding form was far more often spotted in the boxes at Covent Garden than on the benches of the House of Commons.

But although he was wild and sensation-seeking, Delaval took science seriously, filling his Downing Street house with beautiful and precise instruments: orreries and steam engines, hobby horses, singing birds and monkeys that chattered up and down sticks. They were all constructed using the newest mechanics: magnets and flywheels, springs and pressure pumps. The tenacity with which he built his collection quickly gained him other objects too, women in quantity and a hearing in the coffee houses of Covent Garden. When he met Prince Edward, Delaval was already intimate with Samuel Foote and could offer himself to the Prince as an aristocratic bridge to a world he longed to enter.

By the time the Seven Years War broke out in 1756, Delaval was broke. Meeting Prince Edward and paving the way for him to become intimate with Foote might for another man have offered a road back to prosperity. But neither the company of Foote nor the glamour of Prince Edward was enough to keep boredom away for long. War glimmered on the horizon and seemed to promise an excitement and a novelty equal to anything that London had to offer. In 1758, to the astonishment of his friends, Delaval enlisted as a private in the Grenadiers and sailed away for the coast of Brittany in a 150-strong fleet under the command of the young commodore Sir Richard Howe. A few weeks later he was back, dining out on the glory of having been the first British soldier to wade through the surf and onto French soil during a punitive back-door raid.

One expedition was all the war Delaval wanted. He was awarded a knighthood for gallantry and left the Grenadiers in glory. In Portsmouth, Commodore Howe was preparing to sail back to France again, and this time Prince Edward would be with him. Perhaps prompted by Delaval's stories, he asked his grandfather if he could join the navy, and was hurriedly enlisted as a midshipman on the *Essex*, Howe's flagship. Before he arrived Howe was instructed, as he wrote later, 'to act respecting him just as if I had not any such person aboard the ship'. This was difficult since Prince Edward came blithely unprepared, with no uniform and none of the bedding and linen that midshipmen had to bring. Howe took the Prince shopping, made sure he had a bevy of captains to accompany him to the ship when he returned properly clothed, and then left him to weeks of waiting in the Solent for orders and a favourable wind.

When it came, the action was dramatic. The fleet was majestic and substantial. Sailing south-west in close formation down the Channel, were twenty-four ships, the sixty-gun *Essex* in command, the frigates *Pallas* and the *Brilliant*, with thirty-six guns each, and an accompanying swarm of smaller fast boats like the dashing sloops *Swallow* and *Speedwell*, carrying sixteen guns apiece, that could dart in and out of the more cumbersome men-of-war, and the little fireships *Pluto* and *Salamander*, eight guns light and ready to be launched with a following wind into an enemy fleet. The whole creaking · group headed for Cherbourg at the end of August. The town's defenders were caught unawares, and after taking the port and destroying its shoreline forti-fications, Howe sailed round to St Malo, where the Grenadiers were landed on 3 September and given orders to march on the town. But this time the French were ready. The sudden arrival of a well-armed defence force of six thousand soldiers, local militia men and armed peasants, sent the Grenadiers flooding back to the sea. Rescue boats had to approach the shore through a wall of shell and shot fired from the bluffs above the beach, and though most of the soldiers were re-embarked safely, the expedition was abandoned, and the Prince was on his way home.

The next year, though, he was back again, cruising off Brest in the *Romulus*, on the lookout for French men-of-war, but finding, as he put it, 'nothing but Dutchmen or convoys'. Ease and pleasure made the Prince look around him with Covent Garden eyes. A good many 'comical fellows' made up for a lack of women, and Edward went to hear their singing. There were several fiddlers aboard too, who played boldly for him even in rough weather, as he explained to the landlubbers at home: 'The prodigious rolling we had two nights ago had so little effect on me that I had music during that time, and should have continued at it without any inconvenience from it had not a sudden roll overturned the table, fiddlers and all, and another very near canted the base and your humble servant clean over a twelve pounder.'

The blockade of Brittany was interrupted to allow for refitting and supplying in mid-October. Prince Edward requested leave and drove hard up to London, arriving in time for the first events of the season. Although he would have the title of rear-admiral by the end of the war, he saw little action on the water and was always easily lured away to the more comfortable delights of the capital. In the autumn of 1759, he had a particular reason for his sudden abandonment of naval life. He had fallen in love, and not with a Covent Garden dancer or a curvaceous actress, but with a society widow who was upright, severe, and not accustomed to waiting.

Her name was Lady Mary Coke, and she was the daughter of the Duke of Argyle. Witty, pretty and with a host of well-connected relatives, she had been married at twenty to Edward Coke, heir to the Earl of Leicester, a noted agricultural improver and owner of a large seaside estate. The marriage was a disaster from the very first night, and reportedly remained unconsummated. Lady Mary alleged cruelty and her husband cordially acknowledged his hatred of her. They were separated in 1749, and by a stroke of fortune Coke died a year later, allowing Lady Mary to exchange the uncertain status of a separated wife for the enviable pleasures of widowhood on £2,500 a year.

In friends, Lady Mary inspired exasperation and affection in not quite equal measure. She had a slight, captivating figure, a round face and a pert look that was immediately attractive. Quick-witted, good company and well-educated, she was nonetheless unable to see herself in the mirror of irony, and maintained a rigid belief in the sagacity of her judgement and her understanding of character. Yet her heart was a finely adorned and thoroughly old-fashioned temple to social standing. Though, for instance, she was an accomplished lutanist and loved the theatre, she scorned actors and musicians who might have given her variety and pleasure. In the extensive running letters that she wrote in instalments to her sisters Anne and Caroline, reading, politics, gossip and fashion were scarcely mentioned. Lady Mary saw herself as a chronicler of the elevated world of St James's, and little, except her own ill-fortune and comings and goings in the courts of Europe, interested her beyond it.

In an age that now looked forward and out, Lady Mary loved to look back. When she had herself painted by Allan Ramsay in 1762, she chose both a costume and a prop that advertised her devotion to the previous century. Ramsay painted Lady Mary standing up, looking combatively out of the picture and holding the stem of a bass-lute, an instrument she prided herself on playing well, but which had long gone out of fashion, except in pockets of her native Scotland. As if to emphasise her retrospective tendency, she wears an old-fashioned satin gown, with puffed and gathered sleeves, a nipped-in waist and a stiff standing petticoat, quite at odds with the prevailing fashion for loose sacks which hung softly from the shoulder.

Lady Mary presented Prince Edward with a challenge. They first met when he was seventeen, and by the winter of 1758, two years later, when he had passed through flirtations with two married society women, Lady Essex and the Duchess of Richmond, he had fallen in love with her. Lady Mary was thirty-two to his nineteen, and along with her wit and beauty, her ornamental manners and elegant propriety offered a tempting obstacle. For a young man who was used to getting what he wanted straight away, Lady Mary's austere unavailability was suddenly irresistible. He began calling at her house overlooking Green Park; he tried sending her presents and asking to exchange books into which he could tuck a note that would catch her interest. Although he was not a seductive writer and had always saved most of his energies for mimicry and wit, Prince Edward was decently fluent and felt more confident on paper than faced with Lady Mary in all her stagy dignity. Returning a volume that she had lent him some time in the winter of 1758, and referring to himself as a distant object in the third person, he was able to tell her that 'he can never omit an opportunity of assuring her of the regard and affection he has for her', and went on with half-assumed, half-real humility, 'he knows how very imperfectly he can do this in writing, but that he must certainly fail if he ventures an expression on the subject'.

When this sort of appeal failed to move what the Prince called Lady Mary's 'awful and severe' comportment, he tried harder. He sent his own lute tuner to set her bass-lute to rights and followed that up with a note asking if he could visit. Then Lady Mary fell ill, offering Prince Edward a golden opportunity for enquiries sent by his servants and for a shower of letters, notes and awkward flattery. 'Thursday morning, ten o'clock', he wrote, 'Prince Edward should certainly, upon not hearing a satisfactory account of her health on Tuesday, have sent again yesterday, had he not chosen to live in uncertainty concerning what interests him most, than, by following the impetuosity of his regard etc., to run the risk of incurring her displeasure by an overbearing troublesome assiduity. He shall flatter himself therefore to hear that she's awake and better.'

Lady Mary chose to be displeased. Ten o'clock was too early to be writing notes to a lady. The Prince, knowing that she kept very early hours, allowed himself the luxury of an ironic apology. 'Prince Edward sends his compliments to Lady Mary Coke and cannot help making another attempt to enquire how she does. Is provoked with himself for not remembering the fashionable hours better than to enquire after a lady's health at so early an hour, as must oblige her to send back word she's asleep out of complaisance and conformity to an idle, dissipated and unthinking age.'

For the most part, Lady Mary refused to allow light-hearted dalliance. 'Sir', she began in reply to one of Edward's letters which displayed more than his usual tenderness, 'I am extremely sensible of the honour your Royal Highness has done me in the many instances of respectful regard you have favoured me with.' But, 'even the honour of your regard when become too particular may give room for the malice of the world to censure my conduct – and permit me to say, your Royal Highness, that I cannot bear the thoughts of submitting even to the most trifling suspicion. You have too much justice, Sir, I am persuaded, to be offended at my desiring that your Royal Highness wou'd add one more instance of regard to the many you have already honoured me with, by avoiding everything that may make me an object of suspicion.'

Prince Edward chose to take these reprimands not at face value, but as a suggestion that he be more discreet. 'I have troubled you with this letter to assure you how ready I am to obey everything you think proper, but to entreat you at the same time to allow me as frequent opportunities of seeing you as may appear consistent with that prudence you have always acted with', he replied, signing off cheerily, 'your most affectionate friend Edward'.

Lady Mary could never admit the pleasure Prince Edward's devotion gave her. She was a flirtatious rather than a passionate woman, and such a correspondence was delightful and flattering. But in the end she paid too much attention to what she thought convention required and not enough to the workings of her own heart. For underneath her rigidity, Lady Mary began to revel in the Prince's adoration and to harbour a hope that it might eventually flower into something more. But she was unable even to hint at her own feelings. Casting away the chance of happiness, she rebuffed the Prince at every turn. 'Your Royal Highness does me great honour', she wrote in response to another letter later that winter, 'and I am extremely sensible of your goodness, but it is not only the appearances I mean to avoid – those are chiefly for the world and, although always to be regarded, are by no means sufficient to satisfy one that thinks as I have always done. I would have no pleasure in the applause of the world if I did not know I deserved it. Praise unmerited turns to censure. Strictness of conduct as well as strictness of honour must always guide my actions, and it would be highly improper to see your Royal Highness often at my house.'

Prince Edward was undeterrred by Lady Mary's high-mindedness, perhaps because when he did manage to get into her Green Park drawing room he fell under her spell again, perhaps because her very reserve spurred him on. For her part, Lady Mary luxuriated in his devotion. Nothing changed between them through the winter of 1758 and into the following spring. Besides the occasional private meeting, they saw each other often at court, at concerts and at the theatre. Nonetheless it was a lopsided admiration. Prince Edward may have persuaded himself that he was in love, but he had plenty to distract him from Lady Mary's froideur. She, on the other hand, could only sit and wait for his letters and visits, and her impassivity was heightened because for the most part she refused to recognise the milieu in which he moved when he was not at court, despite the fact that its denizens could be seen every day parading in the park beyond her windows.

In Green Park, and in St James's, actors and actresses, courtesans, pickpockets and charlatans mixed with grazing sheep, respectable citizens and the very poor. Sometimes they seemed interchangeable, and very often those who lived on high society seemed more interesting than those who lived in it. Certainly in the winter of 1758 the sensation of the season was not an eligible lady at court, but a nineteen-year-old courtesan, Kitty Fisher. Kitty had an enviable list of admirers, picked and prominent as heroes of a nation at war. In short order she had been taken up by Admiral Audon, Commander Keppel and General Ligonier, and the *Public Advertiser* was equally quick to print an admiring description of her charms. When Kitty rode each day round Hyde Park, crowds bunched along the sandy bridle way as if she were a new object in an exhibition of wonders. 'You must come to town to see Kitty Fisher', wrote a new arrival, Tom Bowlby, to a friend stuck back home in Gloucestershire, 'the most pretty, extravagant, wicked little whore that ever flourished. You may have seen her but she was nothing till this winter.'

Kitty knew she had little time to make her mark and her fortune and that she had to do everything she could to burn brightly in the firmament of stars. On 12 March 1759 she staged an accident that not only would display her to the best possible advantage but would also make the news and allow her to eclipse all her rivals. Trotting out of Hyde Park past the lodge at the top of the road to Knightsbridge, her horse shied at a crimson file of advancing soldiers, and she tumbled to the ground in front of a horrified crowd. Immobile for a few seconds, her black riding habit spread out revealingly on the roadway, she suddenly – so newspaper reports had it – laughed merrily, jumped up, hopped into her gilded sedan chair which had opportunely appeared, and took off.

Sensation followed. The incident was written up in the press and formed the subject of several poems and pamphlets. Scenting a bonanza, the hacks worked overtime. On 27 March, only fifteen days after the fall, an anonymously written imaginary memoir, *The Juvenile Adventures of Kitty Fisher*, went on sale at the popular price of three shillings, and inside promised a follow-up volume the next week. For Kitty herself, the appearance of a spurious autobiography was a godsend. She immediately inserted a disclaimer in the *Public Advertiser* saying that not only was she was suing the printer of the *Juvenile Adventures*, she was also slandered by reports circulating about her. 'Miss Fisher', she wrote, 'is forced to sue ... to protect her from the basenesses of little scribblers, and scurvy malevolence. She has been abused in the public papers, exposed in print shops, and to wind up the whole, some wretches – mean, ignorant and venal – would impose upon the public by daring to pretend to publish her memoirs.'

For Kitty Fisher, who wanted as much publicity as possible, the symbiosis between the press, the public and the notorious individual worked beautifully. She was cheerfully prepared to feed the public with information about herself and to increase the profits of the printers as she did so. Her position as the most fashionable courtesan of the season was assured and her prices rose accordingly. Several racehorses as black as her riding habit were named after her and less than a month after her fall she paid the first of many visits to the studio of Sir Joshua Reynolds. Underwritten by a new admirer, Sir Charles Bingham, she had her image fixed so that it could be engraved and distributed across the country.

Kitty's fame and chattiness soon attracted Prince Edward. He found getting an invitation to her house surprisingly easy, and after a loquacious tête-à-tête, left fifty guineas in cash on her hall table on the way out. Kitty made it clear that she was disgusted. She expected to be paid for her body, but not with cash like a common prostitute, and her time, wit and charm came free. Inferring, as Lady Mary Coke would never have dared to do, that the Prince was both vulgar and ignorant of the modus operandi of her own rarefied world, she forbade him her house. Letting it be known that she had done so, she may have reckoned that advertising her spurning of the Prince would in the end be more lucrative, or at least win her more notoriety, than having him as a client or even an admirer.

While Prince Edward was trying to be both well-behaved lover to Lady Mary and young man about town with no cares in the world, Prince George, at Savile House, was falling mutely, ponderously and helplessly in love. Like a great ocean swell that had gathered far out to sea, his 'daily increasing admiration of the fair sex' crested and crashed against the first beautiful girl he came across. Her name was Lady Sarah Lennox. She was fourteen, newly presented at court and described by the Prince of Wales as 'everything I can form to myself lovely'. The Prince's feelings intensified as the winter went on, leaving him more confused than elated and more miserable than transported. Because he had made Lord Bute the potent repository of his love, Prince George felt he had to offer up even this new adoration to his friend. But, for the first time, he rebelled against Bute's domination, silently hiding and conserving his desire, staying alone to nurture it and watching it grow like a hothouse flower.

Lord Bute sensed the Prince's silent challenge to his authority, and pressed him in the evenings to divulge his secret, subtly threatening a withdrawal of his approbation if he failed to do so. The Prince stubbornly resisted, knowing that if he surrendered it, his love would wither in the light of day and under the Earl's cold scrutiny. 'Dearest Friend', the Prince wrote after having one evening narrowly avoided divulging his secret, 'as to what he hinted at but in the kindest manner kept in, that I can with the greatest truth assure him I have long wished to communicate; indeed it has two or three times been almost out, had not on these occasions a certain diffidence seized me with regard to lessening me in his opinion.'

'I mean to lay my whole breast before you', the Prince of Wales began another anguished letter to Bute that winter. But he still could not give in. It was only as spring was coming that he sat down one morning and wrote, 'What I now lay before you I never intended to communicate to any one', and in a mood of triumphant self-abnegation, told Lord Bute the whole story of his passion for Sarah Lennox, and concluded, 'I don't deny having flattered myself with hopes that one day or other you would consent to my raising her to a Throne.' Putting his fate in Lord Bute's hands was, as Prince George knew quite well, the same as giving up his love, and abandoning his feeble groping towards some emotional independence. 'If I must either lose my friend or my love, I will give up the latter', he told Bute, concluding with histrionic bathos, 'tho' my heart should break, I shall have the happy reflection in dying that I have not been altogether unworthy of the best of Friends, tho' unfortunate in other things'.

Bute's triumph seemed to be complete, and having firmly dismissed the Prince's dreams of Sarah Lennox by writing back briskly, 'the case admits of not the smallest doubt', he made it clear that any unhappiness George felt did not come from his dear friend but from his position in life. 'Think, Sir', Bute wrote, 'who you are, what is your birth right, what you wish to be, and prepare your mind with a resolution to hear the truth, for such alone shall come from me.' The Prince of Wales had already come sadly to the same conclusion. He would, he told his mentor, endeavour to 'keep under' 'this combat in my breast', and he would do it by attention to work, because 'keeping the mind constantly employed is a likely means of preserving those passions in due subordination to it'. So the Prince forced his feelings below the surface. In the spring and autumn of 1760, he continued to see Sarah Lennox at court and to talk to her, but he said nothing, did nothing, and allowed himself to feel almost nothing except his own gratitude to Lord Bute. 'I am born for the happiness or misery of a great nation', he concluded, as if it were destiny itself that had forced his choice, rather than either his own emotional extremity or his ignorance of the way he had been so skilfully manipulated by his friend.

The Prince hinted to Lord Bute that the struggle between his prudence and his 'boiling youth' would be tipped in favour of the former by his marrying. Bute seized on this idea immediately. A young and newly arrived German princess could be no threat to him, he reasoned, and might easily be brought into the circle of his dominance. Although the Prince had abjectly written, 'I thought the just setting down my resolution never to marry an English woman would please my Dearest Friend', Bute decided to prevent any back-sliding by urging the Prince and his mother to start the search for a bride right away. So the trawl through the shoal of available German princesses began. Even the Prince, who hid any tendency to levity behind his shyness and solemnity, and whose love for Sarah Lennox still burned bright, could see the absurdity of the task. 'Our evening has been spent in looking in the New Berlin Almanach for Princesses', he told Lord Bute, adding, 'three new ones have been found as yet unthought.'

In the pages of the almanach the matter lay dormant for a few months. Then, suddenly, on 25 October 1760, George II died of a heart attack. The Prince of Wales, at twenty-two, became king and Prince Edward, recently created Duke of York, became heir apparent. But just when the need for a queen and a new heir became urgent, and he was free to fix on any princess that he wanted, George seemed to lose interest. In the first few months of his reign, Sarah Lennox was on his mind again and he luxuriated in the pleasure and the guilt of his love for her.

Slowly, though, the young King advanced towards his fate and slowly he forced himself to embrace it. Princesses from Swedt and Darmstadt were assessed and rejected because the erratic natures of their parents gave George 'melancholy thoughts of what may perhaps be in the blood'. Better reports filtered through about the character and disposition of seventeen-year-old Charlotte of Mecklenberg Strelitz. Two incognito scouts described her as plain and one, damningly, as without any beauty at all. But she was also said to be, a little more promisingly, of moderate intelligence, with no disposition to meddle in politics and physically suited to childbearing. George, in self-admonitory mood after falling under the spell before of Sarah Lennox's extravagant good looks, declared that although the reports were 'not in every particular as I could wish . . . yet I am resolved to fix here'. He had already explained to Lord Bute his fear of becoming the 'prey' of women, as he put it, saying that 'Princes when once in their hands make miserable creatures'. 'The annals of France', he explained, showed that quite clearly. Having fallen so far and so fast, he now contented himself with the thought that his bride's lack of allure was insurance against a loss of self-control that might give her undue sway in national affairs.

Negotiations with Princess Charlotte's family and preparations for the wedding went on secretly in the spring and summer of 1761. By 8 July, when the Privy Council was told of the King's intention and it became public news, the Princess had already been measured for her wedding gown, and heavy handfuls of jewels had been bought to adorn it. While the gown was being made up to measurements sent from Germany, the jewels were kept well away from court gossips and prying hacks, at Lord Bute's London house. The Duchess of Northumberland, a court servant and a friend of Lady Bute, went along to see them after the marriage announcement. 'There are an amazing number of pearls of a most beautiful colour and prodigious size', she reported. She was impressed by the flashing grandiosity and the workmanship that turned jewels into the encrusted twinkling panel of the wedding gown's stomacher. But, like many other visitors, she was just as interested in adding up the wealth that sparkled there. 'The stomacher, which is valued at £60,000, is the finest piece of magnificence and workmanship I ever saw. The fond is a network as fine as cat gut of small diamonds and the rest is a large pattern of natural flowers composed of very large diamonds, one of which is 18, another 16 and a third 10 thousand pounds apiece. The middle drop of the earrings cost twelve thousand pounds.'

The King, who had a lock of Princess Charlotte's hair, 'of a very fine dark colour and very soft', and a flattering portrait sent over from Strelitz when the marriage had been agreed, met his bride in the garden of St James's when she arrived on 8 September. He seemed unflustered by her striking plainness. Five hours later Prince Edward led her into the Chapel Royal, which was lined for the occasion, like a womb, in crimson. Five tapestries, sewn in imitation of the Raphael cartoons in the Royal Collection, were mounted on the red velvet and framed in broad golden lace. The altar was wrapped round in gold cloth and its steps were covered in diaphanous silver organza. Crimson thrones, lined with silver and fringed with gold, stood either side of it.

Followed by a double line of unmarried aristocratic girls, including a radiantly beautiful Sarah Lennox, Princess Charlotte walked to her future with Prince Edward on one arm and eighteen-year-old Prince William on the other. Feeling her stumble from fear, exhaustion and the weight of her jewels, Prince Edward whispered in French, 'Courage, Princesse, courage', to keep her going. When the service was over the bride was handed to one of the thrones, where she sat for a few minutes while the orchestra played and the guests looked critically on.

If Lord Bute had assumed that the arrival of a tongue-tied and inexperienced princess would do nothing to dent his relationship with the King, he was mistaken. George applied all his dogged stubbornness to his marriage, and, although with much difficulty and in the face of popular and parliamentary opposition he continued to encourage and demand Bute's parliamentary advancement, privately he began slowly to transfer his loyalty and his quotidian love to the Queen. He was determined that his married life should be exemplary, not least to his own family, and so it proved to be.

Until madness severed their closeness in 1788, the King and Queen lived in harmonious union and produced fifteen children.

Before they were crowned later that month, the King and Queen posed for their official coronation portraits to the Scottish painter Allan Ramsay. Ramsay may have painted almost all of the two huge originals himself, but he must have hired many assistants to help with the scores of copies that would be ordered for country houses up and down the land. These paintings were the monarchs' official presentations of themselves to the country, and ordering a copy, or for less wealthy citizens buying an engraving, was a way of displaying loyalty and of joining in the theatre and enterprise of the new reign.

Ramsay painted the twenty-three-year-old King full length, elevated, a little aloof, and presenting, at eye level, fine calves and elegant legs framed by the soft swirls of his ermine-lined and fringed coronation cloak. With his ceremonial sword half-hidden, the crown only just visible and the orb and sceptre absent, the King seemed a handsome, magnificent young man unburdened by his station. He looks out of the picture steadily as if towards the nation's great destiny, and Ramsay has darkened his unfashionably light eyes to a mature and steady blue.

The ermine and brocade of the coronation were soon cast off. In private or in his office the King favoured simple suits of Prussian blue, or buff or brown, with white cravats, a minimum of lace and a short wig curled above the ears in a way that soon looked old-fashioned. Moreover, neither the serenity nor the magnificence of Ramsay's portrait were carried over into his private, family life. The tranquillity to which George aspired was only sporadically to be his lot, and splendour he never wished for. Though he considered it his duty to be a generous patron of artists, musicians, writers, scientists, instrument makers and architects, he gradually honed his personal habits into an austerity which balanced his outward rejection of excessive and dangerous emotion. Like his mother he was convinced that temperate living and a quiet life would make him virtuous and even good.

'The fault of his constitution', the King told the novelist and courtier Fanny Burney in 1788, 'was a tendency to excessive fat', which he averted, he said, 'by the most vigorous exercise and the strictest attention to a simple diet'. Less than a year after his marriage, his daily habits and his diet were set for life. He got up at six, leaving the Queen, who was almost continuously pregnant for the first two decades of their marriage, to slumber on for a bit. After checking any letters and dispatches that might have come for him in the night, he went for a quick ride. Breakfast with the Queen followed, and then, in the early years, one of his brothers would call if the King was in London, and they would ride out together, through Hyde Park to Kensington and beyond. Until dinner at four, when some of the royal children and other members of the family might be present, George stuck grindingly to his official business, and often returned to his study in the evening.

At about seven the King rejoined the Queen and they spent the evening before supper together fitting in visits to the nursery with seeing the King's mother, now the Princess Dowager, of whom George remained fiercely protective and fond. She lived more at Carlton House and less at Leicester House now, although her children still used Leicester and Savile houses, and they still all went to Kew in the summer. Bute remained the Princess Dowager's confidant and the King often met him at his mother's.

During the season, the King and Queen went to the Opera and to the theatre. But their passion was for music, especially German music. In the intricacies of chamber music and the emotional breadth of large-scale oratorios, the King could lose himself to peace and contentment. He played the flute and harpsichord at home, and it was in music that he dedicated himself to his new domestic life, writing for the Queen a tune he called 'The Royal Bride', which was worked up by the court orchestra and danced to by the assembled guests at the wedding ball. Thereafter the Queen put on a concert weekly, patronising musicians and composers from beyond the court and especially from Germany. Prince Edward played his cello and violin, Prince William the flute, while the Queen and Lady Augusta sang and played the harpsichord.

The court cooks were given fewer opportunities to display their talents than the royal musicians. The extravagances that weighed down aristocratic tables were absent from the King's: he liked his meat plain and undressed, and for dessert, instead of trembling jellies hung like ball gowns with loops of crystallised fruit, he ordered simple bunches of grapes or plain fruit tarts. The Countess of Northumberland noticed as early as the spring of 1762 how unvaried the royal family's diet had become. Every day at dinner the King and Queen had soup, followed by 'a large joint of meat and two other dishes such as a pie or a broiled fowl'. On the side table there was always cold meat and a salad. For a second course the cooks made more pies, often of spinach or sweetbreads, and a fish dish like oysters, shelled and broiled in a sauce. Supper, served about ten in the evening, always followed the same monotonous and carnivorous theme, even when there were guests after concerts or cards. 'Their supper consists of two made dishes,' the Countess of Northumberland wrote, usually 'chicken or smoked turkey à la bechamel, a joint of cold mutton, buttered eggs, custard, and constantly veal and chicken broth.'

In front of the simplicity and order of the new life that George created with the Queen, with its low-stake games of whist or pontoon, visits to the fast-filling nursery and hours of country riding, stood Lord Bute and a political situation that was anything but serene. George had made Lord Bute a Privy Counsellor two days after his accession, signalling vigorously his intention that his friend would play a considerable part in the government of the nation. Three months later he was brought into the ministry headed by William Pitt and the Duke of Newcastle, making the government fatally unstable and earning the resentment of many MPs and commentators who saw in Bute's rise an assertion of royal prerogative and a challenge to the authority of Parliament.

Although Bute had no parliamentary seat and no official ministerial post or responsibility, he quickly came to assume a primary role in government both because he controlled access to the King and because he had his trust. With the Earl as his avatar, George put forward the general scheme that his father had long ago proposed to him, of removing party from politics in order to introduce a kingdom-wide reign of disinterested virtue. But in a professionalised political environment, and one, moreover, in which parliamentarians were determined to maintain their predecessors' hard-won distinction between the person of the monarch and his kingly office, such a programme was anachronistic and unworkable.

Besides, Lord Bute, having achieved political power, had no idea how to use it. His talent was all personal, for emotional domination. As a bureaucrat he was inexperienced, and as a negotiator and leader of men in the highly sophisticated theatre that Parliament had become, he floundered and panicked. His fear bred instability, disgruntlement and opposition. The opacity of government gave opposition groups both inside and outside Westminster the chance to claim that the real figure of power was neither Bute nor the King, but the Princess Dowager, a mother secretly manipulating her son for her own ends, a petticoat government that was emasculating the nation. Piggybacking onto this inflammatory claim a series of demands for more representative government and cleverly using the potent weapon of the press, the opposition MP John Wilkes urged his supporters onto the streets. The crowds carried boots and petticoats in caricature of the favourite and the Princess Dowager and vociferously demanded an end to their supposed usurpation of Parliament.

John Wilkes was a brilliant organiser and rabble rouser who was to be a thorn in the King's side for nearly a decade, the more so since personally he flamboyantly represented just what George feared and had with such difficulty suppressed in himself. Wilkes was a relaxed libertine, unscrupulous and charming, witty, conversational and outgoing. He was sympathetic to the demands of many of his supporters for greater representation in Parliament, personally hostile to the air of probity emanating from Carlton House and St James's and quite ready to harness a disparate pack of discontents to pull himself to power. Perhaps most galling of all for the King, Wilkes was able cheerfully to abandon protest when something more attractive came along. After a turbulent decade when he was elected, arrested, tried, jailed, released and re-elected, Wilkes had the last laugh on his opponents by retreating without rancour from the fray, becoming Lord Mayor of London and retiring to bucolic tranquillity on the Isle of Wight.

In the face of all sorts of opposition from both inside and outside Parliament, the first administration of George III's reign was a shambles. William Pitt, who had governed in coalition since the end of 1756, and was regarded as the architect of Britian's gains in the continuing war, resigned in protest at the conduct of the peace negotiations in 1761, leaving Bute and Newcastle to carry on the business of government more exposed than ever to the rage of the opposition. Bute brought the long war to an end, and the Peace of Paris, signed in 1762, added to Britain's possessions a rich necklace of colonies that looped round the world from Quebec to the Caribbean, Louisiana to the Indian sub-continent, right up to Minorca and home. But it was an unpopular peace and left Bute despised and scorned. He wilted and crumbled under the pressure and in a long letter to a friend, written at the end of January 1763, theatrically declared his intention of retiring. 'Tho' in the bosom of victory', he said, he trod constantly, 'on the brink of a precipice', and waiting for his envious enemies to push him off had brought him to a nervous collapse. Bute spared no details. 'My health', he wrote, 'is every day impairing. A great relaxation of my bowels of many years standing is increasing on me continually; the eternal unpleasant labour of the mind, and the impossibility of finding hours for exercise and proper medicine, the little time I get for sleep, the little I ever enjoy, even when abed, become invincible obstructions to the cure of an inveterate illness. My health therefore dictates retirement from the greatest weight that ever lay on any man in this country.'

The tables had turned. The man who had so often urged on his pupil the need to bow to his destiny had flinched before his own. The hard taskmaster who had demanded unstinting labour and mental exertion was overcome by it himself. The King, incensed though he was by the attacks on his mother and loyal though he remained to his friend to the end, was powerless to help. The Duke of Newcastle gave in and went into disgruntled retirement, George Grenville took over the government and Bute retreated, first to Bath, then to Harrogate and finally to his sumptuous estate of Luton Hoo in Bedfordshire. George continued to correspond with his old tutor, still in the same tone of emotional subservience and strain of high emotionalism. He still saw him too until at least 1766, despite the promise he had given to his new ministers to the contrary. But the tide of Bute's dominance was ebbing. Many people, both in government and opposition, continued to be suspicious – and with good reason – of Bute's secret influence, and certainly political turmoil did not cease with his departure. But the King and his Dearest Friend gradually drew apart.

Bute left much of use behind on the rocky shore of the King's personality. He had given George the means to carry on day by day, to work unstintingly and to put his head into the stiff harness of government business. What he had failed to do was to temper the histrionic side of George's personality with any sort of emotional pragmatism. Faced with difficulty or reverse the King still reacted with the characteristic blend of passion and stubbornness that complicated and prolonged both personal and political crises.

With his younger siblings, George felt a deep bond, reserving for them a well of tenderness that had been sunk deep into his personality. Even after his wedding, he saw his brothers and sisters frequently. He rode out almost every day with Edward, William and Henry, and often played music with his older sister Augusta. The little ones, Henry, Louisa, Frederick and Caroline Mathilda, whose ages ranged from seventeen to eleven in 1762, he saw when he and his wife spent evenings with his mother and the whole family attended the Chapel Royal on Sundays. But he never forgot that he was both father and brother to them, and as time went on, his relationship with his two eldest siblings, Augusta and Edward, became less fraternal and more fatherly and monarchical. Indeed, one of his first tasks, as monarch, was to find a husband for Augusta, who was already twenty-three when he became king, and was growing increasingly resentful of her immurement inside Leicester House. Like Prince Edward, Augusta disliked and resented Lord Bute. She took far more interest in politics than George believed was appropriate in a woman, and her love of jolliness and intrigue meant that finding a husband was imperative if only to ship her out of the country before her dissatisfaction turned to disruption.

For two generations the cross-Channel traffic in German princesses had been balanced by the dispatch of English princesses to the Continent. George II's sister Sophia Dorothea had married Frederick of Prussia, while of Prince Frederick's sisters, one had become the Princess of Orange, one the Queen of Denmark and one the Duchess of the small German state of Hesse. Although Augusta, ageing and troublesome, was bound to follow them, George's choice for his sister was more expedient than thoughtful.

As early as 1755, when George was only seventeen, his grandfather had proposed that he marry Caroline, the daughter of the Duke of Brunswick-Wolfenbüttel, a small territory that lay in the southern shadow of the Electorate of Hanover. This plan, like any idea that seemed to come from the King, was instantly opposed by the Princess of Wales, and left dangling in mid-Channel. George II tried to revive it in 1759, but Prince George by then declared that the Duke was 'embittered', and flush with the 'pride that generally attends those petty Princes', and that nothing would induce him to take a princess 'out of that House'. As a consolation for the Duke, though, and in recognition of the long-standing alliance between Hanover and Brunswick, he proposed that Augusta should marry his heir, Karl Wilhelm Ferdinand. Negotiations were slow, but a settlement was finally agreed and in early January 1764 the Hereditary Prince, as he was called, arrived in England to carry away his bride.

In the war that had just finished, Karl Wilhelm Ferdinand had made himself a master of irregular warfare, harrying and hunting down the Austrians and the French. He had also masterminded the siege of Crefeld and led the unfashionable infantry on a gallant charge at the Battle of Hestenbach. Though he was only twenty-nine years old, his face had a satisfyingly battle-worn, weatherbeaten look. The deep blue eyes that gazed out from amongst the wrinkles set off a tall figure and an appropriately military bearing. The crowds loved him, and his officers and men felt a deep reverence for him that no British soldier, not even General Wolfe, who had died in the act of winning Quebec, and Canada, from the French, could command. Robert Murray Keith, a Scottish captain who served under the Hereditary Prince in his German campaign of 1758, wrote a breathless panegyric that caught their adoration. 'Behold him', it ran, 'glorious in the conquered field / George's avenger and his country's shield; / Humanity and Justice by his side / And the loud voice of Liberty his guide.'

Augusta and the Hereditary Prince were married on 16 January 1764, but their departure to Brunswick was delayed by days of celebrations and crowd-pleasing tours. By the beginning of February the King was eager for the couple to leave, but Augusta was enjoying her triumph and the world beyond Leicester House too much to be in any hurry. She and the husband she called 'our hero' finally arrived in the newly renovated stone and half-timbered palace at Brunswick in the middle of February.

Unfortunately it did not take very long for Karl Wilhelm Ferdinand to tire of his boisterous bride. He preferred war and other women, his own illegitimate children and the slow reform of the small German territory he inherited when his father died. He cast a cold eye over the marriage business, explaining years later to a friend that centuries of intermarriage among German princely families was a recipe for genetic and amorous disaster since one of his class had to marry according to certain conveniences, which was a most unhappy thing. The heart had nothing to do with these marriages, and the result was not only to embitter life, but also to bring the most disastrous experience on those who came after. The children, he concluded, were mostly cripples in mind and body. Despite his heroic exploits in the Seven Years War, the Hereditary Prince was anything but dashing at home. He was a cautious and cerebral man, loyal to his own illegitimate children, often taciturn in company, whose care for his small country and capacity for administration held no glamour or interest for his wife. Once she had seen beyond the gilding of his heroism, Augusta came up against the rock of his reserve and against his severe intelligence. Headstrong, rumbustious and used to causing a stir, Augusta was mortified and made miserable by her husband's studied indifference to her, and by the gossip that trickled out of the palace and made its way to London.

News was eagerly seized on and relayed. 'All we have heard about their living very ill together is true', wrote the politician and bon viveur Richard Rigby to his patron the Duke of Bedford some time after Augusta and Prince Karl Wilhelm Ferdinand were married. He added, with all the lusty curiosity of a drawing-room gossip, that although the Hereditary Prince's 'outward behaviour' to his wife was 'respectful and full of attention', he 'made no scruple of all kinds of infidelities', and lived his own life.

Rigby's information came from Henry St. John, a courtier in his twenties who was both intimate friend and Gentleman of the Bedchamber to the Duke of York, as Prince Edward was now called. St. John, or the Baptist, as his friends called him, had just returned from a continental tour with his master that had taken them at breakneck speed through France to Sardinia and on to Florence and Rome where, the Duke wrote to Lady Mary Coke, the Pope paid him 'every mark of distinction possible'. The Duke had travelled through the Continent in defiance of his brother's wishes, desperate for novelty and something to do. George III had not yet come up with any constructive role for his younger brother, and peace had destroyed any hope of a real career in the navy. Without offering him any kind of employment, the King made it clear he wanted his brother to stay at home. Part of George's hostility was that of a man who had neither the means of travelling beyond the borders of his own country nor the desire to do so. Part was a wish for his family's affairs to be decorous, economical and tidy. Arriving incognito in foreign capitals, visiting as a private man and unofficially, but then spending and costing as much as any official visitor, the Duke of York, it seemed to the King, simply caused embarrassment and difficulties for Britain's ambassadors.

Prince Edward saw things quite differently, living it up in Rome, and lamenting his own poverty. Pointing a finger at his brother, he enviously compared his own annual income of £12,500 to the reported papal grant of £55,000 a year that his distant cousin, that other Duke of York – the Young Pretender's brother – received as a cardinal of the Roman Catholic Church. On the way home, Prince Edward veered north and stopped in Brunswick. From there the Hereditary Prince and Augusta joined him on the last leg of the journey back to London. St. John told Rigby that Augusta was over-joyed to be returning to the city she had so cheerfully left a few months before, and had theatrically announced 'that she hoped she should die in England'. Half a century later, in the most melancholy of circumstances, her wish was to come true.

By the time of his summer tour on the Continent in 1764, Prince Edward had made himself the lodestone of a group of rakish aristocrats and men and women who made a living from their restless search for novelty and amusement. Something of the tenor of this coterie, and the emphasis they placed on male friendship, shines out of the portrait the Prince commissioned when he arrived in Venice, on the way back from Rome. In the portrait, William Murray, the British envoy in the republic, stands next to the seated Prince, half extending his hand in explanation or in welcome. Around Prince Edward is a nonchalant group of young men. Two of them, Henry St. John and William Temple, were travelling with the Prince's party; the others were temporarily attached to it. But they were all joined by a similar outlook on life. St. John, tall, eager-faced and sporting the aquiline nose of his father, Prince Frederick's mentor the Earl of Bolingbroke, stands loosely, one hand on hip, the other thrown round the shoulder of William Boothby. Boothby was from a Derbyshire land-owning family, and his brother, Brooke, was to become one of the most fervent disciples of the newly notorious French man of letters Jean-Jacques Rousseau, who would arrive to much clamour in England two years after the painting of this portrait. Behind Prince Edward stand Henry Temple, whose father also served Prince Frederick, and who was now making his own entrance as an MP, and John Fitzpatrick, whose brother General Richard was to become a prominent opposition figure and whose sister Mary would soon marry the celebrated 'sleepy macaroni' and man-about-town, Stephen Fox. At the extreme right of the picture, looking with casual lack of interest over his shoulder, slouches Topham Beauclerk, great-grandson of Charles II, a writer, wit and dope-fiend, who, four years later, would run off with St. John's sister-in-law, the beautiful and talented Lady Diana Bolingbroke.

In London, the personnel was more diverse, but the tone of the circle was essentially the same, and had at its heart the serious commitment to pleasure and innovation to which Francis Delaval had already introduced the Duke. Richard Rigby, who had himself embarked on the treacherous waters of politics in the leaky flotilla of Prince Frederick, and was by now well soaked by inebriation and intrigue, did duty at the age of forty-two, as one of the group's elder statesmen. Alongside him was William Douglas, the hugely wealthy and profligate Earl of March, who divided his connoisseurship between the turf, tables at cards and the youngest singers at the opera. Henry St. John was there intermittently, Francis Delaval and one or other of his brothers and sisters almost constantly, pointing the group now towards the Jockey Club at Newmarket, where the young Scottish peer Alexander Montgomerie, Earl of Eglington, sparkled, sang and joked, and now towards Covent Garden, where more wit than cash was needed to maintain a reputation.

In Covent Garden the presiding genius was still the actor Samuel Foote, whom Prince Edward had first encountered in 1756. Foote was an adipose, bald man, his flat features carved in bas-relief out of his shiny bullet-like head. He had, an observer wrote, an 'archness in his eye', constantly scanning any gathering for objects of ridicule, and enjoying the apprehension he inspired in acquaintances, who knew, as one put it, that he never let truth stand between him and a good jest. Born the son of a minor gentleman and magistrate in Devon in 1721, Foote soon gave up an early career arguing in court as a barrister, and put his talent for manufactured outrage, mimicry and wit to more fashionable use by becoming an actor. By the mid-1750s he had became famous for writing and performing one-man shows in which he imitated the gestures and voices of actors, doctors and politicians well known to his audience, and cruelly parodied their pretensions to artistry and fame. Foote was an entrepreneur of novelty. Nothing and nobody fashionable or new escaped him, and he transformed change into words and profit with a sure touch. Magicians who cunningly used magnetism or electricity, doctors, nabobs newly arrived from India after the rapacious advances of the 1760s, naive Grand Tourists palmed off with fake bits of art in Naples and Rome, politicians, actors a-plenty, and, in the 1770s, a few Methodists – all who were new and meretricious were minced up and spat out, each with absurdly funny and recognisable deformities.

It was a tricky, tightrope life. Foote made a living from satirising his audience, at once casting over it the enchantment of his unsettling personality, and dependent upon it for his fame, his income and his sense of self. Like a charismatic monarch or prophet, he seemed to many only fully alive in the act of performance. He could never extinguish the burning lamps of his own fame and he was well aware of it, writing, 'We that live to please, must please to live.' Prince Edward was one of those Foote charmed, and he must have known, like all the actor's friends, that he might one day find his own mannerisms and habits held up to ridicule on the London stage.

These men, with attendant groups of imitators, formed the inner circle around Prince Edward. They were intelligent chancers, men of wit who sat aslant society and who poured great ingenuity and time into ridiculing social and philosophical endeavour and earnestness. Women from both the highest and the lowest social strata came and went. The courtesan and singer Anne Catley was often among them, and she later claimed in her memoirs to have had two illegitimate children, one by Delaval, the other by Prince Edward. There was also a group of pleasure-seeking court and society women: Lady Harrington, Lady Essex, and Francis Delaval's married sisters. Lady Mary Coke mingled with these women in the drawing room, and was, indeed, never averse to a bit of entertainment provided the patina of respectability was laid on thick enough, or if the excitement got the better of her fear of vulgarity.

In the spring of 1762, for instance, the Duke of York persuaded Lady Mary and Horace Walpole to come with him and visit the Cock Lane Ghost, a spectral emanation that was pulling the crowds to a small alley by St Paul's Cathedral. Jumping into a carriage one night after the opera, the trio drove into the City and pushed through the throng to the small house where the ghost staged its nightly act. That night, sensitive to incredulity, it refused to make an appearance, leaving the party to traipse home disappointed. Two years later, while Prince Edward and Lady Mary still carried on their over-courteous and attenuated relationship, she took two court friends, the Imperial ambassadress and Henrietta Vernon, to the Little Theatre with her and recorded in her diary that she was 'well enough pleased' by Samuel Foote's performance.

Around this inner core whirled dozens of neophytes, dancing attendance on greatness like the fizzing sparks in the electrical machines that were just coming into fashion. No ingénue was ever more eager and more impressed by an unexpected proximity to fame and rank than a twenty-year-old Scottish would-be Guards officer, James Boswell. Boswell had run away to London in the early months of 1760, escaping from the rigours of a small Ayrshire mansion and from his father's disapproval. In the midst of a crisis that was spiritual as well as familial, Boswell went to ground. With supremely fortuitous ignorance, Boswell's father asked his neighbour Lord Eglington to find his errant son, give him a dressing-down and put him back on the narrow high road to Scotland.

Boswell, writing the thirty-nine-year-old Eglington up in his diary in 1762, said of him, 'He is a man of uncommon genius for everything: strong good sense, great quickness of apprehension and liveliness of fancy, with great good humour. . . . He has at the same time a flightiness of reverie and absence of mind, with a disposition to outright trifling.' By 1762, Boswell was using his diary to fashion himself into a man of letters, a city wit in the mould of Joseph Addison who would soon don the frogged red coat of an officer of the Guards. But in 1760, he was a twenty-year-old in the grip of melancholy, middle-sized, with pursed lips and a tendency to plumpness, who was running away from his father into the transcendental certainties of Catholicism. Eglington did not then appear as he did two years later, 'neglected in his education', but rather as Boswell's rescuer, mentor and friend.

In 1760, Eglington hauled Boswell out of his dismal lodgings and brushed off his Catholicism by dangling him in front of more earthly delights. First he sent him to a courtesan to lose his virginity and then he introduced him to Mayfair gaiety and Newmarket gambling. Boswell moved into Eglington's apartments in Queen Street just north of Piccadilly and was swept into what he called 'the circles of the great, the gay and the ingenious' on the tide of his new friend's hospitality. He determined to be equal to the shock, and up to a certain point he was. He held his own with the Earl of March and kept his balance when introduced to and flattered by the novelist Laurence Sterne, whose work in progress, *Tristram Shandy*, was the current touchstone of wit. But when he was called down from his room to meet the Duke of York, Boswell's veneer of sophistication cracked. Unable to understand where drollery ended and coterie wit began, he misjudged the situation completely. He was dazzled by royalty and his closeness to it, and wrote in a poem that he sensibly left unpublished:

> That I, without the least restraint
> Have heard them men and manners paint!
> Talk less of books than of mankind,
> And women fickle as the wind,
> When brilliant wit and humour droll,
> Flash'd instant pleasure on my soul!

After the Prince had said, 'Come Boswell, what have you to say', Boswell joined in. Soon he came to believe that the Prince could be not just his conduit to high society and an army commission, but also his friend, 'simple Ned', as he put it to himself. A couple of weeks later, elated at being elected a member of the Jockey Club at Newmarket, he sat in its coffee room and wrote a rambling poem while the Duke and Eglington pursued their business on the track, and read it to them later. Back in London he ran it round to the printer and made himself a proud, published poet. Called 'The Cub, at Newmarket', the verses played on the double meaning of the cub as a young lion and as an initiate in a circle of glamour, and they were, of course, about himself. Boswell jocularly dedicated his poem to Prince Edward. 'Sir,' he wrote, 'Permit me to take this method of thanking your Royal Highness for condescending to like the following sketch. Or, in other words, permit me to let the world know that this same Cub has been laughed at by the Duke of York, has been read to your Royal Highness by the Genius himself, and warmed by the immediate beams of your indulgence.' Intoxicated by the company he was keeping, Boswell assumed the Prince would be as delighted by his 'genius' as he himself had become. He ended his dedication with breezy familiarity, writing: 'I wish your Royal Highness a long, a merry, and a happy life, and am your obliged, devoted servant.'

Boswell was unable, even at twenty, to make an acquaintance without wanting to turn it into print. Later he reconciled his longing for fame and his habit of reverence with his talent for friendship, and produced a masterpiece that has allowed him gradually to eclipse his subject in renown. But in 1760, his bumptiousness and poor judgement cost him dearly. The Prince's circle might have seemed open and even egalitarian, but it was in fact exclusive and self-regarding. Prince Edward had no wish to open his world to the eager scrutiny of the reading public or to be used by Boswell to court its attention. He had not given permission for the dedication and he still withheld it after the poem's appearance. Eglington was embarrassed by his protégé's naivety. Retribution was swift: a letter to Boswell's father, Lord Auchinleck's arrival in the capital and a slow, melancholy journey home for his errant son.

Boswell kept alive his dreams of a military life, the more easily since they were in fact less martial than fantastic. A commission in the Guards was something of a sinecure, and could leave plenty of time for a wit and man of letters to pursue his calling. Amidst the brown and green of the family home at Auchinleck, Boswell dreamed of the red and gold of an officer's life, but never of the mud and blood of battle overseas. Although his father eventually relented and in the autumn of 1762 allowed James to go back to London with an annual allowance and permission to try his luck, Lord Eglington's important patronage remained tantalisingly out of reach. 'He imagined me much in the style that I was three years ago: raw, curious, volatile, credulous', Boswell wrote in his journal, annoyed that Lord Eglington still saw his younger self. 'I told him I was sorry that my dedication without leave to the Duke of York had been ill-taken, and I insisted that he should make it up and bring us together, which he half-assented to.'

Eglington had no wish to magnify his earlier indiscretion. He made it up with Boswell himself, and promised to push him forward. But neither a Guards commission nor another meeting with Prince Edward ever came Boswell's way. So Boswell drifted away from high society wits and began assiduously to cultivate those whose thirst for reassurance and attention could be at least partially slaked by the gift of his noisily insistent adulation: dramatists, poets, hacks, satirists, men who lived, as he did, in narratives of their own invention.

Other young men who were introduced into the Prince's circle were more circumspect and took more away from it than shame and rejection. One such was Richard Lovell Edgeworth, four years younger than Boswell, but, as the son of an Irish landowner and minor gentleman, occupying something of the same social position. Like Boswell, too, Edgeworth studied desultorily for the Bar, while chasing other dreams. His, though, were not of the glamour of the Guards, but of inventions and devices that should have been useful and even lucrative, but most of them proved most often to be visionary and fantastic. Some, like a jumping mechanical horse, 'that should carry me safely over the highest wall in the country', never got beyond scores of model prototypes. Others, like his 'sailing carriage', an early kind of land yacht, were painstakingly built and tried out in public, to the fear and amazement of those who saw them.

Late in 1765, Edgeworth met Sir Francis Delaval through a connection of his wife's family, and found a perfect partner for his visionary absurdity. Delaval demanded the highest mechanical standards, but he never had any interest in invention as a spur to manufacturing. On the contrary, Sir Francis loved to tread the boundary between imagination and fatuity, and to do it in the exactest manner possible.

Edgeworth and Delaval first collaborated on a phaeton designed without the usual cantilevered driver's seat that made conventional coaches so unstable and liable to capsize and then on a signalling machine that was designed to send Newmarket results to London faster than a courier could gallop them. Then, in the summer of 1766 they planned and practised a show with conjuring tricks and automata in Delaval's Downing Street house that would rival anything seen on the London stage. Prince Edward, numerous actors and 'men of letters and science' all crowded in to see this 'joint exhibition of wonders'. 'Feats were performed by seeming magic', Edgeworth wrote in his memoirs, 'and many were seriously alarmed by the prodigies they witnessed.'

When Downing Street proved too confined for his tricks, Delaval moved outdoors and away from London. Along with Samuel Foote and Prince Edward, he was often to be found at Canons, the country house in Middlesex that was home to his sister Sarah and her husband the Earl of Mexborough. Both scientists and actors had already worked their magic there. The painter and electrical philosopher Benjamin Wilson had daringly collected lightning in a bottle on the lawn one stormy night, pointing a curtain rod to the heavens so the company could watch the sparks blaze round the dry glass interior. Samuel Foote had put on entertainments and plays there too, mixing the spoken word with puppet-shows, grinning matches and sack races in which the aristocratic guests were buttoned up to the chin in hessian flour sacks and made to hop their way to victory.

Perhaps in a jocular spirit of revenge for such indignities, Prince Edward decided on a visit to Canons in early February 1766 to turn the tables on his friend. Cornered by the Prince's teasing, Foote, who was not noted for either his horsemanship or his love of riding, belligerently asserted that, 'although he generally preferred the luxury of the post-chaise, he could ride as well as most men he ever knew'. Triumphantly, Prince Edward demanded proof of his bravado and brought up an unbroken horse that he had ready for the purpose. Foote heaved himself into the saddle and was propelled first away and then, unceremoniously, off. It was, he explained later, 'a royal hand that raised me from the ground'. But his right leg was shattered, and his life and livelihood were both in immediate danger.

Contrite and worried, Prince Edward sent to London for his own surgeon William Bromsgrove. As soon as he arrived, Bromsgrove prescribed amputation to stop any putrefaction spreading, and he performed it then and there. Foote knew that much depended on his reaction, and publicly he played the part of heroic and unembittered invalid with finesse and skill. Alone, though, he feared for his future. His talent was for making audiences laugh, and who, he asked David Garrick in a letter written a fortnight after the accident, would laugh at a cripple? 'Admitting that the best can happen, is a mutilated man, a miserable instance of the weakness and frailty of human nature, a proper object to excite the emotions?'

To Francis's brother Sir John Delaval he wrote more hopefully, 'I am better rather from what I am told than what I personally feel. I am weak from pain and get no sleep but from opiates. But, however, the artery's bleeding is stopped, and they flatter me in less than a fortnight I shall be upon crutches, and then with safety may be conducted to London.'

Prince Edward, having first gone back to town, soon returned to Canons and stayed several days, showing what Foote called, 'singular humanity and generosity'. As the pain receded and anxieties came to take its place, Foote turned his mind to using the Prince's liberality to save him from destitution. When Edward warmly 'expressed a desire of securing me from . . . poverty', Foote had his request ready, as he explained to Sir John Delaval. 'I took the liberty to mention to his Royal Highness that a patent from the Crown for the House in the Haymarket during my life would protect me from want.' Hitherto forced because of the lack of a licence to put on plays as free 'after pieces' to concerts or entertainments, or to perform in the summer season when the two licensed playhouses were closed, Foote saw the way through calamity to good fortune in the acquisition of a third year-round patent.

The Duke of York did his best. Foote did not get a patent to rival those at Drury Lane or Covent Garden, but in July of the same year he was granted a licence to put on plays legitimately every May to September. By then he had had two cork legs made, one dressed in a silver-buckled court shoe and a silk stocking, the other more peg-like and mundane. Foote was back in the Little Theatre, new-shod, in June. True to his habit of drawing satirical comedy out of what he saw around him, he made the most of his one-legged state, even enduring endless puns on his name about his remaining foot. In 1767 he was able to buy the Little Theatre outright. Pointedly renaming it the Theatre Royal, he opened his first season as proprietor with a comic version of his own accident called An Occasional Prelude. Subsequently he wisely drew attention to his cork leg, writing it into his plays with profitable bravado and making it a trademark of which no other actor could boast. In The Lame Lover, which he wrote in early 1770, Foote played his own hero Sir Luke Limp, and made his heroine declare, 'I know how proud Sir Luke is of his leg, and have often heard him declare that he would not change his bit of timber for the best flesh and bone in the kingdom.'

While Foote was still nursing his stump at Canons, Sir Francis Delaval was pressing on with plans for a theatre of his own. Despite his debts and his own expensive life, Delaval gave Richard Edgeworth the commission 'to fit up a theatre in Petty France, near the Gate of the park, and no trouble and expense were spared to render it suitable to the reception of a royal guest'. While Delaval and the Duke of York went up and down from Newmarket, flirting with a string of women whose names Lady Mary Coke entered in her diary with jealous precision, Edgeworth laboured at his task. By October 1766 the theatre was finished, and Prince Edward, on one of the many visits he made to Lady Mary Coke that autumn, announced that he and the Delavals were to perform Nicholas Rowe's tragedy *The Fair Penitent* there. He himself was to play the hero and seducer, the 'haughty, gallant, gay Lothario'. Lady Mary was alarmed. 'Never having heard of a prince of the blood performing in a play after they had passed their childhood, I was concerned the Duke should do anything so contrary to decorum, and so unbecoming the Royal dignity.'

Lady Mary seems to have regarded Prince Edward's portrayal of a rakish seducer – which observers noted was both skilful and 'warm' – as more to be censured than his life. In fact, she might have noticed some similarities, although the Prince preferred more experienced women than the character he played at Delaval's theatre. He liked to surround himself with pretty, and available, women and to spend a good deal of money on them. The Earl of March told his friend George Selwyn in December 1766 that he had been passing his time, 'chiefly with his Royal Highness, the Chevalier Delaval and the Opera people', for some time, adding, 'We live very high.' March had a passion for juvenile singers and dancers. Prince Edward, though, kept up his interest in the capital's most fashionable courtesans. Early in November of the same year, Lady Mary, surveying the park as usual from her drawing-room windows, 'saw the Duke of York walking with Mrs Archer', the reigning queen of London's brightly lit 'demimonde', current mistress of a sea captain, Robert Boyle-Walsingham, and past and future mistress to many others, including the Duke's younger brother Prince Henry.

Dinners with opera girls, visits to courtesans and country houses and gambling at Newmarket did not come cheap. The Duke was perpetually short of money and permanently in dispute with his brother about it. He was afraid to confront the King directly about his allowance, but as early as 1764 he was getting others to intercede on his behalf. The first to ask for an increase was the Prime Minister, George Grenville, and the second Prince William, who had in the last few years become the King's favourite sibling. Both failed, and the King, who spent little on himself, reacted with predictable pique. In fact, as he explained to Lord Bute, Prince Edward's demand made him ill. 'I shall not have the pleasure of seeing my D. Friend tonight from an attack of a complaint that makes me quit the room too often to venture going out', he wrote, adding, 'this is perhaps owing to a little cold I have had, but I rather attribute it to agitation at the demand of my brother.'

Free-spending the King thought bad enough, but jaunting, gambling and consorting with courtesans added to the injury that the Duke of York's profligacy already did to the reputation of the royal family. In spite of the rebuff, though, Prince Edward persisted. After the Duke of Cumberland's death he was given the Duke's old office of Keeper of Windsor Great Park, which came with lodgings attached, though not much money. Prince Edward, besides, had no wish to live in Windsor. He had no interest in country pursuits and since 1764 he had had his own establishment, York House, at 1 Upper Grosvenor Street, a stone's throw from Delaval, Lady Mary and a host of other Mayfair friends. 'This is a better country for a subject to live in than a Prince of the Royal Family', a loyal and credulous Henry St. John told George Selwyn in December 1766, 'there are many rich men of the former class, none of the latter.'

Finally, in the first session of Parliament in 1767, an annuity of £18,000 for the Duke was proposed by the King, and voted through. It was an increase of a few thousand on his income before but in no way commensurate with the Prince's spending. Prince Edward was determined not to use it wisely. One of his first outlays was a theatre of his own. Early in 1767 he asked Benjamin Wilson, the painter and electrical experimenter he had met at Canons, to fit out and manage a small theatre for him in James Street, near the fashionable new developments north of Oxford Street that were being built by his friend and political ally the Duke of Bedford. Wilson was given a precise budget, £600, and an open invitation to dinner at York House whenever the Duke was at home.

Wilson, who had no rosily tinted view of the nobility he served, was surprised at the care the Duke took of the arrangements for performances and the way he excluded the racier side of his life from them. 'The Duke's habits were very exact and orderly', he noted, 'and everything was conducted with the most perfect regularity, silence and propriety'. No opera girls were allowed, and Wilson wrote that, 'Mr and Mrs Garrick were indeed admitted to one rehearsal and two plays, but this was a great favour.' The theatre was designed to seat only fifty. Twenty tickets usually went to Francis Delaval's sisters, Lady Mexborough and Lady Stanhope, while the Duke distributed the remainder himself. Lady Mary Coke, with her sisters Lady Dalkeith and the Duchess of Grafton, each got a ticket for 7 April 1767. They met at Lady Mexborough's house and 'went together to the place appointed. Sir Francis Delaval met us, and showed us into a room where all the rest of the company came.' Benjamin Wilson's entrance to the room was, as he put it, 'the signal for their entrance into the theatre'. Lady Mary, relieved to be in acceptable company, allowed herself to be impressed. 'Sir Francis spoke a prologue made on the occasion', she wrote. 'The play then began and certainly was well performed. The Duke of York, I thought, acted finely.'

Wilson's rewards were to be the office of Painter to the Board of Ordnance, where he produced landscape panoramas of areas where troops might be stationed or have to fight, and an easy intimacy with the Duke of York. Noticing that the Duke's pulse, after a string of late nights and busy days, seldom beat 'less than eighty-six in a minute', Wilson told him that if he kept up such a pace for long, 'this continual fever would become very serious to him'. In reply, the Duke told Wilson that he planned soon to change his way of life. Two weeks before, he had celebrated his twenty-eighth birthday and may indeed have been thinking of somehow or other settling down.

Not just yet though. As soon as the season was over, the Prince announced plans to go abroad for the summer, travelling in stages through France to Genoa and Turin, coming back across the Alps and then on to Paris. The King was furious. He disapproved of the self-indulgent idea of travel as an end in itself, and his mistrust of France, stirred up by the Hereditary Prince of Brunswick on a recent visit, flared up as soon as he learned of the Duke's itinerary. He took particular exception to the idea that his brother might attend the annual review at Compiègne, a supplicant at the celebration of French military might. From his own summer retreat at Kew, where five little children now accompanied him and the Queen, he dashed off a letter to Prince Edward. 'Brother. A report is very prevalent that you have some intentions to be present at the reviews of Compiègne. I cannot give great credit to this as you know how I insisted on your not making any stay in France . . . I am if possible more averse now to any of my Family going there from what I learnt from the hereditary prince.'

Such a letter from the King was almost bound to confirm the Duke in his plans. Taking no notice of his brother, Prince Edward set off at once, dragging with him his two valets and his Gentlemen of the Bedchamber, Captain Wrottesley, Colonel Morrison and Henry St. John. He made straight for the French court, travelling in notional incognito as the Earl of Ulster. French officials and the royal family made sure he was conspicuously well received. Although the Prince was travelling in a private capacity and so could not be officially received, everyone at the French court knew who Prince Edward was and he was treated with a deference and courtesy far beyond that which would have been given to a wandering Irish peer. When the Prince accompanied Louis XV on horseback to review the French army a haughty message sped across the Channel: in Britain, boorish chauvinism might have the upper hand, but in France, courtesy reigned.

Prince Edward stayed in Compiègne until the end of July. Lady Waldegrave, the widow of his old tutor, had been picking up the gossip from France and reported to a correspondent on 28 July that the Queen had told Lady Rochford, the wife of the British ambassador, that the Prince 'spoke French vastly well, and was quite the Frenchman, which is the greatest compliment a French person can make'. 'As his Royal Highness is vastly delighted with all this', she added piously, 'I hope it will change his disposition and tempt him to quit the stage.' Prince Edward had no intention of curtailing any of his pleasures. His interest in the French court waning, he hurtled south to Montpellier. Henry St. John was already wilting and despondent, writing from there to George Selwyn, 'I can assure you I go through a great deal of trouble and fatigue accompanying *mon Prince*. I may, and I am afraid I do, injure my constitution, and I fear I shall never benefit by the honour. We are in such a hurry and travel so fast, I have little comfort in seeing what otherwise I should enjoy.'

The Duke and his entourage whirled on through the Mediterranean heat. From Montpellier they galloped across the marshy Rhône delta to a château outside Toulon, where Prince Edward danced till early morning and then insisted on heading straight into town. The next morning he complained of a chill and fever and that night had to leave a performance put on for him at the theatre. The party struggled on to Monaco, a gruelling heat-blasted journey of at least two days. There, in the Prince's palace, the Duke took to his bed in one room and Colonel Morrison, who was also unwell, lay down in another. Days passed, but despite the Duke's being given James's Powder to bring down his temperature, his fever did not subside, and he became steadily weaker. 'He has great evacuations, is quiet and composed and tho' he does not speak often, possesses his senses', Henry St. John reported on 11 September to the Earl of Rochford, Britain's ambassador to the French court. Heavily, St. John lifted himself from his unease to realise that his master might be dying.

Prince Edward was there before him, and with his characteristic tidiness, he decided to say goodbye. He wrote not to the King, but to his brother William who had interceded for him once before and of whom both he and the King remained fond. The Duke may have been thinking of the row over his allowance when he selected Prince William as his conduit and he may have wanted to make amends for his political opposition to the King. But he had always been his father's favourite son and that made him proud and self-confident. Now he wanted simply to set things right with his family rather than convey any particular message. 'My Dear Brother', the letter ran, 'The weak state I find myself in induces me, while it still may be in my power, to desire you to pay my last weak duties to the King, and if at any time I should have incurr'd his displeasure, I hope the generosity of his temper will at least make him forgive my unheeded past conduct which is all at present I have in my power to offer. Pray say the same to my mother. Pray give my friendship and love to my dearest sisters Augusta and Louisa and Caroline and my dear brother Harry. Adieu my dearest brother, E.'

Prince Edward drifted into unconsciousness soon after writing his last letter and died a week later on 17 September. Dispatching the letter to Prince William, Henry St. John added a note of his own for the French ambassador. Despite his anxiety about Prince Edward's over-exertions, he knew it was not frantic travelling that had killed his master. The Prince was only twenty-eight: malaria not exhaustion had killed him. The Prince, St. John wrote, died, 'after a long illness which ended in a . . . maleary fever', with 'inflammation of the bowels' and 'mortification'.

Colonel Wrottesley set off overland with the melancholy news, and it was left to St. John to accompany his master's body back to London. One of the many British warships cruising the Mediterranean, the *Montreal*, was brought into Monaco harbour. When the Duke's body had been loaded aboard, it sailed out again to a muffled salute from the city's guns, ranged in batteries on the parched cliffs above the sea. St. John felt his master's presence through the wood and lead of the coffin. Sitting and sleeping with Prince Edward's remains, 'constantly under my eyes, during a long voyage of 800 leagues', as he put it, he was horrified by his master's death and tormented by thoughts of his life. Back home in Sackville Street off Piccadilly at the beginning of November, St. John, in his grief, forgot that his friend George Selwyn took an unusually keen interest in death and corpses, and wrote without any trace of the complicit humour that Selwyn's friends usually sprinkled over their accounts of the dying and the dead, 'I am sure you felt for me on hearing of the whole melancholy transaction.'

St. John gradually recovered from the Duke's death. The King reinstated him in the army and subsequently gave him a post in his own household. By 1771 he had married and had become, as he put it, 'acquainted with temperance, chastity and sobriety'. Somewhat to his own surprise he lived more or less within their borders for the next half-century. Francis Delaval, though, hearing the news at the end of September, seemed to shrivel and abandon hope in the future. Richard Edgeworth claimed that the Duke of York had been in love with Delaval's recently divorced sister Lady Stanhope when he left for the Continent, and that Sir Francis had hopes of their marriage. He wrote in his memoirs that 'by the death of the Duke of York Sir Francis found all his schemes of aggrandizement blasted. Though a man of great strength of mind, and of [a] vivacity that seemed untamable, his spirits and health sunk under this disappointment.' More than grief or disappointed ambition, though, it was beef, alcohol and late nights that were sapping Sir Francis's strength. He was only forty-four, but on 7 August 1771, after a huge meal washed down with port, he staggered upstairs to his bedroom in Downing Street, collapsed and died on the spot. His heart, rather than his hopes, had given out.

Samuel Foote, already made prosperous by royal contrition, had suffered little by Prince Edward's death. The royal patent made him rich, his accident even more famous. But when Francis Delaval died, he was shattered. According to one observer, the satirical shield that Foote habitually placed between himself, the public and even his friends, was broken. 'He burst into tears, retired to his room, and saw no company for three days.'

The intensity of Foote's grief may have fuelled the rumours that were beginning to snake themselves around him. Murmurings gathered that he had no interest in women, and was in fact an 'invert' who practised 'unnatural' acts. Finally, in December 1776 his former footman accused him in the court of King's Bench of two attempts to 'commit an unnatural act upon his person'. The trial was bankrolled by Foote's enemy the Duchess of Kingston, whom he had repeatedly lampooned and who had herself been convicted of bigamy a few months before. The charge was thrown out, but Foote's spirit and reputation went with it. En route to France a year later, perhaps to recover his health, perhaps to escape another, crushing, prosecution, he had the last of several paralytic strokes, and died.

Quietly, on 27 October 1777, three mourning coaches left Foote's house in Suffolk Street behind the new Theatre Royal where his body had been taken. They creaked down the Haymarket and Whitehall and round to the side of Westminster Abbey. With the agreement of the authorities, but away from the public gaze he had so craved in his life, Sam Foote was buried by torchlight somewhere under the abbey cloisters, his incomplete skeleton lying only yards from the embalmed body of the Duke of York.

Lady Mary Coke was in Frankfurt when she received news of the Duke's illness at Monaco. She wished he was at home, she wrote in her running diary-letter to her sister, as if she were there too, and not jaunting on the Continent herself. But it was 4 October, and she was back in England, before she could bring herself to record what she never quite came to accept. 'The sad and unexpected news that arrived in England this day sennight has shocked me more than I can well tell you', she wrote to her sister, adding, 'I was not born to be happy and the same ill-fortune that attended me in early life pursues me still.'

Lady Mary was determined to grieve grandly. She pulled the cloak of her misery around herself and refused to take it off. Only her anger and the expression of it in her journal kept her going. Noting, after the Duke's will was published, that he had left his house to his brother William and his diamond insignia to his brother Henry, she wrote balefully, 'They have neither of them his understanding or his manners. He was a gentleman but they are not. . . . Nobody can say anything against the poor Duke, but that he pursued pleasure with so much eagerness and gave himself no rest.' Angry when embarrassed friends left the subject of her loss sitting in the air between them, she was equally furious if they attempted to discuss it. After the hapless Duchess of Norfolk mentioned the Duke's death, Lady Mary wrote in her diary, 'I made no answer. But it has convinced me that either the Duchess hates me or else that she has very little feeling for others.' For the rest of October and into November, Lady Mary waited with horrid trepidation for the *Montreal* and its grim cargo to arrive. On 24 October she wrote, 'I prayed to God to assist me to bear as I ought the seeing myself deprived of every expectation of happiness in this world', and the next morning recorded, 'I have passed a terrible night; could not sleep any time together; yet four times I dreamed the same dream. I thought I was in Westminster Abbey and the funeral service was performing for the poor duke; that I had not resolution to go into the Chapel, but sat down in another part of the Abbey, where I thought the figures on the Monuments moved.'

Still she forced herself to go to the usual functions at St James's, drowning in the memories the place was full of. '*Sunday, Oct 25* – I passed a sleepless night. Was up a little after seven, and went to the Closet [by the Chapel Royal] at eight; luckily nobody was there, for I was so shock'd, that I could not help crying, having constantly seen him there.' She had clung, in her misery, to the belief that Prince Edward must have charged one of his servants with a message for her, words that would illuminate the dark path of her life ahead. But none of them came to see her, even after the *Montreal* had landed. 'That he should not think of me when he was dying is indeed very extraordinary', she wrote on 1 November, 'but in a few days, if I hear nothing, it will then be out of doubt.'

Perhaps hearing of Lady Mary's extravagant misery, Colonel Morrison, who had himself been ill at Monaco and who had also arrived home on the *Montreal*, took pity on her. He came to her house and gave her details of the Duke's last days, 'explaining that after dictating his letter to Prince William', Prince Edward 'seemed to wish to do something more'. But, Morrison added, 'they thought it was of so great consequence to him to keep his mind quiet, that they endeavoured to persuade him not to trouble himself with anything that might agitate him'. To Lady Mary it was obvious what the Prince had wanted to say or even to do – to reiterate his devotion to her and perhaps send a proposal of marriage. Morrison kindly left Lady Mary with her belief in the Prince's love and she placed it reverently in the chamber of grief that she built to keep her memories and her dreams alive. She visited it day and night, in spectral and illusory happiness, determined to live in the past.

In the mid-November gloom, Lady Mary worked in her Notting Hill garden, refusing visits, nursing her loneliness. 'As nobody comes near me', she wrote, 'I wish I had some one person in the house, for I find being entirely alone increases my dejection of spirits, and at times I am so melancholy that I know not what to do.' As the months went by she came steadfastly to believe that not only had the Prince for some time intended to marry her, but that he would have proposed on his return. Her dreams bore out her conviction. 'I dreamed a good deal about Colonel Brudenell', she wrote in her diary on 6 November 1767, a few days after the Duke's body had returned to England, 'relating to the advice he had given the poor Duke not to marry me, and for which advice the Princess of Brunswick said she thought herself so much obliged to him.' Perhaps Prince Edward had proposed some time before his European visit of 1764 and perhaps he had been warned off marriage. Whatever the case, little by little Lady Mary ceased in her own mind to be lonely and deprived and became instead a royal widow. Princess Amelia, her dead Duke's maiden aunt, became her close companion. The courts of Europe from Saxony to Dresden, Paris to Turin became her second homes. She travelled restlessly between them in the years to come. Her journal became a copious outpouring of court gossip, gathered not so much in the spirit of an ardent royalist, but in the belief that it was family news. Although the sight of Westminster Abbey could reduce her to histrionic lamentation, and she displayed a morbid fascination with royal vaults and tombs in every country she visited, she was not, on the whole, unhappy. Oblivious of the slightly ridiculous figure she cut, Lady Mary grew into her role, inhabiting it fully and with conviction until the day she died in 1811 at the age of eighty-four.

3

A Dangerous Prescription

Early in July 1765, a thin, small boy six hundred miles away from London noticed that above the desk at which he sat and mused while his hair was brushed and tied in the morning, a new portrait had been hung. It showed a girl of thirteen, full-faced, blue-eyed, blandly innocent: his first cousin, Caroline Matilda, Princess of England and his bride-to-be. Crown Prince Christian of Denmark, searching the picture for traces of his own features or those of his dead mother, might have hoped that he and Caroline Matilda would find the same happiness as had his parents King Frederik and Queen Louise. But the wedding was planned for eighteen months' time, and the sixteen-year-old Crown Prince was too much occupied in quelling the fantastic demons that stalked his mind and steeling himself to face the world outside to dwell too much on any future state.

Since his mother died when he was two, Prince Christian had had too little love and too much learning. Queen Louise, the youngest daughter of George II and Queen Caroline, had died, like her mother, of an internal rupture. But whereas Queen Caroline had nursed her malady for years before succumbing, Queen Louise had died suddenly and apparently without warning. King Frederik found comfort first in the bottle and then, less successfully, in a new wife, Juliane Marie, daughter of the Duke of Brunswick and aunt to the Hereditary Prince Karl Wilhelm Ferdinand.

Juliane Marie avoided her three stepchildren, treating them even-handedly but offering them neither comfort nor mother-love. After her son

Prince Frederik was born in 1753 she absorbed herself in his care. Prince Christian and his sisters lived in the royal nursery, rarely troubled by visits from either their father or their half-brother and stepmother. Then, when he was six years old, Christian was separated from his sisters, and given his own household and a tutor, Count Ditlev Reventlow. An unremitting academic education began for him, in the texts and theology of Christianity, in Latin and modern languages, in mathematics and military studies, in the history of Denmark and its neighbouring states, and in music and dancing. Reventlow was a harsh and unsympathetic man who sanctioned physical punishment with alacrity if the Prince failed at any of his tasks.

A child whose roots were anchored deep in a bedrock of love might have grown up unwarped by rigour and chastisement. But Christian had no comforting certainty, not even a nurse who could have given him the sort of mother-love he desperately needed, and his sisters, with whom he had practised receiving and giving love, were now removed from him. He was intelligent and sensitive, imaginative and lonely, and his mind was soon clouded with fear.

In 1760, when Christian was eleven, a new instructor, Elie Salomon François Reverdil, was appointed to teach him French language and literature. Reverdil was only twenty-eight, and had grown to maturity as attitudes towards childhood, education and domestic life were softening, and increasing emphasis was being placed on affection in both home and schoolroom. He was also an outsider, born in Switzerland and subsequently a professor at Copenhagen University, unaccustomed to court routines and etiquette.

Reverdil saw at once that not only was Christian intelligent and accomplished, but also he was absorbed in an intense and fearful inner life. Constantly distracted from his work, Christian would study his hands, turning them over and over, scrutinising them intently. At other times he would unbutton his waistcoat, pull his shirt out of his breeches and repeatedly press and feel the tight bands of muscles crossing his stomach, explaining to Reverdil that he was determined to achieve a perfectly hard body.

Alone with his fears, Christian lived in a nebulous and precarious mental world that he felt might be overwhelmed by terrors that lurked beyond its boundaries. Recognising his own vulnerability, and translating it from his mental to his physical state, he was determined to give himself a hard, impenetrable shell. If he could achieve physical perfection, this thin, exquisite, tiny boy believed, he would be invincible, invulnerable and perhaps capable of becoming king. For one of Christian's greatest fears, probably exacerbated by the gruelling public examinations he had to undergo in the presence of his father, government ministers and assorted diplomats, was of having to rule, and it was made more palpable by its inevitability. The idea of physical perfection became his shield of Perseus, which would turn away his fears and make his destiny more bearable.

When he could keep above the surface of his panic, Christian was charming, witty and engaging. His cousin Prince Charles of Hesse, looking back from old age, described him as 'irresistible' in his youth, and, along with other observers, praised the 'beauty of his slight form'. William Cosby, the assistant British envoy in Copenhagen, wrote even more effusively of Christian's talent after an audience with him in the spring of 1764: 'To an amiable and manly countenance, a graceful and distinguishing figure, he joins an address full of dignity and at the same time extremely affable', he reported to London, adding that Christian resembled no one more than his cousin the King of England, 'when His Majesty was of the age the Prince is now'.

In England Princess Caroline Matilda was growing up suffering none of the losses and fears of her husband-to-be. Even her father's death, which had so altered the environment and atmosphere in which her older siblings lived, was for her only a sad story. Born four months after Prince Frederick died, Caroline Matilda knew only the closed worlds of Leicester House and Kew, and her mother's austere protection.

Yet she lacked neither confidence nor company. Although her brothers George and Edward moved out of Leicester House, when she was five, the two establishments overlapped, especially in summer and on winter evenings. Until 1760, moreover, all Augusta's other children lived undisturbed and together. Caroline Matilda, the youngest and prettiest, had her sisters Elizabeth and Louisa and her brothers William, Henry and Frederick to entertain and spoil her. The early death of the infirm Elizabeth at the age of eighteen in 1759 only increased the Princess Dowager's anxious care of her younger daughters, and Caroline Matilda grew up accustomed to attention, determined and observant.

After her brother's accession in 1760, Caroline Matilda must have noticed much that bore directly on her own situation. First and foremost, she was made aware that no royal child was free to marry for love. She may have noticed too, that there was no talk of the Princesses staying at home to marry. Only unmarried princesses, like her father's sister Amelia, had the luxury of remaining in England. Others had to leave, usually for ever. The situation of these royal brides was poignantly shown in the arrival of her brother's wife, Queen Charlotte, terrified, alone and unable to speak English. Three years later, when Caroline Matilda was thirteen, Princess Augusta married Karl of Brunswick, and if she departed happily enough for her new home, she came back a little later with regret in her heart, making no secret of her unhappiness.

Yet while royal weddings continued to be contracted for dynastic and diplomatic reasons, aristocratic marriage, which had hitherto followed it, was changing under the influence of the ideas about domestic happiness that were gaining credence on the Continent. The unmarried girls who carefully carried Princess Charlotte's long train when she married the King in 1761, would mostly be free, within certain limits, to choose their husbands and marry for love as well as land and status. Moreover, no visitor to the theatre, no reader of plays or novels, could have been unaware that romantic love was being brought into the domestic fold and that for novelists and dramatists like Henry Fielding and Oliver Goldsmith true love could sanction the breaking of social barriers and form the foundation of lasting marital happiness. Caroline Matilda, well read and educated in French, English and German, would have been able to dream of love and happiness in three languages. But all the while she knew that in an arranged marriage with a foreign prince she would be very lucky to find them.

Caroline Matilda's childhood offered her other bleak messages too. Though the Princess of Wales professed a hatred of the corruption of courts and the viciousness of aristocratic and political life, after George became king her own household was the centre of secrecy and, eventually, deceit. The serpent in the garden of innocence that the Princess had tried to create for her children was the omnipresent Lord Bute.

After the Earl of Bute's fall from office and his retirement in 1763, the incoming administration more or less made the King promise that he would neither see nor communicate with his old friend and adviser again. Secret influence, though, could only be stopped if all channels from Bute to the King were closed up and the Princess Dowager could only implicitly be placed under the same restriction. So, in a pattern which Caroline Matilda would later see repeated, the King promised one thing and did another. While he assured his ministers, with absolute and obvious veracity, that Lord Bute now played no part in government, he continued to ask for and receive the Earl's advice, with his mother as conduit and enabler. Bute would enclose a letter for the King inside one for the Princess Dowager, and George would collect it when he came to visit. Replies went in the same way.

Caroline Matilda watched and took note. In the spring of 1766, as yet another administration, this time headed by the Duke of Grafton, was on the point of collapse, the King wrote to Bute about his despair, inability to sleep and need of counsel, adding, 'I beg an answer but if possible shall when I have retrieved that, avoid writing till everything is one way or another settled.' Besides the usual need for caution, the King had realised that Caroline Matilda had worked out exactly how letters, visits and replies fitted together. 'I have reason to suspect that my sister watches when I deliver any letters to my mother, not from ill intention I hope, but curiosity and she has also said that ... De Marche us'd frequently at five o'clock in the evening to bring letters from you on days when I went to my mother which she supposed must be for me. All this I beg may be trusted to no living soul; [and] shews how cautious we must be. Pity your unhappy friend for indeed he deserves it.'

Caroline Matilda might have drawn a number of conclusions from her curiosity: that politics and subterfuge went together, that women in courts, even women as retired as her mother, could wield influence in subtle and disguised ways, and that one could say one thing, do another, and still consider oneself innocently above reproach. They were not lessons that she forgot, and they sent her into the world with an understanding that kings might need advisers and women might be both the holders and conduits of political power.

Although Caroline Matilda had known since early 1765 that she was to marry the crown prince of Denmark, it is unlikely that anyone had told her exactly why and even less likely that she knew there had been a good deal of mercenary wrangling over the price her brother would have to pay for her privilege. The British envoy to Copenhagen, Walter Titley, though, had no scruple in laying out the gains in such a marriage. Besides the fine qualities that Prince Christian himself possessed, Titley wrote, Britain needed Denmark's friendship, 'on account both of His Majesty's dominions in Germany and of the British trade in the Baltic'. To this the Secretary of State for the Northern Department, or Foreign Office, Henry Seymour Conway, added 'the common cause of the Protestant religion, the mutual interest of the two crowns' and 'the ties of blood which already unite the two Kings'.

Denmark's small population and relative insignificance in the European land-mass belied its importance. From the great fortress at Kronborg, where the ghost of Hamlet's father once stalked the ramparts, and where patrolling soldiers could peer eastwards through the mists and masts of innumerable ships to the soft outline of the Swedish province of Skåne on the far side of the Sound, Denmark controlled the ebb and flow of trade in and out of the Baltic Sea. As it passed into the Baltic from the west, every vessel lowered its topsails and unravelled its anchor chains, halting in the lee of the tip of the island of Sjælland, or Zealand as the British called it, to pay a toll to the Danish Crown. One visitor to Denmark estimated the resulting income as £100,000 a year in the early 1780s.

Twenty ships a day usually sailed into the Baltic, not in a steady progression but often in great groaning flotillas that had been gathering in the channel beyond Kronborg waiting for favourable westerly winds, their rigging snapping in the easterlies and their crews chafing with boredom and tempted to skip to the neat town of Helsingør on shore. In Helsingør, Hamlet's Elsinore, lived the British agent, Nicholas Fenwick. His fine house, 87 Strandgade, faced east out across the sea. From a lookout on the roof, Fenwick could watch for ships flying the Union Jack and collect information on ships under rival flags. In 1766 he recorded that thirteen hundred British vessels made the journey through the Sound, over two thousand Dutch, and hundreds of French, Swedish, Russian and German ships, heading for the ports of Danzig and Riga, Konigsberg, Stockholm and St Petersburg. Cod, silks, wool, ceramics and luxuries went in, furs, timber, tar, iron, copper and grain came out. With the forests of southern Europe exhausted and Britain's oaks for ships' keels and timbers long gone, Baltic wood and Baltic tar were vital to every naval power in Europe. The whole Baltic seaboard enjoyed a resulting importance, shifting the diplomatic balance northwards and settling the ink-blot outline of the coast in every diplomatic and monarchical mind.

Because of Denmark's control of the shipping lanes, each great nation tried not only to ensure the most favourable trading conditions for its merchants, but also to advance its interests with the Danish Crown at the expense of its rivals. British diplomats in Copenhagen were advised to court the Danish King and his ministers assiduously and to form alliances with the

Russians and friendly Protestant powers to thwart the ambitions of the French and their northern allies, the Swedes. For its part the Danish Crown tended to maintain a canny neutrality which allowed Danish merchant ships to carry goods for both sides in a succession of European wars, to profit from trade embargoes and to play rivals off against one another. So Frederik V, while speaking to the long-serving British envoy Walter Titley of his late English queen, 'with such an overflowing tenderness as filled his eyes with tears', happily accepted a substantial annual subsidy from France, and resisted Britain's efforts to stitch together an 'offensive alliance' of northern Protestant powers that would put an end to Denmark's neutrality.

The Danish Crown was always short of money though, and so even a limited friendship had to be handsomely paid for. Caroline Matilda was one such payment, an item of kingly merchandise that Britain and Hanover exported at a huge loss. As if her dowry of £40,000 and jointure of 40,000 rix dollars from the King's Hanoverian treasury were not enough, Danish diplomats also asked Walter Titley to pass on to London a demand for an annual subsidy as well. Titley resisted that request. But he remained nervous about the bargain he had struck. It was up to Caroline Matilda herself to make good the balance sheet, to offset the cost of inserting her into the Danish court by tipping the balance of interest there permanently towards Britain and away from France. He had heard, he wrote to London as the contracts were about to be signed, that the French, 'place some hopes even in the future Queen, expecting to work upon her youth and inexperience so far as to induce her to favour their cause. Therefore, if it be not presumptuous I would beg leave to insinuate that it were to be wished her Royal Highness, before she comes hither, might be a little prepared and put upon her guard against such impressions, since it is very certain that her authority here will always be precarious, whatever flattering prospects may be held out to her, if any foreign power should prevail to the prejudice of that of England.'

By the spring of 1766, Titley had become more anxious still. Danish ministers were by then asking for the wedding date to be brought forward from late 1767 to the autumn before, only a couple of months after Caroline Matilda's fifteenth birthday. Undermined by alcohol, King Frederik's constitution had begun to give way. As his kidneys failed, dropsy set in and his body was filled with fluid, drowning him by slow degrees. He died on 13 January 1766 and, just before his seventeenth birthday, Christian was proclaimed king. At first, the auguries for his reign seemed good. 'They say that notwithstanding his want of years and experience, he has extraordinary sagacity in discerning the real characters of men, and that he knows the *fort* and the *foible* of all that are about him and makes use of them accordingly', Titley reported to the British Prime Minister Lord Grafton in May 1766. But the young King soon began to display traits that ministers were less happy to advertise: a distaste for the quotidian mundanity of government, a liking for low-life exploits in the brothels of Copenhagen and a propensity towards destruction. Reports circulated of street fights, smashed windows, broken furniture and neglected paperwork. Rumours floated about that Christian's taste in women had a similarly violent edge. Marriage, his ministers thought, might prove a steadying counterweight to the King's frivolity and excessive behaviour. Negotiations over Caroline Matilda's dowry were speedily concluded and the wedding set for October in London. As if to make quite clear the role that national and dynastic interests had played in the choice of her husband, Caroline Matilda's marriage contract would be signed not only by the King and other members of the royal family, but also by William Pitt, now Prime Minister and Earl of Chatham, and the Secretary of State Henry Seymour Conway.

Reportedly calm in the months preceding her wedding day, Caroline Matilda collapsed as the moment approached, overwhelmed by a grief that was as much for her imminent departure from her home and family as it was for a marriage without love and without even her bridegroom present. Although the wedding had been set for seven o'clock in the evening on 1 October, the guests who had assembled in the drawing room of St James's Palace waited nearly an hour before the King and Queen, the King's mother, his aunt, his siblings and his four-year-old son George, Prince of Wales, filed silently in. The Duke of York came in alone a few minutes later, and stood by the table. The Duchess of Northumberland, who attended the wedding, wrote in her journal that, 'before she set out on the procession', Caroline Matilda 'cried so much that she was near falling into fits', and that her brother William, who led her to the table where the Duke of York was standing in for the King of Denmark, 'was so shocked at seeing her in such a situation, that he looked as pale as death, and as if he was ready to faint away'.

The archbishop of Canterbury read one half of the wedding service, the Secretary of State the other. The Duke of York spoke the King of Denmark's replies, and Caroline Matilda, looking, Lady Mary Coke wrote, 'very pretty in the midst of her sorrow', managed hers without stumbling. At the end of the service the Duke of York gave Caroline Matilda her wedding ring, the archbishop read 'the prayer for children', and the weighty contract was signed, which, as Lady Mary crisply put it, 'ended the ceremony'.

As soon as she had become Queen of Denmark, Caroline Matilda had to set off for her new home and new life. The Danish ministers had appointed a household for her, and refused to allow her even one lady-in-waiting from London, wishing to have their new queen shorn of all possible influence from home. So Caroline Matilda took only her trousseau and a letter from her brother to read before she embarked on the royal yacht at Harwich. 'The poor Queen of Denmark is gone out alone into the wide world; not a creature she knows to attend her any further than Altona', wrote the bluestocking Elizabeth Carter. 'It is worse than dying; for die she must to all she has ever seen or known; but then it is only dying out of one bad world into another just like it, and where she is to have cares and fears, and dangers and sorrows, that will all yet be new to her.' Mrs Carter's lament was echoed by the many women in the crowd outside St James's Palace whom the newspapers reported as weeping in sympathy with Caroline Matilda when she emerged the morning after her wedding, crying bitterly as she walked to her carriage. An engraving published at the same time caught this mood. Taken from a pastel by Francis Coates, it shows her heavy-lidded, with eyes downcast, and pear-shaped pearls hanging like heavy tear-drops as earrings and as ornaments for her stomacher and sleeves.

As she rolled down the Essex Road, a detachment of Life Guards and then Light Dragoons trotting either side of her coach, Caroline Matilda had plenty of time to consider her brother's letter. In fact, the King had given her two. The first, dated that morning and clearly written with an eye to other, Danish readers, was a bland assurance that God would guide her steps, coupled with forthright advice to stay out of political intrigue and concentrate on private happiness. God, the King proclaimed, would not only sustain her through the vicissitudes of her new life, but would protect her from 'the malice, deceit and other evils that are the common attendants of courts'. He warned her against expecting too much, reminding her that 'those who are ever running after an extent of happiness this world does not furnish, must of course fail', and added: 'may the most cordial affection ever subsist between you and and the King of Denmark, may you be happy in your children and may you always look on those private blessings as the sole objects worth your concern.'

The King's other letter, nominally addressed to his sister Augusta, briskly swept aside such colourless pieties, beginning: 'Dear sister, I think I can no way so essentially show Caroline my real affection for her, than in giving her a few hints that may perhaps be a means of preserving her from the precipices into which she may else very probably fall.' He went on to lay out just how Caroline Matilda's 'private blessings' were wrapped up in national interests, and that far from remaining detached from them, she was expected to use her private influence for political ends that would serve not necessarily Denmark, her new home, but Britain, her old one. Noting that the King of Denmark was 'fearful of being governed', George went on, 'Caroline cannot therefore in every part of her life too carefully avoid the least appearance of having that weight with him that I hope she will in reality obtain. With that caution, I am almost certain nothing will be able to hurt her in his opinion. He is much inclined to England. This may be improv'd by her throwing out if she finds him talking of England, that her native country will ever treat him with a becoming respect, but that France on the contrary will ever look at her allies as vassals.'

Having clearly laid out Caroline Matilda's duties – and the reason why the British Crown had been so anxious to secure her marriage – George ran through the way she should behave to Christian's grandmother, stepmother and sister Louisa and went on to describe for her the characters and proclivities of the Danish ministers, and of Madame von Plessen, the head of her new household. The latter's appointment had been a particular disappointment to the acting British envoy Robert Gunning, who described her as 'entirely devoted to the French system and interest', and put in place by francophile ministers who counted on Caroline Matilda's youth and impressionability and hoped to bring her round to the French cause. George III, always quick to see galllic duplicity, explained to his sister that Madame von Plessen was 'quite French, very intriguing, and will be most assiduous in trying to ingratiate herself, therefore a double degree of caution is necessary towards her'. He concluded his letter by saying: 'in general Caroline cannot too much keep her thoughts to herself, and try to dive into the real characters of those she sees before she opens herself. This will, I am confident, if scrupulously observed preserve her from inevitable ruin.'

Once over the shock of departure, Caroline Matilda seemed less anxious about impending disaster than her brother. On the way to Harwich, the *Public Advertiser* wrote, 'an easy melancholy at times seemed to affect her on account of leaving her family and place of birth, but upon the whole she carried an air of serenity and majesty which exceedingly moved everyone who beheld her'. Caroline Matilda was a queen but also still a child. She had never seen the sea, a harbour or any ships bigger than those that could get up to the Port of London. Although she was reported in the newspapers as having gazed at the lights twinkling along the marshy Essex coast until they faded into the October gloom, she was delighted at the splendour and size of the royal yacht *Mary*, the other three yachts that carried government officials and their escorting sloops, the *Cruiser*, the *Hazard* and the *Wolf*.

On 9 October after a three-day delay because of inhospitable easterlies and a rough crossing of three more days, the convoy came in sight of the Dutch coast. By then the excitement of the sea had palled. 'We are now within nine miles of Rotterdam,' she wrote in her careful, round childish hand, 'I have been very sick, but thank God I am now quite recovered and am very impatient to leave the yacht.' Passing with her entourage and her own kitchen staff of four cooks, two clerks of the kitchen and two wine men, Caroline Matilda travelled from one continental principality and duchy to another, sped on her way by parades, poems, crowds, flowers and cavalry. She glided by water from Rotterdam to Utrecht, and then bumped overland to the River Ems, crossed into the bishopric of Münster and the electorate of Hanover, and finally, after ten days, up to Altona on Denmark's southern border, arriving there, as anxious Hanoverian officials noted, at five-thirty in the evening of 18 October. There she said goodbye to her suite and her last British companion, Lady Mary Bowlby, and passed into the care of Louise von Plessen, who had been sent from Copenhagen to meet her.

Remembering her brother's advice, Caroline Matilda approached Madame von Plessen with caution, interpreting her attempts to make her feel wanted and at home with derision, writing proudly home on 20 October and entrusting her letter to her returning escort, 'I think I am very safe from being deceived by Madam de Plesse [sic], as she has the appearance of a very false woman. She tells me the whole day how she and the rest of her country people love me, though they have not seen me, and she cannot help crying when she thinks how like I am to my aunt. I like the Dame D'atour, much better. She is very civil, and does not flatter me. They appear not to be very fond of one another, which gives me no bad opinion of the latter.'

At Altona, Caroline Matilda's English-speaking life ended. Henceforth she would talk to her attendants either in French or in German, saving

English only for reading or writing letters to her brother and her other siblings at home. Her new husband, perhaps taught by his English-speaking mother, could certainly read and speak the language, and when they wanted privacy in a court of ears, he and Caroline Matilda may have spoken it together. But German was the language in Copenhagen, Danish the language of everyday life, and French the tongue of international exchange and diplomacy. Caroline Matilda must soon have been thinking and dreaming to new sounds and patterns of speech. Her name, too, was remade into German and Danish, adding an h and dropping an a; she was Mathilde, or sometimes Mathilda, now, and soon began thinking of and signing herself that way, abandoning the resonance of the English queen she had been named after, and returning herself to her family's German roots.

Travelling slowly north through the German-speaking lands of Schleswig and Holstein, Caroline Mathilde was introduced to the colours and the contours of her new home. It was a land of shallow undulations, of copses, hedges and dense chocolate-brown soils, saturated with the rain that would keep the grass green right through the winter. In the villages the houses were long and squat; wooden-framed, clapboard-coated, with cruciform windows evenly spaced on the ground floor and looking out from the end gables. Set back from the road, larger houses of tenant farmers running round three sides of a square were built in the same modest style, rendered and painted, like the village houses, in deep chalky red, ochre or the yellow of winter jasmine. Aristocratic manors, some moated and still protected by drawbridges, also took their colour from the land about them and their small red bricks, thin as sandwiches, were baked from the clay they sat on. Only Denmark's capital city showed much influence of the rococo and classical styles that had swept Europe in the last few decades, and the great surge of country-house building, which in England was rising on the dividends of professional politics and a fast-expanding empire, was absent in the Danish countryside.

More animals than people greeted the new Queen, herds of chiaroscuro cows chewing the last of the autumn grassland, families of pigs nosing through the woods, snouting for acorns and berries and grubs. In every farmyard and village, flocks of geese pecked the verges, white as the simple rectangular bulk of the Lutheran churches. Listing the principal 'natural productions' of Denmark, the British envoy first came up with 'grain of all sorts', and then added 'cattle, bacon, salted-meat, butter, cheese, tallow, skins, leather, wool', and feathers. Despite this abundance, Denmark's was a relatively static rural economy. Its landholding and farming patterns had more in common with countries to the east like East Prussia and Russia than with Sweden to the north or Holland to the south. Most land was held in large estates, leased in smaller units to peasant farmers, who had no right of movement beyond their own districts. They had to work for the landowners, and, if necessary, to serve as conscripts in the army.

Some of the first peasants Caroline Mathilde saw were in fact the freest, beneficiaries of the reforms of Count Hans Rantzau-Ascheberg, who, in 1739, had given the tenants on his large estates in Holstein some rights to buy leaseholds and to work the land freely. But though such reforms were discussed by the landlords and government officials, they were more admired than imitated. Nonetheless, if they lacked the sorts of liberties by which the British defined themselves, Danish peasants were by and large better educated. The Lutheran Church was far more energetic and influential than its plump and otiose Anglican counterpart. Rural pastors ran elementary schools in every village and literacy was widespread.

Nevertheless, without a free press, there was in Denmark no diffusion of political sentiment similar to that in Britain: no blizzard of broadsides and sophisticated cartoons, no massed crowds wielding symbols like the boot and petticoat that had been intended to humiliate Caroline Matilda's mother, no low-level pamphlet wars, no satires and squibs. Power struggles were confined to the capital city. The visual culture, in the crude woodcuts that were allowed to circulate, had a style that to a modish English eye was almost a hundred years out of date. Moreover, if public culture was less obviously developed, the presence and size of the army and the navy, in relation to Denmark's small population, dwarfed those of Britain, though unlike in neighbouring Prussia there was very little militarisation of the executive or the state. Denmark was a neutral power and it guarded its neutrality with a large navy and a sizeable standing army, and a reserve that could be swiftly mobilised. Despite its neutrality, the administration nursed imperial ambitions and its colonial possessions in the West Indies and the Far East demanded expensive naval and military support.

If the thick brown land seemed to give Denmark some stolidity, the sea, ever-present and glinting at the tree-lined shore, pressed up against it, mercurial and always changing. The nation was a land of islands, and even the peninsula of Jylland, or Jutland, on which Caroline Mathilde began her journey, was pitted with countless lakes, as if the sea were pushing up inexorably from underneath. In the long harsh winters the Baltic Sea, and the Great and Little Belts between Denmark's main islands, shrank back from the narrow beaches and often froze over. When the spring finally came, the ice released the fishing boats, the brown-sailed trading ships and the national fleet of thirty-two ships of the line, sixteen frigates and four thousand seamen. Inside many a Danish farmer was a fisherman or sailor: 'herrings and other salt and dry fish, oysters, mussels', Gunning's list of produce finished up. To them, indeed, it would have seemed quite appropriate that the young queen's forthcoming arrival in 1766 was celebrated with the launch of a bristling new seventy-gun ship of the line, built in Copenhagen and christened the *Caroline Mathilde*.

Despite the nation's colonial holdings and its Atlantic dominions of Norway and Iceland, Christian VII had relatively few subjects. Population surveys were always kept a closely guarded secret because they had a bearing – especially in a country of tied peasants like Denmark – on the nation's military strength. Diplomats spent a good deal of time trying to calculate populations and Gunning, in 1766, made an estimate that the Danish peninsula, its archipelago and its German-speaking lands had about three and a half million inhabitants, while Norway, Iceland and the Faroes added another nine hundred thousand. But another, probably more accurate, survey in 1769 halved that figure, estimating the total population of all the Danish lands at just over two million, roughly a sixth of that of England, Wales and Scotland. It is likely that those who worked the land made up three-quarters of the people. Only a quarter of the population were free agents, carrying on or being supported by labour, trades, skills, professions: servants, merchants, seamen, lawyers, craftsmen, prostitutes, the indigent and, at the other end of the scale, independent landowners and their families.

As Caroline Mathilde would have been taught before she left England, Denmark, by virtue of the *Kongeloven*, or 'Royal Law', of 1665, was an absolute monarchy. Ultimate and unlimited legal and executive authority were vested in the king. Not only did he crown himself, he also had the power to appoint all office-holders. There was no legal means to replace or declare the King unfit to govern, because he himself was the highest authority. In practice, though, Denmark was run by dynasties of Crown servants much as Hanover had been and absolutism rarely impinged on the daily life of Danes beyond the court, who had long-established systems of local government that contained sufficient checks and balances to be relatively equitable.

Denmark's old system of elected kings had been replaced by an absolute monarchy in 1660, after disasters at war with Sweden nearly destroyed the country. Although the transformation was brought about by a virtual coup d'état, it had been accompanied by a reform of the executive into a series of centrally run departments which were opened up to men below the highest ranks. Newcomers might, in theory, rise as high as their talents could take them, acquiring titles and estates along the way. The system was perhaps more meritocratic than the one Caroline Mathilde had left behind, although the career of a commoner like Sir Robert Walpole, who became Prime Minister and retired an earl, showed there were parallels. But usually, in both countries, influence and acreage still rose hand in hand. Differences, however, were also stark. Whereas in Britain Parliament had seized the right to stand in judgement over the monarch and to limit his powers, in Denmark there was no body that represented the third estate, and no fourth estate at all. There were professional state servants, but there could be no parliamentary politics, and no theatre of power subject to the scrutiny and ridicule of a free press. In Denmark, careers, animosities and passion were all still fermented in the hot-house of the court at the royal palace of Christiansborg, and politics there still carried the tang of the jostle and gamble of ambitious men.

Nowhere was Denmark's absolute state better displayed and advertised than in its magnificent royal palaces, which offered Caroline Mathilde a choice of residences far more splendid than any Britain had to show, and far grander than any Danish aristocratic home. Instead of the modesty of Kew or the draughtiness of Windsor, she had a choice of four country palaces within a day's drive of Copenhagen: Frederiksborg Slot, north-west of the capital, towered and spired and sitting in the middle of its own lake; 250-roomed Hørsholm or, in courtly German, Hirschholm, completed forty years earlier in hunting country north of the city; the more modest manor of Fredensborg; and, for the quickest getaway, Frederiksberg Slot, a rococo palace and formal garden up a gentle hill to the west of Copenhagen. In town, instead of the cramped medieval quarters of St James's, the unloved interior of Kensington Palace, or Leicester House with the noise and swell of London life pressing up to its courtyard gates, Caroline Mathilde would have the massive, dominant bulk of Christiansborg Slot, rising half a dozen sheer storeys from its encircling canal, commanding the city as no London palace had ever done.

Christiansborg was as much a site of power as a place to live. Built into and clustering around the royal palace itself, with its newly decorated Great Hall and suites of rooms for the King and Queen, were the royal stables and indoor exercise hall, the royal theatre, rooms for hundreds of courtiers and servants, and almost all the offices of the executive. The Supreme Court, the Privy Council and the State Exchequer were all housed within the main palace buildings. In the basement gold and specie were kept, like ballast to stop the giant structure toppling over. It was as if St James's Palace, the Royal Mews, and much of Whitehall had been squeezed airlessly together with a garrison, two small gardens and water all around. The narrow brick-and-copper stock exchange, with four roguish dragon-tails twisting up its spine, was edged onto the north-east corner of the castle island by Christiansborg's great bulk: monarchy, not mercantile endeavour, was Denmark's biggest business.

Christiansborg was guarded and gated, but not impermeable. Many aristocratic officials and many courtiers with families lived outside its walls, either a stroll away down Kongens Nytorv or in the newly built baroque palaces of Amalienborg in between the old town and the moated citadel, the Kastellet, on its northern edge. They came and went daily, civil servants, clerks and craftsmen, hawkers, idlers, musicians, soldiers and sailors from the navy yards and harbour just beyond the castle walls. The monarchy was the city's life-blood, Christiansborg its biggest building site and place of work. Nonetheless it was a forbidding place, especially in the winter when the bitter and unceasing wind whipped round its sheer stone walls and ruffled the iron-grey water in the canal that girded it. From the docks and wharves to the north and east, the palace seemed oppressively dominant and closed in upon itself. Only from the west, where its great courtyard ended in trellised gates, did it open out and invite the eye to linger, drawn in across the open ground of the manège, where in the spring the royal horses took the air.

Caroline Mathilde's first meeting with her husband was not in the confines of Christiansborg but at Roskilde about twenty miles out of the capital, where, inauspiciously, the Danish royal family went to be buried as well as to crown themselves and to be married. Having met, they immediately parted again, and Caroline Mathilde entered Copenhagen alone in her carriage, to go through a second marriage ceremony at Christiansborg. This time she had her small and slender husband by her side, dressed in a silver suit while she stood plump in her white brocade. Many Danes had seen their new Queen on her journey up to Copenhagen, but after a wedding ball and a week of festivities at Christiansborg and on the streets, court life closed over her. Although she might be seen still from a distance, at the royal theatre or the chapel, face-to-face meetings, especially for the British envoy Robert Gunning, proved difficult. Caroline Mathilde was beyond outside influence, dependent on the love and favour of the King and on her own resources.

Robert Gunning was well aware of the importance London attached to his keeping in touch with the Queen and gaining her confidence. He was a career diplomat, Irish, ambitious and well connected, a loyal servant of the Hanoverians and naturally suspicious of reforming zeal. A serious man, who discharged his duties with little lightness of touch or evidence of pleasure, he knew when he arrived in Denmark in the summer of 1766 that he was taking over a posting in which the hardness of the task was not compensated by any of the glamour that was attached to other northern embassies – Berlin, for instance, or St Petersburg. Nobody wanted Copenhagen much, and Gunning's predecessor Walter Titley had been allowed to stay in the job for thirty years, and still stayed on now even though he was mortally ill.

Pretty soon, Gunning would have the melancholy job of accompanying Titley's coffin to the grave. For the moment though, he was just the plenipotentiary, given the power of Titley's office while waiting for the title to become available. His task was not an easy one. He had to try to find a way to Caroline Mathilde's parlour and her friendship. He set off on the back foot, believing that the failure of the negotiations surrounding Madame von Plessen and the composition of Caroline Mathilde's household had ceded ground to France even before she arrived in the country. But even getting an audience with the new queen proved very difficult. He could not amble casually up to the gates of Christiansborg as a private man. The reception of foreign ambassadors was a cumbersome and magnificent ceremony of the kind that Christian VII had already come to loathe. Arriving in his court clothes at the palace, Gunning would be led through several ante-rooms, accompanied and handed over by pages and courtiers who dropped away one by one to leave him alone in the great audience chamber with the King, who had to stand under a canopy by his silver throne. Ambassador and monarch were then closed in together and left to talk in as private a situation as absolute monarchy could devise. But the ceremony, the waiting and the hushed sense of occasion terrified Christian, bringing all his fears of ruling and having to be king swimming to the surface. Soon after his accession he began to avoid seeing ambassadors if he could, and without an audience with the King, Gunning was cut off from the Queen as well. 'All access to either the King or Queen of Denmark is rendered so difficult', Gunning reported to London on 18 November 1766, 'that without being furnished with some pretext I can never expect to approach either of their Majesties but in public.'

Gunning saw Caroline Mathilde in relative privacy at the beginning of December, about three weeks after her arrival in Copenhagen, and was impressed by her maturity, telling General Seymour Conway that 'the sweetness of her disposition and the uncommon degree of prudence and discretion she is endowed with must ensure her a large share of happiness'. This may have been guarded banality, because Caroline Mathilde was already unhappy and discontented, and Gunning may have known it, preferring to keep the Secretary of State in the dark rather than risk his own reputation at such an early stage in the Queen's marriage. George III, however, was soon in no doubt about his sister's feelings. Caroline Mathilde was feeling neglected and unwanted, and Christian was planning to leave Copenhagen as soon as the weather permitted in the spring and travel down to Holstein without his wife. 'I fear that I shall not go with the King this spring to Holstein', Caroline Mathilde told her brother on 9 December. 'He seems to think there is no occasion to be troubled with me. He told it to me when I had not been here longer than a week. I wish it was in my power to write more openly to you but you know it is not my fault.'

Declaring that her reticence was forced upon her, Caroline Mathilde invited her brother to see the larger dissatisfaction beneath her words. But she did not seek either help or solace. In fact she had already made it clear to George that advice was unwelcome and that she intended to rely upon her own judgement to steer her across the whirlpools of court life. Three weeks after she arrived in Denmark, she revised her early assessment of Madame von Plessen, and wrote to the King: 'You remember what I said of her from Altona. She is not what I took her for, and I think that she has been of some service to me, by giving me a few people's characters.' Remote from her brother, Caroline Mathilde need not have written anything about her new affection for Madame von Plessen. But she did, advertising clearly not only her rejection of his advice but the transfer of her trust. Similarly, when George asked anxiously for an account of how she passed her time, she replied strictly to the letter of his enquiry, ignoring altogether its spirit and saying blandly, 'I go often to the play which is really my greatest amusement, as the French comedians are very good. I have been several times in sledges but I cannot say that I amuse myself much with these parties. We had last Thursday the third masquerade but there is not enough people here that one can be long unknown.' She may have been lonely, confused by her husband's indifference, and fearful about the future, but she clearly did not intend to confide in the brother who had decided her fate and sent her into the unknown. Instead she sought the stern but present protection of Louise von Plessen, the very figure in her household whom her brother had warned her against.

When duty or pleasure took her across the bridges separating Slotsholmen, the castle island, from the rest of Copenhagen, Caroline Mathilde saw a tidy and austere city, diminutive in comparison to London, much better regulated, and, with several Guards regiments quartered on its outskirts, more martial in tone as well. With seventy thousand inhabitants, Copenhagen was smaller than Norwich or Bristol. East from the central square of Kongens Nytorv along the wall of the new canal dug a hundred years earlier to bring merchant vessels into the city, it was only a few minutes' walk to the water's edge with open shipping lanes to the north and, across the water, the naval quarter of Christianshavn. The other way, half an hour took the walker into market gardens and summer houses beyond the bastions, ramparts and canal at the city's western edge. One traveller measured Copenhagen's circumference at 'between three and five miles'. Although his estimate must have been too low, a brisk rambler could comfortably have made it round from Christiansborg, along the waterfront, round the zig-zagged southern edge of the citadel, down the western fortifications with their elevated views of the flat lands west of the city where windmills turned in the constant breeze, and back to the southern façade of Christiansborg palace in an afternoon.

It was a compact town too, built four or five storeys high with flat façades and steep mansarded roofs that drew the eye to the pale sky above. The older houses from the previous century were timber-framed and stuccoed, washed in dove-grey and ochre, wintry blue and greying pink. The newer aristocratic buildings north of Kongens Nytorv were stone, light buff and modestly ornamented. Magnificence stayed inside, while the buildings themselves sat square on their streets without railings, courtyards or driveways.

Copenhagen had its own repertoire of sound, different from an inland capital like London's. Beyond the roar and clatter of hooves and wheels on stone, was not the shush of trees in the breeze, but the incessant slapping of water against hull and thud of rope against mast. Instead of gossiping sparrows, gulls brayed sarcastically as they rode the wind searching for offal and fish-ends. The real tumult of Copenhagen, though, was not in its traffic, but in its weather. In the bitterness of the long winter the wind whined incessantly on street corners and against buildings and the city was often furred with snow, its encircling waters turned to a mosaic of shifting ice blocks. Wrapped in Norwegian fur, heads down to the bare pavements, Copenhagen's wealthier citizens struggled against easterly winds and made for the stove-warmed comforts of home as soon as they could on dark evenings, leaving the poor to shiver outside. Spring was sudden and short, summers intense, humid and often hot, a reminder that Denmark was a Baltic kingdom as much influenced by the great continental land-mass to its north and east as by temporising Atlantic currents.

That first winter, Caroline Mathilde confronted two arduous challenges: to ingratiate herself with the King and to find a place for herself at court. Stepping into Christiansborg may have seemed to her more like stepping back into the vibrant and vicious English Stuart courts of the Restoration than walking about the dry, dull and increasingly powerless place St James's had become. But if her task seemed insurmountable, she did have at least a working knowledge of one crucial aspect of court life, the power that women could wield there. Beyond this, and equally importantly, Caroline Mathilde had the appetite, and some of the toughness of her namesake Queen Caroline, and she set about the task with a will. In the months after her arrival in Copenhagen, wrote the officer and courtier Otto von Falkenskjold, 'she took great pains to learn the Danish language and in a short time she spoke it with a fluency that greatly flattered her subjects'. Symbolic though her endeavour was, it had practical application too. Danish was the language of daily life, of servants, of rumours and of spies. Speaking it, Caroline Mathilde was much more likely to keep the trust of those working in the lower levels of her household, her coachmen and seamstresses, carpenters and cooks, and to hear from them the news and gossip that ran down the back-stairs and along the endless corridors.

Caroline Mathilde also soon realised that she had no place in her husband's affections, and could hope for no more than reserved politeness from the King's stepmother, the Dowager Queen Juliane Marie, and her son Prince Frederik, and for benign tolerance from Christian's grandmother, Sophia Magdalena. Each member of the royal family had his or her own rooms in the palace. Days passed with Christian in his grand and gilded suite on the main floor and Caroline Mathilde in her own rooms, quite separate. According to one observer, Christian 'dispatched with reluctant haste the most important concerns of the state', leaving as much as he could in the hands of his chief ministers Counts Bernstorff and Reventlow. Caroline Mathilde, meanwhile, was left with her books, music, ladies-in-waiting and occasional sorties out. Reverdil, taking his role as tutor very seriously, claimed in his memoirs to have encouraged Christian to sleep with his wife. But although the King and Queen met in public to discharge their official court duties, and dined together as well, they did not see one another in private often enough to produce an heir.

To a large extent, Christian's indifference towards the office that he held and his fear of governing did not matter. Daily life in the executive went on unimpeded by the King. Administrations were small and could function efficiently. When Caroline Mathilde arrived, for instance, the Foreign Ministry under Count Bernstorff had only about ten officials including its clerks, and senior officials often sat on more than one of the councils that made up the executive so that they could share information and decisions. Political life was a combination of this stolid bureaucracy and rumour-carried intrigue. For months or years, administrations might be stable. New ideas of governance and new personalities, however, did combine at intervals to demand or force change. Then the smooth surface was ruptured by promotions, realignments or dismissals and the ripples spread out through the court and the vast complex of Christiansborg and into the nation.

Diplomats spent much of their time and a good deal of money, ears to the ground, listening out for vibrations of subterranean movement and change. Every country with interests in Denmark had spies above- and below-stairs in Christiansborg. News came in from other courts as well. Robert Gunning's dispatches and information were relayed by his tireless messengers Mr Bothwick and Daniel Ardonin, who spent their lives trekking along the sides of an arduous rhomboid defined by Copenhagen, Stockholm, St Petersburg, Berlin and the free port of Hamburg, the great centre of spying and communications that served the whole of northern Europe and the

Baltic. Letters were also continually sent to and from Nicholas Fenwick in Elsinore, and Gunning relied especially on his close friend Ralph Woodford, the British envoy to Lower Saxony, who lived in Hamburg and picked up gossip that made its way down the Jutland peninsula or that filtered through from the courts in the east.

Bothwick and Ardonin were charged with protecting diplomatic correspondence and carrying it as speedily as possible. Most dispatches from Copenhagen went to London via Hamburg and The Hague, in a relay from courier to courier. The most important and urgent were carried by a single messenger all the way, a journey which depended a good deal on the weather and might take anything from a few days to two weeks. The dispatches themselves were numbered and important information was written in cipher. The ciphers – each of them given a letter of the alphabet that was indicated in the dispatch – were one of the diplomat's most vital tools, kept under lock and key in embassies and passed with great care from outgoing to incoming envoys. They could of course be cracked if dispatches were intercepted and copied, especially since most were fairly simple strings of quartets of numbers punctuated by dots. But cipher was as much a screen from prying and spying eyes within offices and embassies as it was a protection for information that travelled from country to country. At its destination, each dispatch was deciphered, trusted officials helpfully writing out the words in the broad spaces left between the lines of numbers.

Caroline Mathilde's letters to London were sent not through British channels, although she could have sent verbal messages that way, but through Denmark's envoy in London, Count Bothmar, who presented them to the King at an audience, or passed them along to the Secretary of State. She came quickly to be convinced that her correspondence was read and selectively edited before it even left Denmark. In the spring of 1767, when her dissatisfaction with her situation and with her husband was turning from hurt to anger, and when she had begun to take an interest in the intricacies of political intrigue in Copenhagen, she wrote to George III mentioning various diplomatic upheavals, but also complaining that her letters were not getting through. 'I fear that my letters do not always arrive to London, as all the family reproach me that I do not write to them, in particular Louisa, to whom I never miss a week writing.'

Although the authorities in Denmark may have had good reason to stop accounts of Caroline Mathilde's misery seeping out of the country, Danish officials may not have been the culprits. London was equally vigilant, and George III may have wanted to protect his sickly sister Louisa from any unpleasant revelations about life abroad. Moreover he wanted, as always, to make sure that no news should reach the opposition or the press.

Although the King and Queen lived very separately in Christiansborg, Christian was well aware of the need for an heir. Egged on by Reverdil, who believed that Madame von Plessen was both prudish and obstructive, he did continue to visit Caroline Mathilde's chambers at night. Although she seems not to have told her brother, by the beginning of May 1767 Caroline Mathilde was pregnant, a sixteen-year-old mother-to-be. Perhaps learning that news gave Christian the excuse he needed to leave her behind when he travelled south that summer. Reverdil, who accompanied the King, and who liked to think he still occupied the fatherly role in his increasingly raucous retinue, wrote in his memoirs that Christian displayed little tenderness towards his wife. But he was in awe of her and having promised himself a diverting and disorderly trip, did not want to be impeded by the consciousness of her presence and disapproval.

The King's plans for his journey may have had a sexual element that he wished to hide from his wife. But his behaviour had other motivations, too, which were rising to the top of the bubbling cauldron of his fears and desires, and beginning to take hold of his personality. First and foremost was his now powerful wish somehow to cease to rule and even to stop being king. Travelling away from Copenhagen, from his court, his wife, his ministers and his duties, was one way of suspending the kingly state, of trying to forget that it could in fact end only with his death. Once in Holstein, Christian began to experiment with games that combined this fugitive impulse with another propensity, the urge to violence, and especially to have violence directed towards him. Reverdil reported that Christian dreamed up a game in which, tied to a chair, he pretended to be a criminal bound to a wheel, the most exalted man in the kingdom imagining himself the most outcast and reviled. Once fettered and bound, Christian demanded that one of his companions hit him with a roll of paper, play-acting a scene of execution and extinction. Reverdil noted, though, that such games only increased the King's anxiety, agitation and disposition to melancholy. Christian was still overwhelmed by fears of his own powerlessness and Reverdil still tried to talk and soothe him into calm.

Reverdil erroneously believed that if Caroline Mathilde were allowed more sway over the King he might be dragged back from the descent. During the summer in Holstein he wrote a series of tender letters to the Queen himself, which Christian grumpily agreed to copy out and sign, provided that they were not too long. Caroline Mathilde seemed to be delighted to have received them, or at least to have chosen to believe that though the words were not the King's, the sentiments they expressed might be and the good intentions certainly were. When she heard, at the end of the summer, that the King's entourage was approaching the southern edge of Copenhagen, Caroline Mathilde drove out to meet it. But the Christian who listlessly climbed down from his coach and into Caroline Mathilde's and who sullenly accompanied her into the city was not a new king, but the old one, more determined than ever to shed his royal dignity in search of another kind of life.

That autumn, Christian took his quest out beyond the gates of Christiansborg, onto the streets of Copenhagen and into its brothels. With his friend Count Holck and a small band of courtiers and pages, Christian took to tramping the streets incognito, walking into brothels, and, after using their services, indulging in his newly unleashed taste for violence by smashing up furniture and breaking glasses, bottles and windows. On other nights, Christian and his band threatened passers-by, challenging them to fight, seeking confrontation and mayhem. Caroline Mathilde, as if released from her confining role by the King's erratic behaviour, began her own, much milder version of her husband's forays. As the year and her pregnancy advanced, she surprised Copenhagen's citizens by walking through the city streets accompanied only by Madame von Plessen and a footman, often wearing a simple black cloak pulled round her bulky stomach. It had never been seen as respectable for noblewomen to mix with ordinary citizens in this way, but Caroline Mathilde's habit of strolling along the city ramparts to Frederiksberg Street and up through the old town was quickly taken up by other women of the court, and one observer noted that from then on women of all classes started to walk casually through the whole city.

Much more shocking for the court and ordinary citizens was the King's acknowledgement that he had a mistress, a lively courtesan of obscure origins who was known as Støvlet-Cathrine, or 'Catherine of the bootees', because of her small and beautiful feet. It was suggested, as so often with successful courtesans, that Støvlet-Cathrine was of noble stock, born on the wrong side of the sheets and fallen on hard times. Her real name was agreed to be Anne Cathrine Benthagen, but accounts of her career diverged from there. One had her a dancer at the opera and then mistress of Sir John Goodrich, an Englishman living in Copenhagen. A second had her a common prostitute, rescued by Goodrich from the streets, but then mistress of the Venetian envoy. Whatever the case, Støvlet-Cathrine caused ministers much more trouble than a discreet aristocratic mistress. In the first place, she drew Christian even further away from court life and its duties. In the second, she, and he, became visible to ordinary people, causing confusion and consternation among Copenhagen's citizens. At night she and a rag-bag entourage of courtiers might be encountered anywhere – prowling the streets round the old market Gammeltorv, or filling sailors' taverns by the docks and navy yards. Though many people knew perfectly well who the tiny, beautiful, childlike man was who led the band, none knew how to behave towards him. No one could restrain the King – indeed it was a capital offence to lay hands on him – and no one dared to tell him to stop his destructive forays. His behaviour was the more shocking because Copenhagen, unlike London, was a safe city whose inhabitants, one British visitor noticed with surprise, did not expect to have their pockets picked or be accosted by marauding drunken gangs.

In the absence of any way of checking or commenting upon the King's behaviour, Cathrine herself became the target of hostile attention. Crude prints showing her saucy-faced, skirted and booted emerged from several of the city's twelve printing shops. Each one was an implicit condemnation of the manners of the King and the indignity he brought to the Crown, and none was intended innocently to celebrate and advertise Støvlet-Cathrine's charm and sway.

Not content with meeting his mistress on the streets of the capital, Christian brought her into Christiansborg as well. Reverdil, who had wearily tried to keep the King's conduct within bounds that would not arouse too much comment, protested, suggesting to Count Holck that Cathrine's presence in the palace was an unnecessary impropriety and an insult to the Queen. He was promptly sacked and left the country. Count Holck henceforth became the King's constant companion. Night sorties, masquerades and acting projects proliferated, all fiercely resented by the Queen whose bitterness about the first was compounded by her exclusion from the others on the grounds of her advancing pregnancy.

The antics and visibility of Støvlet-Cathrine ruptured the delicate transparent membrane that both joined the King to and separated him from his people. Seeing the King, on the streets and every inch a human being, opened the monarchy up to criticism and threatened its claims to absolute power. Støvlet-Cathrine could not be allowed to last long. After a few riotous months the King was persuaded to pension her off. Thankful officials drew up a contract in which she agreed to leave the city and move to Wandsbeck in Holstein in return for a generous annuity. After signing it on 6 January 1768, Cathrine was transported by marshals beyond the city boundary on and rode off into a prosperous retirement.

Although Cathrine's departure temporarily stopped the King's nocturnal wanderings, the masquerades and frantic jollity went on. On 6 January 1768, Robert Gunning reported that, 'His Danish Majesty has of late taken great delight in theatrical entertainments in which he performs several parts himself; the foreign ministers and almost all the nobility are invited by his brother to see him perform the character of Osmanoro in the tragedy of Zaire at the theatre of the court this evening.' Voltaire's play combined an alluringly grisly end with a forbidden love between a Muslim sultan – played by the King – and a Christian slave. A perennial favourite since its first performance twelve years earlier, it hinged, like many contemporary tragedies and farces, on mistaken and confused identity. Gunning's tight-lipped disapproval may have stemmed partly from a feeling that it was unseemly to see the King perform first murder and then suicide onstage. But it was compounded by his belief that it was wrong for Christian to be throwing everything into acting out his inner life so soon before Caroline Mathilde's expected confinement.

The young Queen was reportedly in poor health, and through the medium of her friend Madame von Plessen, she was anxious for the King to know it. 'Her mind is too good and fine not to be deeply hurt by the lack of tenderness and politeness with which she is being treated', Madame von Plessen wrote to the chief minister Count Bernstorff. Any poor outcome to Caroline Mathilde's labour, she hinted, would be laid at Christian's door.

The royal heir, born just forty-eight hours after Christian VII performed *Zaire* in front of the assembled court, was a small baby, but both he and Caroline Mathilde survived the ordeal of birth. In his very last dispatch the next day, Walter Titley, delighted to see the union he had brokered bear fruit before he died, wrote: 'The Queen, God be praised, and the new-born Prince are this morning both as well as can be expected . . . the birth of a male heir to the crown has completely fulfilled the ardent wishes and prayers of the public, and consequently spread a real joy through all ranks of the people here.' Christian was delighted by the birth of Crown Prince Frederik too. It meant that he had fulfilled his duty to his country and so lessened the pressure he had felt to visit Caroline Mathilde at night. With an heir tucked safely in his cradle, moreover, he felt emboldened to move against Madame von Plessen, whose disdain of his fears and disapproval of his riotous attempts to distract himself from them made him angry and uncomfortable. At the end of February 1768, despite prolonged and vigorous protests from Caroline Mathilde, Madame von Plessen was dismissed through the agency of Count Bernstorff. To underline his authority Christian replaced her with Madame von de Lüke, the sister of his companion Count Holck. Louise von Plessen was ordered to leave the country and eventually settled beyond the arm of the Danish Crown at Celle in the electorate of Hanover.

In London, George III had chosen to ignore his sister's poor relations with her husband. His congratulatory letter on the birth of the Crown Prince, though, caused him some difficulty. He abandoned the first draft after finding he had written that he 'could easily conceive the sensation' Caroline Mathilde's safe delivery would occasion in the King of Denmark. The second try was discarded when George came to a halt having written that he saw the birth 'as the foundation of . . .'. Finally he settled on a bland formula which managed to describe the exact opposite of Caroline Mathilde's relationship with her husband, saying that 'this great event will endear you still more to the King and to his subjects, and will, I trust in heaven, be a source of endless felicity'.

Caroline Mathilde was indeed delighted with her son, and followed the newest aristocratic fashion in motherhood by breast-feeding him herself. But Prince Frederik's birth did not bring the royal couple any closer together. Caroline Mathilde for her part remained furious that she had lost her motherly confidante and friend and that Madame von Plessen had been replaced by someone she had no particular love for. The King, for his part, was planning a long journey that would remove him far from court squabbles, from his duties as king and from his wife. Christian announced his intention of travelling under pseudonym through Hesse and Holland and going thence to Britain and to France.

George III did not receive this news equably. He was in a nervous mood in the spring of 1768, rattled by a General Election that had produced an uncongenial administration headed by the famously dissipated Duke of

Grafton, and annoyed by the return of his mother's tormentor, John Wilkes, from exile on the Continent. Wilkes returned to test the law that had forced him into exile and he immediately set about inflaming popular grievance against the government. In a tumultuous poll he was elected MP for Middlesex, and declared his intention of applying for commutation of the sentence of seditious libel that had been pronounced against him in 1763, on the grounds that the general warrant that had been used to arrest him was illegal.

Between Wilkes's election and his sensational rearrest on 27 April, which sparked weeks of rioting and bloodshed in London, George III tried as forcefully as he could to put pressure on Christian VII not to come to England, claiming that his travelling incognito made it difficult to know how to receive him. 'I am so to acquaint you', the new Secretary of State wrote to Robert Gunning on 8 April, 'that however agreeable it might be to the King, in some respects, to see the King of Denmark in England, yet many difficulties in point of etiquette, which must necessarily arise upon so unusual an occasion, as that of a visit from a crowned head in so close a family connection with His Majesty, and travelling incognito with the title Count of Aldenbourg (so it is reported) make the King wish very much, upon the whole, that such a journey may not take place.' In fact, George did not want Christian either as count or king. In May his twenty-year-old sister, the semi-invalid Louisa Ann, died, compounding his anxious gloom. Three weeks later he wrote to Lord Weymouth about the visit with ferocious underlining: 'you know very well that the whole of it <u>is very disagreeable to me</u>.'

George was writing this letter on the very day that Wilkes's case was being heard by Lord Mansfield in the Court of King's Bench. Memories of recent riots and his personal dislike of Wilkes, whom he described as an 'audacious criminal', made him more exasperated. If he had to play host to Christian, he would have preferred to be able to display a loyal realm and a peaceful capital city. Instead he was threatened with more insult to his mother and Lord Bute, continued riot and scandalous incidents that found their way into the foreign press. Only a few weeks before, the Austrian ambassador Count Seilern had been forced from his coach. In reference to the suppressed edition of Wilkes's magazine, the *North Briton*, which had sparked the first disturbances five years earlier, 'No 45' was chalked on the soles of the ambassador's shoes. 'I fear anarchy will continue till what every temperate man must dread, <u>I mean an effusion of blood</u>, has vanquished', the King wrote on

30 April. The last thing he wanted was for Christian to see the capital city of the most powerful nation in Europe controlled by a mob and the law held up to ridicule by a man who had shamefully dragged his mother's good name into the dust.

Caroline Mathilde was no less annoyed. On 8 April she had written to her brother saying of Christian's proposal: 'I am in hopes that he will not be abroad so long as we had at first reason to fear, though for the present he is determined to go to England.' Her optimism was misplaced; Christian was determined to go and to go in style. Though he occasionally called himself 'Graf von Traventhal', he did not really travel incognito, and the journey to Britain soon took on the colouring of a state visit even though it was never officially classed that way. While minor princes like Ferdinand of Brunswick could travel as semi-private individuals, a visit from the monarch of a major power was, for George III, without precedent, and, as it turned out, without sequel too. Christian's announcement threw both ministers and servants in disarray. It fell to them to organise lodgings for the King and his suite, and to manage meetings and tours that would flatter and acknowledge Christian's rank without forcing George III to spend too much time in his cousin's company. George III quickly began to see Christian's summer-long ramble not only as an insult to his sister, left behind for the second year in a row, but also as an imposition upon himself and upon the innocence of Queen Charlotte and his young family. Only the fact that the court was still in mourning for Princess Louisa offered him the chance of any relief. The mourning would have to be broken to stage any entertainments, but it gave George a perfect excuse to keep any contact between his family and his guest to the lowest possible level consistent with kingly good manners.

The last place George wanted Christian was at the Queen's House itself, and he ordered that the entire Danish suite be housed at St James's where forty-two rooms were set aside for it. Renovating the best apartments for Christian and his senior officials was said to have cost £3,000, and George also undertook to pay for the food for all fifty-six of Christian's party, at a daily cost of £84, thus guaranteeing that the longer his cousin stayed the more his presence and prodigality would be resented.

Reports of Christian's behaviour on the first leg of his journey amply confirmed George's forebodings. Christian left Copenhagen in the first week of May 1768, accompanied by Bernstorff the chief minister, von Moltke the still powerful Count Marshal, his own favourite Count Holck, several other nobles and a full complement of servants. After travelling down through Schleswig and Holstein and stopping near Ahrensburg, close to Hamburg, where a young physician, Johann Friedrich Struensee, was added to the party as physician-in-ordinary, the King donned his pseudonym of Graf von Traventhal and crossed into German territory. Leaving his suite to make its own way to Amsterdam, Christian, with Holck and Bernstorff, sped south to Hanau and the hospitality of his sister Louise and his brother-in-law Prince Charles of Hesse. The dowager princess of Hesse was Christian's aunt and George III's too. She lost no time in sending her impressions of the young King to her sister Princess Amelia, who read the letter to Lady Mary Coke. Lady Mary was happy to report that King Christian's behaviour fell short of the high standards set by the late Duke of York. Indeed the dowager princess told her sister that not only did Christian apparently curl his hair 'very high', in the fashionable French style, but that 'he seldom spoke to anybody except his favourite'. He was erratic, too. On one occasion he ordered a masquerade but then set off to look at battlefields from the recent war, returned at eleven o'clock at night and went straight to bed. At one in the morning he got up, dressed and went to the masquerade, 'the company having waited for him from early in the evening'.

After a whirlwind journey from Frankfurt to Coblenz, across land to Bonn and Cologne, Christian joined his suite in Amsterdam and went on to The Hague and Brussels, received everywhere by enormous crowds. George III had sent the royal yacht *Mary* to sail the party across to Dover, and Christian landed there on the morning of 9 August. Messengers, for George III and for various newspapers, must have galloped up to London with the news, because as Christian was reluctantly enduring the greetings of the clergy and municipality of Canterbury and remarking with more wit than tact that the last time the Danes had entered the city they had left it in ashes, a large crowd was gathering outside the gates of St James's Palace to see him.

For centuries crowds had been a forceful element in London's political and cultural life. They grew quickly at election hustings, they came together at the call of opportunists like John Wilkes, they massed when great beauties or famous courtesans walked in Hyde Park or St James's, and when criminals swung at Tyburn. Crowds sent strong visual messages to those in authority, the Crown, its ministers and the judiciary, and they gathered and transmitted news, coagulating on rumours passed along pavements and in alehouses. When Christian landed at Dover, there had been no time to print the news of his impending arrival in London, but the news spread from messengers to idlers bunching on street corners, to street-sellers and servants, gossip-mongers and curious passers-by. London's streets, especially in summer, were so thick with people that like a conjuror's magnet pulling in iron filings, a new excitement drew a crowd to itself in a few minutes.

All through the spring of 1768 the crowds had been busy and threatening. At the beginning of May, after strikes by coal-heavers and sawyers, four thousand sailors demanding a pay rise came from the dockyards at Chatham, and with flags and ensigns flying rowed upriver towards the King's summer house of Richmond Lodge. 'I find they have just passed Kew Bridge, and have in consequence ordered the gates to be shut, and the Guards to keep every thing quiet. I have ordered the servants to say I am out', wrote the King dramatically to the Secretary of State on 7 May. The sailors were pacified, but the very next day a huge crowd of John Wilkes's supporters gathered in St George's Fields across the river from Westminster and advanced on the King's Bench prison demanding his release. Magistrates who went out to read the Riot Act were shouted down and guards pelted with mud, bricks and stones. An instant martyr was created of a young man called George Allen who was shot dead by soldiers.

The crowd that collected wherever the King of Denmark went was benign, curious and full of women, who tried to touch and even to kiss him. It was more a testimony to the magic of royalty and the simple pleasure of massing for an event than evidence of any hostility to authority. Indeed Christian had the effect of temporarily deflecting attention away from the government's troubles. 'The King of Denmark', wrote one MP to another, 'is the only topic of conversation. Wilkes himself is forgotten, even by the populace.' But the London crowd was obliquely commenting on its own monarch too. No such enthusiasm accompanied George when he rode out from the Queen's House or drove from Richmond to London in his carriage. The adulation which had greeted him when he succeeded to the throne and his popularity in the first two years of his reign had been dissipated during the years of Bute's public ascendancy and in the scepticism that was still prevalent about his continued influence. It would take two decades, a bout of madness and a revolution in France to bring it back. King Christian's tumultuous reception galled George III not merely on his sister's behalf, but also on his own. It was over a week before he honoured his cousin with a state dinner at the Queen's House, and he made it abundantly clear that he was welcoming Christian more as etiquette demanded than as an honoured monarch and a close relation.

In fact the last thing Christian wanted was to be treated like a king, to be preached at by clerics and bowed to by ministers. In the midst of the pomp of his visit he was still nursing his impossible dream of slipping through life unnoticed with the anonymous exterior of an ordinary man. The new physician-in-ordinary, Johann Struensee, in whom the King very soon began to confide, later wrote that while they were in France, Christian proposed 'very seriously to run away with him', into the army, because, as he put it, 'he wanted to owe his happiness to no one but himself'. Christian's choice of alternative profession was indeed a common one for young men who wanted a fresh start, as James Boswell's attempts had shown. But it also harked back to his early desire to be invulnerable and strong, and derived, too, from his recent reading of Voltaire's biography of Carl XII of Sweden, a warrior king who was killed fighting the Danes in Norway in 1718. Voltaire's biography of Carl, published in 1731, portrayed him as an idealist who faced down compromising officials to fulfil his martial destiny, a glorious man-of-arms who had no court or even fixed capital, who fought Russia, Poland and Denmark for nearly two decades and was defeated only by fate. Staying in palaces with a fifty-strong entourage, Christian perhaps longed not only for the toughness embodied in Carl XII but also the open-air privations and freedoms he imagined came with the military life.

In England, Christian's own three personae of king, gentleman-traveller and low-life hellraiser each had a packed itinerary. As they competed with each other for time, the King's whole visit developed a nightmare quality that terrified his attendants, baffled observers and did little to lift his own mood of bitter mania. By 13 August Christian had already been presented to the King and Queen and the Princess Dowager, visited the City of London and the special exhibition staged by the Society of Artists in his honour, sent orders to Garrick to act a tragedy before him, begun sittings with the portraitist Angelica Kaufmann, and been to Ranelagh and dined in the open booths at Vauxhall with the Duke of York's flirtatious friends Lady Harrington and Lady Bel Stanhope. On the evening of 13 August he went to a performance of Niccolò Piccinni's opera *La buona figliola* at the Haymarket and sat in the box and great velvet chair of his late uncle Prince Frederick. Despite his supposed identity as a German count Christian had brought some of his royal regalia with him, his sash, star, sword and crown, and at the opera he threw aside his incognito and dressed like a king.

The opera, however, seemed to bore him, and as soon as it was over, he went straight to Carlyle House in Soho Square, where the most famous impresario of the day, Teresa Cornelys, gave an impromptu entertainment for him. 'Mrs Cornelys had put the apartments in all the possible order that a few hours notice would admit of', the *Annual Register* reported, 'and the whole was splendidly illuminated with upwards of two thousand wax lights.' Paying guests crowded round while Christian danced minuets, English country dances and French cotillions, and seemed, according to the *Annual Register*, 'very much pleased with his reception'.

This frenetic activity continued unabated. Christian filled his days with visits to historic and commercial sights, his evenings with grand entertainments. On 19 August, for instance, he went to Westminster Abbey, the Tower of London and the Royal Armoury, the Mint, the Bank of England and St Paul's Cathedral. In the evening he drove out of town to Gunnersbury where Princess Amelia and a huge party of three hundred people awaited him, and the evening was passed with supper, fireworks and a ball. He seemed scarcely to look at anything. Bernstorff excused him by saying he was shortsighted and could make out nothing in the middle distance, but Christian made no attempt to wear glasses, and rumours began to circulate that his odd behaviour was due to something more than defective eyesight.

At the beginning of September Christian set off on a whirlwind tour to the north of England, travelling up the east side of the country and then going across to Manchester. There he asked to be taken to the end of the new Bridgewater Canal and expressed 'astonishment and pleasure' at the wharves and docks and the low brick-lined tunnel that allowed the Duke of Bridgewater's coal to be floated right into Deansgate in the centre of the town. Struensee and the King went shopping, too, buying yards and yards of fine velvets to be sewn into suits. Struensee selected a shimmering blue velvet which impressed observers when he wore it back in Denmark, and packed up the cloth to take down to the capital where it could be made up in Spitalfields.

Back in London, Christian could still be witty, good-humoured and generous, scattering coins from his pockets whenever crowds gathered round him and never seeming to mind when people tried to touch or kiss him. He and Struensee spent empty afternoons at the riding school of Philip Astley, a former horse-breaker for the British army who was regarded as the finest horseman of his generation, and who worked under the dashing title of 'the English Hussar'. A few months before Christian arrived in London, Astley had opened the country's first circus at Halfpenny Hatch, a field on the south side of the Thames between Westminster and Blackfriars Bridges. There, in a nightly show that included rope-dancers and tumblers, Astley displayed his equestrian skills, rather like one of the conjurors who performed in the Little Theatre across the river. Later he added automata and other magical elements to his show, but at the beginning he relied on feats of horse-training and -riding. He played the pipes while riding two horses, one leg over each. He stood on his head on a pint pot balanced on the saddle while his horse Billy went round the ring. He trained Billy to lie motionless on the ground, 'dead, apparent at your sight', and then rise to life at a word of command.

Astley's equestrian shows were immediately popular and fashionable and he capitalised on their success by giving lessons in horsemanship to both men and women during the day. For Johann Struensee, Astley's instruction could help him sit well and manage a horse with the aplomb demanded of an ambitious young doctor who wanted to rise in the world. But he was also eager for Christian to tire himself out, to exhaust his body in the hope of giving his weary mind some rest at night. For Christian was finding it more and more difficult to sleep. 'I have to talk to him all through the night, or read to him', his new valet Frederik von Warnstedt told a correspondent. Warnstedt was both amazed and terrified by the King, writing, 'such an extraordinary imagination and so much wit are given to few people. He notices everything that happens around him and afterwards points out all the things that annoy him, as well as the oddest and most ridiculous. In this way words stream out of him the whole night through, and I sweat with fear and try to hide my reserve and fatigue with trivial answers. Often things happen that I can in no way understand.'

Those things were often violent and extreme. Christian was rumoured in London to have gone to the docks and the slums of St Giles disguised as a common sailor and to have stirred up brawls in both places. Struensee admitted that he had regularly smashed up his lodgings and that the furniture in St James's was 'nearly all broken' by the end of their visit. When not living in the world of his violent and troubling thoughts, Christian kept up the same frenetic pace. He went to Windsor and Oxford – where Struensee and several of Christian's ministers were given honorary degrees – and

Blenheim. He watched Garrick duly perform *Hamlet* for him at Drury Lane, and attended a magnificent day-long entertainment on the river that culminated in a banquet in the City of London. On 24 September George III, at the end of his tether and mindful of the daily charge on the royal purse of the Danish suite, put on a grand 'farewell entertainment' for Christian at Richmond Lodge. His cousin pointedly did not take the hint, stayed on, and at the beginning of October went to Newmarket.

Throughout his London visit Christian had mixed with the circle of the late Duke of York, so it naturally fell to the Earl of March to look after him when he went to the races and out with hounds. Like many others, the Earl was far more anxious about than flattered by his task, particularly since the King insisted on following the pack on his own horse when he went hunting. 'We had a great deal of leaping, and he would go over everything', March complained to Selwyn, adding, 'I was very glad when we got him safe home, and he was mightily pleased with the chase, and satisfied with himself, which put him in better spirits than I ever saw him . . . He is to see a cock fight this morning, and sets out for London about one.'

A week later, to the immense relief of George III, Christian hosted a grand valedictory masquerade at the Opera House in the Haymarket, which he hired for the night. The public was allowed in the gallery and two and a half thousand guests who had paid for tickets filled the pit and the stage. Princess Amelia surveyed the scene through her mask sitting in a box and even George III attended, although, as the *Gentleman's Magazine* put it, he stayed 'in a private box, apparently shut, with transparent shutters'. His brothers William and Henry, now twenty-five and twenty-three, mingled with the crowd, the former in a crimson mask, the latter in purple, both with arching white feathers in their hats. Fashionable eastern themes predominated among the costumes, a brash sartorial celebration of colonial expansion and the wealth that it would bring. Prince Henry's friend the Earl Grosvenor was in a splendid suit, 'of the Turkish fashion'. Representatives of the City of London were out in force and one of the most grandly dressed of the guests was Lord Clive, whose victory at Plassey five years before had delivered the south of the Indian subcontinent and its riches to the East India Company. He came, appropriately, as a 'nabob'. In general, commented the *Gentleman's Magazine*, 'the quantity of gold and silver tissue made into Indian, Persian and Chinese habits, together with the quantity of diamonds with which these habits were decorated, is past belief'. Two days later,

Christian finally left London, giving a thousand guineas to the servants at St James's and scattering coins amongst the poor who pressed round his carriage. In Dover, he once more boarded the *Mary*, and grateful British officials sped him on his way to France and the hospitality of Louis XV.

Back in Denmark, Caroline Mathilde made the most of the unease created by the rumours of the enormous expense of Christian's travels. Although she was only just seventeen, she already knew perfectly well the value of a gesture, and pointedly spent the summer in thrifty retirement at the castle of Frederiksborg west of Copenhagen. Despite carrying out few official duties in her husband's absence, Caroline Mathilde took care when she was at the magnificent castle to visit the poor in the village of Hillerød across the lake, reminding her subjects that royal money could be more usefully spent on relieving poverty than in assuaging the boredom of the King. She also allowed Robert Gunning to drive out, visit her, and see the Crown Prince. In the late autumn she arrived back in Copenhagen, stood in for Christian at the inauguration of the great bronze statue of Frederik V in the middle of the bare paved square at Amalienborg and then retreated to Christiansborg to wait for her husband's return.

Christian, though, had no desire to hurry home. Copenhagen was already cold and unwelcoming, and heavy, besides, with the burdens of kingship. At the end of November, after he had been in France for six weeks, Christian sent to Caroline Mathilde to write to her brother in effusive terms about his London visit, and she dutifully declared to George III that 'the King has ordered me to tell you that he is much more pleased with England than with France'. But despite this diplomatic grace, Christian was a francophile by education if not by birth, and a much better French- than English-speaker. He was well read in French literature and the writings of the philosophes. While in Paris, besides visiting all the usual sites that any Grand Tourist took in – the Théâtre français, the Opéra, the Sèvres factory, Marly, Versailles and the Trianon – he also held a dinner for twenty philosophes. Many of the guests were associated with the *Encyclopédie*, the great new compendium of knowledge and thought begun in 1751, suppressed in 1752, relaunched and proscribed completely in 1757 and continued semi-secretly until its completion four years after Christian's visit. At the dinner Christian sat between one of the *Encyclopédie*'s editors, Denis Diderot, and Claude-Adrien Helvétius. Hélvetius's long and rambling *De l'Esprit*, or 'On the Mind', published in 1758 and immediately condemned by the Sorbonne, was one of the most widely read and diffused texts of the new view of the world that was being constructed, article by article, in the *Encyclopédie*. Christian impressed the assembled *Encyclopédiastes* with his knowledge of their work and his devotion to the intellectual godfather of their endeavour, François-Marie Arouet, Voltaire, who was sitting out his self-imposed exile near Geneva. So too did Christian's new doctor and friend, Johann Struensee. Struensee was placed between Baron von Grimm, the private secretary of the duc d'Orléans and confidant of Catherine the Great, and the lawyer-playwright Bernard-Joseph Saurin. Later he made sure that he paid a private visit to Helvétius himself, as admirer, disciple and thorough reader of his inflammatory text.

La Condamine, a French scientist who visited London in 1763, told James Boswell that Helvétius's *De l'Esprit* was a dangerous book in the hands of young people whose principles were unfixed and fluid. Indeed, its mixture of unbridled materialism and unapologetic libertinism unanchored to any reverence towards social norms or structures was likely to be heady stuff for bold young rebels. But for Struensee, Helvétius was one step, and by no means the last, on an intellectual journey that he had begun fifteen years before and that was now coming to conclusion and fruition.

Johann Struensee was born in Halle, a small town in northern Germany, in 1737. The second son of a prominent Lutheran minister, Adam Struensee, he was also grandson of a doctor who had risen to become physician-in-ordinary to Christian VI of Denmark. Johann, his brother Carl August, two years his senior, and their siblings, grew up in a strenuously religious environment strongly influenced by recent upheavals in the Lutheran Church.

By the early years of the eighteenth century the vigorous Lutheranism of the Reformation and the seventeenth century had settled into social and religious orthodoxy, ensconced in a position of comfort and no longer much interested in great questions of faith. A reforming movement, Pietism, grew up, imbued with revivalist enthusiasm, impatient with doctrine and flushed with a democratic confidence in individual experience of divine revelation. Struensee's father Adam became a prominent leader of the Pietist movement, and even though some of its emphasis on overt displays of the experience of conversion and revelation declined after the 1740s, the pastor's children were nurtured in an atmosphere of belief, certainty and very active faith.

Quickly outgrowing Halle's grammar school, Johann was enrolled to study medicine at the ancient University of Halle in 1752 on his fifteenth birthday. Struensee was already a brilliant student, with a forging, enquiring mind. At Halle, in the medical school, he ran straight into one of the many controversies stirred by the ramifications of the greatest and longest debate of the eighteenth century: the tussle and agonies produced by the linked questions about the nature of the soul, the body and the mind. Doctors, whose professional province encompassed the last two, were to be central to the debate both as thinkers and as fledgling men of science who took up and applied the idea of the efficacy of empirical experiment propounded by Newton and by Locke. Most of Struensee's fellow medical students stuck to learning about anatomy, surgery and dispensing medicines. But others could already see, as they laboured over their dissection and anatomy, that studying the body raised questions about the nature of the soul, and the very principles upon which life was generated and governed. Sitting behind the idea of the mind and the soul were, after all, the deity and the afterlife. The stakes could not have been higher.

By the time Struensee entered medical school, crucial philosophical, physiological and religious questions had risen to the top of the great frothing cauldron of enquiry which had produced both Newton and Locke. Were the soul and mind separate from the body, or did the body produce them? If body and soul were separate, upon what philosophical and physiological principles did the soul and mind operate? Did the deity provide a 'vital spark' from which soul and mind developed, or was the soul inserted, fully formed, into inanimate matter? If, conversely, the mind was the product of sensation, and so of the body, what happened when the body ceased to function? If the mind died with the body, what price the soul, and where, crucially, did that leave the deity? The century-long debate over these questions formed the core of the great philosophical endeavour, loosely called the Enlightenment and epitomised both by the production of the *Encyclopédie*, and by the bitter and continuing reaction to it. Some of its protagonists, like Voltaire, were explicit about the aims of the project and their role within it; others, like Newton, perhaps, or even David Hume, were drawn in by the implications and brilliance of their contributions and conclusions. But at its essence, in thousands of fractured, unfinished and even unwitting fragments, the Enlightenment was, and remains, the boldest attempt ever mounted to shift human consciousness from a god-centred to a man-centred view both of the world and of the life that could be lived in it.

In the field of medicine the first solid steps towards setting the profession on a foundation of clinical study and scientific experiment were taken by Herman Bœrhave, Professor of Medicine at Leiden University until his death in 1738. Bœrhave was a wide-ranging philosophical practitioner who abandoned any belief in the separation of mind and body in favour of seeing the body and mind as a single organism created together by a deity and functioning according to observable natural laws. He was clinician, philosopher, chemist and botanist all rolled into one and became the most influential and charismatic medical professor of his time. Voltaire was by no means the only non-practitioner of medicine who travelled to Leiden to hear him speak, and Bœrhave's fame spread throughout the Continent. With it went the notion that medicine could be a respectable profession rather than a trade so infiltrated by charlatans that it had no credibility. At Halle, Struensee was educated in the ambit of Bœrhave's influence. He rushed through the syllabus with great speed, graduating with a degree in medicine when he was still only twenty, and was appointed town physician at Altona the following year. Altona was the German-speaking Danish town on the northern bank of the Elbe opposite Hamburg, and there Struensee began to put Bœrhave's general principles to work.

Struensee became a doctor when not only was the professional standing of physicians changing, but also the way in which they were used. This was especially evident in capital cities and other urban centres which attracted young and ambitious practitioners who had graduated from the ancient universities of Germany, Scotland and Holland. The new professional status of doctors and their growing intellectual self-confidence was apparent in the way they were contributing to debates which questioned the very purposes of man's existence. More than thirty contributors to the *Encyclopédie* were physicians, and medicine and its language of sickness and cure became both testing ground and linguistic bedrock of what the philosopher David Hume called 'the moral sciences'. Voltaire was fond of describing his grand secularising project as a struggle for health, and religion as 'a sick man's dream'. Diderot, himself the son of a doctor, repeatedly insisted, more modestly, that health and happiness always went hand in hand, and made one of the three protagonists of his secretly circulated fable *La Rêve d'Alembert*, written in 1769, the doctor Bordeau. Doctors, Diderot implied, could be standard bearers for thought and experiment about the nature of man and the society that man moved in and created.

At the same time, and paradoxically, the very methods that doctors now developed to treat their patients began to mean that the doctor was sometimes regarded by his clients – often with his own encouragement or connivance – as a worker of miracles akin to a priest. If the body, the mind and the soul were no longer seen as separate, it made empirical sense for doctors not simply to observe the effluvia of their patients' bodies, but to consider their minds as well. Although a science of diagnosis was not formulated until the end of the century, and although there was as yet no systematised idea of noting down a patient's medical history, it must have seemed obvious, if mind and body were intimately or even causally linked, to ask the patient how he or she was feeling.

In the mid-eighteenth century this was a very loaded question, an enquiry on three levels. It asked first what the patient's physical sensations were, secondly what his or her emotions were and thirdly, in the most common of contemporary philosophical links, how the first connected to the second, since sensation had still a double meaning of both feeling and the physical operation of the nerves. The patient might reply in many ways, but if he or she attended to the second or third valences of the doctor's question, the doctor might rapidly become a recipient of confidences, and in Protestant lands, where religious fervour was cooling and religious feeling finding new outlets, occupy the old role of the father confessor. Add to this the doctor's perceived ability to effect cures for disease, made spectacularly obvious when smallpox inoculation was widely introduced in the 1720s and 1730s, and his presence at moments of vulnerability and fear, and the conditions were created for him to become, to some patients, more priest and miracle-worker than simple dispenser of prescriptions and medicines. When the doctor was young, confident and handsome, and his patients afraid, trusting and female, a miasma of sexual longing might pervade the relationship. If for one side it carried excitement and danger, for the other came the certainty of professional advantage and a heady sense of personal power. London's first aristocratic medical elopement came in 1760, when Caroline Keppel, daughter of the 2nd Earl of Albemarle, rose nimbly from her sickbed to run off with her handsome young doctor, Robert Adair. Adair rapidly turned romance to professional advantage, and ended his career as surgeon-general to the King himself.

By all accounts, Johann Struensee was just such a charismatic young man when he took up his post in Altona in 1758. Almost six feet tall, big-boned and broad-shouldered: voluptuous muscularity radiated from him. His fair hair, deep-set blue eyes, long prominent nose and full, well-defined lips made his face memorable and compelling. He wore his own hair, moulded at each side of his head in two butter-like curls, and casually tied at the back with a simple black ribbon. It was sometimes powdered, sometimes left in its natural state. This strong physical presence, combined with what one writer later called 'a merry look', easy charm and a quality of attention to people whom he met, made it simple for Struensee to win over both men and women. He was soon widely regarded as a good doctor, his practice flourished and he began to acquire friends and patrons among the town's reforming aristocracy. Prominent among his early supporters were Count Rantzau-Ascheberg, then beginning to give his peasants small freedoms, and his son Major Schack Carl Rantzau-Ascheberg. With the Rantzaus, luck seemed to be on the young doctor's side. The younger Count's wife contracted virulent smallpox soon after his arrival. Although inoculation was by this time widespread, for those not inoculated, like the Countess, there was no cure for the disease, and the only chance of survival lay in a confident doctor's doing nothing other than giving liquids and counselling rest. The Countess lived, Struensee took the credit, and his reputation spread.

Along with the Rantzaus, Struensee also treated the families of the Baron von Söhlenthal and Privy Counsellor von Berketin. Von Sölenthal's son, Enevold Brandt, became Struensee's closest local companion. Brandt shared with Struensee a strong commitment to radical thought and libertine habits and exploits. Struensee also soon counted Berketin's wife as one of his patrons, and when she moved to Copenhagen after her husband's death to take up a post in the household of the Hereditary Prince Frederik, he established the first outpost in the expanding empire of his renown. It was through these and other local dignitaries that Struensee was introduced to Christian VII's favourite Count Holck when the King travelled to Holstein in 1767, thus first planting himself in the minds of the King's advisers as a competent, forward-looking physician who might be called upon to help if Christian's condition worsened or his staff needed strengthening.

In Altona, too, Struensee always had interests beyond those usually found even in a successful and well-connected young doctor. He spent his twenties practising and improving his profession, meeting and seducing women and reading widely. In July 1763 with his friend the man of letters David Panning, Struensee started a monthly magazine, *Zum Nutzen und Vergnügen*, rendered into contemporary English as *For Instruction and Amusement*, but better translated to reflect an intellectual outlook that was both practical and libertine, as *For Use and Pleasure*. The magazine contained articles on medicine and history as well as poetry and satire. But it folded after six months; perhaps the editors, having made their mark as young men with ambition, got bored with the effort of its production. Struensee's only direct contribution seems to have been an essay called 'Considerations of a Doctor on National Population', in which he argued for the economic benefits of population increase. Nevertheless, with its self-consciously cosmopolitan outlook and its evident francophilia, *Zum Nutzen und Vergnügen* had more in common with the headier atmosphere of the free-thinking port of Hamburg south of the Elbe than the careful town of Altona to the north, and it signalled its participants' desire to measure themselves against big city rather than provincial life.

In the decade after his establishment at Altona, Struensee undoubtedly worked his way through Voltaire and Rousseau, parts of the serial volumes of the *Encyclopédie* and other radical literature making its way over the German border. A knowledge of two works in particular seems to have found its way into his circle through the publishing underground, *L'Homme machine* by the French doctor Julien Offray de La Mettrie, and Helvétius's *De l'Esprit*. Struensee almost certainly studied Helvétius closely; La Mettrie he must have known at least by report, although it is unclear whether he actually read all the way through his work, and, according to one writer, he denied having done so.

La Mettrie, whose description of 'the great art of healing' as man's 'noblest activity' would have endeared him to any dedicated young physician, held degrees in both natural philosophy and medicine before he went to study with Bœrhave at Leiden in 1733. A prolific author of practical clinical manuals as well as a translator of and a commentator on the works of his master, he first practised as a doctor and then, in 1742, became a physician in the French army during the War of Austrian Succession. After a bout of fever and delirium during the campaign, La Mettrie concluded that his wayward thoughts had sprung from his diseased body and, as his protector Frederick the Great of Prussia put it, 'filled with these ideas during his convalescence he boldly bore the torch of experience into the night of metaphysics'. The uproar provoked by the resulting book, *The Natural History of the Soul*, published in 1745, drove La Mettrie from France, and its sequel

L'Homme machine of 1748 frightened even the liberal authorities at Leiden and led him to seek sanctuary in Prussia, where he died in 1751.

La Mettrie's two books, and especially *L'Homme machine*, succinctly brought together the wide-ranging debate about the body, the mind and the soul. In *The Natural History of the Soul* he suggested that mental processes were physiological in origin, but in *L'Homme machine* he went further, asserting that the soul and the mind alike were simply the production of organic processes. If everything thus had a material cause, any idea of the deity was simply a chimera produced within the body. Free will was invented and morality a by-product of physiological processes. Man was neither free nor infused with the divine: he was just the workings of his own body, a machine for life.

La Mettrie's explosive and prescient theory was repeated and garnished with a lot more smoke and a little less flame by Helvétius a decade later. Helvétius put La Mettrie's ideas in a social context and transformed a philosophical treatise into a rambling but exciting social manifesto. He drew back from the godless implications of La Mettrie's materialism, declaring that God said to matter, 'I endow thee with power'. But having given the deity a starting role, Helvétius shunted him to the very back of the theatre to watch the drama of man's passions play itself out. Physiologically induced passions, Helvétius said, were the primary motive for human actions, and he added that 'they prompt man to heroic actions and give birth to those grand ideas which are the astonishment and admiration of all ages'. There was, moreover, no merit in established social position and no disgrace in social ambition prompted by the desire for pleasure. It was this social analysis that disturbed Helvétius's critics and animated admirers like the ambitious young Struensee.

'Let us suppose', Helvétius wrote, 'that a man, born without a fortune, but fond of the pleasures of love, has observed, that the women comply more easily with the desires of a lover in proportion as the elevation of his rank will reflect the greater honour on her; and that being thus filled with ambition by his passion for women, he aspires to the post of general or prime minister; in order to obtain these places, he must apply his whole care in acquiring abilities or in forming intrigues.' Few who read *De l'Esprit* would have thought of putting any of its ideas to the test. It was a book drunk on its own extremity, and its rambling examples from past cultures offered illustration rather than incited imitation. But it was a book for young men who wanted to make a stir, who wanted to upset the established order and flaunt their allegiance to the new ideas coming from France. Johann Struensee would not have swallowed it whole. By 1758, when it was published, he had a mind well stocked with a wide variety of reading and a way of thinking about the world in which women probably never occupied a commanding, primary position. But Helvétius did offer him a portrait of the kind of man he already believed, by virtue of temperament and education, that he might one day become.

By 1768 when he was thirty-one and his influential patrons had secured him the position of physician-in-ordinary to Christian VII on his travels, Struensee was almost certainly a materialist who believed with La Mettrie that both sensations and the mind were produced within the body by organic processes. He had probably, as an observer put it later, 'carried freedom of thinking as far as any man', and had become 'deficient in both . . . morality and religion'. But this new lack of belief was held within a cast of mind that was as fierce and unforgiving as the Lutheranism into which he had been born. Struensee had nothing of the humane indolence of a man like the philosopher David Hume, who enjoyed his own life too much to give the question of God's existence a starring role. In contrast to many pragmatic deists and a few self-confessed unbelievers, Struensee was an ex-Christian, a fierce ideologue who was constructing a new system of beliefs to replace the old, a new set of rules to unshackle mankind and allow organic desires to flourish.

No doctor in a small provincial town, however, would jeopardise his social or professional standing by voicing such ideas publicly. When Christian VII passed through Altona on his initial summer tour in 1768, Struensee was known first as an excellent physician and only second as a man of reformist views who moved in liberal circles and was something of a libertine. Once with the King's party, though, Struensee seized his opportunity for professional advancement with an alacrity that would have impressed Helvétius himself. As his mania grew on him, Christian had more need than ever of a competent and sympathetic doctor. But he also wanted someone who would sit with him at night and drive away the demons that marauded through his head. Warnstedt, his valet, did his best, but he was a young man who had no experience of the kind of thoughts that possessed the King. Struensee not only had a fund of knowledge with which to distract Christian, he came as a doctor who was used to having authority over his patients and he had no hampering reverence for Christian's exalted station. Struensee later wrote that he thought the King's malady prevented him from having any feelings towards others. Nonetheless, by the end of the long European journey of 1768, Struensee had become more than Christian's temporary doctor. He had gained his confidence and the King did not want to give up his services. Soon after the party passed through Altona on the way back to Copenhagen in January 1769, Struensee was appointed surgeon-in-ordinary to the monarch. Taking his chance he disbanded his practice and moved to the Danish capital.

In the first few months after he arrived in Copenhagen, Struensee's main objective was to retain the King's confidence. It had been fairly easy to build a close companionship on their travels, but the court at Christiansborg contained both competing attractions for the King and dozens of potential rivals for his new doctor. By his own later admission, Struensee decided to stay within the boundaries of his appointment, concentrating on consolidating his position among the court doctors and taking stock of the volatile world around him. In the absence of the King and his chief minister, government in Copenhagen had proceeded with its usual digestive slowness. When Christian returned, Bernstorff, anchored by the might of Catherine the Great's Russia, resumed his commanding position. But the position of the government was bound to be uncertain and the political situation volatile because now no one knew when the King's illness would strike and what he would do when his mania descended. In this uncertain sea swam not only Bernstorff's administration but also the King's stepmother Juliane Marie and her son Frederik who lived somewhat in retirement but nonetheless at an angle to the court at Christiansborg, and the Queen as well. Caroline Mathilde had had ample time to reflect on her position in the five months of the King's absence. At the beginning of 1769 she was still only seventeen and a half and was reported to have grown both upwards and outwards while Christian had been away. But she had certainly considered her own grievances and determined to combat her isolation and unhappiness by asserting herself at court.

Caroline Mathilde had no idea of forming the nucleus of any political party herself. Rather her strategy was to attach herself to her husband and try to gain prominence, amusement and a greater sense of her own status through him. So, although she disliked Bernstorff and probably held him responsible for the removal of Madame von Plessen, her interest was more in supplanting the King's favourite Count Holck than in forcing any kind of political change. Johann Struensee she ignored altogether. He was merely one of the King's doctors. He had no title of nobility and was thus debarred from attending court ceremonies, and he was, besides, standing carefully aside from political involvement or any behaviour that might attract attention.

At first Caroline Mathilde's strategy seemed to be having some effect. Robert Gunning, anxious to send London some good news, allowed himself to believe that not only had Christian abandoned his night sorties and disdain for the Queen, but that Caroline Mathilde would now see off any royal favourites. 'Your Lordship has already been acquainted with the change that appeared in his Danish Majesty', he told the new Secretary of State, the Earl of Rochford, on 18 February 1769. 'Those amusements in which he used to take delight no longer afford him any. Her Majesty will now, no doubt, obtain that just and proper degree of influence, which her numberless amiable qualities entitle her to.' Caroline Mathilde, longing for more friendly faces, persuaded Christian to invite her brother William, now Duke of Gloucester, to visit Denmark in the summer. But nothing much else came of her push for a greater public role. The King may have gone out less. But Caroline Mathilde was not keeping him inside. In the first place his mistress had been decorously removed and his circle of carousers broken up. In the second, he was becoming more incapacitated and spending more time indoors and with his doctor. He was soon spurning Caroline Mathilde in public once again. It was rumoured in the early spring that if the King and Queen chanced to meet on one of Christiansborg's long corridors, they would advance towards one another with their attendants and pass in silence, each without making any acknowledgement of the other. Duty sometimes required the King and Queen to be together, but mostly Christian preferred to live completely apart from his ample wife.

This strained monarchical duet had to be played with conviction, at least on Caroline Mathilde's part, during the Duke of Gloucester's visit in July. Prince William's visit would coincide with Caroline Mathilde's eighteenth birthday and since the celebrations had been muted for the last two years, a series of entertainments was planned. But the twenty-five-year-old Duke was not the ideal party guest. He was George III's favourite sibling, a ponderous, stubborn young man, ill-at-ease in unfamiliar surroundings and uncertain how to behave at Christiansborg. Caroline Mathilde was not in a very good position to play the relaxed hostess. She was angry and frustrated, and her brother's visit must have reminded her forcefully of the dynastic and diplomatic reasons for her unhappy marriage. She may or may not have known that the Duke had been sent to Denmark partly to remove him temporarily from an unsuitable romantic entanglement, but she must have suspected that he and his suite had been asked to check up on her, on the King and on the political situation in the country.

Caroline Mathilde's response was to stage a series of spectacular entertainments for her brother at which she sat alongside Christian or acted as chief spectator and so disguised her isolated position and marginal role in the life of the court. Prince William was treated to a review of the massed Life Guards and the troop of regiments stationed in Copenhagen, to balls and summer lunches, and two days of festivities for Caroline Mathilde's birthday. During the celebrations the King and a group of courtiers performed a 'carousel', a whirling musical horseback ride worthy of Philip Astley, and then led out the Life Guards and a large band in procession, 'richly dressed in Turkish dress'. One day the Duke, King and the Queen were driven north in what Gunning described as 'very fine, hot weather', through the rustling stands of beech, ash and lime to Elsinore and Kronborg Castle. Nothing much seemed to impress the Duke of Gloucester; not the steepled castle with its smooth mint-green roofs, not the massive star-shaped ramparts with their broad grass terraces, not the dozens of gun batteries whose ten- and thirteen-inch mortars faced menacingly out to sea, and not the Danish man-of-war that sped them back to Copenhagen with the slender Danebrog snapping beyond its masthead. He sat silent and florid through all the magnificence, eating his way through huge meals and earning himself the meaty sobriquet of 'the English ox'. After three weeks he and his suite left. They had brought no comfort to Caroline Mathilde and took no good news away. The Queen, they must have reported, was unhappy, slighted and full of resentment.

All through the summer and autumn, Johann Struensee was making steady strides in the King's esteem and methodically widening his ambitions. In May 1769, when he was thirty-one, he was appointed State Councillor, a rank rather than an office, but a rank which, in the highly stratified court, allowed him to attend official functions and thus to understand how influence was distributed. By the summer he had begun to translate the ambitions of his years in Altona into practice, thinking perhaps to cut a larger figure on his new stage by presenting himself not simply as a doctor, but as a natural philosopher as well. So 'The Considerations of a Doctor on National Population', written six years earlier for *Zum Nutzen und Vergnügen*, were practically solidified into a detailed survey of the population of Denmark and its dominions, with the occupations of adult males and the rates of births and deaths. It was drawn up under his supervision and acquired by Gunning – or perhaps by his spies, who could lay their hands on secret material – in the middle of August.

Caroline Mathilde had shunned Struensee on first acquaintance. She was convinced that he was bound to be hostile to her because he was a new favourite of the King's and she was besides determined to dislike everything associated with her errant husband. But Struensee was intent on keeping clear all possible avenues of advancement and took care to present himself as open, sympathetic and prepared to mediate between the King and Queen. By the summer of 1769 Caroline Mathilde's belief in the doctor's hostility had been transformed into a willingness to see him. During the royal family's brief residence at Frederiksberg Castle after the Duke of Gloucester had left, Christian insisted that Caroline Mathilde spent time in Struensee's company, or perhaps simply refused to send the doctor away at times when he was forced to be with his wife. Shortly afterwards Caroline Mathilde chose to consult Struensee when she was unwell, eager to engineer the sort of intimacy that the sickroom permitted, when court etiquette was laid aside and where the deference that was still due to the Queen was balanced by the authority vested in the doctor. Caroline Mathilde's lady-in-waiting, Elisabeth von Eyben, with whom Struensee was having an affair at the time, later reported that one day while the court was still in residence at Frederiksberg, Caroline Mathilde was paying her a private visit when there was a knock on the door to her room. 'I ran to the door', she said, 'and it was Struensee. I told him to go away and said that the Queen was still there, so I could not see him. The Queen immediately asked who it was, and when she heard it was Struensee she wished he had come in.'

Back in Copenhagen that autumn, though, Caroline Mathilde found herself as isolated as ever. Made miserable by her loneliness, she observed her husband not merely hostile to her but increasingly ill and incapacitated. Seeing no change as she looked forward from her eighteen years to a blighted future, she withdrew from public appearances, overcome with melancholy. When she finally wrote to George III in England, he reacted with grumpy pique, as if Caroline Mathilde's sadness was being directed at him. 'Your long silence', George wrote on 12 November, 'I was in hopes had been occasioned by the hurry you commonly are in. I was much hurt at finding by the letter I have received from you that it was owing to illness, which had even obliged you to keep your bed. Forgive the anxiety of a brother that tenderly loves you, and to that attribute the earnest entreaty that you will be more careful of your health. . . . I shall order Mr Gunning to be very constant in his accounts of what so nearly concerns me.'

Robert Gunning, in fact, had always wanted to safeguard his own professional future by writing as little as possible about either the King or the Queen of Denmark. Relaying the news of the King's madness or the Queen's melancholy might look too much like a negative assessment of the whole project of uniting the British and Danish royal families, an implicit criticism of his employers in St James's that might hamper his plans for a more ample and glamorous posting. Now, though, Gunning was forced to risk incurring the anxiety of the Secretary of State in London and the concern of the King, by writing directly about Caroline Mathilde. On 21 November, after seeking information about her illness at court, he wrote to the Earl of Rochford with ungrammatical reluctance, 'I am extremely sorry to acquaint your Lordship that the state of the Queen of Denmark's health has lately presented some very unfavourable symptoms, which have given such apprehensions to her physicians as to make them think that a perfect reestablishment may be attended with some difficulty unless Her Majesty can be persuaded to pay more attention to herself.'

Four days later Gunning wrote that 'the remedies' prescribed to Caroline Mathilde had 'begun to take effect'. But in the course of his enquiries, Gunning realised for the first time the ever-increasing importance of Johann Struensee in the Queen's life. He was enough of a professional politician to realise that Struensee was a man of talent and ambition, and to have a hunch that he was already bringing instability to the Danish court. Count Holck, he told Lord Rochford, was still an important figure, 'but the mainspring, the first mover of all the present intrigues is discovered to be another person, of whom it cannot easily be determined whether his talents are more formidable, his principles more relaxed, or his address more seducing. These qualities, combined with almost constant attendance on the King, have contributed to give him the most alarming ascendancy over His Majesty. When I consider at once this gentleman's supposed predilection in favour of French politics, his consummate artifice, and behold at the same time the chain of royal confidence which binds him to the throne, it becomes hard to judge whether it be less easy to remove him or more dangerous to suffer his continuance.'

Gunning's intelligence was timely, but his last phrase was wishful thinking. There was no chance of either removing Struensee or of 'allowing' him to continue. The doctor himself was already manipulating events and the political landscape was changing rapidly. He was no longer just the close friend of the King. Caroline Mathilde had fallen quickly and completely in love with him.

Caroline Mathilde lost her heart easily and swiftly. Round about the beginning of November 1769 she had consulted Struensee about the melancholia which still dogged her. Perhaps for the first time, an intelligent, confident and physically commanding man asked her in confidence, in private, and paying the closest attention, about the state of her mind and her health. Together and alone, he enquiring, she responding, he acted as adviser, and she happily forgot her status as queen. She fell under the dense enchantment of his presence. She sought more meetings, followed his advice, laid herself open to him and then for him. Melancholy fell away; passion, excitement and joy took its place.

By the winter Struensee was visiting Caroline Mathilde alone. In the middle of January, the Queen used her influence to get him lodgings in Christiansborg. In the evenings and after dark he began to make use of a dark, unlit staircase from his rooms on the mezzanine floor to reach the first floor, walking with his candle through the large room known as the hermitage, which was deserted and empty at night, to the Queen's rooms beyond. This nocturnal wandering must have added illicit pleasure to their meetings. But even without the shared excitement of the forbidden, Struensee overwhelmed Caroline Mathilde and then himself with his recklessness and his heady sense of a power that was both political and personal. Caroline Mathilde's fall was headlong and Struensee had to decide quickly what to do with her love when he realised he had it. He did not hesitate. By February 1770, and despite the fact that sleeping with the King's wife was a capital offence, Struensee and Caroline Mathilde were lovers.

Caroline Mathilde was stepping into the unknown by allowing herself to fall in love with a man so outside her circle and station, a man whose status hovered uneasily between that of tradesman, professional and priest, and who was neither a courtier nor a nobleman nor a Dane. It was a measure of her desperation and her loneliness that she did so, but a measure too of her tough and fearless disregard for the rituals of court and royal life. It was indeed Struensee who was taking the greater risk, and with far less pragmatic justification. By the time he met Caroline Mathilde he had already started to widen his attention beyond the consulting room. He saw himself once again, as he had in Altona, as a natural philosopher, but this time on a national stage. Perhaps he was already thinking along the lines of the classical analysis of the state, that it was a body with the King at its head, that it was not just the King who was sick, but his kingdom as well, and that he had the means and the ambition to cure it. Promoted to the rank of state councillor and enjoying the complete confidence of Christian VII, he could soon unseat Count Holck and use his new position as the King's favourite as a springboard from which to launch a political career. For that, he had no need of the Queen's help or advice, especially since she had little power of her own within the court.

She, on the other hand, had great need of him. Even in the midst of her tumultuous love, Caroline Mathilde must have realised that Struensee, in the space of a few months, had won what she had wanted for three and a half years. He had the trust and love of the King, and because of that he had the means to help her acquire the position of influence and stability within the court that was her due as Queen. Perhaps at the still centre of her love was a shard of shrewdness. She was intimately familiar with the presence and role of the royal favourite, having grown up in the ambit of her mother's fondness for Lord Bute and the aura of secrecy and dependency that characterised her brother's relationship with him. But she never had any intention of reproducing either relationship. She was, as someone who observed her closely wrote, 'not only clever, but had a good mind', and in Struensee she had found someone whose intelligence matched her own. Knowing how a favourite could act as a trojan horse in an impenetrable circle of power in the court, she may have calculated that Struensee, already possessed of her love, could supply her other needs as well.

Indeed, the doctor was soon working on the Queen's behalf. He began to mediate between Caroline Mathilde and the King, trying to work her into the position of influence she had long wanted in the court, so that she would be recognised as the reigning queen, replete with status and influence. At the same time, he continued in his professional role and the suggestions he made to help her return to health worked to startling and visible effect.

Caroline Mathilde rode and walked daily. Abandoning the unbalanced delicacies of side-saddle, she put on breeches, boots, frock-coat and spurs and rode like a man astride her horse. Many observers declared that she looked ungainly and unfeminine in her new riding habit. But though they ostensibly rejected her costume on aesthetic grounds, hinting that the Queen was too plump to wear belt and breeches, it was the assertive manliness that worried them every bit as much as the Queen's too obvious curves.

On fine days Caroline Mathilde rode out into the countryside beyond Copenhagen. In the sleety dank of the winter she dashed round the sand-covered floor of the great riding hall that stretched along the northern side of the palace. Her melancholy vanished and her presence by the King's side seemed to indicate a reconciliation between them. At the same time, though, rumour and contradictory reports began to drift like smoke through the corridors of Christiansborg, hanging in the air, making it difficult to see what was happening. In November 1769 Robert Gunning had complained that 'all avenues to authentic information (notwithstanding my having spared no pains nor expense to obtain it) are now absolutely shut up'. Struensee may have been emotionally reckless in private, but in public he was extremely careful, and he confided in no one about his relationship with the Queen.

Later, two of Caroline Mathilde's chambermaids, Bruun and Horn, together with her lady-in-waiting Anna Petersen, claimed that as early as the New Year of 1770 the Queen was making no attempt to hide her feelings for Johann Struensee. A few months later, Bruun and Horn decided to take matters into their own hands and to confront her about the nocturnal comings and goings. They had been conducting their own experiments and taking note of the evidence of the Queen's affair, and now devised plans to check up on Struensee's movements in the night. They got a maid to sprinkle powder on the floor outside Caroline Mathilde's bedroom, and found large footprints in it the next morning, as well as their whitish doubles on the carpet inside. The King, they said, 'never came that way', and besides he had the delicate feet of a young boy. The maids also put wax in the keyhole of the door to the Queen's bedroom and found it on the floor outside, showing that Caroline Mathilde had unlocked her door and crept out into the darkness. After such night traffic, the maids found the beds dirty, the sheets rumpled and stained and marks on the Queen's sofas and towels which, as they said, 'modesty' forbade 'them to mention'.

Horn and Bruun decided to confront the Queen, 'to save her royal reputation' and to safeguard their own. Sobbing as they told her of their suspicions, they called forth Caroline Mathilde's sympathy and she comforted and caressed them, asking anxiously what was wrong. Bruun said it was rumoured that Struensee came to her in the night and that they feared it was true. Caroline Mathilde's first instinct was to ask her lover's advice and she ordered her maids to go and get him. After he had gone, she told them that they should not say such things about a queen. But the maids stood firm, saying they had their evidence and hinting that they might have to use it, and it was Caroline Mathilde who retreated. She asked them humbly if they thought that the rumours would subside if she was closeted with Struensee less often. Horn and Bruun replied that in order for the stories to die down, Struensee should only come now and again and should never stay for long.

For two weeks, 'this warning worked', as Bruun and Horn later put it. But then Struensee's visits lengthened again. Caroline Mathilde threw caution away. She couldn't give Struensee up, she told her maids. He had such 'a good mind', she said, he helped her with so much and he was always on her side. She had decided, she concluded, not to care what people thought of her. Having recklessly confided everything to her maids, and receiving no sympathy in return, Caroline Mathilde belatedly decided to put them at a distance. She ordered all her waiting women to stay in their own rooms and only come to her when they were called.

Despite the difficulty he had in getting accurate information, Gunning had an acute sense of the implications of what he too suspected. He was convinced from the beginning that Caroline Mathilde's new confidence and Struensee's unprecedented emergence were not merely domestic changes, but would have political consequences. Writing with cryptic fervour to Rochford on 2 January 1770, he declared that, 'the politics of Denmark seem incapable of any other production than that of intrigue. Scarce a week passes without a new one being set on foot and some by persons the least suspected of engaging in them.' Day-to-day government continued undisturbed, however, and Bernstorff, the chief minister, was unmoved by the liking the King and Queen had begun to show for Struensee. With the disdain of the lifelong professional for the untried amateur, he declared that the doctor understood neither the court nor the people, and could thus never pose a threat to those who were running the country. In the spring he ignored another signal that Struensee was confidently advancing up the hierarchy at court, and quickly gaining an absolute authority over the King.

Frederick Lewis, Prince of Wales, in 1735-6, painted by Philip Mercier. Loathed by his parents, he was a good father but an unsuccessful politician.

Augusta, Princess of Wales, painted by Allan Ramsay in 1755, sad and austere in her widowhood.

Princess Caroline Matilda when she was three, painted by Jean Etienne Liotard in 1754, and already looking at the world with some shrewdness and mistrust.

FACING PAGE:
(*Above*) Prince George and Prince Edward Augustus about 1748, painted with their tutor, Francis Ayscough by Richard Wilson. Staring boldly out, knees up off the sofa, Prince Edward is already the jollier of the two.
(*Below*) Richard Brompton's group portrait of Prince Edward, Duke of York with his friends in Venice in 1764; a cheerful, convivial man about town.

Henry Duke of Cumberland, his wife and her sister, painted by Thomas Gainsborough in 1783-5. The Duchess of Cumberland, glamorously centre stage, proved a kind and loyal wife to her rackety husband.

Prince William Henry, Duke of Gloucester, in Rome in 1772, his unmistakable Hanoverian features caught by Pompeo Girolamo Batoni. Recovering from a severe illness, the Duke was also nursing a long-kept secret.

Maria Walpole, Countess of Waldegrave, engraved from a portrait by Joshua Reynolds. Then considered one of the most beautiful women at court, she planned to use her looks to take her all the way from illegitimacy to an ermine gown.

Allan Ramsay's coronation portrait of George III, 1760. For him ermine was a necessity more than a pleasure; he dressed plainly, lived modestly and revered virtue.

As he had done with Caroline Mathilde, Struensee secured his new position by taking a considerable risk. This one, though, was short-lived. In the midst of an outbreak of virulent smallpox in Copenhagen, which was claiming hundred of lives, Struensee inoculated Crown Prince Frederik against the disease. There was considerable opposition to his initiative. Struensee was not the King's chief physician, and the Crown Prince, at two and a half, was very young. Behind this lay the pedigree of inoculation itself. Inoculation, despite having been diffused through Europe from Britain, had been championed by Voltaire, and so it was associated with radical thought, anti-clericalism and France, and disapproval of any one of them could colour views of it.

Prince Frederik's inoculation, though, went easily and well. Inevitably, it brought Struensee and Caroline Mathilde even closer together. The Queen rarely left her son's room while he was getting better, and the doctor was in constant attendance. Her gratitude was added to her love, and, as Robert Gunning explained, it was soon made public. Letting slip his fear of Struensee's 'French' sympathies, Gunning wrote to London that the operation 'was performed on his Royal Highness on Thursday last, by Monsieur Struensee, physician to the court; upon which occasion, and as a mark of the great esteem their Majesties bear to this gentleman, he is raised to the Rank of Conseilleur de Conferences'. To the title of *Conferenzrath* was added that of Reader to the King, a post that Struensee had in a sense occupied from his first acquaintance with Christian, and a handsome, though carefully inexcessive, salary.

Indeed, Struensee was now less reader and companion to the poor King than his keeper. By early 1770 Christian's condition was a good deal worse in degree if not in kind than it had been a year before. Two years later, Struensee wrote an assessment of the King's illness. It was a detached, measured and humane account, assembled from observations that he had made as a trained physician and natural philosopher who sought to be worthy of Newton. It was written in French and thus obviously intended for an audience beyond the German-speaking world of the Danish court. In it Struensee presented himself as a natural philosopher in the mould of an *encyclopédiaste* assessing and trying to understand what he saw. Although it was a carefully crafted document, which offered between its lines a justification to the wider world for some of Struensee's political actions, it nonetheless clearly set out the difficulties of dealing with a king who was inimical to and progressively less able to deal with the task to which he had been born.

Underpinning Christian's complicated imaginary world lay the belief that things were different from the way they seemed, and that he himself was either working towards or already possessed the secrets of this mysterious universe. In the first place, in a world in which thousands dreamed about playing a royal part, the one man in Denmark to whom that part belonged and who could never be separated from it, wished it was not so. Christian told Struensee repeatedly that he was not the son of Frederik V. He was a changeling, he said, or he was the son of Lord Stanhope, the Earl of Chesterfield, who had written a book of advice addressed to an illegitimate son, or his birth was a mystery that would one day be revealed. He would not be king for ever, he insisted, because he was changing day by day, approaching a happier and better state, and when he had got there he would leave Copenhagen and see the world as it really was. That world – where, he told his doctor, he had killed large numbers of people and been given opium so that he would forget the deed – was far superior to the world he saw around him. Men were better there, soldiers stronger, entertainments more brilliant. To prove he was, as he had believed in his childhood, 'advancing' towards it, Christian would hit himself in a test of his strength or rub his body all over with whatever was to hand – hair powder, pomade, snow, or even burning wood from the fire. In that world, where he was invincible, and where he would be able to jump from great heights and land without a scratch, lived a woman called De La Roquer. She was hugely strong and she would hit him and he would hit her in return. Never, Struensee noted, did Christian show any longing to be loved or to give his affection in return.

Christian's desire for violence, and to be treated with what Johann Struensee called 'indignation', became stronger as the years passed. Struensee believed that the reason why the King repeatedly smashed up the furniture in his rooms, or hurled it out of windows, and the reason why he would often swear uncontrollably at those around him and at the Queen, was that he wanted the same treatment himself. He liked Caroline Mathilde to wear her male riding habits in his presence, perhaps because the breeches, boots and spurs conjured up a pleasurable fear of chastisement and because his real queen became mixed in his mind with the immensely strong woman of his imaginings.

When Christian's excited thoughts filled his head he would talk about them for hours on end, night and day, without stopping. He talked to whoever would listen, but especially to Struensee or to Warnstedt. When the imaginings subsided, however, he could be plunged into black melancholy, convinced that he would die. Then he would talk of rushing out of the palace and killing the first person that he met. Always he returned continually to his lifelong desire not to be king.

Struensee diagnosed Christian as having, 'among other things, a certain lack of feeling in his nerves', because he could hit himself without seeming to feel any pain. In medical opinion, lack of pain and lack of feeling were connected, so Struensee may have believed that Christian's insensitive behaviour, especially towards Caroline Mathilde, was a consequence of a disorder of the nerves. Nowhere in his report did Struensee write that Christian was mad, although he did describe him as falling into melancholy frequently. Listening and watching the obsessive and unchanging parade of the King's ideas and habits, Struensee became convinced that Christian's condition was incurable. At the beginning, he wrote, he, Warnstedt and Count Holck tried to persuade Christian 'that all his imaginings were false'. But reason only made the King 'sad and melancholy', and unable to find any distraction in his amusements. So Struensee began a regime of containment that allowed Christian to keep his ideas but helped those about him to control his physical behaviour. He insisted that Christian live to a strict routine, that he take cold baths and regular walks. In the daytime he was kept busy with amusements, 'lectures, music, card games', and 'thousands of other little children's games'.

The way of life Struensee devised for Christian had to cope with his erratic outbursts of violence and his habit of frequent masturbation, both of which needed to be concealed as much as possible from everyone beyond his inner circle. Christian's moods and fears had to be managed so that he could carry out the day-to-day business of government, reading and signing documents, and could appear now and then in public, if not at ceremonial occasions. Luckily, Christian's desires coincided very nicely with Caroline Mathilde's. Although Caroline Mathilde was eager for a more central place in the life of the court, stiff ceremony bored her too, and kept her away from Struensee. For his part, Struensee found his own position firmly consolidated by the wishes of both King and Queen to live within the compass of a small and intimate circle.

It was not surprising, then, that Struensee's first overtly political public action was to explain, in the name and person of the King, why there had been no official celebrations of Caroline Mathilde's nineteenth birthday on 11 July 1770, and no creations of new titles, as was customary on such occasions. Assuming the voice of the King, he wrote to the Queen Dowager, Juliane Marie, on 30 July, and announced, 'The Queen's birthday was not celebrated this time because she has wanted it this way herself, and because we both think that the usual tedious ceremonies come less from the heart than ought to be the case on such an occasion. I have neither handed out medals nor made appointments because I have decided only to do so in extraordinary cases for the time being, and because of the great number I have promoted in previous years.' Struensee's letter did indeed express the wishes of the King and Queen, but it dovetailed neatly with his own concern too, for fewer handouts of titles and offices and for greater economy in the court. But there was also another signal for Juliane Marie, although she was probably unaware of it. Henceforth, Struensee would be the King's head; Christian only his hand, a signatory to whatever Struensee, or Struensee and Caroline Mathilde together, decided to do.

After the failure of the Duke of Gloucester's visit to Denmark the previous summer, George III decided to send his mother to ferret out the reasons for Caroline Mathilde's wayward behaviour, to warn her of its possible consequences and to bring him back a first-hand report on the results. Accompanied by the Duke of Gloucester, the Princess Dowager set off for the continent on 9 June. The journey was taxing for her, because although she was only fifty, she was troubled by a persistent throat complaint and her health was failing. Fifteen years of childbearing and nineteen years of widowhood, half a lifetime of living through her children and her pinched passion for Lord Bute had left Augusta an old woman. She was going back to her homeland while she still could, visiting her daughters in Brunswick and Copenhagen, saying several kinds of farewell. It was to be a melancholy journey.

No one in Copenhagen was eager for the Princess Dowager to arrive. Christian's dislike of lengthy ceremonies was undiminished, and Caroline Mathilde could not have wanted to give her mother hospitality and receive in exchange a severe judgement on the way she was living. Struensee, who had no love of Britain, had equally no wish for George III to receive any first-hand reports on what was happening in Denmark. Through the medium of the King, he devised a way round the difficulty. Christian announced that since the court would not be in residence in or around Copenhagen when the Princess Dowager proposed to come, he and the Queen would travel out of Denmark and into George III's German territory to meet her. That way he could avoid the excessive formality that accompanied a state visit, and Caroline Mathilde would meet her mother on her own terms.

Ten days after the Princess Dowager and her son left London, Christian and Caroline Mathilde rolled out of Copenhagen. They were accompanied by an entourage of 280 officials, staff and servants. Among them were Count Holck, Warnstedt, many members of the Queen's household, Count Bernstorff and, of course, Johann Struensee. Four days later at Gottorp Castle in Schleswig they were welcomed by Christian's sister Princess Louise and her husband Prince Charles of Hesse, who was regent of the King's German-speaking duchies of Schleswig and Holstein.

Years later, when time had added wisdom to his memories, Prince Charles remembered Caroline Mathilde at Gottorp as a lost woman, and he wrote in his memoirs, 'I confess it grieved me to see this Princess, endowed with so much sense and so many good qualities, fallen to such a point and into hands so bad.' He chose to believe that Struensee terrorised the Queen, forbidding her to speak to her friend Princess Louise alone and keeping a close eye on whatever she did. Caroline Mathilde, Prince Charles recorded, 'was always ill at ease with me when Struensee was present; at table he invariably seated himself opposite to her'. Like many who observed the love affair between the Queen and the doctor, Prince Charles attributed malign motives to the social upstart and saw corrupted innocence in the young Queen. That Caroline Mathilde's anxiety lay at least in part in her fear that her love would be discovered and publicised to her wide European family did not square with the Prince's commitment to the idea that she was the passive victim of a calculating and cruel libertine.

As soon as it was practically possible, the Danish party left Gottorp and travelled south through the light undulations of green land to Traventhal, a royal castle nearer to Altona and the border with the German states. Traventhal was a small castle, unsuitable for the accommodation of a large entourage, and Struensee used its size as a pretext to turn back to Copenhagen many of those who had accompanied the royal party. Three of Caroline Mathilde's ladies-in-waiting and several officials were sent home. Most significantly, Count Holck was also sent away, and Christian appeared to care little that he was gone. When the party arrived back in Copenhagen they learned that they had all been dismissed. Holck was given a sizeable pension, but the others got nothing to take the edge off the loss of income and prestige.

By taking the King away from Copenhagen and into the relative isolation of the German-speaking duchies, and now by removing Holck and the courtiers and officials associated with him, Struensee and Caroline Mathilde could begin to remould the court and solidify their power within it. Ralph Woodford, the British envoy to Lower Saxony who was trying to complete the tricky arrangements for the meeting between the Princess Dowager and her daughter, believed that Bernstorff, though still with the royal party, had not been informed of the dismissals before they had been handed out. 'Mr Bernstorff and the officials appear to be entirely ignorant of these little arrangements, the royal confidence running in quite another direction', he wrote. But Woodford felt slighted as well. No access to the King or Queen was possible and no information about them leaked out. 'With regard to the court's movements at Traventhal nothing is known', he wrote to the Earl of Rochford on 13 July, 'for everything is kept a secret from those who, by their employments, ought to be informed.'

Bernstorff was not as complacent as Woodford supposed. He had already noted ironically that the King, and those around him, had developed, 'an extraordinarily excessive taste for solitude', and he could see quite clearly that Holck's dismissal was accompanied by two ominous arrivals. First to come was Struensee's Altona friend Enevold Brandt. Brandt was from one of Altona's most prominent families and was Struensee's near contemporary, born in 1738. Although Robert Gunning described him witheringly as 'too light and insignificant to mention', Brandt had been a brilliant student at Copenhagen University who had risen rapidly in the early years of Christian's reign, when he was a page at court and one of the King's companions in riot. He had been banished from court after falling out with Holck and had spent the previous three years travelling through Europe, where he made his way to France and paid his dues to Voltaire at Ferney. In Paris in 1769 he made a point of ingratiating himself with his old employers during Christian's stay, but was not allowed back to court. Finally, on Caroline Mathilde's birthday in 1769 the door to his rehabilitation was inched open with a minor appointment in the government of the county of Oldenbourg and the title of chamberlain. A year later Caroline Mathilde and Struensee flung it wide.

Schack Carl Rantzau-Ascheberg, another companion of Struensee's provincial days, soon followed Brandt. Born in 1717, Rantzau was twenty years older than Struensee, and more of an old-fashioned rake than a man whose personal conduct was prompted by a desire to live out any strictures of recent natural philosophy. Long before La Mettrie and Helvétius, Rantzau had been living a libertine life, scheming and pursuing women. Originally a career officer in the Danish army, he had left under a cloud in 1756 and travelled through Europe and Russia as a gentleman-mercenary and adventurer. Rejoining the Danish army a decade later, he was dismissed after two years and retired to Holstein where he inherited his family's large estates and maintained his father's reputation as a liberal and reforming landlord. Bernstorff and other court observers saw Rantzau as a force for instability and intrigue. Gunning, with typical severity, declared that 'it would be difficult to exhibit a character more profligate and abandoned'. Having tangled with him two years earlier, Bernstorff saw in Rantzau's reappearance the first ominous sign that Struensee was preparing to push his influence beyond the royal family itself and into the government of the country.

Caroline Mathilde, on the other hand, was delighted with the new arrivals and while the court was at Traventhal, Bernstorff noted that he had never seen her 'so beautiful and cheerful'. Encouraged by Struensee's indulgence and his wife's good spirits, Christian too blossomed that summer. He was allowed to indulge the more harmless of his fantasies free of almost all his tedious Copenhagen paperwork, and was accompanied everywhere by his favourite dog, Gourmand, who travelled in convoy with him through the countryside. While the King led the way in an open phaeton, Gourmand followed behind, seated in his own carriage with a runner in front. The carriage was decorated with a royal monogram and a sign that read proudly, 'Gourmand, Grand Chien Danois du Roi'. Gourmand tolerated his rolling captivity, Christian was delighted, and his blackest thoughts seemed to recede in the sunshine.

When Brandt arrived in Traventhal he was surprised but in no doubt that he found the Queen and Struensee in love. They had abandoned all royal etiquette, he said later, and took little care to conceal their movements. 'Their intimacy showed that they loved each other, searched for each other and were happy when they found one another', he said, adding with careful wonderment, 'their love showed in a way that can be noticed but not described'. Some mornings Christian went to the Queen's bedroom. But on most days she had tea in bed alone and then the tea table was re-set for two in her parlour and Struensee would arrive. Caroline Mathilde's maids then withdrew, leaving the two together, with the windows that opened on to the castle garden carefully blinded, leaving only slivers of sunlight in the room.

Merchants arrived from the cities of Hamburg and Lübeck, and Struensee and Caroline Mathilde went on a joyous spending spree. She ordered two grand pianos and from the piles of lace, ribbons, silks, stockings, embroideries and linen, he bought a pair of red embroidered silk garters. They became the symbols of her love for Struensee, her 'sentiments garters' she called them: her 'ties of feeling'. Caroline Mathilde began to wear them every day, and they joined a clutch of things that she kept near her which stood for Struensee when he was not there; a cross made with garnets that she wore round her neck and hid in her bodice, a pair of gold and enamel buttons, and a drawing of Struensee done in Altona that same summer which she kept first between two leaves of her diary and then in a special gold box with green enamelled sides.

As a belated birthday celebration on 22 July, the royal party shed even more of their attendants and drove over to Rantzau's estate at Ascheberg, returning home late and cheerful. Two days earlier, Caroline Mathilde had signalled her approval of Rantzau's rehabilitation by donning full regimental uniform and reviewing his two companies of Life Guards in the square before the castle at Traventhal. Soon afterwards, she, Struensee, the King and a few of their closest associates returned to Ascheberg to stay for several days. Bernstorff, who was not in the party, could only report that the visit was 'exceedingly amusing', all play and no work, and that the courtiers took a delight in mingling with Rantzau's peasants and behaving with as much rustic abandon as they could.

In fact Caroline Mathilde and the rest of the group lived as if they were at an English country-house party, preferring not to dress for dinner, like many English aristocrats in the country, and dancing simple country dances in self-conscious celebration of their pastoral personalities and responsibilities. Caroline Mathilde lounged around in her favourite riding costume. She sang while Brandt played the piano and the King was allowed to perform his riding tricks. Caroline Mathilde and Struensee, it was true, took very early morning drives alone into the woods. But otherwise the visit, and the masquerade with which it ended, was a recognisable country holiday. Slipshod merriment, dogs underfoot, riding, hunting, dancing and informal dressing were mixed with political gestures that were meant to be noticed. Mingling with Rantzau's peasants signalled Struensee's interest in the problem of the peasantry. Taking the King with them, without any of the officials who worked in the executive, sent a clear message to everyone left at either Traventhal or in Copenhagen that Struensee and the Queen were firmly in charge of him. Bernstorff understood that the message was directed first and foremost at him and did not bode well. As a professional politician he wanted to hang on to power; as a shrewd observer of men he was beginning to suspect that his retirement was imminent.

All through the summer Struensee and Caroline Mathilde had been stalling about a meeting between the Princess Dowager and her daughter. They refused to pack up and move on to Brunswick, where the Princess was staying, saying that Caroline Mathilde was unwell and unable to travel that far. The castle at Lüneborg, a few hours south of the Danish border in George III's Hanoverian dominions, was then proposed as an alternative. Rather than risk inciting the anger of all her siblings as well as her mother, Caroline Mathilde agreed to a meeting there, although Bernstorff's message was only relayed to frantic officials in Lüneborg on 14 August, giving them less than two days to organise lodgings, food and a meeting place for two royal parties. Johann Albrecht, the Hanoverian high commissioner at Lüneborg, had suddenly to make the castle ready for seventy visitors. But before he had time to write any furious letters of complaint to his superiors, the two parties were upon him. The Princess Dowager arrived from Brunswick at midnight the next day with a suite of twenty-two officials and the Duke of Gloucester, who travelled up separately from the city of Hanover. Albrecht requisitioned the kitchens of the local monastery, whisked buckets and brooms round the castle and hurriedly made up deficiencies in its furnishings with table linen, silverware and even chandeliers from his own house.

Christian and Caroline Mathilde travelled incognito and officials seem to have been confused about both the progress of their journey and the size of their suite. Ralph Woodford in Hamburg wrote privately to Robert Gunning on 14 August that 'their Danish Majesties passed through here incog. last night'. But if he was right they must have dawdled the rest of the way to Lüneborg, because they only finally arrived there on the evening of the 16th. Albrecht counted the royal party as fifty people, but others suggested that it was a good deal smaller. Whatever was the case it included several cooks, for Albrecht reported that the food he hastily brought in was prepared in the castle kitchen by Christian's own staff.

The first meeting of the two royal parties was at this late and hurried dinner, and it passed off frostily. Both sides soon retreated to their bedrooms. Despite the time, Caroline Mathilde insisted on making what were later described as 'changes' to her room so that Struensee might visit her in the morning. The next day she asked her maid to forestall any enquiry from the Princess Dowager's party by saying that she had not been called for and did not know whether her mother was up. Then she had tea as usual in bed and had the tea table put in an ante-room. When Struensee arrived soon afterwards, they went next door and pointedly did not emerge until two in the afternoon.

All observers agreed that the second meeting between Augusta and her wayward daughter went even worse than the first. Caroline Mathilde refused to meet her mother alone, thus pre-empting any attempt by the Princess Dowager to talk to her by herself or pass on any private messages from George III. So the Princess Dowager was thwarted from the outset from warning her daughter that rumours about her conduct had reached London and were disquieting her brother. Caroline Mathilde, moreover, flaunted the object of her mother's anxiety at each opportunity. Struensee came with the King and Queen to the meeting and Caroline Mathilde insisted that he remain.

Once in the room, Augusta began to speak to her daughter in English, trying to find some privacy behind the cloak of their common language. But Caroline Mathilde cut her short, spurning her mother's appeal to family and childhood ties. She replied in German, which everyone knew was Struensee's native language, saying that she had forgotten her mother tongue and tacitly demanding that Augusta speak German too. The ensuing conversation was thus public and bound to be merely distant and polite. Her ruthlessness in refusing to be daughter as well as queen sent a clarion message to the Princess Dowager that her daughter's new way of life was more important than her duty to her family, her brother and her native country. Caroline Mathilde was not serving British interests; she was, in the person of Struensee, demonstrating her own. Unlike her mother, she was not prepared to live a loveless life and she wanted her mother and her family to know it. The Princess Dowager was humiliated and defeated. The meeting was brief and both parties left Lüneborg the next day, clattering off in separate directions. Caroline Mathilde, at least, did not look back. She was never to see her mother again.

In Copenhagen rumour was now spreading about Struensee's ascendancy, brought by Count Holck and the other officials dismissed at the beginning of the summer. Bernstorff's hold on power seemed suddenly shaky, and when the King and Queen returned to Christiansborg and then immediately left again with Crown Prince Frederik, Robert Gunning concluded, 'their Majesties go into retirement in Hirschholm and Frederiksberg to elude the scrutiny of the public eye', so that 'if certain dissmissions are resolved upon they may be effected with greater secrecy'.

At Frederiksberg Castle on the western edge of Copenhagen, Caroline Mathilde and Struensee laid down the foundations of new, and linked, ways of both public and private life. The freedoms they demanded and tried out for themselves there they also proposed to offer to Denmark's unwitting citizens. Struensee now became Caroline Mathilde's constant companion. They usually had breakfast together and, later, went out riding and returned together for lunch. At night the servants noticed how often Struensee made his way to Caroline Mathilde's room, and once, at two in the morning, Caroline Mathilde disturbed Prince Frederik's nurse when she crept through the nursery going the other way. One of the footmen noticed them kissing in broad daylight in the cabinet next to the Prince's bedroom. Struensee and Caroline Mathilde shared an illicit love, but it scarcely remained a secret for long, partly because nothing could be hidden in castles with scores of servants crossing and recrossing courtyards, standing in ante-chambers and running up and down the back-stairs, and partly because they seemed carried away by the novelty of their passion and defiantly careless about hiding it.

Despite the time he spent with Caroline Mathilde, Struensee did not neglect politics. In the second week of September Bernstorff received a letter signed, if not written, by Christian VII. It dismissed him as chief minister with a pension that was scarcely sumptuous for a lifetime's work in the service of the Crown. Although his privy council place was left to him, Bernstorff bowed out gracefully, resigning his remaining office on 15 September and leaving Copenhagen a fortnight later.

Bernstorff's sacking was meant to signal the end of the system by which ministers in council, in tandem with a more or less active monarch, had governed the country for the last century. The decrees which Christian issued the next day were the first loud shout in a new form of government and a new way of life. Struensee was far too ambitious merely to be content with reform of the executive. Politics were to him the means to a wider end that had been his abiding interest since his days in Altona: the unshackling of all people from the chains of custom, belief and ignorance. The practical doctor and natural philosopher was at heart an idealist and an ideologue who saw himself putting bureaucracy and law to work to start the great work of the philosophes in Denmark, reordering the consciousness of the nation and of every individual – nobles, clerics, serfs, men, women, children – within it.

To make it clear where his philosophical sympathies lay, Struensee deliberately opened his programme of reform on 4 September by issuing, in the King's name, a decree which declared complete freedom of the press. The demand for freedom of the fourth estate had been primarily associated with Voltaire, and Struensee had already written to his aged hero asking him to write a letter to the Danish King extolling the wisdom of his decision.

The exchange of letters took some time and the old sage's laudatory epistle, signed at Ferney on 15 January 1771, obviously arrived too late in Copenhagen for any of its sentiments to be incorporated in the decree of 4 September. When it did come, though, it was handsomely printed and bound up for distribution with some of Voltaire's poems and an essay by David Hume. Struensee embellished the September decree with comments of his own, grandiloquently declaring the press free so that it could stimulate impartial investigation of the truth, further the common good and clear away misunderstanding. No one, he added, should be deterred from attacking abuse and exposing prejudice by exaggerated respect for 'persons, regulations or preconceived opinions'.

Struensee's words were carefully chosen. Behind the abstraction of the word 'persons' stood the nobility, behind 'regulations' the judiciary and behind 'preconceived opinions' the clergy. It was at these three entwined groups that much of Struensee's reforming fervour was to be directed in the coming months, and on 4 September he was giving everyone freedom to question them as fearlessly and as vigorously as he intended to do. He was taking a huge risk, though, with his very first reform, for he must have been aware that he was handing to any enemies he might have, or make, a weapon of immense and far-reaching power. Once emboldened, his critics would not hesitate to use the new freedom of the press and once out of the bottle it was a genie very difficult to put back. More than that, Struensee had created at a single stroke the most liberal climate for opinion anywhere in Europe. Not even the press in England, where the Crown and the executive were at least partially protected by the law of seditious libel, had such unlimited licence.

Struensee lost no time in beginning to dismantle obstacles to the sorts of freedom he insisted the Danish people have. By the end of autumn 1770 he had begun to curb the power of the Council of State, reducing it from a body with enormous practical executive authority to one which merely advised the King on matters of finance, foreign affairs and policies at home. He had struck a blow at entrenched habits and privileges with an order that all candidates for offices of state should be able to demonstrate their qualifications, and appeared to slight the Lutheran Church by abolishing several religious holidays.

Knowing that her brother would not react well to Bernstorff's dismissal and Struensee's increasing influence, Caroline Mathilde, apologising for her tardiness, wrote blandly to London on 1 October, 'We have had a great many changes here since I wrote last to you, but I hope they are now at an end. I should have answered you sooner if I had not been hindered by illness.' Robert Gunning, however, felt obliged to report that it was Caroline Mathilde herself who was widely held responsible for the upheaval. The new measures, he wrote, were ascribed by many people, 'without scruple to the Queen of Denmark, whose power they affirm to be unlimited, and on whose [wishes] all depends. If these assertions are not made without reason, your Lordship will judge how much those persons who are honoured with Her Danish Majesty's confidence have misrepresented the state of affairs to her, in order to make her assent to what is so evidently against the system this court has for some time adopted.' The idea that Caroline Mathilde was a cipher with no views of her own was a comforting one both for ministers in London and her brother George. It was easy to sustain because Caroline Mathilde did not often write to her brother and now never saw the British envoy alone. In a letter written in French, and therefore almost certainly in collaboration with Struensee, on 10 December, Caroline explained that Bernstorff was dismissed because he was overbearingly powerful in Denmark and because he was 'l'esclave de la Russie', Russia's slave. But whether this was her own view, a view she shared with Struensee or simply a convenient explanation to offer, no one in London could know. Certainly it ran counter to rumours in Copenhagen which ascribed responsibility for Bernstorff's sacking to her as revenge for his dismissal of her confidant Madame von Plessen three years before.

Any belief that Caroline Mathilde was an empty vessel into which Struensee poured his views was obviously fantastic, owing more to prevailing views about the role of women in politics than anything that observers saw or reported. The Queen herself was perfectly happy to shatter convention. At the same time as she was writing to George III about Bernstorff, Caroline Mathilde was composing and sitting for a portrait that showed her as anything but weak and pliable. Commissioned from the portraitist Peder Als when the royal party returned from Holstein in September, it was begun in December 1770 and completed the following summer. Caroline Mathilde intended the portrait to be a commemoration of her visit to Ascheberg in the summer and she presented it to Count Rantzau when it was finished.

The large full-length canvas was as different as possible from the demure wedding portrait made four years earlier by Cotes and engraved by James Watson. The drooping young girl with dipped head and laced stomacher was gone. In her place is a straight-standing, mannish queen, very tall-seeming, looking almost saucily out of the frame and confidently holding the eyes of her subjects. Caroline Mathilde dressed herself in a specially adapted copy of the uniform of the Danish Life Guards. As Peder Als himself put it in the notes he made in December 1770 to help him think himself into the mood of the painting he was about to begin, she was dressed as a man but in such a manner that she would be clearly recognisable both as 'frauenzimmer', a woman, and as a queen. Caroline Mathilde wears black knee-high boots with spurs, white silk breeches, waistcoat and cravat, a heavy tasselled sash and a sumptuous version of the gold-edged frock-coat worn by the soldiers themselves. By her side, below a hand gloved in solid buff pigskin, hangs a carved and chased ceremonial sword. In her other hand she holds a black tricorne hat and behind her lean the regimental flags with her monogram in the corner. On the wall behind hang two grisaille paintings. One shows a Roman scene, the handover of a battle standard, which viewers might have interpreted as an allegory of the transfer of power which Caroline Mathilde and Struensee had just brought about. The other is a portrait in profile of Caroline Mathilde herself. Although clearly incorporated into what Als called the 'tableau' to demonstrate the Queen's femininity and royalty, it also bears a striking resemblance to another grisaille portrait, that of Catherine the Great of Russia painted a few years earlier by the Danish artist Virgilius Eriksen.

Behind and beyond an obviously imaginary version of the castle at Traventhal where Caroline Mathilde had inspected Rantzau's regiment of guards in the summer, and through a fantastic triumphal arch, the soldiers line up stiffly. They form an unbroken line, standing with muskets raised, waiting for the Queen to arrive. But in comparison to her they are insignificant, distant and tiny. It is the Queen who dominates; the soldiers are just props in the shadow of her glory.

Sword, boots, breeches, spurs: Caroline Mathilde's uniform shouted manliness, authority, assertion. There were, indeed, precedents for such flaunting of male attire, but they were hardly reassuring to those who saw her clothing and her picture as an abnegation of her feminine qualities and her duties as a woman and a wife. Queen Christina of Sweden, a century earlier, had refused to marry, ruled her country alone before abdicating, and frequently wore male dress, especially on her many long travels. More ominously, Catherine the Great famously wore and had had herself painted in the olive-green uniform of the Semenevsky Regiment only eight years before, holding up an unsheathed sword, booted, spurred, wearing a tricorne hat and pigskin gloves, bestriding equally her white stallion and her nation.

Only a few months before Virgilius Eriksen painted Catherine in her moment of triumph, she had deposed her weak-minded husband to become empress of Russia and was commonly regarded as complicit in his subsequent strangling. Caroline Mathilde was undoubtedly hostile to any Russian influence over Danish affairs. But she may not have been averse to a comparison between herself and a fiercely intelligent, ruthless sovereign who saw herself as a francophile and ran her huge and expanding empire with a series of favourites and lovers for diversion and support. Prints of Vigilius Eriksen's equestrian portrait circulated throughout Europe, and although hers was a private rather than a public statement, Caroline Mathilde may have wished to suggest a direct parallel between her own behaviour and the accomplished fact of Catherine's assumption of power in Russia.

While Als was at work, on 10 December Caroline Mathilde wrote to her brother announcing another bold step in Struensee's takeover. 'Le Roi', she announced to him, 'vient d'abolir le Conseil d'Etat, et de congedier les ministres qui l'ont composés autrefois': the King was going to abolish the Council of State and retire its ministers. Christian, she went on, wanted to rule his kingdom, 'lui seule', on his own, according to the Lex Regia. But he had no intention of changing the political system or of allying Denmark with any outside powers, least of all France. By writing to her brother in French, Caroline Mathilde was signalling that, for the moment at least, the private, family correspondence between them was at an end. For George III, put on guard by his mother and brother as well as by his diplomats in Copenhagen and Hamburg, Caroline Mathilde's last two letters were confirmation that her confidant stood behind her shoulder all the time. He was not to receive another private letter from her for many months.

On 27 December Christian issued a decree that set the seal on the changes that Caroline Mathilde had alluded to in her letter to George III. It began in rolling splendour, giving the King all his many titles, 'King of Denmark, Norway, of the Goths and the Wends, Duke of Schleswig-Holstein, Stormarn and the Dittmarsches, Count of Oldenburg and Delmenhorst', but went on to explain more prosaically that, 'as the affairs of state in an absolute government are only confused and delayed when many of the nobility take part in them', and as he had, 'nothing so much at heart as the zealous promotion of the general good', he therefore thought 'fit to abolish and absolutely suppress our former Privy Council', and 'restore the constitution to its original purity'.

In two bold moves, the highest level of the Danish executive had been removed. On 8 December all members of the Privy Council had been dismissed; on the 10th it had been abolished. On 18 December Struensee had been created Maître de Requêts, a post that enabled him to take decrees directly to the King for signing, making him the fount of all legislation. In not much more than a year, the thirty-three-year-old doctor from Halle had grown from being the King's physician and friend into the lover and confidant of the Queen and then the unchallenged ruler of a country where all decrees issued by the King had the immediate force of law. Struensee always had a clutch of friends to advise and support him, mainly fellow German-speakers from the south. But in its swiftness and completeness his was a rise to power unparalleled anywhere in Europe. The malady of the King and the love of the Queen had placed a nation in his hands.

4

A Lewd and Adulterous Conversation

Three months before Christian VII abolished his Privy Council, Robert Gunning wrote to the Earl of Rochford saying that should the preservation of Denmark's system of government, 'be thought worthy of the King's attention, your Lordship will, I am sure, think it necessary that the Queen of Denmark should be acquainted with His Majesty's sentiments as soon as possible'. George III may indeed have written Caroline Mathilde a letter of remonstrance. But as far back as the summer, when she had so publicly snubbed her mother, she had made it quite clear that she was no longer interested in advice from London. Traded into marriage for diplomatic and dynastic ends, she now, in her happiness, saw no reason to conciliate the brother or the country that had put her to such use.

In any case, George III may have been looking at events in Copenhagen with only one eye over the previous eighteen months. At home, he was still battling against the consequences of the Middlesex election of 3 February 1769. Twice the populist candidate John Wilkes had been returned; twice the ministry, acting through its majority in the House of Commons, had quashed his election. The third time round, the ministerial candidate, Colonel Luttrell, was forced by the House onto the angry and defiant voters. Luttrell's election provoked new riots, squibs, prints and general unrest in London. Together with the hostility of the Americans towards attempts to tax imports into the colonies, it crystallised opposition to the administration. More and more, as well as being acted out on the street, this wave of

147

discontent was verbal, public, debated and directed at individuals, particularly the King, and his successive Prime Ministers, the Duke of Grafton and Lord North.

By 1769, according to the opposition *Middlesex Journal*, sixty newspapers were printed each week in London alone, and dozens more circulated in the provinces. Newspapers were beginning to be big business and their writers and publishers known to the public and sometimes feared by politicians. Above the clatter of the presses, no voice in Grub Street sounded more loudly that that of Junius, the star writer in the *Middlesex Journal* and its sister daily the *Public Advertiser*. Junius's impenetrable anonymity created around him an alluring mystery that made his writing seem oracular rather than personal. But his success lay in using his own visceral hatred of the administration and the Crown and combining it with both direct, unsparing personal attacks on public figures and with abstract issues about the franchise, the constitution and the colonies. From the time of his first letter, printed in the *Public Advertiser* in January 1769, Junius became the mainstay of the newspaper. Adored by his supporters and imitators, he was greatly feared by members of the government who felt stalked by an unknown infiltrator with an outsider's anger and an insider's knowledge.

The wider truth of Junius's success was that under the warm cloak of anonymous scribbled notes and quiet coffee-house chats, publishers were discovering the commercial and political potential of stories about individuals. A change in the stamp duty in 1757 made it fortuitously cheaper to publish bigger- rather than smaller-format newspapers and the newly available space was duly filled with political news and stories about individuals as much as it was with advertising. The obvious appetite of readers and a weak law of personal libel made proprietors unashamed about printing whatever salacious or compromising details they could come by. To avoid prosecution and imprisonment for libel, it was enough to refer to individuals by initials and blanks, or by known euphemisms. Publishers habitually referred to the King, for instance, as 'a very great personage', and to Lord North simply as L—— N——; readers quickly became adept at filling in the blanks. So when, just before Christmas 1769 the newspapers reported that 'an assignation at the White Hart at St Albans, between L—— G——, and a certain great D——e, was disconcerted by my lord's gentlemen', coffee-house gossips would have speculated happily, and aloud, about the duke's identity and waited, with salacious expectation, for the next chapter in the sorry story. George III, though, if he read the paragraph in the respectable monthly *Gentleman's Magazine*, to which he subscribed, might not have been surprised. Even though the papers had the story only two days after the event, the King, like most of the reading public, probably already knew that the duke in question was royal, his younger brother, Prince Henry. A scandal involving the royal family was now not just news in the metropolis and larger cities, as it had been in their father's day; it was a national event, producing hundreds of columns of newsprint, pamphlets, prints and, by the end, at least two novels. In the thirty years since Prince Frederick's quarrel with his parents, scandal had joined forces with a new fascination in the lives of celebrated individuals to produce a heady cocktail of entertainment and profit. In a royal story, moreover, opponents of the government found yet another opportunity to attack the Crown and embarrass the hapless monarch.

Born in October 1745 at the height of the Jacobite rebellion, Prince Henry Frederick, the Duke of Cumberland, was seven years younger than the King. Although he had what one observer called 'the thick speech' and the light complexion common to all Prince Frederick's children, he was slighter than the King and fairer too. In form and colouring he was closer to the Duke of York, sharing his small frame and startling white eyebrows. But he quite obviously lacked Prince Edward's intelligence and eye for detail; his own sister Augusta writing from Brunswick in 1764 declared in faint praise that, 'dear Henry' would be generally approved of, 'if he can learn to think before he speaks'.

Like his older brother, however, Prince Henry liked to mix low-life intrigue with high-life flirtation, going from courtesans to countesses, Newmarket to the opera, Covent Garden bagnios to levees at St James's Palace. His behaviour caught the eye of diarists and the press as soon as he began to be seen beyond St James's. In November 1766, when he was twenty-one and newly independent, Lady Mary Coke reported him flirting with Lady Anne Stanhope, the vivacious sister of his brother's friend Sir Francis Delaval, a woman who was never averse to an eye-catching dalliance especially with a prince.

Notionally enrolled in the navy, where he eventually had the title if not the duties of an admiral, the Duke of Cumberland established his own household in Pall Mall and spent most of his time in pursuit of women. He seemed to be an amiable man, a lover of frolic and frivolity, given to cards and hunting, to dancing and chat. Thoughtless rather than vindictive, slight rather than pompous, he inspired more indifference than hostility, although Lady Sarah Lennox, the King's first love, took to calling him 'the white pig' after she met him at court in the early 1760s, and hinted that she found his attentions unpleasant rather than merely annoying.

At Windsor, where he took over his uncle's office of Ranger and Keeper of the Great Park in 1766, Prince Henry chased hares, foxes and women together. Soon after his arrival he installed a young woman, Polly Jones, as his companion and playmate. According to the famous courtesan Ann Sheldon, Polly Jones was spotted as a girl on the streets of London by Mrs Mitchell, a notorious procuress who ran one of the many brothels in King's Place near the clubs and mansions of St James's. Small and auburn-haired, with dark eyes and an inviting smile, she was persuaded to abandon her meagre living selling salad stuffs to passers-by and to go into Mrs Mitchell's house as a friend and guest. Once there, she was groomed to be sold as a virgin to one of Mrs Mitchell's clients, men who would pay hundreds of pounds for young, beautiful, inexperienced girls. Soon after her initiation, now plying her trade as an ordinary prostitute under Mrs Mitchell's beady eye, Polly was noticed by the Duke of Cumberland parading along the walks at Vauxhall Gardens. After handing over £70, the Duke took her down to Windsor as his exclusive property. There Ann Sheldon met her, and her memoirs reported, 'I now made frequent visits to Miss Jones, and used to accompany her and the Duke in their walks, which seemed to be chiefly taken in order to amuse His Royal Highness with her tumbling in the grass . . . While she was tumbling heels over head, and throwing herself into indecent postures, he used to laugh with a degree of violence that I never beheld before or since.'

Apparently, the Duke soon tired of his entertainer. He told Ann Sheldon that Polly's vulgarity 'quite disgusted him', and added 'a proposal to me to succeed her in his affections and protection'. Ann not only declined, but in the spirit of defiance and friendship often shown in courtesans' memoirs, told her friend what Prince Henry had done, whereupon they abandoned him, decamping together for London. Soon afterwards, Polly began a vendetta against the Prince. Though it may rarely have happened, there was an expectation that cast-off royal and aristocratic mistresses should receive some sort of maintenance from their former employers. Polly claimed in the press that far from giving her an annuity, the Duke took from her everything but the clothes she sat in, sending 'the proper officers to dispossess me of my household furniture, which had been provided at his expense, and left me destitute, friendless, and almost penniless after he had professed the greatest regard, esteem and even love for me'. Luckily, she was at pains also to tell the press, a gentleman of the Prince's train, 'who had long entertained a tendre for me, no sooner knew of my distress than he offer'd me his assistance ... [and] he has proposed being united with me upon the most honourable terms'. Polly, it seemed, was not completely without cash. She gave her new beau a bond for £3,000, which readers would assume came from the royal purse, and later successfully sued him for money due on it. Eventually, in the early summer of 1770, that favourable judgment was reversed on appeal in the Court of Chancery, but by that time, Polly had made sure that the Prince's name had been in the newspapers for over a year. The publicity had added no lustre to the royal name, convincing many that the King's reputation for meanness was proved by the ungenerous actions of his brother.

In the autumn of 1769, Prince Henry found himself the subject of one of the first exposés, or 'Tête à Têtes', as they were titled, in a new, and immediately popular, 'Repository of Knowledge, Instruction and Entertainment', called the *Town and Country Magazine*. The *Town and Country* was a scandalous review that took its cue from the secret histories that were first published about court life in the Restoration. In a bow to its spiritual father, Anthony Hamilton, who had largely written the scandalous *Mémoires de la vie du Comte de Gramont*, published in 1713, the *Town and Country* described itself as 'printed for A. Hamilton Jr'. Although it had sentimental stories, snippets of 'foreign intelligence', gardening instructions and mathematical puzzles every month, the highlight of each issue was the 'Tête à Tête', which exposed the amorous adventures of public men with accuracy, panache and a moral colouring that offered a justification for the exposé without ever detracting from its value as entertainment.

The *Town and Country* called Prince Henry 'Nauticus', and was banteringly sarcastic about his naval career, telling readers that he had risen, 'by his merit only to a command in the navy', and explaining that 'In the course of [two] ... voyages, Nauticus has been present at several battles, that have been purposely fought to give him a proper idea of naval engagement; and from which he has reaped the intended benefit, without the least injuring his health'. It went on to detail a number of his affairs – with the young Venetian singer and dancer Anna Zamperini, with the famous courtesan

Grace Elliot and with Polly Jones – before telling the story of his latest liaison, with a *soi-disant* Polish countess, Camilla D'Onhoff.

Camilla, Countess D'Onhoff was one of the shadier figures in the undergrowth of London society. Although she claimed to be the widow of a Polish count, she was rumoured to have in fact been the mistress of the King of Poland, and to earn her living as the highest sort of courtesan. She kept an elegant new house in Cavendish Square just south of Oxford Street where she held routs, assemblies and card parties. The *Town and Country* hinted that she was really a business woman rather than a hostess, and that her entertainments were 'supported by subscription'. Furthermore her declaration that she lived on a Polish pension of £400 a year was nonsense. She was maintained by Prince Henry and, indeed, he had already bought her 'a snug retreat near his hunting seat' at Windsor.

If George III were privately unhappy about Prince Henry's frequent appearances in what the *Town and Country* called 'the annals of gallantry', he never let it show, riding with his brothers each morning in town and hunting with them on winter weekends in the country. But he must have known that the consequences of Prince Henry's new appearance in the press at the end of 1769 would be public and scandalous. L—— G—— was Henrietta, Lady Grosvenor; her sister was Caroline Vernon, maid of honour to Queen Charlotte, and her husband was none other than Richard, Earl Grosvenor, Prince Henry's own friend and partner by the track and on the streets. The public and the royal family knew that more revelations were on the way, and that the press would never let such a possibility for making both an attack on the Crown and a tidy profit from eager readers pass by. Sure enough, details soon began to emerge about all the principals in the drama.

From the very beginning, Richard, Lord Grosvenor seemed to have had in his character both a strong streak of expediency and a marked indifference to the feelings of the many women he encountered. In 1763, when he was thirty-one, he was paying noticeable attention to Henrietta Molesworth, the young and beautiful daughter of his near neighbour in Grosvenor Square. On 5 May of that year, in the middle of the night, fire engulfed Lady Molesworth's house, trapping Henrietta and her mother in their second-floor bedroom above the drawing room. As smoke filled the room and flames pushed up from the floor below, Henrietta, with terrified determination, threw herself out of the window, smashed against the railings on the pavement and crashed into the basement area. Her mother, paralysed by fright and thinking of her younger children asleep on the nursery floor above, stood watching at the window. Gathering onlookers urged her to jump, but she stayed there motionless until the floor collapsed beneath her and she was incinerated by the inferno. Henrietta Molesworth was carried to Grosvenor House next door, where her smashed leg was amputated. Over the next six months she gradually recovered. She lost her lover with her limb, though; Lord Grosvenor's romantic attentions soon stopped.

The Earl was already well known as a lothario, and his doctors, the newspapers later reported, urged him to marry to repair a constitution badly damaged by serial bouts of venereal disease. Described as a tall, thin person of black complexion, with a long nose and heavily marked with the small pox, Lord Grosvenor was scarcely the handsomest of men. But he was one of London's richest, owning much of Mayfair and a large estate in Cheshire, and deciding to take his doctors' advice, he lost little time in finding a bride. In the spring of 1764, dodging a sharp shower, he ducked into a lodge in Kensington Gardens and found two young women, Henrietta Vernon and her sister Caroline, already there. Offering them a ride home in his carriage, and hearing Henrietta's coquettish praise of its soft upholstery, he was said to have declared that she could be mistress of it whenever she chose. Henrietta, a chestnut-haired brunette with the soft dark eyes that the Earl was particularly fond of, came from an ambitious gentry family in Staffordshire, and was in London to find a husband. She was worldly enough to spot a good match in the making and she knew that with the carriage came Grosvenor House and the lucrative freeholds of the streets around. In a month she was Lady Grosvenor; in a year she regretted it.

With her nose for misery and her constant observation of the royal circle, Lady Mary Coke was quick to notice that, by 1766, Lady Grosvenor was more often with the royal dukes than with her husband. At the Drawing Room of 24 August she sidled up to her, overheard snatches of conversation and duly recorded in her journal, 'Lady Grosvenor was in the most joyous spirits I ever saw. She twice burst out into such violent fits of laughter that she was obliged to hide her face behind her fan . . . I heard her say she had been at Tonbridge and was now going into Cheshire. It was something that Prince Henry said to her that made her so merry.' It was also rumoured that she flirted with the Duke of York. 'A story was generally propagated', a pamphleteer wrote later, 'that his Lordship had detected some familiarity which had passed between the late Duke of Y[ork] and her ladyship, and that his lordship forgave her infidelity on condition that she would never see him again in private.'

Beneath the veneer of Lady Grosvenor's public vivacity, however, lay a real despair and misery. Lord Grosvenor had two abiding interests, street girls and fast horses, and by the time of his marriage he had been a habitué of both Newmarket and the brothels of Piccadilly and Covent Garden for over a decade. He did not intend to stop now, whatever his doctors said, especially as it seemed that Lady Grosvenor would sooner or later satisfy his dynastic ambition and produce an heir. Lord Grosvenor, Ann Sheldon's memoirs recorded, 'certainly was not in the habit of feeling compunction for the very low career of his amours'. He liked street girls and blondes, and at some point Ann Sheldon began to find them for him. Ostensibly meeting him to ask a favour about the Lying-in Hospital of which he was, ironically perhaps, a patron, she soon broached the real subject of her visit. 'We entered into a long conversation about the ladies of our profession', her memoirs recorded. 'As we were both upon a subject which we pretty well understood, it was easily exhausted, and as I discovered in the course of it that Lord Grosvenor had a very great partiality for lasses with golden locks, I offered to recommend him one of that description, whom I had every reason to believe would meet with his approbation.' More commissions followed; Ann Sheldon would gather girls for him and Lord Grosvenor would take his pick, though she noted tartly that he was quicker to accept their services than to pay for them.

Henrietta Grosvenor, meanwhile, was soon telling her friends that she was disappointed in the bargain she had struck, 'tied to such a mate ... for the sake of rank and title at the time she was a universal toast'. From the vantage point of her early twenties she looked at a long, bleak and lonely future that not all the mansions in Mayfair could invest with happiness. Not much more than a year after her wedding she told her brother Henry Vernon that her husband 'used her extremely ill', and that she was miserable. With the birth of an heir to the Grosvenor title in March 1767, part of her dynastic duty was done, and she threw herself back into scenes so brightly illuminated that the icy lump of her unhappiness was melted in the glare. By the end of 1768 the Duke of Cumberland's admiration of her beauty and gaiety was becoming more insistent and pointed. At the beginning of 1769 they began to try to meet where they thought they would be unobserved by servants or their own relations.

On 1 March 1770, three months after the discoveries at the White Hart, Lord Grosvenor's lawyers, Partington & Garth, formally entered a Libel on his behalf against his wife in Doctors' Commons, the consistory or ecclesiastical court of the diocese of London. The Libel was presented to the court and immediately leaked to the press by officials who regularly supplemented their income by making more copies than legal procedure demanded and hawking them round coffee houses to the highest bidder. In the Libel, Lord Grosvenor was necessarily described as 'a man of sober, chaste and virtuous life', who, 'always behaved towards his Lady with true love and affection, and did all in his power to render her completely happy'. She, on the other hand, 'being unmindful of her conjugal vow, and not having the fear of God before her eyes, but moved and instigated by the devil, did contract and carry on a lewd and adulterous conversation with His Royal Highness [Prince Henry] Frederick. . . . The party therefore prays that justice may be done in the premises, and that the said Richard Lord Grosvenor may be divorced from the said Henrietta Lady Grosvenor, his wife, because of adultery.'

The Libel's invocation of the devil and the charge that Lady Grosvenor had forgotten her duty to God were reminders that Doctors' Commons was an ecclesiastical court which could order the dissolution of the religious component of a marriage but had no civil jurisdiction. Lord Grosvenor was not asking the court for a legal end to his marriage, but for a judgment that would allow him to separate from his wife without paying alimony or returning any dowry she might have brought him. A successful action could be followed by a parliamentary divorce, which would leave both parties free to marry again. But a case in Doctors' Commons was very often preceded by a civil suit or action for criminal conversation, in which an aggrieved husband sued an accused lover for damages to his property: that is, to his wife and to his own person and honour. A crim. con. suit, as it was habitually called, had the useful side effect of establishing a wife's guilt, which did not obviate the need for a suit in Doctors' Commons, but certainly would go some way to making it a formality.

Lord Grosvenor's suit in the consistory court was an angry attempt to beggar and humiliate his wife. But it carried a real risk. Under ecclesiastical law Lady Grosvenor had the right to counter-sue her husband on the same grounds, and if she were successful the two suits would, in effect, cancel one another out. Lord Grosvenor would be able neither to divorce his wife, nor force her into a penurious separation.

Believing, or being advised, that his wife was unlikely to mount a suit of her own, Lord Grosvenor went ahead. His lawyers spent the months after they had lodged his Libel identifying witnesses, persuading them to testify and bringing them to the court to make statements or depositions. The depositions were copied carefully down by the court's proctors, Mr Lushington and Mr Heseltine, witnessed and signed. But the proctors were practical as well as attentive. They made extra copies of the depositions and sold them to the press. When the depositions came out as a pamphlet a year later, their editor used public demand to justify their publication. 'The great importance of the cause, in the process of which the following depositions have been taken', he wrote, 'hath excited so universal an attention, that an apology may easily be made for their publication by those whose profession it is to contribute to the gratification of public curiosity.'

Proctors Lushington and Heseltine were unhurried and Lord Grosvenor's witnesses well briefed by his lawyers. From the great stack of statements, mostly made by the humblest actors in the grisly drama, a story emerged that was both banal and poignant. Far removed in its grandeur from everyday life, it was still so replete with ordinary longing for happiness, so full of mundane betrayal and hatred, that it rose beyond its gilded confines to become a story about human happiness that touched all sorts of readers. It was a topic, one pamphleteer wrote, 'that has universally agitated the tongues and pens of the scribblers and tattlers of the present age'. Beyond its human elements, though, the affair also brought to the surface smouldering worries about the meaning of divorce and adultery, and the role and place of younger members of royal families.

From the depositions of the witnesses, it was obvious that Lady Grosvenor had no confidante among her own staff and, in particular, no lady's maid to whom she could entrust the secret of her growing closeness to Prince Henry. Her isolation within her own household made communication with her admirer extremely difficult once they had moved beyond a public flirtation to a private and intense affair. For a woman in Henrietta Grosvenor's position privacy was often not wished for and certainly not expected beyond the door of her own bedchamber. She was well known in Mayfair, at Ranelagh, at the Opera, at Vauxhall and at court, and her husband's coach and livery were instantly recognisable throughout London. The Prince, with his distinctive Hanoverian white eyebrows and lashes, and his royal coach and attendants, was even more visible, and watchers were at every known vantage point in the city. By 1769, London newspapers were eagerly following the lead of the *Town and Country* and reporting aristocratic dalliances, and there was money to be made by anyone spotting a well-known figure in a compromising position.

In the spring of 1769 Prince Henry and Lady Grosvenor began to meet at Lady D'Onhoff's house in Cavendish Square, probably paying her for the use of her rooms. The Prince no longer supported Lady D'Onhoff himself but he must have thought he was buying her silence and her goodwill. He was mistaken. Lady D'Onhoff was happy to make money as the lovers' go-between, but she proved an unsteady friend, as ready to sell her secrets as any less well-heeled informer. At the beginning, however, the arrangement worked perfectly. Sending a note, 'by D['Onhoff's] servant', Lady Grosvenor asked Prince Henry to reply in the same way, saying, 'the boy has my orders and will bring it to me'. Her love was now on paper, dangerous and frank. In reply to a letter from the Prince saying that he was unwell, she wrote, 'I thank you for your kind note, your tender manner of expressing yourself calling me your dear friend, and at this time that you should recollect me. I wish I dare lie all the time by your bed and nurse you – for you will have nobody near you that loves you as I do, thou dearest angel of my soul. O that I could but bear your pain for you I should be happy. What grieves me most is that they who *ought to feel* don't know the inestimable prize, the treasure, they have in you.'

It was not long before both Lady Grosvenor and Prince Henry realised that they must have a safer place to meet, especially since Henrietta was seven months pregnant with her second child and propriety demanded that she should be seen less in public. In April the Prince's aide-de-camp, Captain Foulkes, paid a visit to Mary Reda Vemberght, a forty-five-year-old widow who ran a milliner's shop a few doors down Pall Mall from Cumberland House. A man visiting a milliner's was not unusual, as Captain Foulkes would have known perfectly well. Unlike most household goods traded by women, millinery was men's business too. Lingering over lace for cuffs and silk for cravats was as acceptable for men as spending five minutes leafing through the latest cartoons in a print shop. But many successful courtesans started life as milliner's assistants, and milliners often ran profitable double businesses, selling the goods both on and behind their counters. Mrs Reda knew about and was probably party to Lord Grosvenor's taste in young women, and for a fee she would also help Prince Henry. In the first place the Prince and Lady Grosvenor wanted to use her as a go-between instead of risking Lady D'Onhoff's servants. But Captain Foulkes had also been instructed to enquire about the empty apartments above Mrs Reda's shop.

Although Mrs Reda claimed later that when Captain Foulkes asked about the empty rooms, 'she supposed it was for *something bad*, that it was for girls', she raised no objections at the time, and the two quickly came to an arrangement. Two of Mrs Reda's friends took the empty rooms above the shop and rented them on to the Duke. That way neither the press nor the freeholder would be alerted to the Duke's presence, a deception that was the more necessary since the freeholder was the Earl Grosvenor himself.

Prince Henry and Lady Grosvenor had only a few weeks to use their secret hideaway. On 7 June 1769 she delivered a son, Richard, in Grosvenor House, and began her tedious month of lying-in, lounging in bed and receiving visitors. Soon afterwards Prince Henry was ordered to sea aboard the aptly named frigate *Venus*, nominally in charge of a fleet that was to conduct naval exercises in the English Channel. Full of first love, unable to imagine how he could get through the six weeks he was to be away without seeing his Henrietta, the Prince poured out his heart to Mrs Reda, 'cried very much and seemed almost distracted'. He 'said he should die', if she did not forward Lady Grosvenor's letters to him. Mrs Reda promised to pass on the Duke's letters and to send him Lady Grosvenor's in return. In the following six weeks over thirty parcels were delivered to her by one of the Duke's porters, and she had to find ways of getting them into Grosvenor House. Some she sent in band-boxes amongst the packaging for summer hats, some she sent on to Lady Grosvenor's sisters Caroline and Lucy Vernon, and some she took up personally, announcing that she had come to see Lady Grosvenor about trimmings for gowns that she would be wearing again now that she was no longer pregnant.

At sea, Prince Henry thought little about starbord, port and studding sails. His mind was still on the silks of Mrs Reda's shop and the delights of the rooms above it. The day after the fleet left Portsmouth he took advantage of a weak easterly to tell Admiral Barrington not to sail, and the whole flotilla anchored offshore. 'The wind was not so contrary but we could have sailed', he boasted to Lady Grosvenor. But he proudly told the admiral that he had 'dispatches of consequence to send to London', and sent a frigate back to port with his letter of love, leaving thousands of men to swab the decks and scrub their quarters while his amorous words sped across the water. 'Indeed my dear Angel', he wrote to Lady Grosvenor to make quite sure she appreciated his audacity, 'I need not tell you I know you read the reason too well that made me do it, it was to write to you, for God knows I wrote to no-one else nor shall I at any other time but to the King.' The Duke admitted to a touch of queasiness at sea, though it blended so easily with his lovesickness that the two were indistinguishable. Once aboard, he told Lady Grosvenor, he was unable to eat so he went to bed, kissing the lock of her hair he had brought with him, and praying for her. His dream was exciting, its end memorably sad. 'I then lay down and dreamt of you', he wrote, 'had you on the dear little couch ten thousand times in my arms kissing you and telling you how much I adored you and you seemed pleased but alas when I awoke I found it all delusion, nobody but myself at sea.' 'I shan't forget you', he concluded, as if he were going to be away for months and months, 'God knows you have told me so before – I have your heart and it lies warm in my breast ... thou joy of my life, adieu.' The next morning, before sending it off he sat reading, 'in Prior' and added some lugubrious poetry of longing and separated swains to his long letter, saying, 'such is my amusement to read these sorts of things that put me in mind of our mutual feelings and situations.'

About ten days later this and other letters docked at Mrs Reda's, and she ferried them round to Lady Grosvenor's sister in St James's Palace. Caroline Vernon, sixteen, pretty and poor, perhaps saw in her sister Henrietta's loveless marriage a vision of her own probable future. She was a willing accomplice in her sister's affair with Prince Henry, caught up in its secrecy, excitement and hope. When she got the package from Mrs Reda she hurried the few hundred yards from St James's to Grosvenor House and sat with Henrietta while she read, sharing her happiness and their complicity.

Disaster struck when they were surprised by Lord Grosvenor. The Earl came into his wife's bedchamber and demanded the letter she was holding. Henrietta refused to hand it over, and he leaned over the bed to grab it from her. Rushing to her sister's aid, Caroline Vernon tried to pull Lord Grosvenor away, tugging from behind at the tails of his frock-coat. Angrily he turned round, pinched her hand and then pushed her away, snatching the torn letter and glancing through it as he stood there. Then he turned to go, 'seemingly very cool', as Caroline Vernon later put it, and said to his wife, 'My dear you need not be afraid of showing me the letter, for there is no harm in it.'

Lord Grosvenor was indeed cool. Tiny Richard Grosvenor, sucking at his wet-nurse's breast and apparently completely forgotten by both his parents, was his second male heir, and barring disaster his patrimony was now safe. He did not need his wife any more, and instantly decided not to keep her much longer. He copied the Duke's letter and kept the mangled original. Somehow he found a way of intercepting some of his wife's letters too, and had them copied before they sped on their way, accumulating proof of her guilt sheet by sheet. At the same time he began to stay away from her, not coming to her bedroom at night even when her month's lying-in was up. A separation, as he must have known, was usually refused by the courts if a husband continued to sleep with his wife after he had discovered her adultery. Lord Grosvenor was taking no chances. Careful to avoid Henrietta, he instructed some of his more trusted servants – particularly his second coachman Charles Cock who drove Lady Grosvenor round London – to keep a close eye on her movements. But he was deceitful too, keeping an even temper and kissing his wife on the cheek when he said goodbye.

For her part Lady Grosvenor was initially terrified, certain that her husband had found out everything and afraid of what he might do. She told her maid Hannah Birch 'that she must go out of the house that night, for that it was impossible for her to stay, after what my lord had seen in those letters'. But her husband's studied behaviour calmed her, and she began to convince herself that he had not been able to piece together the torn fragments of the Duke's letter well enough to read its most incriminating parts. 'My dearest friend', she wrote to Prince Henry in the morning, 'he seems rather in better temper today, so I'm in great hopes he did not get enough of the letter to make out much.' After a few lines she heard her husband coming up the stairs to the bedroom, and scribbled quickly, 'I shall resume tomorrow.' The next day, still light-headed with risk, relief and fear, she went on, 'Yesterday he shook hands with me, and this morning he came and kissed me and said he was going out of town to Walthamstow to dine with his brother. Perhaps he is gone to ask his advice. But I don't care, he may take what measures he pleases with me if you will but love me. I'd a note from Mrs Reda this evening. She says she is certain he dares not say a word to her, but she wishes he would above all things, for she knows very well how to answer him, for that she knows enough of his intrigues for him to be afraid of saying anything to her.'

Caught up in the deceptions of the minute, Henrietta was thinking only of the weeks ahead and how she could see her lover, trusting his words of adoration and dreaming securely of a future full of love. Her main worry was not what her husband was plotting but how she would manage to stay in London when the family usually travelled up to their sumptuous estate at Eaton in Cheshire. 'I think I've laid a good scheme', she wrote to Prince Henry on 19 June, eager to share her petty deviousness, 'I've already complained I've got a pain in my side and I intend to say it's much worse at the end of the month and that I cannot bear the motion of a carriage. . . . at the end of five or six weeks I'll grow very ill and send for Fordyce the apothecary and make him send me a quantity of nasty draughts which I'll throw out of the window. Only think how wicked I am, for in reality I'm already as strong and as well as ever I was in my life.'

While his wife marvelled at her own audacity the Earl Grosvenor calmly laid his plans. Prince Henry arrived back in London towards the end of July, and the Earl's coachmen recorded Lady Grosvenor's secret meetings with him at his Pall Mall house, his lodgings in Kensington Palace, and, as if by chance, at Vauxhall, Ranelagh, the Opera and Almack's. William Venen, Lord Grosvenor's first coachman, later said he often left Lady Grosvenor by the gate of Kensington Gardens. Sometimes the Duke of Cumberland seemed to be waiting inside – and the door-keeper John Baker recorded that he would walk up and ask him whether Lady Grosvenor had come – sometimes he arrived immediately afterwards in a hackney carriage. Taking the driver of one of the hackney carriages to an alehouse for a drink while he was waiting for his mistress to return, William Venen confided his suspicions, and the two heartily agreed that the Prince and the Countess were lovers. Charles Cock, Lady Grosvenor's usual driver, took to following her on foot after he had dropped her off, checking, for instance, that although she said she was visiting her sister in St James's Palace, she actually went into the park, met the Duke of Cumberland by the back gate of his house, and disappeared inside with him. Cock talked to Prince Henry's coachman as well, who told him jokily that he knew whenever he spotted Lady Grosvenor's coach in the street he would be ordered to turn round and follow it.

Alerted by gossip among London's hackney-carriage drivers, a stealthy army of informers also began to watch out for the lovers. Towards the end of the summer Lord Grosvenor received an anonymous letter, signed 'your unknown friend Jack Sprat', that both suggested how he could catch his wife and lover and less than subtly demanded payment for the tip-off. 'If you have a mind to see your wife go off with her gallant', it ran, 'place yourself at

Kensington Gardens garden door at a little before eight and you will see her and her little sister go with him to his own back door a little way off and so return the same way at half an hour after nine. If you are fool enough to disavow this information or not be thankful for it, you shall have no more.' Lord Grosvenor, though, was not yet ready to strike. To sue his wife for adultery, or to sue the Duke of Cumberland for criminal conversation with her, he needed to catch the lovers together, not ambling side by side through Kensington Gardens, but in bed, and he needed at least two witnesses to the event. So he bided his time, keeping away from his wife, spending days out of the house and weeks out of town. Lady Grosvenor and the Duke of Cumberland went on meeting, blissfully unaware that traps were being laid for them, and happily congratulating themselves on their ingenuity and skill at subterfuge. Punctuated by the intervals of his sea voyage and her lying-in, their affair raged as strongly as ever, he proud of his passion, she of her adoration and trust.

In the last week of October 1769 Lord Grosvenor left London for Newmarket and Lady Grosvenor reluctantly set off for Cheshire, where the family was to spend the two months before Christmas. Usually, as her husband was quick to notice, Lady Grosvenor travelled up in the family coach, private, resplendent, comfortable and speedy, using two sets of his fine horses, changing them as she needed to and arriving at Eaton in a few days. This time, though, she decided to travel post, hiring horses and going by well-known, slow stages, from inn to inn.

From London, Lady Grosvenor took the old Roman road of Watling Street straight up to St Albans, then branched off to Towcester in Northamptonshire. The post route ran on to Coventry, through the burgeoning industrial landscape of the Black Country to Wolverhampton, and into Shropshire. At the Cheshire border, Lady Grosvenor would turn north for the village of Tarporley, which lay on the western edge of the Grosvenor estate. Shadowing her, sometimes lagging behind her coach and sometimes leapfrogging it to gallop in front, was Prince Henry, accompanied by his friend and gentleman porter, Robert Giddings, and a single manservant called John. When Henrietta Grosvenor and her family stopped for the night, so did the Prince, and on the road they danced around each other in happy parabolas all the way to Cheshire.

Innkeepers, chambermaids and waiters at the inns along the route, though, saw the progress of the three strange horsemen differently. Thieves, pickpockets, card-sharpers and even highwaymen lurked round inns and on the roads and this trio was obviously shifty and odd. One of them, in his late forties, seemed to be guarding or shepherding a second who was so heavily bundled up in outsized clothing that he disappeared inside it. A third tagged along behind like a lookout after a raid. They were obviously up to no good, and roused suspicions immediately.

Prince Henry's difficulty was that prints, written descriptions and the occasional foray out of town had made him so instantly recognisable that disguise seemed imperative. In his saddlebags he had stashed several changes of costume and different wigs, planning to travel in the character of a Welshman or a farmer, as place and occasion suited. At the Saracen's Head Inn at Towcester in Northamptonshire, the Duke declared himself to be a Mr Jones, while Giddings took the name of Tush. They told the innkeeper, William Pratt, that they were were meeting a farmer there to settle a debt, but Pratt was suspicious. Mr Jones, he reported, not only kept his great-coat buttoned right up but had his hat 'pulled so low over his face that he could only see his nose and cheeks'. When the Duke and Giddings went upstairs and chose a bedroom, Pratt mounted a guard on them, believing that they were card-sharpers out to fleece his customers. Nothing happened, however, and, when neither a farmer nor Lady Grosvenor arrived, the party left at twelve o'clock, riding off into the night on the Coventry road.

The lovers had agreed before they left London that whoever arrived at an inn first would try to choose nextdoor rooms. At the White Hart in St Albans they were lucky enough to find two rooms with a connecting interior door: in other places Giddings told the chambermaids that if they saw his companion in the passages, 'or anywhere about (as he was apt to walk in his sleep), not to touch him or go near him'. They took his advice, but were still worried by the Duke's demeanour and appearance.

On 27 October, four days out from London, the travellers arrived at the Red Lion at Whitchurch, on the border between Shropshire and Cheshire, where the Duke, prompted by their closeness to the Welsh border, now called himself Griffith, after having spent a night at Wolverhampton as Morgan. Robert Giddings chose to be Trusty, a pseudonym he liked enough to hang onto thereafter. John Richardson, the ostler at the Red Lion who stabled their horses, was convinced that all three were highwaymen. Mary Spencer, who worked indoors, was particularly alarmed by the Prince, now dressed 'in a claret coloured great coat, with a brownish coat under', and a theatrical black wig with turned-out curls that came right down his fore-head. His behaviour was strange and 'silly', and she decided to keep an eye on him even though Giddings explained that 'the young person was a little foolish', and that he was employed to look after him.

Walking along the corridors upstairs, the Duke alarmed Mary Spencer by whipping a length of chalk out of his pocket and making a long stroke down the door of the bedroom he had chosen. Soon afterwards Lady Grosvenor arrived and insisted on taking the room nextdoor. Mary Spencer explained that a pane of glass was broken in the window, but Lady Grosvenor was immovable, declaring grandiosely that as long as her children had a good room, 'she did not care if she lay in a barn'.

When Lady Grosvenor finally arrived at Eaton, the Duke of Cumberland, still taking the name of Griffith, stayed first close by at Tarporley and then in Chester, where he and his companions lodged at the Falcon Inn. Despite appearing to be Welsh farmers or travellers, they startled everyone there by talking French at dinner. In the next few days they were spotted lurking around the edge of Lord Grosvenor's estate or taking coffee and meals at convenient inns. William Roberts, one of Lord Grosvenor's tenant farmers, saw John leading two saddled horses down a lane, and asked about his absent companions and who they all were. 'Staffordshire graziers come to buy cattle', came the answer quickly.

By 28 October Henrietta was confined in Eaton Hall like a caged bird, flying to the windows to see if she could catch sight of Giddings arriving with a message from her lover. A few times she managed to meet the Duke in the fields or park, arriving back with her gown wet and flecked with red Cheshire clay, which made her servants instantly suspicious. When Lord Grosvenor wrote to say he was on his way, the Duke beat a hasty retreat to London, galloping down as Lord Grosvenor came up, passing him somewhere on the road and grateful for his hat, wig and voluminous great-coat.

Once at Eaton, Lord Grosvenor seemed to be interested only in equine genealogy, and his wife was both astonished at and grateful for his distrac-tion. 'He will sit for half an hour with his eyes fixed on a table or a chair and then apply to Tom or anybody that is by, "Do you know what mare such and such a filly was out of"', she told the Duke. The Earl was brooding on tactics as much as horses. After his return from Newmarket he had received another letter from 'Jack Sprat', running, 'Once more and no more, if I have not often enough pointed out ways for you to be convinced of the truth, I am not your friend, but if you have not a mind you will take no notice, perhaps, of a certain person who is gone in disguise and lies at every inn where she does. Examine your servants and they will be able to tell you more of his constant attendance. He is now about your house and gardens in the country.'

Jack Sprat's information was already old, however. The Duke's disguises and his gauche attempts at rustic behaviour had alerted many on the estate to his presence, as Henrietta told him in some alarm: 'My maid tells me there has been some of our servants telling her that it is all about here that you have been here and she has really told me every particular – that you came down with us and that we met here in the fields and lanes.' She was sure, though, that her husband knew nothing, and wrote happily to her sister Caroline about her return to London for Christmas, 'What a vast deal of talk we shall have – I'm all in a twitter, dreading every moment he may come in, so dare say but little as it would betray all and undo us. He has never mentioned that name so all seems quiet. I pray God keep it so – I don't fancy he has heard anything.'

In the middle of November Lord Grosvenor took action. He ordered his butler Matthew Stephens to intercept Henrietta's letters and copy them, taking himself off to his neighbouring estate at Halkin to allow the lovers to set their own trap. In his absence the Duke of Cumberland made another dash to Chester, meeting Lady Grosvenor twice in the wintry park and fields. After his visit her hopes rose and despite hearing from her sister Caroline that malicious stories were going round London, she wrote exuberantly on 5 December, 'Never mind what any of them says nor let them vex you. I've a vast good plan to tell you of. . . . I know you are laughing and think I am building castles in the air, but see if you don't find it as I say – I assure you I will.' The same day she wrote to Prince Henry, saying, 'the best thing we can do now is to make him believe it is all over between us, and we really have, I believe, blinded him for some time. At least he has no proof about us and I hope to God that by degrees his suspicions will be lulled and then we may form some plans for meeting happily.' 'Only think,' she went on, 'he said yesterday he had so many horses and so much to do at Newmarket he believed he'd go there every fortnight.'

If Henrietta had no fears about what her husband was up to, her sister did. Caroline Vernon was filled with foreboding, knowing that if Henrietta were ruined she herself would lose her job as maid of honour to the Queen and with it her lodgings, salary and opportunity to find a suitable husband at court. After reading a press report that Lord Grosvenor, coming back from a decoy visit to the country, had gone to Mrs Reda's shop, 'and forcing open the front room on the first landing discovered his Lady in bed with her gallant', she wrote to her sister begging her to stop seeing the Duke. Telling Henrietta that the Queen and the Princess Dowager were already angry with her, and that stories were spreading about the summer meetings in Kensington Gardens, she retreated from her earlier position as one sister supportive of another's bid for happiness. 'I am wretched to find', she scribbled disjointedly, 'that a passion for a certain person wrongly entitled to it has so much got the better of you that the loss of your own reputation, and mine, and both our happinesses are to you of no consequence; and could my simple advice be of any service to you I would implore you on my knees, nay serve you as a slave night and day, that you would for ever banish from your thoughts them whom you style your "Friend", for I know if you don't that the rest of your life is destined to be wretched – not only the bitter pangs of the whole world being against you, but you must be banished from all your relations who dearly love you by reason of this.'

This letter, sent up to Eaton and sequestered by the Earl's servants, probably never reached its destination. Lord Grosvenor left Cheshire on 14 December, loudly announcing that he was going to Newmarket before he went on to London. For his part the Duke of Cumberland had dispatched an exhausted Robert Giddings back up to Chester, from where he sent Lady Grosvenor another of his letters signed with his nom de guerre of R. Trusty. Having met Giddings, Henrietta announced she would set out for London immediately. Surrounded by her husband's spies and accomplices she left Eaton with a light heart and an arrangement to meet her lover again at the White Hart in St Albans.

The White Hart was not the wisest choice of rendezvous. In the first place the Duke and Henrietta had already spent a night together there two months earlier. Secondly the old coaching inn was right in the middle of things, the start of many journeys north out of London. It was loud with the clatter of horses and carriage wheels and the shouts of servants, full of smoke and buzzing with business and gossip, a place where few went unremarked and fewer still unrecognised. Henrietta and the Duke arranged to take the two connecting rooms on the first floor exactly as they had in October. This time, though, Lord Grosvenor's servants were ready for them. While

Henrietta was down in the inn's dining room eating supper, the Earl's trusted butler Matthew Stephens crept upstairs and bored two small holes in the door of her bedroom. When she came back he waited for a while and then knocked on the door with a cup of negus in his hand, which she took unsuspectingly, not thinking that his motive was less to serve her than to check that she was there.

At a quarter to eleven Stephens made his way back upstairs, this time accompanied by several witnesses. His brother John, who was adjutant of the Cheshire Militia and a loyal servant of Lord Grosvenor, as well as a man trained in rough business, was beside him. Making up the rest of the group were the coachman Charles Cock, the groom John Anderton, Robert Betton the under-butler and no fewer than three of Lord Grosvenor's footmen. This time Stephens was confident of bagging his catch. Much to his chagrin, he found he had miscalculated his drilling. With his eye pressed to one hole and then the other, he could scan most of the bedroom. But the corner where the bed stood, beyond the fireplace, was out of sight. Though he could hear rustlings and amorous noises, and, as Stephens put it later, he was sure 'they were in or upon the bed', he could see no part of either of the lovers themselves.

Knowing that his master wanted irrefutable evidence, Stephens decided to break down the door. Several of the party put their shoulders to it and shoved, not standing on any ceremony. On the floor above Robert Giddings was wrenched out of sleep by the rend of the lock giving way, and rushed downstairs to a scene of confusion. Lady Grosvenor was frantically fastening the small buttons that ran up the front of her light brown 'jesuit dress' when the crowd of men burst into the room. She tried to run away and tripped over her own disordered skirts. The Duke, 'much confused', with his cream waistcoat undone, tried to run through the door that connected the two rooms. His way was barred by Stephens and his brother standing in the doorway holding up the pokers from the fireplace.

The Duke held fast to the efficacy of his many disguises, especially the dark wig he was still wearing. 'Do you know who I am?' he demanded of the posse of men filling the room. 'His Royal Highness the Duke of Cumberland,' they all confidently answered. The Duke paused, stunned, and then changed tack, declaring that 'he was not in her Ladyship's bedchamber, and that he would take his bible oath on it'. When Giddings came running in, the Duke whispered loudly to him him, to say nothing, and to 'go, go along, or something to that effect'. Stephens meanwhile was efficiently going about his business. He called up the servants of the inn and asked them to examine the bed, which Robert Betton described as being 'much tumbled from top to bottom, in a very extraordinary manner, all the bed clothes being much rumpled'.

Three separate parties left the White Hart the next day. The Duke went back to Cumberland House to lick his wounds and wait for a summons by the courts. Lady Grosvenor went quietly with her children to anonymous lodgings. She knew she could never go back to her husband and that she would be reliant on her lover's charity and the support of her brother and sisters. Stephens and the other servants went back to Grosvenor House with their statements and information. Two days later the press and the country had an astonishing story to enliven Christmas. In the Vernon family there were few festivities, though. Lady Grosvenor's mother, lady-in-waiting to Princess Amelia, immediately severed all links with her daughter; Caroline Vernon knew she would lose her job.

In the grey of the new year, Lord Grosvenor hired a firm of lawyers, Partington & Garth, to gather witnesses and bring them to London to testify against his wife. In anticipation of a criminal conversation suit, the Duke of Cumberland also began to assemble a legal team, instructing the firm of Buxton & Windus to act on his behalf. In fact, Lord Grosvenor did not immediately begin proceedings against the Duke. Instead he lodged a Libel against his wife in the consistory court of Doctors' Commons, beginning the lengthy process of a legal separation. Such an action was unusual because the consistory courts were notoriously tardy and while a case continued an accused wife held her title and dignity intact. A crim. con. suit, which would establish a wife's guilt and was generally over in a couple of days, was the usual prelude to any Libel and divorce trial because after it a disgraced wife could generally be ousted from the family home. After 1 March, opinion in the press, which had initially favoured Lord Grosvenor, turned against him. It was whispered that the Libel was itself a front and that Lord Grosvenor's real interest in lodging it was not to get a divorce, but to blackmail the Crown. A dukedom was what he wanted, it was said, and one pamphleteer even went so far as to suggest that he 'paid a visit to a certain great Personage to obtain a d[ucal] c[oronet], on condition whereof he promised to stop all proceedings'.

The matter, however, may have been more procedural than premeditated. By the late spring preparations for a crim. con. suit were also under way.

In an effort to create sympathy for his case and to counter some of the reports that were now circulating about him, Lord Grosvenor gave copies of all the letters he had intercepted between his wife, her sister and Prince Henry to John Wheble, publisher of the *Middlesex Journal*. He did not do so out of sympathy for Wheble's anti-government stance, because he was and remained a staunch Tory, but because he recognised Wheble's genius for scandal and nose for public opinion. The *Middlesex Journal* was read everywhere in London, and the longing letters of the Duke aboard the *Venus* and Lady Grosvenor's artless replies began appearing in it from mid-June 1770 onwards. Lady Mary Coke was dining with her friend the Duchess of Norfolk on 16 June when, as she recorded in her journal, 'the Duchess showed me in the *Middlesex* a long letter of the Duke of Cumberland's; it seems that HRH's correspondence with Lady Grosvenor is to be printed in that paper. One of her ladyship's followed in the next, and tho' I never had any great idea of her delicacy, I own the indecency of her style quite shocked me.'

From the *Middlesex Journal*, and perhaps directly from Wheble himself, who was more than happy to make extra money embarrassing the Crown, the lovers' letters found their way into newspapers everywhere, so that by 1 July, when the trial was held, a mood of happy anticipation gripped the country. This was especially true since efforts by both Crown and government to define and strengthen the law of libel had just been frustrated. In the previous few weeks, three trials for seditious libel, including one between the King and Henry Sampson Woodfall, publisher of the *Public Advertiser*, had taken place. Despite the judge's recommendation to juries to find for the plaintiffs in each case, in only one out of three cases had they whole-heartedly done so. The verdicts effectively gave publishers carte blanche to go on printing attacks on easily identifiable public figures. Hacks, copyists and engravers responded with gusto, expecting that a court case between an aristocrat well known for his taste in young street girls and the brother of the King would make plenty of work for all of them.

Like the libel case of *Rex v. Woodfall*, *Grosvenor v. Cumberland* was heard at the court of King's Bench before its formidable sixty-five-year-old chief justice Lord Mansfield and a special jury from the county of Middlesex. The court of King's Bench, though one of several common lawcourts in the City of Westminster, did not in practice deal with ordinary criminal business, but was used for high-profile and test cases. It sat, as befitted its status, in Westminster Hall, the massive and ancient edifice rising above the jumble of buildings along the Thames that housed both Parliament and many other government offices and departments.

Westminster Hall had been built as a formidably imposing building sitting on the banks of the Thames where the river made its swan's-neck arch northwards between Vauxhall and Charing Cross. It was a grand and sombre space, 240 feet long and 68 feet wide, rising 92 feet towards the heavens, with a soaring hammerbeam roof that dated from the fourteenth century. By the 1760s the church-like space of the medieval hall had been broken up, and made into a series of very earthly meeting places. In 1740 the two courts of King's Bench and Chancery were pushed to the southern end and divided off from the remaining space with a lacy rococo screen designed by William Kent. The benches of the courts could clearly be seen through the screen's theatrical tracery, and sound travelled easily through its openings. The body of the hall had become a general meeting place rather like the privy garden in Whitehall, sheltered from bad weather and conveniently lined with shops selling books, prints, pens, ink, and lawyers' wigs. Dogs loped across the flagged floor while copyists, hacks and throngs of the casual public milled about in the huge open space, pressed up against the screens to watch sensational trials and often fell silent when Lord Mansfield pronounced his eloquent and simple judgments.

A large crowd filled the hall for the opening of *Grosvenor* v. *Cumberland* at eight in the morning on 5 July 1770. Barred by legal procedure from the court itself, none of the principals were there, despite the fact that at least one popular print showed them all standing before the judge and having their say. Lord Grosvenor and his wife stayed at home, while the King pointedly took his younger brother out riding in Richmond Park, well away from town. Looking up the length of the hall, the court of King's Bench was on the left. Alexander Wedderburn, Lord Grosvenor's able Scottish counsel, sat on one side with his six-strong team. Opposite him were John Dunning, his deputy Mr Skinner and two other lawyers who represented the Duke of Cumberland. The jury sat at the far end, the judge above it and copyists and admitted members of the public, hacks among them, along the sides. 'The Court was never known to be more crowded than it was upon this occasion', the *General Evening Post* reported. Lord Grosvenor's lawyers had brought dozens of witnesses, the Duke of Cumberland's many fewer, but all of them, from the Duke's secretary to a Mrs Howe, a prostitute described in one account as 'one of the dirtiest of all the women coming from about Long Acre', were crammed into the Court of Chancery next door. Muslin curtains had been tacked onto the inside of Kent's screen and hung down to the floor to stop the curious public staring at them as they waited to be called.

Well aware of what these women would have to say, Wedderburn's opening remarks avoided the encomiums to the chastity and cleanliness of his client that his team had put into the Libel lodged in the ecclesiastical courts. Instead he simply demanded damages for Lord Grosvenor of £100,000, justifying the enormous sum by pointing to the 'high quality of the accused' and claiming that the Prince's standing made the damage to the Earl's honour and property much greater than in cases where plaintiff and defendant were of the same rank. 'No sum', he concluded with a rhetorical flourish, 'could be a recompense for the loss of everything dear to a British peer.'

Such a crim. con. suit should have been a relatively simple matter. Once the jury was satisfied that the Duke of Cumberland had indeed damaged Lord Grosvenor's property, their job was simply to assess the degree of damage and award a commensurate sum to the plaintiff. But as Wedderburn knew, damages varied hugely. In the dozen cases of crim. con. that Lord Mansfield presided over in his long career, the average amount juries awarded was £200, and the sums ranged from one shilling to £3,000. The £100,000 demanded in this case, then, was partly because the rank of the defendant, a prince of the blood, had no precedent, and partly because public ridicule and interest were inflicting on Lord Grosvenor's honour a grievous blow. It was a risky strategy, all the same. If John Dunning on the Bench opposite, a counsel who had an unrivalled reputation for sharp reasoning, could cast slights and shadows on Lord Grosvenor's own character, the jury might regard him as already dishonourable and tailor the damages they awarded accordingly.

Wedderburn began his presentation of evidence by solemnly reading out every letter that Lord Grosvenor had intercepted from the time of his wife's lying-in. Not just the court but the pressed crowd in the hall beyond fell silent to listen. When he came to the Prince's long ungrammatical, unpunctuated declaration of love, 'aimons toujours mon adorable petite amour je vous adore plusque la vie même', his straight face and the Prince's lamentable French produced a knowledgeable and superior titter. But Prince Henry's sad awakening aboard the *Venus* to find his happy dream, 'all delusion, nobody by me but myself at sea', provoked gusts of laughter that filled the court and spread to the hall beyond. The letters between the parties, the *General Evening Post* reported, 'occasioned much entertainment to the whole court, as they may truly be said to add to the novelty of epistolary writing'.

More merriment was caused by the witnesses, taken through the story of the lovers' meetings at Lady D'Onhoff's and Kensington Gardens and their trysts on the road to Cheshire right up to their eventual entrapment. Bad French, disguises, wigs, the Prince's blustering denials, his fondness for Welsh pseudonyms, his acting simple, the fears of locals that he and Giddings were highwaymen or cardsharps: the story was more like a Drury Lane farce than conduct befitting the brother of the King. Lady D'Onhoff herself was not in court. Willing, perhaps for a fee, to give a deposition on behalf of Lord Grosvenor in the separation case before Doctors' Commons, she was conspicuous by her absence at King's Bench. Could it be, the newspapers hinted, that the Prince had seen fit to buy her off? Her evidence in Doctors' Commons was damning; she swore to having interrupted the lovers and to having caught them together on her drawing-room sofa, the Prince with his breeches down, the Countess with her petticoats splayed out to receive him. Without her, Dunning had only to deal with the fiasco at the White Hart, not the scenes at Cavendish Square as well.

Summing up for Lord Grosvenor, Wedderburn took advantage of the temper of the court and pressed again for high damages. Widening the argument too, he declared that the case was not just about damages to his client but also about how a prince should behave. The Duke of Cumberland he declared, should be deterred 'from setting a bad example to the subordinate classes of society', and a costly rebuke would encourage him to follow the example of the King, 'whose conjugal attachments, abstracted from his other virtues, not only ornamented the throne he filled, but shed a bright example to his subjects in general'.

John Dunning, speaking in his soft Devonshire accent and pulling his famously ungainly body up off the Bench, began his defence of the Prince by asserting that the damages Wedderburn was demanding were far too high whatever the outcome of the case. Without elaborating, he then proceeded to suggest that the case was anyway not proven. Addressing Lord Grosvenor's counsel he said, 'My learned friend thinks the fact sufficiently established by the extravagant professions of love and attachment to be found in the letters. I contend for the reverse of the proposition. The language of lovers, after enjoyment, is not so violent. These letters are too ardent, and too passionate, to have been written by any lovers whose passions have been previously gratified. I will allow the Duke of Cumberland and Lady Grosvenor have been imprudent, blameable, inexcusable and censurable. I can suppose everything to have passed between them but the criminal act upon which this action is founded.' The two, he added, had never been caught *in flagrante*, as the law demanded, and finding for the Duke of Cumberland could thus set a bad precedent. In support of his implication that the Prince and Lady Grosvenor had never slept together, Dunning's deputy, Skinner, called Robert Giddings, who testified that, although his master had confessed to him that he was 'in love with Lady Grosvenor', he stayed near them all the time they met in the fields near Eaton, but all they did was, 'sit upon the grass . . . and that His Royal Highness read a play or some book to the said Lady Grosvenor'.

Leaving the jury to consider the startling possibility that the lovers had kept their affair unconsummated for nearly a year, Dunning turned his attention to the character of Lord Grosvenor. In the weeks before the trial, one pamphleteer reported, the Duke's solicitors Buxton & Windus went into many of the common bawdy-houses and houses of known ill-fame and repute in and about London, to find women prepared to give evidence against Lord Grosvenor. One by one Skinner called five women, Mary Howe, Mary Waten, Ann Tremilly and Mary Smith, all of them common prostitutes, who testified to having known and done business with Lord Grosvenor; another, Abigail Mary de Boisgermain, admitted that she had known Lord Grosvenor for three years, but made it clear that, though she was prepared to come to court, it was not to do the Duke of Cumberland any favours. Acknowledging 'that she knew Mr Giddings, the Duke of Cumberland's porter very well', she told the court spiritedly that 'he came to her lodging to bring her the subpoena; that she told Mr Giddings the whole story some time ago, and came there merely to serve Lady Grosvenor, and to support the cause of her whole sex'.

If the day was going well for any of the protagonists in the drama it was indeed the absent Lady Grosvenor, caught as she seemed to be between a feckless if ardent lover and a pock-marked husband who scoured London's streets for young girls and the commonest prostitutes. The law, though, was uninterested in the miseries of marriage. At six-thirty in the evening Mansfield began his summing-up. He rarely took notes or intervened while evidence was being presented, though many people noted his habit of very obviously reading the *Public Advertiser* if he thought lawyers were wasting the court's time. When he came to sum up, onlookers crowded up to the screen in front of the court to hear what he had to say, and surprise and murmurs of dissent greeted his direction to the jury to disregard the rank of the Duke of Cumberland, to consider the case merely 'a question between A and B', to decide how much damage had been inflicted on the one by the other, and to tailor their award accordingly.

Aware of Lord Mansfield's reputation as a judge who favoured the Crown, many of the spectators signalled their strong disapproval of his advice. Although the saga of John Wilkes's defiance of the Crown and Parliament was all but over there were many in Middlesex and in the rest of London who remained hostile to the government and to the King himself in equal measure. In *Grosvenor* v. *Cumberland* they saw an opportunity to hit out again at the reputation of the Crown, and regarded Mansfield's insistence that the rank of the defendant should be immaterial to the size of the damages awarded as a craven admission of his own political leanings.

Mansfield himself was not a man either to linger in the courtroom or to bow before criticism. At about seven o'clock he left the hall and went back home to his large new house in Bloomsbury Square on the Bedford estate. The jury deliberated until ten o'clock and then, summoning four carriages, set off north to deliver their verdict with several officials from the court. 'Upon the arrival of the jury at Lord Mansfield's, in Bloomsbury Square', one account recorded, a number of people, whose curiosity was very great, had collected together round the door; and before the jury had got well into the house, many rushed in with them. Lord Mansfield . . . received their verdict and immediately withdrew. Some of the people who were nearest the door, after having heard the verdict, communicated it to others, and a loud huzza was heard, as approbatory of the jury's conduct.'

The verdict was guilty, the damages set at £10,000. It was only a tenth of what Lord Grosvenor had demanded, but it was nonetheless a huge sum, a blow to the Duke, and by implication, to the Crown. One writer insisted that the jury would have hit the Duke harder if it had not thought that the sum would probably come from the Treasury in the end and 'be a charge upon the public'. In private some members of the royal family agreed with the jury. Princess Amelia, with whom Prince Harry, as she called him, had been something of a favourite, decided to cut off communication with him, telling Lady Mary Coke that 'the little remorse he seem'd to have for having ruin'd a whole family quite shocked her, and the little feeling he had for himself, though abused and ridiculed in every public paper, considering his rank, shocked her to the last degree'. Keen to reap some moral advantage from an action that had seen his name blackened every bit as much as that of the man he had sued, Lord Grosvenor ostentatiously declared that he would donate the entire sum of the damages 'to the most useful and beneficial public charities'. The newspapers recorded his intent but not the final destination of the money.

In any case, Prince Henry was incapable of paying his erstwhile friend. As the papers predicted, it thus fell to the King to come up with not only the damages but the lawyers' bills too, £13,000 in all. Prince Henry dithered until the last minute and then went to the King with his brother Prince William to help and intercede for him. Within hours of his brothers' visit the King had written to his Prime Minister asking him to authorise the payment from the Civil List, saying that he could not raise the money himself because he could not be seen to be involved in such a sordid affair. 'Lord North', he wrote on 5 November, 'A subject of a most private and delicate kind obliges me to lose no time in acquainting you that my two brothers have this day applied to me on the difficulty that the folly of the youngest has drawn him into; the affair is too public for you to doubt but that it regards the lawsuit; the time will expire this time sevennight when he must pay the damages and the other expenses attending it. He has taken no step to raise the money, and he has now applied to me as the only means by which he can obtain it; I therefore promised to write to you, though I saw great difficulty in your finding so large a sum as thirteen thousand pounds in so short a time; but . . . [he pointed out to me] that the prosecutor would eventually force the House, which would at this licentious time occasion disagreeable reflections on the rest of his family as well as on him.' Adding that 'whatever can be done ought to be done', the King signed off by saying, 'I ought as little as possible to appear in so very improper a business.' The faithful Lord North got straight to work and was able to report the same day that he was confident that Parliament would authorise payment of the money. 'This takes a heavy load off me', the King wrote gratefully back.

Perhaps waiting to have Lord North's confirmation more officially, the King did not immediately pass on the good news to the Duke of Cumberland. Indeed Prince Henry, meeting his brother on 8 November, could only suppose that the King's silence boded well. Writing to Mr Le Grand, his treasurer, the next day, the Duke advised him to hope for the best, as 'the cost of [the] suit must be in Buxton's hands on Monday morning as that evening they are together with the adverse party to finish this very disagreeable business'. Le Grand got the money, and the King was quick to tell his Prime Minister that he had given his brother a slice of his wisdom to accompany it. 'I flatter myself', he wrote, 'that the truths I have thought it incumbent to utter may be of some use in his future conduct.' The press was equally forthright with its advice, keeping the story going with an avalanche of commentary that ranged from sentiment to humour and to a vigorous debate about the meaning of adultery and the role of young members of the royal family like the Duke of Cumberland.

Now that criminal conversation between Prince Henry and Lady Grosvenor had been proved in a court of law many in the press assumed that an adultery trial and a parliamentary divorce would follow quickly. A divorce would open the way for the lovers to marry. Because of that, the *Middlesex Journal* reported on 28 July, 'a very Great Personage and his amiable Lady have expressed a wish to L[ord] G[rosvenor] that he not sue for divorce, fearing that an alliance, by no means to be wished, would be the consequence'. It is unlikely that the King would have intervened so dramatically in an affair of the kind that, he told Lord North, 'my way of thinking has ever taught me to behold as highly improper'. He approached the problem purely personally, condemning his brother's actions and ashamed at the figure he cut in public. The first king for three hundred years who was responsible for more than two royal princes, he was both unable and unwilling to think about giving his brothers' lives meaning beyond the symbolic and dynastic. Their job, as he saw it, was twofold. First, they must marry foreign princesses and increase the royal stock. Secondly they might adorn the army or the navy, in a mostly decorative way, as titular generals or admirals, lending the dignity of the Crown to Britain's military might.

The press, though, was less reticent, both about the trial and about the Prince. One pamphleteer called the case 'the most important and remarkable trial ever to come before a court of judicature', and multiple editions of the lovers' letters and complete transcripts of the trial were published to meet public demand. For months afterwards, while the consistory court continued to collect witness statements for the forthcoming adultery trial, writers talked over the issues the trial had raised. In an inflammatory pamphlet that condemned just about everyone involved in the case, an anonymous writer echoed the King's own formulation of the relationship between himself and his subjects, and went on to declare that his brothers were a part of it. 'A king of Great Britain', he wrote, 'is the master only of his own servants; he is, or ought to be, the father of his people; his subjects are his children, and his indulgence in acts of gallantry would be a kind of civil incest.' The royal princes were bound by the same rule, and therefore their moral conduct was 'a matter of national as well as private concern, such a dangerous influence do they derive from their titular and elevated station'. Several other writers echoed the belief that Prince Henry's disgrace dragged the honour of the Crown, and the nation, into the mud. One addressed the late Duke of Cumberland in a verse of dogged rhyming couplets entitled simply, 'The Adulterer, a poem'. The poem compared the prowess of Cumberland as the victor of Culloden with the shame of his nephew and namesake, saying,

> See, how dishonouring his Noble Race
> Thy nephew earns reproaches and disgrace
> Whilst a vile deed of rapine and of fraud
> Shall spread his Name with Infamy abroad
> And foreign nations shall this land abuse
> – For who shall dare th'atrocious Act excuse?

The object of all this scorn lay low through the barrage, escaping on a tour of northern England at the end of July. Arriving at Alnwick Castle, he was 'saluted with twenty-one guns', and must have felt his self-respect revive. The Earl Grosvenor left town as well, heading for Newmarket and his jockeys and grooms. Shown in prints with the horns of the cuckold firmly stuck on to his wig, he was mercilessly attacked in the press and ridiculed in the *Town and Country*, where he was dubbed 'the Cheshire Cornuto' and his amorous history laid bare. As soon as the Earl 'was convinced of the intrigue between his Lady and the D[uke] of C[umberland]', the *Town and Country* asserted, 'he no longer made any secret of his amours, but publicly appeared with Miss Charlotte Sp——r, a nymph well known in the circle of amorous pleasure'. Another writer went further, printing a letter purporting to be from Lord Grosvenor to Mrs Charlotte Hayes, perhaps the most notorious of all the brothel-keepers in St James's, who specialised in finding young and beautiful girls for aristocratic men. 'As I have now got rid of my wife', Lord Grosvenor was supposed to have written, 'I propose having any good piece that you recommend. I shall not mind delicacy so much as health – . . . She must be tall, and have good teeth; and I would chuse she should have dark eyes.'

The only principal in the case whom the press treated with any leniency was Lady Grosvenor herself. A print rushed out at the time of the trial had her declaring, with arch double entendre, 'My case shall be laid before this Court, and I have nothing to fear from an upright judge.' But elsewhere she was portrayed as the innocent bystander in a tawdry low-life world, giddy and silly, but a pawn in the great game of dynastic ambition, passed on to a profligate aristocrat by her ambitious family and only turning to Prince Henry when her husband had ceased to need her. The three novels published about her story, *The Divorce, A Full and Complete History of His Royal Highness the Duke of Cumberland and Lady Grosvenor, the Fair Adulteress*, and *Harriet, or the Innocent Adulteress*, all made her their heroine, and their mostly female readers must have sympathised with her plight.

Lady Grosvenor, though, could not survive on sympathy alone. By the autumn of 1770 she had been living for over six months in lodgings, with a small staff, desperately short of cash. But if she hoped that once the long divorce process was complete she would be lifted out of her difficulties into the ermine robes of a royal duchess and the splendour of Cumberland House, she was soon disabused. From his sloping cabin on the *Venus*, Prince Henry had carefully copied out Prior's lines, 'No time, no change, no future flame shall move / The well plac'd basis of my lasting love'. But he soon forgot the poet's lofty sentiments. By the autumn of 1770, Prince Henry had abandoned his mistress, leaving her hopes dashed and her purse empty. Before the year was out he had found a new mistress, the courtesan Mrs Hailey, and cheerfully paraded her through the streets of London, delighting the press and scandalising his brother the King.

It was surely for this reason that Lady Grosvenor decided to contest the suit that her husband had started in Doctors' Commons. If she counter-sued Lord Grosvenor and showed that he had been unfaithful before she herself strayed, then the court would not allow any divorce, merely a separation. Knowing now that she would never marry Prince Henry and certain that her tainted past would make it unlikely indeed that she could ever marry again, she no longer had any interest in letting the case run all the way to a parliamentary divorce. Proving her husband as guilty as herself would mean that he had to pay her an annual jointure for maintenance, whereas she would be left penniless if his Libel were upheld and he went on to divorce her.

In the autumn of 1770 Lady Grosvenor set about finding witnesses to her husband's low life, offering rewards to those who would come forward. Her solicitors, Buxton & Windus, who had already acted for Prince Henry, were charged to find 'strange women of loose character and prostitutes, at lodging houses, and at public places of resort . . . and at houses of ill fame and reputation.' It was not difficult, and the evidence they came up with was squalid and damning. Prostitutes counted for nothing in the hierarchy of London life, and visits to them were mere peccadilloes lasting no more than minutes. But once stories and faces were put to names, Lord Grosvenor's tastes became shocking even to those who saw procuring and prostitution as just incidental elements in aristocratic life.

Out of London's teeming jails came Elizabeth Roberts, her clothes pawned and her person thrown into the Marshalsea Prison. She had her debts paid and her clothes restored with Lady Grosvenor's money, and she testified that in May 1770, in the very weeks before his crim. con. case came to court, she had met Lord Grosvenor, 'accidentally', in Cranbourn Alley to the east of Leicester Square one evening, and he took her to the Leicester Fields Hotel. Her friend Elizabeth Newton told a similar story, while Elizabeth Elwes, confined for debt in the King's Bench Prison, recorded two encounters with Lord Grosvenor at about the same time. Mary Muilment of Crown Court off Cheapside in the City, gave evidence of having found various girls for the Earl. Abigail de Boisgermain who had already come forward to testify for Lady Grosvenor at the earlier trial, admitted that she had known him for three years and Mary How, 'sitting at her work' in the house of 'one Mrs Lisle in Glastonbury Court, Long Acre', in May 1768, remembered that Lord Grosvenor had spotted her there and come to see her three times.

Most damning was the evidence of a Cheshire girl, Alice Tipping, who was also known in efforts to escape both her creditors and her past as Alice Williams, Charlotte Gwynne and Charlotte Williams. She seems to have met Lord Grosvenor in 1765 when she was seventeen, and to have been sent down from Cheshire to Mrs Hayes's house in Little Duke Street off Piccadilly, to be available for him when he needed her. After some time, she said, he proposed to get Lady Grosvenor 'to advertise for a maid servant, and that she should take the deponent as her servant', and then, 'everything would be snug'. Charlotte refused this subterfuge. But by 1767, according to Lady Grosvenor's brother Henry Vernon, Lord Grosvenor had married her off to a Mr Williams and set them up in Craven Street off Piccadilly where he could drop in at will. By the time of the crim. con. trial he had abandoned her and she had left her husband, completing her descent by becoming Alice Tipping, a common prostitute and down on her luck. Her money had run out and she had gratefully agreed to testify against her former benefactor in exchange for board and lodging from Henry Vernon and Lady Grosvenor herself.

After the court case, these and all the other prostitutes, grooms, ostlers and chambermaids who had briefly written themselves into the future with their testimonies, disappeared back into the largely unrecorded world of servants and of the streets, their lives as insecure and as poor as they had ever been. Even courtesans, protected from the worst that prostitutes suffered by having better living conditions and fewer clients, had short working lives and were more likely to die of consumption and other diseases of overcrowding and poverty than retire on their earnings to gentility on the south coast. Ordinary women of the street who began working as teenaged girls lived brutal, lousy lives. Ann Sheldon recorded finding two girls for Lord Grosvenor on Westminster Bridge, 'covered in vermin', and most would have come and gone that way, sick, young and quickly forgotten. For Lady Grosvenor, though, they served their purpose. When the Consistory Court finally got round to assessing all the evidence on 22 April 1771, it did not take long to reach a verdict. If Lord Grosvenor had proved his wife's infidelity, she had amassed more than enough evidence to show that, as her lawyers put it, he himself 'hath led, and doth continue to lead, a vicious, lewd, and debauched life and conversation, by visiting, corresponding with, and carnally knowing, diverse strange women of loose character'.

Lady Grosvenor was allowed the right to live separately from her husband and to receive from him an annual allowance. At £1,200 it was not going to keep her in Grosvenor House style, but banished from court and estranged from her family, her needs would be small. The settlement gave her no freedom to dissolve her marriage, however, and so she remained in shady retirement, unable to remarry or live in society. She paid for her nine months as Prince Henry's mistress with a life of modest living outside the ballrooms and theatres in which she had been so conspicuous as a girl. Many years later she met a much younger man, a soldier, Lieutenant-General George Porter, who represented the borough of Stockbridge in the House of Commons. His family were determinedly reticent about their liaison, refusing to name it in their family histories. But when Lord Grosvenor's rackety life ended in 1802, Henrietta, released from her purgatorial anonymity, became the humble, and happier, Mrs George Porter, until she herself died four years later.

As for Prince Henry, he seems never to have seen Lady Grosvenor again after he left her to fend for herself in the early autumn of 1770. While she stayed in her obscure lodgings, he was soon cheerfully out and about, at Windsor and in London. He saw little of his brother the King, perhaps because the burden of his debt to the Earl Grosvenor still hung heavy between them, so George III was surprised when he turned up uninvited at Richmond Lodge on 3 November 1771. The two men walked out together into the autumn woods beyond the gardens, the thirty-three-year-old King still slim and muscular, his twenty-six-year-old brother much smaller, fairer and slighter. After a good deal of small talk, Prince Henry, according to the King, suddenly stopped, pulled a letter out of his pocket and gave it to the King, who read it as he stood, in ominous silence and with rising feeling. Prince Henry was not much more of a letter writer now than he had been on the *Venus* three years before. His sentences still veered about uncontrollably, their messages lost in thickets of unpunctuated dependent clauses. His meaning, though, was clear. 'Sir', the letter began, 'it is impossible for me to describe the emotions whilst I impart an event which I feel I never should have kept a moment secret from you if I had not found myself incapable of offering you the cruel alternative of either being involved in any inconvenience by giving your consent to it; or of pronouncing my future misery for life by your refusal. Sir, I am married to Mrs Horton Lord Irnham's daughter and nothing now remains to make me one of the happiest of men but your approbation which I trust the sensibility of your heart and the amiable qualifications of the object of my choice will strongly plead for and fully justify.'

Prince Henry signed himself, 'your most anxious and dutiful brother', and he had every reason for his temerity. There was nothing in the law of the land to stop him marrying. The Marriage Act of 1754, which required banns to be posted in advance of any ceremony and witnesses to be present, did not apply to the royal family, and the Prince, at twenty-five, did not need the consent of his mother or the head of his family. But the King saw it as his duty to direct both the private and the public lives of his siblings, and Prince Henry's insouciant bid for self-determination enraged him. Indeed the King's anger, so disproportionate to the offence, had deeper roots than he could acknowledge. That Prince Henry had flouted his authority George III was prepared to say loud and clear. But he had done much more than that; he had followed his heart, married a commoner and turned his back on the prescribed recipe of a foreign princess who could have no political or dynastic ambitions in her adopted country. It was the very opposite of the way he had felt compelled to act a decade earlier, and the Prince's defiance opened the King's old wounds so immediately and cleanly that at first he could not speak.

At first George refused to accept what his brother had written. 'After walking some minutes in silence to smother my feelings', he wrote, 'I without passion spoke to him to the following effect, that I could not believe he had taken the step declared in the paper, to which he answered that he would never tell me an untruth.' To his mother the King wrote, 'the more I reflect on his conduct, the more I see it as his inevitable ruin and as a disgrace to the whole family'. Writing to his brother Prince William, who was recovering from illness in Florence, the King allowed himself more emotion, and unselfconsciously reached for the vocabulary and subjects of his childhood essays for Lord Bute. 'Dear Brother', the King wrote, 'It is grievous to me to be obliged to acquaint you with an event that as it disgraces the family must cause you pain. The D[uke] of Cumberland, not content with his unwarrantable conduct in the St Albans business, his attendance on Mrs Hailey, and his connection with Fetty Place and Newmarket grooms, has now stooped to marry Mrs Horton, Lord Irnham's daughter. This cruel blow I had to meet whilst in agonies on account of you and to break to my mother. . . . In any country a Prince marrying a subject is looked upon as dishonourable, nay in Germany the children of such a marriage cannot succeed to any territories. But here where the crown is but too little respected it must be big with the greatest mischiefs. Civil wars would by such measures again be common in this country; those of the Yorks and the Lancasters were greatly owing to intermarriages with the nobility.'

The King must have known that the notion of a civil war between the Hanoverians and any supporters of his renegade brother was an absurdity. His excess reflected his high emotion and the feeling he had that with his mother's decline, the Duke of Gloucester's illness, the increasingly bad news from Denmark and, now, Prince Henry's insouciant flouting of his authority, his control over his family was slipping away. After Prince Henry had left for the boat that would take him out of the country to France, however,

George's anger subsided. Despite his recourse to history, it was not the fact of the marriage that made him angry. It was the Duke's very public acknowledgement of it and his assertion of his right to decide the course of his own life that really bothered the King. 'It is impossible I can ever receive her or ever look on him again unless he will promise not publicly to acknowledge', George explained to the Duke of Gloucester with ungrammatic emotion, adding, 'the story has been too industriously spread by her family for anyone to doubt the truth; but if he does not avow, her people will by degrees grow doubtful and I can without disgrace see him. . . . His retiring out of the kingdom is the only decent thing he has done. I could not write but I have sent Deaken with my firm resolution of never seeing him again unless he consents to let this affair remain doubtful and that he never names the subject to his mother or me.'

By this time the Duke of Cumberland had sent the King a second letter 'from on board the packet', that was probably intended for the press but threw the gauntlet down to his brother as well. After copying his first letter word for word, the Duke added, 'No person whatsoever knew of this transaction but one lady and the clergyman who married us on Weds 2nd of October 1771. We are just sailed for Calais, shall go to St. Omer and remain there for a couple of days then proceed to Arras in Artois, where I shall stay till I hear from England.' Still enamoured of disguise, and still short of money, the Duke concluded: 'To avoid suspicion I have taken the name of Thomas Johnson Esq. as I was obliged to have correspondence with a banker.'

While Mr and Mrs Johnson enjoyed their short, late-autumn holiday, her relations in London were busily passing this information on to the press. Sensationally, her family was well known in Grub Street. Anne Horton's brother was Colonel James Luttrell, the erstwhile government candidate for Middlesex who had stood against John Wilkes in 1769 and had been returned to the House of Commons against the wishes of the electors. He had been pilloried by Wilkes's heckler-in-chief Junius in the *Public Advertiser* and he knew as well as anyone how quick Junius was with news and how well he could use it. Notwithstanding his treatment at Junius's hands it was to him that the new Duchess of Cumberland's relatives went. Junius knew he had a scoop, writing excitedly to John Wilkes on 6 November, 'Since my note of this morning, I know for certain that the Duke of Cumberland is married to Luttrell's sister. The Princess Dowager and the Duke of Gloucester cannot live and the odious hypocrite is *in profundis*. Now is your time to torment him with some demonstration from the City.'

Wilkes, though, no longer had much interest in tormenting George III. Since his three election battles he had shifted his ground, giving up on Westminster. He had headed for the City, become an alderman and begun his journey back into the moneyed respectability from which he came. That the Duke of Cumberland should marry into a disreputable family seemed to many journalists merely a fitting sequel to his earlier adventures and it was announced in the *Public Advertiser* on 8 November under the heading 'Intelligence Extraordinary but True'. The new Duchess herself was largely spared personal attack, perhaps because she was disarmingly alluring. Taller than her husband by several inches, she was as statuesque as he was slight, with what one commentator described as the most amorous eyes in the world, and eyelashes a yard long. Calculatingly flirtatious, she was well aware of her good fortune and was determined never to be modest about it or about the charms that had won it for her. Painted by Gainsborough with the Duke in 1783 at the age of thirty-five, she firmly took centre stage, shimmering in gauzy silk and gold trimmings, edging her little husband to the side of the picture. But Anne was to prove more solid, and more loving, than the press and commentators supposed. Although she was delighted to flaunt her new status she had few airs and graces, and was happy to live beyond the ambit of the court. With no particular wish to endure the *longueurs* of evenings at the Queen's House or the formalities of levees at St James's she delightedly displayed her ermine and would soon turn the drawing room of Cumberland House into a place of raucous laughter, gambling and levity.

From Arras the Duke of Cumberland sent his brother another letter reiterating his decision to stand by his marriage, saying he was 'ready to do anything in the present situation of things that was consistent with my character and did not in any way alter the solemn vow I had made before the supreme Being'. To the King's suggestion that they could still be on terms if he simply said nothing to confirm or deny his marriage and did not give his wife the title of a royal duchess, the Duke went so far as to pretend incredulity. 'The King does not desire that I disavow my marriage', he wrote to George III's envoy Colonel Deaken on 25 November from Lille, 'but my wife is to be called Mrs Horton and in the above condition alone I am to be admitted to His Majesty's presence – that is the King's commands – I have transcribed them from your letter. I am not logician enough to be able to understand this paradox. She can only be my wife or not.'

The King was in no mood for levity, declaring to the Duke of Gloucester that the marriage was 'a stain the D of C has put on me'. Once it became clear that the Duke would not publicly disavow his marriage, although he was happy enough not to call his wife the Duchess of Cumberland, his brother had had enough. When asked on 1 December by Lord Hertford, the ambassador to Paris, what foreign ministers were to be told about the Duke, the King replied that they could be informed he would not see his brother. A public announcement in the *St. James's Gazette* made his displeasure clear; anyone visiting Cumberland House would no longer be welcome at St James's and foreign courts were expected to honour the King's displeasure too. 'I now wash my hands of the whole affair and shall have no further intercourse with him', the King told his mother.

November and December 1771 were very difficult months for the King. Bad news seemed to arrive too often from Denmark and the Duke of Cumberland made light of his banishment from court. Worst of all, the Princess Dowager was dying. The King's beloved mother had already seemed tired and aged when she had travelled to meet Caroline Mathilde in Lüneborg the year before. A couple of months later she began to show signs of a serious disorder, unable first to eat, then to swallow and finally to talk, as a tumour grew into and across her throat. In mid-November 1771, the King wrote to his brother Prince William that 'her speech grows less intelligible, she hourly emaciates, and has dreadful faintings towards night'. Beyond asking for her daughter Augusta to come to her, the Princess Dowager refused to acknowledge her mortality. She kept rigidly to her usual hours and insisted on receiving the King and his family three evenings a week as she had done since their marriage, and visiting them herself on a fourth.

Unable to confide any longer in his mother and unwilling, as he had always been, to involve his wife in any discussions that might shade into politics, the King relied on the support of his absent brother, Prince William, the Duke of Gloucester. Prince William, five years younger than the King, was less intelligent and less physically robust too. But they had similar temperaments, quick to condemn, slow to forgive and proud of their honesty. A week after the Duke of Cumberland's revelations, the King finally heard that his brother was out of danger and recovering in Livorno from the attack of asthma and fitting which had laid him low. As his brother travelled south towards Naples in search of temperate winter air, George wrote to him in relief, 'I expected no other account than that Heaven had taken you from me, though thanks to God my mind is now at ease. I can scarcely relate what I have suffered without tears, but this has only taught me how much I love you. You are the only friend to whom I can unbosom every thought.' Prince William, eager to deserve such approbation, wrote back on 22 November from Pisa that Prince Henry's 'behaviour in this last instance is inexcusable and weak beyond measure. He has got into very bad hands and we know is easily led to anything. I own I greatly fear for some subsequent follies.'

In the heat of his anger towards Prince Henry, the King declared to the Duke of Gloucester, 'I must . . . on the first occasion show my resentment.' He himself had children, he went on, 'who must know what they have to expect if they could follow so infamous an example'. The fact that his son and heir Prince George was only nine years old seemed then, to the King, to be irrelevant. Summoning his Prime Minister Lord North, the Lord Chancellor and the Lord Chief Justice, Lord Mansfield, the King put together a Bill in December 1771 and January 1772 that would stop once and for all marriages like that of the Duke of Cumberland. Writing to Lord North on 26 February, the King made it quite clear how important the measure was to him, and would be, too, to the Prime Minister. 'I do expect every nerve to be strained to carry the bill through the House with a becoming firmness', he wrote, 'for it is not a question that immediately relates to Administration but personally to myself, therefore I have a right to expect a hearty support from everyone in my service and shall remember defaulters.'

The Royal Family Marriage Bill was presented to the House of Commons, with a message from the King as a preamble, on 4 March 1772. From the start it was contentious and its passage through the House was rocky. 'I do not remember', wrote the historian Edward Gibbon, 'ever to have seen so general a concurrence of all ranks, parties and professions of men. Administration themselves are the reluctant executioners, but the King will be obeyed and the bill is universally considered to be his.' In essence the Bill claimed for the Crown the right to approve or forbid the marriages of all the descendants of George II until they were twenty-five, when they might marry as they wished if they gave the Privy Council twelve months' notice. The ground for this claim was set out in the Bill's preamble, which demanded 'that the right of approving all marriages in the royal family (which ever has belonged to the kings of this realm as a matter of public concern) may be made effectual'. This claim caused a storm in Parliament and in the country for many reasons. In the first place, many in Parliament, and in the House of Commons in particular, did not agree with what they saw as the King's formulation of his rights. Ever since George III's accession in 1760 opposition Members of Parliament and those who were suspicious of the Crown had been alert for any signs that the King was trying to extend his prerogatives and thus diminish the powers of Parliament. Such vigilance – and the belief that the King wanted to accrue more power to himself – was behind almost all the political agitation of the preceding twelve years, from the furore over the role of Lord Bute, to the libel trials of 1770 and the demands of the angry crowds demonstrating on behalf of John Wilkes.

It was this fear that lay behind the vehement opposition to the Royal Marriage Bill, for the fact was that since the Act of Settlement in 1701, Parliament had indeed encroached on the private life of the sovereign, and many members saw the Bill as an attempt to erode that hard-won right. Under the terms of the Act of Settlement, no member of the royal family who was married to a Catholic could inherit the throne and anyone who did so marry was immediately disbarred from the succession. In agreeing to the terms of the Act in 1701, the Crown had implicitly agreed, not that Parliament could determine the marriages of members of the royal family, but that Parliament had the right to decide, on the basis of such a marriage, how the succession would fall and thus who would be king.

To many the King's demands now represented an attempt once more to stretch his prerogative and so to limit the powers of Parliament. In the debate that followed the first reading of the Bill in the House of Commons on 4 March, one MP, Mr Dowdeswell, put this case quite bluntly. It was dangerous, he said, 'even to admit of such a claim, lest other prerogatives might find their way down to these doors, however sad and contrary to the interest of the people, and might, under alike colour and pretense, pour fast upon our Liberties and obtain the concurrence of the House'.

Members of the House of Lords, skirting delicately round the belief of many that the King was not to be trusted, nevertheless decided to submit the King's claim that he had the 'right of determination' to the judges in their midst. The Law Lords' answer was equivocal. The King, they said, did have the right to determine whom his own children, grandchildren and the heir presumptive to the Crown might marry, but they could not decide how far his right extended. A group of powerful Whigs in the Lords, led by the Duke of Richmond, who was himself a descendant of Charles II and whose family had long championed complete freedom of marital choice, entered a detailed protest to the Bill on 2 March. It was not just the danger that the Bill represented an encroachment by the Crown on the powers of Parliament that they rejected. They pointed out too that it had nothing in it about the marriage of a reigning king. If, once the Bill was law, they implied, a king, Protestant and unmarried at his accession, chose then to marry a Catholic, Parliament would have to invoke the Act of Settlement and unseat the monarch, a recipe for just the kind of conflict that had so riven the nation the previous century. Other peers, trying to diffuse the political tension by opposing the Bill on moral grounds alone, claimed that marriage was both 'a natural right inherent in mankind', and sanctioned by the Bible. The last Marriage Act, in 1754, had indeed brought marriage into the ambit of the civil law, but it had made no attempt to limit the choice of any citizen.

In the Commons the fight soon became personal. Lord Folkestone, knowing that in the background to the debate hung the King's sacrifice of his own happiness a decade earlier when he had renounced his love for Lady Sarah Lennox in order to marry a German princess, stood up and said pointedly, 'I must now say a few words as to the supposed dishonour of the crown from an alliance with a subject. ... I will never persuade myself that any British king, much less one who publicly gloried in "being born and educated a Briton", could so far forget the natural equality of all mankind, the boasted independence of every individual in this nation, as to think dishonourable a stream of British blood in the royal veins.' By this time the House of Commons was in an uproar, packed and angry. Lord North had the utmost difficulty, despite his handsome majority, in steering the Bill through the debates and its committee stage. On 23 March, when an amendment to limit the Bill for the duration of George III's reign went to a vote, he survived with a majority of only eighteen. Twenty-four hours later, after a long night of persuasion mixed with carefully bestowed promises of favour and office, the Bill passed the House of Commons by 168 votes to 115.

A grateful king made his Prime Minister a Knight of the Garter at the end of the parliamentary session. The Act would indeed have its uses, but not for this generation of royal children and not for over a decade. But the oddest aspect of the whole episode was that it reflected, more than anything else, the King's desperate desire to assert some power over his family when he felt at his most impotent and helpless. For George knew, not officially or openly but with as near a certainty as made no difference, that the only person to whom the provisions of the new Act might seem to apply, his beloved brother Prince William, the Duke of Gloucester, was secretly married already, and married to an English woman too.

5

A Daughter of England

For Caroline Mathilde in Denmark, the troubles of her older brother Prince Henry in 1770 must have seemed uninteresting and far away, even if she read about them in the continental press. She spent much of that autumn at the castle of Hirschholm in the wooded hunting country north of Copenhagen. There she lived as she had at Traventhal, informally and congenially, abandoning altogether the long days of court and government business that were so inimical to King Christian. Struensee took over more and more of the King's duties, and Christian took his place in the family as part uncle, part unruly child.

Eighteen months later, Struensee maintained that after the long summer holiday, the King's mental state improved for eight months, although he showed no appetite for governing or for etiquette. Christian had never lost his edgy wit and sometimes now his old brilliance flashed out. One day, wearied of signing appointment papers for new officials, and noticing Gourmand slumbering at his feet at dinner, he announced to the assembled company that his dog too should have a government office. He would be Councillor Gourmand, the King announced, and demanded that the whole company drink his health. Another time, half distracted and half parodying the very idea of absolute rule, he came across the servant who lit the great ceramic stoves in each room of the castle, walked with him into the great hall where the rest of the party was assembled and declared, 'I appoint this man my chamberlain,' to the embarrassment of everyone there.

Hirschholm, away from Christiansborg and the gossip that swirled around it, seemed an idyllic backdrop for Caroline Mathilde's experiment in family life and her bid to enjoy the privacy of ordinary citizens. Life there, however, was magnificent as well as pastoral and domestic. Unlike at Windsor or at Kew, there was no abstemious dining, no frowning on frivolity and no penny-pinching economy. Indeed it was precisely the combination of unrestrained superfluity and demonstrative domesticity that confused and scandalised observers. Caroline Mathilde was queen and countrywoman, lover, mother and occasional wife, blurring the boundaries between them, and, perhaps deliberately, making her visitors feel uncomfortable. 'This court has not the most distant relationship to any other under the sun', one shocked British observer wrote in the autumn of 1771 after trying to present himself at Hirschholm with the usual etiquette.

Like many Danish royal palaces, Hirschholm was a shimmering double castle, sitting above its reflection in a shallow lake. Finished only twenty years before and built in the French classical style, it had a steep mansarded roof and turrets and towers. Many of Hirschholm's 250 rooms were lavishly decorated with marquetry, carving, gilding and stucco. Visitors walking through its formal spaces were taken aback, watching their images endlessly repeated in silver-framed mirrors and rows of columns inlaid with silver, sandalwood, mother-of-pearl and coloured glass. Winking crystal chandeliers hung above them and bright rococo paintings sailed across the ceilings.

Outside, the garden was just as embellished. It was French in inspiration, formal, symmetrical and stiff, with forty-eight fountains, a square parterre garden with walks, pools and low planting, an arcade, an island, bridges, a summer-house theatre and shady walks. The whole complex, lake, garden and castle, was encircled by beech- and pine-woods, like a shining jewel on bright green velvet.

By the beginning of 1771, the households of the King and Queen were perhaps smaller than they had been a few years earlier. Fewer courtiers in attendance meant that fewer cooks, chambermaids and stable hands were needed. But splendour was still everywhere. Christian and Caroline Mathilde, with the marshal of the palace at one end of the table and the chief lady of the household at the other, dined off gold plate and were served on bended knee by a team of pages. If Struensee was not eating with the King and Queen, eighty covers were laid in the room next door for him, Brandt, any visitors and the rest of the household.

Many visitors were horrified by the combustible combination of luxury and vice, especially since women, whose nervous systems were regarded as particularly weak, were seen as vulnerable to both. At Hirschholm, loose living, a sensuous woman and a disordered kingdom were all tangled up. 'Nothing could be more licentious than the court of Mathilda in 1770 and 1771', one commentator wrote several years later. 'Her palace was a temple of pleasure, of which she was the high priestess. Everything was found here calculated to excite and gratify sensual desires.' Stories about the lovers' behaviour came out with returning visitors, and with the postboys and merchants who supplied the royal household. Struensee spent hours alone with Caroline Mathilde, it was said, walking with her into the woods and breakfasting in her rooms. She for her part often went secretly to his suite, by the back staircase from her rooms.

The charge of licentiousness seemed to be confirmed by rumours that the Queen was pregnant. There was no certainty about the expected arrival's parentage, but no scruple either in awarding it to Struensee. Robert Gunning, worried that mentioning Caroline Mathilde's pregnancy was tantamount to advertising her immorality and thus further injuring himself both in Copenhagen and in London, kept quiet about it for as long as possible. Finally, on 12 February 1771, probably anxious that the news would get to London some other way, he wrote sheepishly, and with less of the rhetorical flourish that usually accompanied notice of an heir to the throne. 'As no declaration has yet been made of Her Danish Majesty's pregnancy, I have long entertained scruples with regard to the propriety of mentioning it, but as nobody now seems to make the least doubt of its truth, I am at length convinced I ought no longer to suppress so important a piece of intelligence.'

At nineteen and a half, Caroline Mathilde had no need to lounge her way through the nauseous and tiring early months of pregnancy. But she did stay as long as possible at Hirschholm when winter closed in and the court would usually have been back in the comforting mass of Christiansborg. She was kept there not just by her enjoyment of the casual routine but by her two-year-old son, who had been removed from Copenhagen and installed in the country. Caroline Mathilde loved Prince Frederik and her devotion was obvious to everyone who saw them together, the Prince in his mother's arms or toddling about clinging on to her skirts. Having breast-fed him according to fashionable prescription, Caroline Mathilde now proceeded to give her son an early life which was as near to Jean-Jacques Rousseau's fierce instructions in his *Emile* as she and Struensee could make it.

Rousseau's *Emile, ou De l'education*, published in 1762 and immediately banned and burned by the French authorities for its anti-clerical stance and tone, was a book owned by both Caroline Mathilde and her lover. Begun as a treatise, finished as a novel, it was an inspiring rag-bag of assertion, advice and flights of fancy. Rousseau was less an original thinker about childhood and education than a brilliant and emotive populariser of ideas which had been swirling about in print and discussion for many years. His injunction that mothers breast-feed their infants, for instance, was successful not because of the philosophical or medical arguments he advanced, but because he appealed to women themselves. Breast-feeding and loose clothing for infants soon became necessary badges of motherhood for fashionable aristocratic women. Nowhere was *Emile* more popular than in England, and so Caroline Mathilde, deciding to breast-feed Prince Frederik in 1768, was doing exactly what many rich young mothers were doing in her native country, even though it was perhaps the first time in centuries that an English princess had not handed her child straight to a wet-nurse as soon as it was born.

Many readers chose to ignore *Emile's* combustible blend of social primitivism and political radicalism, but this too Caroline Mathilde and Struensee seemed to be following. Rousseau declared the modern world of cities, fashions and theatres corrupt, and by implication he condemned with it the existing social order. By asserting that all men were born equal as well as free and by insisting that his model child be removed from the city to the unsullied purity of the countryside, where he would learn to trust sensory experience and the lessons nature offered, Rousseau claimed that he could produce a man unwarped by the vices of modernity, as free and good as the day he was born. Practical advice it may have been, but it came underpinned by a philosophy that was profoundly unsettling to his detractors. Put a prince in the countryside, educate him side by side with a peasant, and who could tell the difference between the two?

When news began to circulate of the way Crown Prince Frederik was being brought up at Hirschholm many responded with predictable alarm. Their reaction had less to do with exactly what the little boy was doing day by day, more to do with a fear that the court of Caroline Mathilde and Struensee was replacing established order and ceremony with something topsy-turvy and terrifying. Robert Gunning certainly thought that Rousseau and the levelling principle were both at work. 'As no step taken in the education of a prince is without its importance, his nursery may sometimes present a scene not unworthy of attention', he wrote with bitter sarcasm to the Earl of Rochford on 6 October 1770. 'The philosopher of Geneva would hail the dawn of a more enlightened age could he behold (as he might here) the son of a monarch left from his cradle to crawl unassisted upon his hands and knees (like the nursling of a Norwegian peasant) and condemned to lose his meals most philosophically unless he could discern them by the sagacity of his nose. Such are the maxims which obtain in the Royal Nursery of Denmark.'

Prince Frederik was not being neglected, but Rousseau's prescriptions were indeed being followed with unusual avidity. All three adults with an interest in the Prince's welfare had reasons to be inclined to a Rousseauian education. King Christian, his father, had only frightening memories of his own childhood and of the rigidity and cruelty of his tutors. Caroline Mathilde was a perfect subject for Rousseau's visions of a pre-lapsarian rural life because she had spent her summers in family solitude at Kew and her notion of a rural idyll was sanctioned by 150 years of English pastoral romance. Moreover, her father and four of her siblings had died young and she was likely to seize upon any prescription that offered to toughen both body and mind. Struensee, as a doctor, would have agreed with Rousseau's entirely conventional insistence on fresh air, exercise and the development of physical endurance. As a natural philosopher he believed that the mind was formed by sensory experience, just as Rousseau said, and his broader philosophical bent made him temperamentally inclined to favour Rousseau's thoroughgoing experiment.

Many of those who saw Prince Frederik at Hirschholm seemed to forget that he was a toddler and not yet in need of any lessons. What really shocked them, however, was that he had neither nurses and maids around him nor the sort of half-private, half-public life that was usual for heirs to Europe's thrones. Instead he lived the Rousseauian way, very lightly clothed, and sometimes, it was said, barefooted even in winter. He was able to do what he wanted, allowed to try his strength, fall over, graze his knees and pick himself up. His food was very simple, sometimes cold and uncooked. Worst of all, children were brought in to play with him and when he was about two and a half he was given a companion, apparently called Karl. Reports about the Prince's companions were confused – some, including Reverdil, said he had two playmates – but Karl, malicious or perhaps fanciful reports made out, was the son of a doctor. Count Andreas Bernstorff, nephew of the dismissed minister, told a correspondent that Frederik was 'not subject to any restrictions; he eats when he is hungry, falls asleep when he is sleepy and goes to bed when he wants'. He added that Caroline Mathilde and Struensee were 'delighted when he argues with his playing mates. If they get into a fight it is forbidden to separate them.'

Struensee later strongly denied, in his capacity as both doctor and natural philosopher, that the Prince's treatment had been in any way inhumane or even unwise for an heir to a throne. But he and Caroline Mathilde seem to have been aware of hostile reports, because in July 1771 they commissioned a portrait to counter them, to be entitled 'Mother and child'. Peder Als, who had just finished his portrait of the Queen in male clothing, was given the commission, a clear signal that Caroline Mathilde and Struensee were confident that he knew how to put their wishes and ideas onto canvas.

Since the 1740s, portraiture had mirrored the growing fashion for domesticity, and paintings of family groups playing music, reading and writing, sitting out of doors and posing with bows and arrows or dogs and horses, hung on walls all over Europe. Even royal portraiture had become more familial and informal. Peder Als never finished his painting of Caroline Mathilde and her son, but in July 1771 he sent her a series of ink and watercolour sketches that showed the group and setting she had in mind. One showed Caroline Mathilde with her newborn baby, two others with her son.

Als's new commission was far removed from the booted and spurred splendour of his first picture. It was to show Caroline Mathilde as a mother, in soft pink, with plaited hair and silk slippers, book in hand, languidly feminine. Both the construction of the sketches and their setting was startlingly simple. Nothing in them suggested that the two-year-old boy was a prince or his mother a queen. In one sketch Caroline Mathilde sits, in the other reclines, in an unadorned space that opens out into Hirschholm's garden and the gauzy blue sky of a northern summer. In both, her bare hand is folded over Frederik's in a gesture of intimacy and acceptance. The Prince is painted in just the sort of loose frock that Rousseau advised, but his stockings and slippers are more luxurious than anything prescribed in *Emile*, and belie, perhaps deliberately, the reports that were circulating about his running about barefoot. In the most Rousseauian gesture of all, Frederik is holding in his other hand a pint-sized watering can.

Rousseau made gardening the centrepiece of the practical instruction he advocated for the early years of childhood. It offered an array of sensory lessons: the touch and smell of the rich loam, the buzz and chatter of insects and birds, the sight of nature itself vigorously growing. Digging taught the child the practical results of work, and the fruits of the land the notion of property itself. Emile, Rousseau declared, would make the land his own, 'by planting a bean', and this simple act of possession, earned by his own labour, was more 'sacred' and more 'worthy of respect' than any grand imperial conquest. Cultivate your own garden, Rousseau was saying, echoing Voltaire, anchor morality in your own social sphere, and virtue will follow as surely as Emile's plants struggled upwards from the ground. 'We come every day to water the beans and watch them coming up with the greatest delight', Rousseau declared, and Caroline Mathilde, posing with Frederik clutching his watering can, could not have set out more plainly her adherence to his beliefs.

Caroline Mathilde's desire to teach her son life's lessons from nature was echoed in Struensee's policy. He determined to pass on the benefits of the outdoors to all the citizens of Denmark and in the spring of 1771 he decreed that the gardens of Rosenborg Castle in Copenhagen, and Frederiksberg, just outside the city, should be opened to all citizens. Provocatively hinting that nature might offer more solace and pleasure to them than established religion, he deliberately advertised their Sunday opening by adding the diversion of military bands.

Something of the magic and mysteriousness of Vauxhall Gardens and Ranelagh, which Christian and Struensee had visited two years before, soon spread into the gardens at Rosenborg. Shrubberies and groves were illuminated by strings of lights. Dining booths like those at Vauxhall were put up in the summer and music played, even on Sundays. The Lutheran Church was implacably hostile to Sunday music and fun, but the Danish people took immediately to this little slice of Eden, this nature turned to wonderland. Its spirit lived on, magnified and illuminated, in Copenhagen's Tivoli Gardens. Tivoli's illuminated alleys, its candy-flossed strolling, its concerts, flowers, fountains and nightly fireworks were Struensee's and Caroline Mathilde's most visible legacy, and the ice-cream innocence of the garden, like its millions of shiny lights, is firmly entwined around the nation's heart.

The opening of Rosenborg and Frederiksberg gardens was just one ripple in the torrent of change that poured out of Christiansborg after the court returned there at the end of January 1771. Although they had a clear underlying philosophy, many of Struensee's reforms were straightforwardly bureaucratic and in that way were the high crest of a wave that swept round the Baltic in the mid-eighteenth century, from Stockholm to St Petersburg, to Berlin and back to Copenhagen, pushing before it French philosophy and English liberty. So Caroline Mathilde looked in some ways to Russia, and she showed it by setting up a foundling hospital in December 1770 that emulated not only Coram's Hospital in London but also the more recent establishment in St Petersburg. Struensee's reformist model was different; he hoped to replicate not only the efficiency of the Prussian administration, but also Frederick the Great's own magnanimity.

Although Struensee was the architect and often the writer of the decrees issued from Christiansborg, he did not work or think entirely alone. A number of reforming aristocrats grouped themselves around him and, to begin with at least, his friends Rantzau and Brandt backed up his grand designs. Rantzau had a post in the War Department and was generally regarded as Struensee's confidant, although Gunning for one regarded him as temperamentally unsuited to the long game of politics. 'Rashness and revenge', he wrote, 'form a very striking feature of his character.'

Brandt acted as Christian's private and constant companion. But his task became harder and harder as time went on. After the summer of 1771 the King had fewer long periods of lucidity and his melancholy became steadily more debilitating. Brandt was not merely the King's keeper, he had to be his friend and caretaker as well. So to ease the burden Moranti, a former slave or child of a slave, was installed as the King's companion, just as Karl was Frederik's, making Christian less a king and more a pitiful version of his own son. As a relief from this arduous task, Brandt took charge of the Royal Theatre in the south wing of Christiansborg Castle. He set about expanding its repertoire, bringing in Italian opera and French comedy and provoking the anger of the capital's clerics by staging Sunday performances and the disgust of the court by occasionally opening the theatre to ordinary citizens.

To the Foreign Ministry, a key position in a state which relied on diplomatic strategy to support its neutrality and maintain its revenue, Struensee had in 1770 appointed Adolf von der Osten, another German, who had served the Danish Crown in Russia and Poland since 1754. Osten was experienced and respected, a man, according to Gunning, 'of great acquired abilities, joining to a happy memory the closest application to business, he has read much and is master of most of the modern languages.' Osten's professional pride and years of experience sometimes did not sit well with Struensee's headlong zeal, but he skilfully managed to keep Denmark free from the undue influence not just of Russia, but of France and Britain too. Struensee, speaking as usual for the King, rebuked Gunning's attempt to use Caroline Mathilde's new prominence to claim a greater role for Britain in Danish affairs by telling him at an audience at the end of March 1771, 'as His Majesty did not wish for any other foreign country to meddle with the internal regulation of his government, he should himself be as little as possible inclined to meddle with those of his neighbours.' Osten's brief was to maintain this policy and he steered a fine course through waters cluttered with international animosities and personal vendettas.

To work alongside Osten, Struensee appointed a Danish career officer and friend from Altona, Otto von Falkenskjold and another acquaintance, General von Gëhler. The latter Gunning described as 'a smooth, designing, self-interested man, submissive, cool, deliberate and timid', while the former, on the contrary, he defined as a man of 'boundless' ambition. Struensee's brother, Carl Auguste, a professor of mathematics working in Prussia, came to help reorganise the country's financial affairs.

Although Gëhler and Osten had previously had government posts, the others were outsiders who did not know the time-honoured ways of Danish bureaucracy. But even the existing executive struggled under the snowstorm of decrees now issued under the King's name. Struensee intended to leave no part of the civil, royal, clerical and military administration untouched. The government of the city of Copenhagen was to be reorganised, and its citizens' lives regulated by numbering each house and naming and lighting the streets. Orders went out to curb the police and Struensee outlawed brutal penalties for minor crimes. Punishments were to be codified according to the law, and no longer left to the discretion of judges. Torture was to be banned as a means of getting prisoners to confess to crimes. 'It is better to let a guilty person go free than to punish someone who is not guilty, which is so repugnant to the liberties and rights of mankind', Struensee wrote. Fines for adultery were abolished, public shaming of adulterers was banned and illegitimacy declared free of stigma. 'Immoral conduct,' Struensee declared, pursuing his goal of allowing individuals freedom to behave as they wished, 'if it have no directly injurious influence on the quiet and safety of society, must be left to the conscience to condemn.' The police force, therefore, would no longer have jurisdiction over the moral conduct and behaviour of the population, and would no longer enter and search people's homes but would concentrate instead on activities that had a bearing on public order and safety.

At court and in the national government, Struensee wanted to pursue a policy of both reform and retrenchment. Throwing out the very widespread system of lackeying or office-holding struck a blow at the otiose bureaucracy of the executive. A canny decree that lifted the immunity from noble debtors hastened the exodus of court officials, who drained out of Copenhagen to their country estates rather than face shameful and costly prosecutions by their creditors.

Decrees went out to overhaul the Revenue Board, the Admiralty and the War Office. Struensee demanded savings in Danish legations abroad and at the court, pensions were curtailed, office-holders dismissed, the royal stables reduced and all embellishments to palaces stopped. Still royal expenditure did not seem to slow. By the summer of 1771 a new College of Finances had been established, the old Customs Board abolished and the ruinously expensive royal manufacturies proposed for closure. As if all this were not enough, before Christian's signature was dry on these decrees, and certainly before the new practices and institutions had had time to become fixed components of national life, Struensee was planning to press on. He wanted to turn his attention to reform of the army and to the most urgent moral and economic problem of all, the peasantry.

Reform produced backlash more quickly than benefit. Copenhagen was a small capital and by the time the court left once more for Hirschholm in the summer of 1771, the city's streets were thronged with the dispossessed and the aggrieved. Some had seen their hopes of lifelong security dashed, some had lost pensions, offices or influence. Artisans and contractors, like the stonemasons and carpenters who worked on improvements at the royal palaces or the seemingly endless construction of the Marmorkirke in the new Amalienborg district, which Struensee had stopped with the walls halfway up and the huge round structure open to the sky like a northern coliseum, joined them in complaint. The newly free press gave them unrestrained voice. For every moderate man and every reformer whose activities had much in common with men in governments throughout northern Europe, there was an office-holder humbled, a family impoverished, a clergyman enraged and a tradesman diminished.

It was not only the citizens of Copenhagen who turned against Struensee when their interests were threatened. Robert Gunning now also regarded him with a bitterness born of professional disappointment. 'His conversation discovers nothing of that vivacity and grace by which other men in a disadvantageous situation have won their way to royal favour', he wrote to London. 'It is universal matter of wonder', he went on, 'how he has managed to gain so entire an ascendancy over their Danish Majesties.'

The British envoy was only too aware that his information about Caroline Mathilde and the circle around her was painfully inaccurate, despite the money he had paid out to spies and informers. From the sheets of Gunning's dispatches and the running numbers of his ciphers a concocted portrait of the Queen wafted up in which she was an innocent prevailed upon by her doctor, a young woman who had misguidedly given him all her confidence and over whom, in consequence, the upstart exercised a 'vast influence'. Accompanying this fetching cameo, which Gunning must have known bore little resemblance to the stout, headstrong and recklessly determined woman the little Princess had become, was an assumption that if Struensee could be dismissed, Caroline Mathilde would return untainted and unchanged to the bosom of her family.

Caroline Mathilde knew that Gunning was hostile to the way of life she had made for herself, and cordially disliked him. On 26 February 1771 she wrote to her brother asking for Gunning's removal, and calling him 'an obstacle . . . to friendly and confidential intercourse'. Lord Halifax, Secretary of State in Lord North's new government, and perhaps King George as well, decided that fresh blood was needed in Copenhagen. They wanted a man free from association with Bernstorff, who might be able to reach Caroline Mathilde on her own, fondly imagining that they might somehow persuade her to abandon Johann Struensee. 'Foreseeing' the need for better political relations, George wrote to his sister on 22 March, saying that he was 'removing' Gunning to the court of Berlin, and sending in his place a new envoy, Robert Murray Keith, whose 'prudence', he hoped, 'will make his conduct approv'd of'.

Writing candidly about the Danish King was almost as difficult for Gunning as being frank about the Queen. Christian was first cousin to George III and melancholy was thought to run in families. Any hint that the King was irretrievably sinking under the grip of mania might be regarded as a slight on the British King, who himself had suffered an alarming and mysterious illness in 1765 that was rumoured to have driven him temporarily mad. So in April

1771 he said only that 'those talents and that vivacity which his Danish Majesty displayed with such advantage on his accession to the throne have, by a wonderful change, given place to indifference, apathy and dejection of spirits'. The 'new ministry', he added, 'though they pretend to have restor'd the sovereign to the most perfect free agency, keep him in reality in a state of bondage and confinement more mortifying than anything he could have experienced before . . . it is said His Majesty sometimes shews a very poignant sense of his present situation and that he has sometimes been surprised in tears. As far as the Drawing Room or Playhouse have for some time furnished me with the only opportunity of seeing His Majesty, I may add from my own observation his countenance had carried strong marks of melancholy and dejection.'

Few in Denmark attributed the King's mania to cruel treatment or imprisonment. His unpredictable behaviour, on the contrary, was often alarmingly obvious. The courtier and official Bolle Luxdorph described an incident in early April 1771 when Christian began to hurl objects from his balcony at Christiansborg. A crowd immediately formed a safe distance away in the street below, and, with faces upturned, watched as books, porcelain dolls and a poker sailed down, followed by a white drift of pages of sheet music. Three weeks later came a repetition and Luxdorph wrote with worldly-wise economy in his diary, 'balcony again'.

Copenhagen's citizens suffering from melancholia or mania were confined, and even caged, at St Hans Hospital beyond the west gate of the city. The King, however, was never put under guard, although it was obviously necessary to restrain him when he was gripped by his fears or when the desire for violence strengthened his body and urged him to scenes like those noted by Luxdorph. By the summer of 1771, Brandt had had enough, despite the respite that Moranti gave him. He had tired of the job and Christian had tired of him. In June, with the royal family back in the seclusion of Hirschholm, Struensee wrote to Christian's old tutor Elie Saloman François Reverdil asking him to come back to Denmark and share the burden.

After some hesitation, Reverdil accepted. His first interview with the King when he arrived at the castle gave him hope that reports of Christian's illness had been exaggerated. The King made a speech that seemed both coherent and to the point. But Reverdil's second meeting convinced him that Christian had simply learned and repeated what he had been told to say. Once they were alone, Christian began to talk incessantly, braiding strands of nonsense one over the other. 'You are Brandt,' he said assertively to his old tutor and companion, and then launched into a garbled version of several verses from Voltaire's *Zaïre*, which he had acted with Reverdil four years before. That led him to declare Reverdil to be first 'Denise' and then 'Latour', two French comedians who had once been employed at court.

In the days to come Reverdil saw that Christian's mood could turn in an instant and he could veer from grandiloquence to self-hatred in a few phrases. After boasting of his magnificent reception in London, Christian called himself pitifully 'der kleine Man', the little man, small and worthless. Often he spoke forcefully about killing somebody, usually himself. He was fed up with himself, he could not hang on any longer, he was going to throw himself out of the window or dash his brains out against the walls. One day, being rowed across Hirschholm's ruffled lake, Christian announced that he was going to hurl himself into the water. Over and over again he said sadly that he was confused, that his head was full of noise and that he had lost his way.

But even in the fog of melancholia, Christian's language and his violence could hit on embarrassing truths. One day, when the royal party had rowed out to picnic on an island in the middle of Hirschholm's lake, Christian picked up all the dining tables one by one and threw them into the water, where they drifted about among the diaphanous flotsam of tablecloths and napkins, as lost as the King felt himself. Another time he told Reverdil with casual indifference that the King of Prussia was sleeping with the Queen. Then he added, with a nod towards his minister's admiration of Prussian government, that the King of Prussia was Johann Struensee.

Even so, what struck Reverdil about life at Hirschholm was its ordinariness. There was 'no tone of indecency' about the royal family, he wrote, although he was offended nonetheless by what he called 'je ne sais quoi de bourgeois et d'ignoble'. The lack of etiquette distressed him as much as any obvious immorality might have done. A Swiss outsider who had made his mark in the service of the Danish Crown, he wanted more royal behaviour, not less.

Caroline Mathilde still longed for the opposite. Early on in her relationship with Struensee she had said to her maids that they must be much happier than she was, because they could marry whom they pleased, and she added that if she became a widow she would marry a private person whom she loved. By the summer of 1771 she had begun to behave as if she were indeed already married to Struensee. She sat with him at table, walked out with him and even endured his infidelities.

On 7 July, Caroline Mathilde felt her first labour pains. Her second labour was more like that of a private woman than that of a queen. The host of officials and onlookers who usually attended a royal birth were completely absent. There were no ministers of the Church either; a male *accoucheur* but no midwife. It was Struensee, in his old role as doctor and his new one as a kind of husband, who was there throughout. One of his hands held one of hers. The other he put under her neck, supporting her through the contractions and talking to her through her pain. As her maid Cathrine Boye noticed, Caroline Mathilde looked steadily into Struensee's face, drawing her confidence from his own. After her daughter, who was also Struensee's daughter, had slithered into the world, and everyone had gone away to allow them to recover, Caroline Mathilde ordered Boye to bring her pocket book in which she kept the portrait of Struensee, and gazed at it as if he had not just left. During her month's confinement, Struensee came regularly, drinking his tea and coffee and eating alone with her.

Caroline Mathilde named her daughter Louise Augusta. Louise remembered both Christian's mother and sister, and Caroline Mathilde's own sister Louisa Anne, who had died three years before. Augusta was for her sister the Duchess of Brunswick and, out of politeness, her mother the Princess Dowager, who wrote to congratulate her daughter in her execrable diplomatic French, as if they were now the representatives of two nations speaking to one another.

As if to make a record of the new three-cornered marriage that they now all lived in, Caroline Mathilde and Struensee commissioned, about this time, a trio of matching oval portraits of themselves and King Christian. Each was single in its frame but they formed a group: a wife and two husbands. The commission was given to the twenty-six-year-old Jens Juel, who would subsequently mature into the country's most expressive and successful portrait painter. Juel had painted Caroline Mathilde in 1768 in a fur-edged gown and ruched bonnet, looking out over her left shoulder, withdrawn and girlish. In 1771 he painted her in the same pose. But this time she was mature woman and looked far older than her nineteen years in the portrait. The same slightly protuberant Hanoverian eyes gazed out, but now something mocking and challenging was added to their hooded languor. Her mouth, cherry-like and smiling up at the corners in the earlier portrait, was now full, straight and determined. For a queen, her clothing was modest again: matching jewels in her ears and holding back her grey silk veil, a single gathered line of lace round her low neckline. Half under a loose silk bow at her bosom hung the insignium of a new noble order she had created a few months earlier, the Order of Mathilde, a pink ribbon striped with silver, and, hanging from it, a medallion topped with a crown and a sinuous M picked out in diamonds.

Christian, with silvery powdered hair and raised collar, also looked much older than twenty-two, stiff and rigid in his frame. His face was pinched and thin, his body flat and stiff, as if the painter had used a mannequin to paint from and not the King himself. It was Struensee who seemed to have looked most directly and openly at the painter. He posed for Juel sitting straight on, with his bull head turned slightly to the left and inclined just a little forwards, as if he were listening as well as being looked at, open and engaged at the same time. He wore the Order of Mathilde too, but was otherwise simply dressed in a dark blue frock-coat and waistcoat with lace borders and large round gold buttons.

Presenting himself thus, Struensee seemed not to be flaunting the two new titles he had accrued in the middle of 1771. But, on 22 July, when Princess Louise Augusta was christened, he and Enevold Brandt were both ennobled, becoming counts. The honour confirmed suspicions that he was the baby's father and that Caroline Mathilde rather than Christian was responsible for the honour. His other title, however, she did not want him to take, and made plain her opposition to his actions some months later. A week before the christening, on 14 July, Christian had issued a decree that brought Struensee out from behind the chimera of royal governance, making him Privy Cabinet minister and announcing that 'all orders which I [Christian] may give him orally shall be drawn up by him in accordance with my meaning, and he shall lay them before me for signature, or issue them in my name'. Struensee, it was obvious, had wearied of the charade of absolutism and had decided to do away with the need to force an unwilling and sometimes incapacitated King Christian to sign every decree. Struensee's action may have been a first indication that he had begun to mistrust his associates, because it meant that none of them could go to Christian independently and put a decree for signature in front of him. The decree also declared that all orders that went out to the new government departments, or colleges, should be signed by Struensee himself, 'and no longer effected through an order in the college'.

By striking Christian out of the day-to-day workings of the government and by elevating himself above his colleagues, Struensee made himself dangerously exposed to hostility from bureaucrats and ordinary people whose support for the monarchy was unwavering and whose affection for the King deep-seated. The new British envoy Robert Murray Keith concluded in his first long dispatch from Copenhagen at the end of June 1771, 'the whole attention of the public (hitherto divided between three or four persons) will from henceforth be turned on Mr Struensee alone'.

Keith had not had an easy beginning to his new posting. Robert Gunning was leaving sad and disgruntled. He had lost his wife in Copenhagen and also his professional pride. 'I am sorry, my dear G, to find you so dispirited', a friend wrote from Munich in May 1771, adding, 'God knows I did not mean to upbraid you as guilty of reserve.' Gunning's sense of failure made him hostile to his successor and prompted him to drive a hard bargain with Keith for the contents of his sumptuous residence in Amalienborg. Keith had written on 6 April about the cost of the lease on the house, and added, emolliently and unwisely, 'Your wines, coach houses and kitchen utensils I shall take at whatever price you put on them.' Gunning took him at his word. 'I have hired Mr Gunning's house', Keith told his father when he had arrived, 'and the impossibility of finding a furnished one here made it *absolutely necessary* for me to purchase his furniture, for which I paid him, two days ago, five hundred and twelve pounds! From this one ruinous article you may judge of the rest . . . Climate, comfort, society, *all against me* – the ruin of my fortune into the bargain would be too hard.'

As Gunning probably knew, Keith was not a rich man, having spent his life in the rougher side of service to the Crown. He was a veteran of the Seven Years War, a worldly-wise and well-connected soldier. His father had been ambassador to the courts of Vienna and St Petersburg for many years, before retiring to the austere splendour of Edinburgh's New Town and the society of writers and philosophers. In 1747 he had got his seventeen-year-old son a commission in a Scottish regiment in the service of the Dutch Crown, where Keith stayed for five years before transferring to the German army under the command of Prince Karl of Brunswick. Picking up languages, commissions and military glory along the way, Keith ended up a lieutenant-colonel and commanding officer of the 78th Foot, a Highland regiment fighting in Germany.

Stood down and put on half-pay when the Seven Years War ended with the Peace of 1763, Keith idled away some time in Paris, before settling in London and joining the 'gang' around Richard Rigby. Known as a war hero, but ambitious too for a softer sort of fame, Keith wrote music and poetry, eventually publishing three volumes of strictly regulated verse in 1773. But the stipend of a half-pay officer was never going to be enough to keep up with the hard-living jollity of his London circle. So, with no prospect of another war, Keith decided to shift into the diplomatic service. On the recommendation of his friend Henry Seymour Conway and to the fury of career diplomats on cheerless postings all round northern Europe, he was appointed British minister to the court of Saxony in 1769.

Keith saw himself as a man of action grown hardened in nearly twenty years as a serving and half-pay soldier and a romantic who hoped to settle down one day. He was at ease in male company and remained a bachelor, a man about town with a mistress in London and friends around the world. 'I certainly am a good-natured fat gentleman, and the forlorn state of an old bachelor has not yet soured my soul', he wrote to one of his sisters when he was thirty-nine and had just arrived in Dresden. He made the most of his single state there, amusing himself with concerts, balls, drinking and brisk solitary walks in the countryside. Bedded down at the small court, pampered by its women and soothed by its heavy wines, its music and its cards, he was half reluctant to take the promotion to Copenhagen. Even before he had got there and read the papers waiting for him, he wrote to a friend, 'I am very willing to exert my utmost powers for the King's service in Denmark, but it is not to be expected that I should wish to make a long stay in that most comfortless country.'

No one made Keith's task easy in Copenhagen, and there were plenty of people waiting for him to fail. Foremost among them was Ralph Woodford, who had perhaps hoped for Dresden himself and certainly longed to get out of the spies' nest of Hamburg. Woodford described himself to Gunning as 'going grey in the service without having ever received a reward'. He resented Keith's sudden elevation and described him with ironic underlining to Gunning as 'our friend Mr Keith'. So he was happy to report to Gunning in the autumn of 1771, 'I do not find Keith is in any degree of favour either with Br, the Q, or S' – Brandt, the Queen or Struensee – and added, to emphasise his loyalty to his friend, 'I have never had a line nor ever desire to from him.'

It was perfectly true that neither Caroline Mathilde nor Struensee had any particular interest in the success of Keith's mission. Keith inherited from Gunning the fiction of her innocence, and would risk much by bluntly over-turning it. But the story of an innocent woman corrupted also appealed to his temperament as a gallant man who believed that men and women occu-pied different worlds. It was difficult for him to believe that, far from being cowed or imposed upon by Struensee, Caroline Mathilde was happier than ever before and had absolutely no wish to be separated from her lover through the agency of the British Crown. The notion, fondly maintained in London, that Struensee might somehow be persuaded to step aside and leave the country and that Bernstorff might then return, was founded upon the fable of the Queen's innocence. Because of that, if for no other reason, it was bound to fail. When Caroline Mathilde refused to see Keith alone and declined all invitations to confide in him, she was behaving not as Struensee ordered, but as she herself wished. The story invented by Robert Gunning, promulgated by Robert Keith, gratefully accepted by embarrassed officials in London and fiercely believed by George III, was already producing nonsense and would soon produce confusion.

London pursued its hopeless approach to Bernstorff in exile. A letter was sent to him through Robert Gunning in Berlin, declaring on behalf of George III that the King wanted to see the elder statesman return as Danish Prime Minister, and that 'nothing will be left unattempted that can contribute to replace you in that situation'. Keith, meanwhile, could only watch and grumble from the sidelines. Convinced that his letters to Lord Suffolk in London were being intercepted and copied, he took to sending his dispatches via Elsinore or Hamburg. 'My situation', he told his father in August, 'is exactly the same as when I dispatched my first letter. An intercourse of an hour, once a week, with the court – a formal supper once in a fortnight with the fashionable people – make the whole of my public appearances.' Alone in Amalienborg, with only Shakespeare for company, Keith had ample time to ponder whatever was rotten in the state of Denmark. Like many of his countrymen for whom Shakespeare was historian as well as dramatist and poet, Keith was only too happy to accept Hamlet's own hostile assessment of his countrymen. 'A man may smile and smile, and be a villain' in Denmark, Keith wrote to his father, and added, as if Shakespeare's Elsinore and his own were one and the same, 'Hamlet knew his countrymen.'

It was not surprising that Keith soon began to see cunningly concealed villainy everywhere. Struensee, whom he had first described as 'assiduous to the greatest degree, enterprising and intrepid', he now called a 'malignant leveller', a man intent on pulling down the recognised structures of Danish society. Besides that, he was offended by Struensee's apparent unfaithfulness to Caroline Mathilde despite the 'unlimited confidence' she had given him. Probably correctly, Keith surmised that Struensee's beliefs had a single root, his denial of the afterlife and consequent insistence than man could shape his own conduct and his own future. 'His morals are founded on this single principle', he wrote to London on 29 October, 'that a man's duties begin and [end] with himself, <u>and in this life</u>. The weakness of avowing openly a secret so profligate and dangerous, can only be equalled by the ingratitude with which he has acted upon it in his haughty and imperious behaviour to the person who, with unwearied perseverance, continued to heap upon him all possible obligations.'

Whatever Caroline Mathilde's response to Struensee's insistence that, as he himself put it, 'the happiness of a human consists in the freedom to express his desires', their bond was not loosened by his infidelities, nor by the hostile response that they provoked in some sections of the court. Indeed, Keith wrote in astonishment, the Queen's 'partiality for Count Struensee seemed to gather strength from opposition'.

Most of the opposition, though, continued to be political. Struensee's reforms ran on apace in the autumn of 1771. Some were primarily economic, like the disbanding and re-formation into one body of two ceremonial troops of the Household Cavalry and the King's Guard. Money was saved, but the economy threw many officers onto half-pay and into instant opposition. Others were, once again, social. Having already curbed the powers of the police, Struensee further clipped the wings of the judiciary by declaring that adultery trials could no longer be brought by the authorities, but only by a directly interested party, an injured husband or wife.

Many of Struensee's huge number of decrees proved difficult to enact. A whole political class had been swept away and the new ranks of career civil servants brought in to replace them struggled to cope with the burden. Bolle Luxdorph described an episode of 'bloody fighting in the chamber' of the Finance Ministry, a protracted quarrel first of words, with sheets of written complaint by one official about another, then of anger and raised voices and blows. Keith, reporting hearsay from inside the new departments, wrote to London at the end of September 1771, 'It would seem as if the genius of the

Prime Minister had wasted itself in the hasty strides made to gain the summit of power. Daily experience shows us that he has formed no steady plan either with regard to the interior affairs of Denmark or her foreign connections. From such a man it is natural to expect the most decisive and even headlong acts would distinguish an administration of which he had the sole direction; instead of which, the business accumulates in every department of state, and only a few desultory steps have been taken, which lead to no important or permanent consequences.'

One reason for tension in the College of Finance was that despite constant economies, spending was still not under control. The men Struensee had brought in, including his brother Carl August, were able and committed. But court entertainments were as splendid as ever, harvests had been poor and damp, and, worst of all, the state was engaged in a complex and expensive war in the Mediterranean.

For hundreds of years, the Barbary States of North Africa had been raiding shipping in the Mediterranean, taking prisoners and demanding and extracting tributes from northern European powers. Despite their hugely superior navies, northern states had been more willing to pay tributes of both cash and gifts than to wage war, partly because the costs were lower in the end, partly because catching the corsairs was arduous and partly because blockades and bombardments of well-fortified Barbary capitals were difficult and often ineffective. In 1766 the new dey, or ruler, of Algiers, Baba Mohammed ben-Osman, demanded new gifts on top of those usually paid. The Danish government under Bernstorff had handed over some extra presents but balked at giving everything the dey demanded. For over three years the Danish consul in Algiers stalled and ben-Osman threatened. Finally, at the beginning of September 1769, he declared war, taking several ships and their sailors as hostages.

The response of the Danish government was desultory and inadequate. On 3 May 1770 a squadron of four ships of the line accompanied by two frigates, two bomb ketches, a transport and a hospital ship finally set off from Copenhagen, but its bombardment of Algiers was ineffective, its sailors fell sick and its bomb ketches were damaged by the heavy recoil of the guns they carried. After Bernstorff's dismissal, the unsatisfactory and expensive action dragged on. Perhaps to demonstrate to Denmark's allies and enemies alike that he was no less ambitious than Bernstorff for the honour of the nation, and no less prudent about the need to protect its trade, Struensee allowed the war to continue. In defiance of his own policy of economy he ordered the construction of eight flat-bottomed bomb ketches, which would be sailed to the Mediterranean, anchored beyond the range of the dey's gun emplacements and used to pound Algiers into surrender.

In the naval dockyard the work ran late. In September 1771, the double skins of oak that formed the hulls of the first two ketches were still being fitted onto their sturdy rib-cages. The Norwegian crews who had been brought to Copenhagen to man the ships milled around restlessly. There were always soldiers and sailors on the streets of the city: Life Guards garrisoned in the new barracks in Sølvgade, seamen waiting for orders to embark or visiting the naval hospital, and troops billeted on grudging householders. But the Norwegians were different, unpaid, unemployed and angry. In the second week of September a group of them decided to petition the King for their wages and marched out to Hirschholm in a posse two hundred-strong.

News of their march arrived ahead of them. Struensee and Caroline Mathilde feared an insurrection and the royal family, along with Struensee, Brandt and a few servants, hurriedly decamped to a neighbouring estate, Sophienberg, a couple of miles away. They left Hirschholm in a straggling line of carriages, driving away in obvious haste. Rumours quickly followed, and suggested that the Queen and Struensee had discussed with their friends Otto von Falkenskjold and Anne Sophie von Bülow the possibility of fleeing to the fortress of Kronborg. But more prosaically and plausibly, they sent an aide-de-camp to negotiate with the sailors who had begun to crowd up to the closed ornamental gates of the castle. Pacified with a promise of full redress, the Norwegians trudged back to Copenhagen, to a liberal distribution of spirits and a full restitution of their unpaid wages.

Though the stories of panic may have been false, the court's short flight from Hirschholm to Sophienberg was undeniable, and showed the first narrow fissure in the edifice of Struensee's administration and the way of life that was bound so closely to it. Pamphleteers began vigorously to use the freedom of the press against the government that had granted it, and hostile observers like Robert Murray Keith began to take heart. "It has been whispered about', Keith wrote to Lord Suffolk on 25 September, 'that, upon the late disturbances . . . [Struensee] betrayed some unexpected signs of fear, and the natural result of this suspicion is to loosen the attachment of persons whom he has trusted, and to diminish the awe which is necessary for the maintenance of his unbounded authority.' But Struensee had no fears about any personal enemies he might have made. He was far more fearful of popular unrest that might compromise, if not defeat, the pace and objectives of his reforms. Two weeks after the sailors' march on Hirschholm, a hundred weavers protested in their turn about the closure of the royal silk manufactures. They too were placated. Struensee ordered that silk production would be resumed until other work had been found for them.

The dockyard workers posed the biggest problem. Thousands of them laboured and lived around the naval yards on Nyholm, and at the wharfs at Gammelholm within sight of Christiansborg, and at Flådens Leje, where the ships of the line lay at anchor in the winter. While they recaulked hulls, replaced barnacled and rotten timbers and repaired rigging in the bitter winter winds, they were always likely to foment their grievances too, and their numbers made them formidable in dispute. New regulations, partly designed to speed up the work on ships destined for Algiers, had particularly incensed them, and the government decided on a 'festival of reconciliation' for them, intending to dilute any tension in schnapps and to add feasting and dancing for the sailors and their families. An appearance by the royal family was promised, but at the last minute Struensee received a report that unknown enemies planned to assassinate him as he mingled with the crowd.

According to his memoirs, Otto von Falkenskjold advised Struensee to go to the festival and walk about undaunted. But he seized the moment to suggest that Struensee be more cautious, go more slowly with his reforms and stop unpopular measures. Brandt backed him up, but Struensee was adamant. 'No,' he replied, at least in Falkenskjold's account, 'no! I will give up nothing that promotes the welfare of the state.' He did not take Falkenskjold's advice about the festival either. None of the royal party went to Copenhagen that day, and the sailors were left to drink and dance alone.

As winter advanced, Caroline Mathilde and Struensee lingered in the country, heavily guarded and nursing a mood of fatalistic levity. Reverdil wrote that some time after the fiasco of the 'festival of reconciliation', Brandt went round the small party asking each of them how they would survive if they were forced to flee. For his own part, he declared, he would carry on his life as the manager of a theatre. Struensee, still nursing his fading dream of agricultural reform, said he would take a farm far away from Copenhagen and live on it, 'as a philosopher'. Caroline Mathilde, who shared her family's talent for music and had a fine voice, said she would become a singer, a profession which could be lucrative but was scarcely ever respectable.

Belatedly, Struensee attempted to dissipate popular hostility. The Norwegian sailors, still without employment, were sent home on half-pay. Christiansborg was guarded more tightly and visibly than before and, after Christmas, when the court had returned to Copenhagen, the King and Queen were closely protected whenever they went out. Robert Murray Keith noted in his dispatch of 7 January 1772 that, 'the apprehensions of the Prime Minister are very visible by the warlike parade with which the court is surrounded. Dragoons are posted on the market places and patrols in the streets. Twelve pieces of cannon are kept constantly loaded in the Arsenal. The entrance to the French Playhouse is lined with soldiers, and their Majesties, in going from the palace to the Opera House, though the distance is not above three hundred yards, are escorted by an officer and 36 dragoons.' About himself, though, the doctor was headstrong, telling Falkenskjold, 'The purity of my views is my protection.' Although he made sure that the King and Queen were guarded from an angry public, he was heedless about his own safety within the royal palaces themselves. No guards walked with him in Christiansborg in the daytime, and at night he slept in his mezzanine quarters with only his valet between himself and attack. All his reading had failed to warn him that regimes are destroyed by inner collapse as much as from outside tumult. So, although he made a half-hearted attempt to stop criticism of his government in the press and curtail anonymously written satires, he took no action where it was needed most, within his own circle. Perhaps baffled that an administration founded upon a doctrine of removing all forms of restraint and constriction from individuals should have come itself, after less than eighteen months, to a state of fear and suspicion, he disdained to impugn the loyalty of his own advisers. Haughtily committing himself to the public good, Struensee could not believe that messy personal ambition, so much like his own, might sully a project unprecedented in Europe. But, by the end of 1771, not just many officials, but friends too, were preparing to abandon the government and jettison any idealism they might have had left.

This volatile situation was further inflamed by Struensee's decision, just before Christmas, to disband the Life Guards who protected the monarch and the palace of Christiansborg. The regiment of Life Guards was an elite corps which made much of its traditions. Its officers, much like their British counterparts, were young men from noble families. Rather than let themselves be absorbed into other regiments, as Struensee ordered, the Life Guards mutinied and occupied Christiansborg. Copenhagen's citizens rallied to them, sending food and sympathy up to the palace. Struensee backed down, offering the men free discharge, and not insisting that they join other regiments. But the incident was further proof to any waverers that their futures might be better secured by inclining towards a new administration than by remaining loyal to a faltering experiment.

By the autumn of 1771, Struensee's enemies were gathering. Coalescing around Schack Carl Rantzau, who carefully maintained a veneer of loyalty to his friend, they were men made bold by discontent and ambition. Foremost amongst them were the army officers Hans Henrik Eickstedt and Georg Ludwig Köller; Hereditary Prince Frederik's private secretary Ove Guldberg; the army officer and adventurer Magnus Beringskjold; and the bureaucrat Joachim Otto Schack-Ratlou. The presence of the army officers was vital not only to secure Christiansborg Palace itself, but also to demonstrate decisive control of the capital and the state. Between them, Eickstedt's Zealand Dragoons and Köller's Holstein Guards shared the task of guarding Christiansborg, and sometimes they were on duty at the same time.

If Guldberg, Beringskjold and even Rantzau were prompted to start a conspiracy from motives more personal than political, the Queen Dowager stood firmly opposed to everything that Struensee and Caroline Mathilde represented. Struensee's enemies turned to her because, with her son seventeen-year-old Prince Frederik, she gave both gravitas and a royal authority to the rapidly growing conspiracy. Juliane Marie was forty-two years old, upright and stiff, temperamentally and politically averse to the gold-plated informality of the little court at Hirschholm. Caroline Mathilde and Struensee had both made it abundantly clear over the years that they had little interest in the ceremonious royalty that she upheld, and despised its religiosity, its stately dignity and its rigid etiquette. Although Juliane Marie and Prince Frederik were regularly invited to Hirschholm during the long summer residence in 1771, they were pointedly left out of the remade royal family, and when they did come they were welcomed with neither warmth nor ceremony. In so radically changing her life, Caroline Mathilde had broken not only with her mother and siblings in England, but with the whole closely woven northern European royal family, of which the Hanoverians were just a part. Juliane Marie came from Brunswick, where Caroline Mathilde's sister was duchess, so any snub to Juliane Marie was also felt in the small palace there, and washed back through all the territories with which it was dynastically linked, including Berlin, Hesse, London, The Hague and Hanover.

Juliane Marie agreed to put herself forward as the titular head of any plot against Struensee and the Queen after Rantzau and Beringskjold had sent her an address in October 1771 which made their intentions clear enough to bring her out from her studied retirement from the court. On 7 October she apparently wrote to her son Prince Frederik, in an English that neither of them used or spoke, 'The Almighty has chosen [you] to be the instrument by which your brother the king . . . [may] be fortified on his throne, and the subjects have in you an inferior [member of the royal family] who may plead their causes . . . Be not horrified at the danger you should meet with.' Prince Frederik agreed to let his name too be associated with the conspirators, and it added more weight to their cause.

The plotters knew that success depended on three elements: ensuring that the whole of Christiansborg was under their control; seizing Struensee, Brandt and Caroline Mathilde; and, most importantly, getting quickly to King Christian and inducing him to sign whatever papers would give their coup a semblance of legality. Rantzau and Beringskjold may have put the idea of a conspiracy forward, but detailed planning was left to Ove Guldberg, a careful, religious man who was unshakeably loyal both to the royal family in the person of the King and to the idea of Denmark as a nation unsullied by German-speaking outsiders. Guldberg soon came to see himself as the instrument chosen by God to save his country and his king from outside influence and irreligiosity.

By the time the conspirators all met together on 13 January, a simple plan had been formed. They agreed that they would strike on the night of 16 January, when a grand masquerade was to be held. Any comings and goings would be unnoticed in the crowds arriving at the theatre and the King and Queen, as well as Struensee and Brandt, were all sure to be under one roof. Soldiers under the command of Eickstedt and Köller would secure the palace, the King be seized and surprised with a series of warrants to sign, and then Struensee, Brandt, Caroline Mathilde and their closest associates be arrested one by one. The plotters had taken the temperature of the city of Copenhagen and the army well. They had no reason to fear any uprising in favour of the Queen, and they knew that Struensee had neglected his own safety, as if flagrantly daring his enemies to do their worst.

Once arrested, the prisoners would have to be dispatched from

Christiansborg under guard. Struensee, Brandt and their closest male advisers would be taken to the citadel, others confined to their homes. Crown Prince Frederik would have to stay at Christiansborg. Guldberg, with his characteristic reverence for royalty, did not want Caroline Mathilde roughly treated, and suggested that she be confined at Hirschholm and that the six-month-old Princess Louise, whom she was still breast-feeding, should be allowed to go with her. Juliane Marie, though, was adamant that Caroline Mathilde should be transported so far away from the King that it would be impossible for him to reach her. She demanded that the Queen be sent to the biggest fortress of them all, Kronborg, which sat as far away from Copenhagen as any castle on the island of Zealand, was inaccessible through its banks of earthworks and was guarded against land and sea attack by heavy cannon. The Dowager Queen got her way, the plan was agreed and the conspirators dispersed.

The masquerade in the Royal Theatre on 16 January 1772 was neatly emblematic of the way of life that Struensee and Caroline Mathilde stood for. Expensive, luxurious and free-wheeling, it was at the same time open to all of Copenhagen's citizens who could afford a ticket, and its doors stood open even though soldiers guarded its entrance and the streets round about. Under Enevold Brandt's direction, the Royal Theatre had been splendidly decorated. It had walls of pearly white, and gilded columns supported two tiers of rounded boxes that flounced round the auditorium like the ruchings on a ball gown. Brandt raised the floor to the level of the stage and stacked away the benches to make one long horseshoe-shaped space for looking and dancing. High above on the ceiling, a summer sky sailed through creamy clouds and gilded sunbeams. Thousands of candles burned steadily in fluted glass shades along the corridors and up the stairs, doubled in the mirrors which ran round the walls at the back of the stage.

At eight in the evening the conspirators and guests began to arrive. Ove Guldberg came quietly, with the documents he had written for Christian to sign hidden in his muff. In the theatre boxes, tables were set for cards. But Caroline Mathilde, who arrived at ten o'clock with the King and Struensee, preferred to dance, turning across the floor with her lover in joyous high spirits. It was reported that when Prince Frederik arrived an hour later, Caroline Mathilde, noticing his flushed and strained face, said gaily, 'You've arrived very late, brother; what have you been doing?', to which the Prince replied, 'I have had some business to attend to.' 'It seems to me', said Caroline

Mathilde, as if she had been called to write an epitaph on her brief happiness, 'that you ought to think more of pleasure than of business on the night of a ball.'

Reverdil reported that Prince Frederik was not invited to dine in the royal box where Caroline Mathilde and Struensee sat with the King and their friends against the backdrop of plush purple hangings, but was forced to queue at the buffet with the ordinary guests. But, despite the slight, Prince Frederik stayed grimly on, through supper and cards and dancing. At twelve the King retired. But it was three in the morning before everyone else had left and Enevold Brandt, as manager of the theatre, gave the order to lower the chandeliers and extinguish the candles one by one.

An hour later, after creeping through the penumbral spaces of the great palace, the conspirators met in the apartments of Queen Juliane Marie. By four o'clock eight people were gathered, already secure in the knowledge that Eickstedt and Köller had stationed guards at all the palace gates, stopping up both entry and escape. Besides Juliane Marie herself, her son Frederik and the two officers Köller and Eickstedt, there was an ex-valet, Jessen, who knew the geography of the palace on the darkest of nights, and Rantzau, Beringskjold and Guldberg. In the dim light of the Queen Dowager's parlour, Guldberg reminded each of the men there of his duty and, kneeling with them, called upon God to bless their enterprise.

Guided by Jessen, with two softly hissing torches to light their way, Juliane Marie, Prince Frederik, Ove Guldberg, Rantzau and Beringskjold, accompanied by several armed soldiers, carefully walked the short distance from the Queen Dowager's rooms to the apartments of the King. In the ante-chamber Christian's valet, Brieghel, was soundly sleeping. Roused by one of the conspirators, Brieghel agreed, with a mixture of fear and sympathy, to wake the King. But Christian slept on his own, with the door locked from the inside. So the whole party had to tip-toe up to the mezzanine floor, down again and up the servants' staircase to the tiny ante-room where the chambermaids filled the stove in Christian's bedroom from the outside, and where there was another door, to which, presumably, Brieghel had the key.

The King's bedchamber, with its inlaid parquet floor and hangings where golden dragons flew in skies of blue damask, was in darkness. In the torch-light the gilding on the doors and the panelling glimmered softly. The great bed with its heavy canopy was set against the back wall, separated from the rest of the room by a golden balustrade. In its depths, Christian slept, small and vulnerable. All his life he had lived in fear of the night and of beings who might materialise from the inky blackness and threaten him. Now that they had come, he started up in bed and cried out in terror. 'My son, Your Majesty,' Juliane Marie then began, according to the account later written up by Köller, 'we are not here as enemies, but as your true friends.' But, overcome herself with fear and emotion, she could not go on, and Rantzau was thrust forward to explain to the cowering King that his stepmother and half-brother came to liberate him and to free the nation.

Characteristically Christian then seemed to lose both interest in and understanding of what was happening. He called for a glass of water, asked whether Eickstedt were there too, and only demurred a little when he was told that Caroline Mathilde was plotting against his life. Rantzau pulled from his pocket the two orders written by Guldberg for Christian to sign. This, to the King, was a familiar duty, even if he was not usually called to perform it in darkness and in bed. Although he was said to have exclaimed, 'My God, this will cost streams of blood,' he sat up against his pillows and wrote out his name, as he had done countless times before.

These first two decrees, countersigned by Prince Frederik, gave the conspirators all the powers they needed to take over the country. Having thus, with a simple movement of his hand, handed the government from Struensee and Caroline Mathilde to Juliane Marie, his half-brother and their followers, the King got up, was dressed by Brieghel and was led away to Prince Frederik's apartments on the floor above, newly captive and fearful enough now to sign anything put in front of him. Later many of these documents, along with all the conspirators' written plans, disappeared: Guldberg, despite his faith in divine intervention, wanted to make sure that if the earthly powers turned against him, there was no evidence of what he had done.

Once he was sure that his fellow conspirators had made their way successfully to the King's chamber, Köller, accompanied by a band of soldiers from the palace guard, marched without either stealth or ceremony to Struensee's apartments on the mezzanine floor. Struensee's rooms were luridly described by pamphleteers as hung with damask, winking with silver and mirrors and with curtains and bed-curtains of deep purple velvet fringed with gold. Despite this magnificence, however, they were unguarded. Only his valet lay between Struensee and an intruder, and Köller and his soldiers easily forced the young man to open first the ante-chamber and then the door of the doctor's bedroom.

A book lay on the floor by Struensee's bed and his ball clothes were heaped up on a chair; he had undressed and read himself to sleep. When Köller prodded him awake and ordered him to get up, Struensee blustered and then demanded to see the warrant for his arrest. 'Do you know who I am?' Köller reported him as saying. When Köller threatened him at sword point, he was said first to have asked for time to think, then for a cup of chocolate, and only when that was peremptorily refused did he agree to surrender and to dress. Köller, thinking that his valet would try to help Struensee escape, refused to allow them to go into the adjoining closet to choose new clothes. Struensee was forced to put on what lay on the chair, his shimmering rose-coloured breeches and a coat and waistcoat of fine light-blue velvet. Hustled by Köller's soldiers, he was led out and down to the courtyard below.

Once Struensee had been arrested, a Colonel Sames, recently discharged from his post as commandant of Copenhagen, set off to find the sleeping Brandt. Unlike his friend, Brandt had sensed the change of mood in Copenhagen and had said to Falkenskjold months before at Hirschholm, 'I have a sentiment that this regime will soon be overthrown.' When Falkenskjold replied that Brandt would be in trouble if it was, Brandt said insouciantly that he had studied the law and would be able to take care of himself. So, when Sames came knocking on his door, he opened it, meeting his captors with a drawn sword, and said with confident aplomb, 'I am a minister of state, and have committed no crime for which I can be arrested.' Sames told him he was acting on the orders of the King, to which Brandt replied simply, 'Very well, I will follow you quietly,' and made no more resistance.

Writers telling the story later, with only Köller's account to follow, were happy to take his lead in playing off the two endings against one another. Brandt, the theatre manager and jester, light-hearted and bold, was an aristocrat at heart; Struensee, the upstart and voluptuary, was angry and fearful, cutting a poor and shameful figure: Brandt the Dane and Struensee the German, the one warrior-like in the face of misfortune, the other weak and full of regret. The idea of Struensee's demanding hot chocolate at four in the morning, with the kitchens closed, his valet arrested and his life in danger, was surely a grace note, added to show that he was a confirmed voluptuary for whom sensual indulgence came before everything else. In similar vein, Brandt's aristocratic self-possession was thrown into high relief with the nice detail that before leaving his apartment, he put his flute into a pocket – or perhaps slipped it down the length of his breeches – so that he might amuse himself in whatever captivity awaited him.

Soon, both prisoners, heavily guarded, were bundled into two carriages. Flanked by mounted guards, Struensee in the first carriage and Brandt in the second, they were driven out of Christiansborg. The night, as many later remembered, was very cold and still. Frost glazed the city and shards of ice gathered, crystal by crystal, in the water of the harbours and canals. The small convoy turned quickly north outside the palace, driving through Charlottenborg, flanking the new quarter of Amalienborg, where Robert Murray Keith slept unknowing in Robert Gunning's mansion. At the city's edge was Kastellet, the fortress, sunk in its star-shaped ramparts and five gun-topped bastions. The buildings themselves were modest, stuccoed and painted barn-red, but with the drawbridge up and the gatehouse guarded, the compound was impregnable, unless perhaps it were bombarded from the sea. By five-thirty in the morning, Brandt and Struensee were locked into bare cells. Before the day was out they were shackled and chained, bound hand to foot and then to the wall like common criminals.

In the Queen Dowager's apartments, King Christian had been signing his name with abandon. Arrest warrants were soon made up for everyone in the circle around Caroline Mathilde and Struensee. In the next few hours, Otto von Falkenskjold, Struensee's brothers Carl August and Adam, Lieutenant-General von Gëhler and his wife, Major-General Gude, Rear-Admiral Hansen, the cabinet secretary von Zoëga, Struensee's old friend and private secretary David Panning and half a dozen other members of the government were taken to gaol or put under house arrest.

Morning was approaching and the conspirators still had to deal with Caroline Mathilde herself. The King had written her a note in the past tense, which would be presented to her when she was arrested. It told her what was going to happen as if it was already a fait accompli. 'Madam,' he wrote, putting one ungainly phrase after another, 'I have found it necessary to send you to Kronborg, your conduct obliges me to it. I am very sorry, I am not the cause, and I hope you will sincerely repent.' Christian signed and dated it, 17 January 1771, forgetting that the year had already turned. Perhaps it did indeed seem to him that everything had already happened long ago. Then from Guldberg's drafts he copied one order for his wife's arrest, another for the head of the royal stables to prepare the coaches for her removal and a third to Andreas Hauch, the commandant of Kronborg Castle, telling him to prepare an apartment for her.

When the ball had finished, Caroline Mathilde had gone to the nursery to feed her hungry six-month-old daughter Louise. When Rantzau, accompanied by the King's valet Brieghel, knocked on her doors at seven o'clock, she was still fast asleep and so was Ansbach, her chambermaid. No one wanted to walk straight in on the sleeping Queen, and, after a consultation, Brieghel woke Ansbach up and ordered her, at seven-thirty, to go into the Queen's bedroom and tell her that Rantzau and other officers were waiting in the ante-chamber. Caroline Mathilde immediately understood why. Her mind ran to the man she loved, thinking both of his safety and of his protection. Jumping out of bed, not bothering to dress, she ran straight out of the room. 'Where is the Count? Where is the Count?' she shouted loudly, as if hoping that he could hear her. Rantzau, flanked by three soldiers, said nothing, bowed and handed her the King's note.

Unlike Brandt and Struensee, who went quietly with their captors, Caroline Mathilde fought fiercely. She was outraged, as queen, at the way she was being treated, and furious, as a woman, at her own powerlessness. First Rantzau's soldiers and then her own maids had to restrain her as she hit out and tried to escape. Rantzau stood back from the scuffles while Caroline Mathilde ran first one way and then another like a cornered animal. Her maids were sent to fetch her clothes and eventually she allowed herself to be dressed. But then she jumped up again, and tried to run along the corridor to the staircase that led Struensee's apartment below.

Rantzau decided he needed someone in the room whom the Queen might at least listen to, and so Osten was hastily called upstairs. Awake to the conspiracy and prudently siding with its immediate successes, Osten persuaded Caroline Mathilde that she had no choice but to comply with the contents of the King's note. Defeated, shocked and emotionally drained, she agreed. But she still had the presence of mind to capitulate only on condition that her children were allowed to go with her to Kronborg. They were both the objects of her love and the guarantors of her safety and she knew that she must insist on having them with her. She had no idea what had happened to Struensee or where he was. If she read Christian's note with any attention she must have realised that he was only listlessly complying with the demands of the men in front of her, but she may not have had time or the presence of mind to look too carefully at the way her husband wrote.

Osten, evidently aware of the discussion on 13 January, refused to allow Crown Prince Frederik to leave Christiansborg. He knew as well as the Queen that handing her the Prince gave into her hands both the future of Denmark and a symbol of legitimacy that the new regime could not afford to be without. With the Prince, moreover, Caroline Mathilde could appeal to the people as a mother who deserved their sympathy. Little Louise Augusta, though, was another matter. Although acknowledged by Christian as his daughter, and described as such to all the crowned heads of Europe, she was widely regarded as illegitimate and contemptuously called, 'la petite Struensee'. Giving her to Caroline Mathilde made little difference to the conspirators now and they could always remove her later if they wanted. Besides, Louise was still being breast-fed, and one person the conspirators had not thought to recruit to their cause was a wet-nurse. The little Princess might languish and suffer while one was found and the new government did not want any impediments, no matter how tiny, to their progress. Most of all, allowing Caroline Mathilde to take her daughter might induce her to go more quietly.

So Osten gave the Queen Princess Louise in exchange for her compliance. At nine o'clock, as Caroline Mathilde left Christiansborg, she sat in the carriage with her arms wrapped tightly round her daughter, holding in her love and warding off the cold. A single lady-in-waiting, von Mösting, went with them, and the small convoy was accompanied by a detachment of dragoons riding several deep around it. To the left of the carriages, beyond the city, the leafless stands of lime, beech, oak and ash parted to reveal neat farms, half-timbered and deep in mud. To the right, when the sun had come up over the Baltic, slices of ruffled water glinted, colourless and translucent, with lacy lengths of wave turning on the narrow shore. Lumps of ice floated here and there, and in another fortnight the island of Zealand would be stuck fast, captured by the frozen sea.

By ten in the morning Caroline Mathilde had passed the entrance to Hirschholm. At midday, with the temperature recorded at nine degrees below freezing, and the weak light of midwinter already peeling away to the west, the carriages and riders were clattering along the narrow main street of Elsinore. Ahead of them was Kronborg, the sea round three sides of it, three deep moats on the other, with thirty-foot ramparts zigzagging round its promontory and cannons at every apex. As the carriage passed over each moat a drawbridge rose behind it, and when it reached the castle courtyard, Caroline Mathilde became an unreachable prisoner, locked in and encircled by water. Juliane Marie's insistence that Caroline Mathilde be imprisoned in Kronborg told her family and her friends that the new government intended her imprisonment to be harsh and unrelieved.

According to later accounts, Caroline Mathilde and her daughter were taken across the stone-flagged courtyard of the castle building and up to the second floor. There they were said to have been left in a small octagonal room that looked north-east to Skåne and the lowlands of southern Sweden. The little vaulted tower room grew out of the end of what was called the Queen's Chamber. It was scarcely big enough to hold more than a couple of armchairs and too small for a bed. With its barred windows facing freedom and the earliest light of dawn, it was a poignant element of Caroline Mathilde's imprisonment, but could not have been her gaol for long.

William Coxe, a British cleric who went to Kronborg a decade later, asked in Elsinore where the Queen had been imprisoned, and the people there told him that she was confined in the commandant's own quarters. Hauch's own nervous and tetchy reports sent down to Copenhagen confirmed that he and his family had made way for the Queen, and that she and her suite stayed in his quarters on the ground floor of the great castle from the first night. The rest of the castle was unfurnished and unsuitable. Kronborg did indeed have a magnificent set of state apartments, created and finished by Christian IV when the castle was rebuilt after a disastrous fire in 1629. But they were stripped of their furniture and had been unused for years. While the commandant and his family shifted themselves grumpily to one of the outlying buildings in the compound, Caroline Mathilde and Princess Louise stayed in Hauch's six rooms, closely watched by the sixty soldiers who stood behind the doors and patrolled the ramparts outside. Having got the Queen to Kronborg, the government was going to make sure that she could not escape, that no one could reach her and that she could not smuggle any message out, especially one to King Christian, who might relent and order her release.

So when Robert Murray Keith picked up the news of Caroline Mathilde's arrest, she was already out of his reach. Getting up late after the night's ball, it was eleven o'clock by the time he reached Count Osten's house and demanded to see the Foreign Minister. Keith knew that the way he and his masters in London together dealt with the sudden crisis would not only change the course of his own life, but might also lead to war. That the reigning Queen of a major European power should be arrested without a published charge, removed from the capital city and thrown into a fortress was shocking enough. But the fact that this Queen was the sister of the King of Great Britain, who was head of state of the most powerful nation in Europe and perhaps in the world, meant that this could never be seen as a merely domestic disaster. If George III decided to use force on his sister's behalf, Russia and France, the other great powers with whom Denmark had treaties and trading links, might be drawn into the fray. That could entangle not only Prussia and the other German states, but also the Austro-Hungarian Empire, and Europe might find itself at war.

It took about ten days to get a messenger to London, more sometimes if the weather turned ugly, and the same time to get a reply. Three weeks was too long for Keith to sit in Amalienborg and do nothing, and he had to use the powers given him to act in place of George III. Family legend had it that, believing Caroline Mathilde's life to be in danger, he 'forced his way into the Council and denounced war against Denmark, if a hair of her head were touched'. But this must have been a story that was woven afterwards. There was no council on the morning of 17 January, because as yet no council had been formed, and Keith, who had maintained good, if cool, relations with Osten, had no need to force his way anywhere. The new Danish government was from the start extremely nervous about the reaction of St James's to Caroline Mathilde's arrest. Osten knew that his first task after trying to calm down the Queen was to placate the British envoy, playing for time while Guldberg and his allies decided what to do next.

So if on the morning of 17 January Osten was temperate, Keith was angrily impatient. Whatever Keith said at this first meeting it terrified Juliane Marie and the new government. Fearful that Keith's dispatch to London would recommend immediate hostilities to free and reinstate the Queen, Osten, after consulting Guldberg and Juliane Marie, tried a softer path. He came to Keith's house in Amalienborg at ten o'clock the same night and gave him, 'by order of the King, the strongest assurances that the Queen would be treated in her present confinement with every mark of respect and dignity'. Osten's visit testified to the government's fragility and its understanding that conflict with the most powerful naval power in the world spelled disaster.

Every hour that passed solidified the new regime and made it more difficult for Caroline Mathilde to return to Copenhagen. Nonetheless, Guldberg decided very early on the morning of 17 January that the government must swiftly display the symbol of its legitimacy, the exhausted and terrified King Christian VII. Christian had had a busy night. After signing the arrest warrants he had to copy letters to be sent to all the courts of Europe explaining what he had done. When he wrote to London, though, his letter was addressed not to his cousin and brother-in-law George III but, because Guldberg wanted to make sure that Caroline Mathilde's arrest was treated as a family matter and not an affair of state, to the Princess Dowager instead. 'The conduct of the Queen my wife, your Royal Highness's daughter,' he wrote, 'has placed me under the sad necessity of sending her away from my court and my person.' He insisted that he could not have done otherwise and signed off with what quickly became the formula of words that the new government would fall back on in all the hostile negotiations that followed, that Caroline Mathilde would be treated with all the regard due 'à son naissance': to her birth. She would be treated, that is, as an English princess; but no accompanying promise was given to treat her as the Danish queen. The letter was not given to Keith, but sent instead to the Danish envoy in London, von Diede, who would hand it over to Lord Suffolk. Its journey would be slow, for the simple reason that the fledgling government had no interest in its swift arrival.

When he had put his signature to Guldberg's careful and formulaic declaration and finished his other copies, the King was led out onto one of the balconies at Christiansborg and presented to the crowds which had been collecting in the street below, his half-brother by his side. At first he seemed nonplussed by the cheering, and by his half-brother's bowing repeatedly. But he had always enjoyed tumult, and as the noise grew, he joined in, applauding the country's liberation into a new world that, for him, would soon hold more terrors than the one he had half-unwittingly brought to an end. At midday, dressed in stiff and splendid court clothes, Christian was driven out of Christiansborg in an elegant curlicued state coach. But his mood had abruptly changed and he gazed out over the rumps of the eight white horses drawing the coach and the running footmen alongside it, expressionless and apathetic. Euphoria was everywhere but on the face of the King. The playwright and novelist Dorothea Biehl noticed him, 'pale as a corpse', against the velvet padding of the carriage as the procession passed under the windows of her mansion at Charlottenborg.

Guldberg cast his new government in the image of himself, unimpeachably Danish, loyal to the King and strictly Lutheran. The joy at his coup made it quite clear how far Struensee had miscalculated in his belief that emancipation and reform were a public good that would inevitably be welcomed. Guldberg stressed his own version of duty to the common good and cast it in emotively religious language. 'Taking part in these events I felt God's hand', he wrote, 'and my heart was filled with joy that He chose me to be the instrument of saving the King, the Royal Family and the Fatherland.' Osten, whose dealings were for the most part eminently secular, did not hesitate to tell Juliane Marie that they had on their side 'Dieu, la virtue et la justice de notre cause': God, goodness and the justice of their cause. Joachim Schack-Ratlou, who soon became an important figure in the new government, was a lawyer at heart, careful and manipulative. But he too described the conspirators as 'ceux donc Dieu s'est servi comme d'instruments pour sauvez le Dannemarc': those whom God had used as instruments to save Denmark.

To justify this high-minded righteousness, Guldberg had quickly to find evidence of crimes that would justify the intervention of the deity. Despite Caroline Mathilde's obvious and proudly unhidden love for Struensee, he did not want to have to rely on a charge of adultery alone to justify his government and oust Struensee and Caroline Mathilde. In cases of adultery circumstantial evidence was difficult to substantiate and he presumed that neither of the lovers would confess. An anonymous correspondent, perhaps one of his old Copenhagen spies, spelled out Guldberg's dilemma for Robert Gunning. 'As to the intimacy, the Queen had no confidants and Struensee was very close and reserved upon all points. The laws in Denmark too are very rigid as to the proofs required on that head: people of a low class are not admissible evidence, I believe, against a crowned head.'

Instead the new government let it be known that it had found evidence of a conspiracy by Caroline Mathilde and Struensee to force the King to abdicate. They wrote a letter, dated 10 January, making the King copy it out to make it look more authentic and threw out hints not only of its existence but also its contents. Christian, it was said, addressed Juliane Marie, pleading for rescue from his captors and saying he feared for his life. Only four days after the arrests, Reiche, the Hanoverian Resident, reported to his superiors in Germany, 'As is known unofficially, but from credible sources, the intention was apparently to force the King to resign and declare the Queen regent. A declaration of renunciation and abdication is said to have been found prepared.' A week after the arrests this news had reached Hamburg and begun to spread out all over Europe. An anonymous correspondent told Robert Gunning that 'An Act for Abdication is said to have been prepared with Justitz-Rath Struensee's own hand'.

Moral indignation and poisonous rumour produced a febrile atmosphere in Copenhagen. Riots had followed the euphoria of Christian's triumphal ride through the streets. First brothels were sacked, then the houses of those who supported Caroline Mathilde and Struensee. But once roused, the angry and excited crowd began indiscriminate looting that lasted for many hours before soldiers were brought in to stop the destruction and patrol the city.

Violence made the government jumpy. A volatile people might turn against them, particularly if the King showed any signs of repenting what he had done. Guldberg and Juliane Marie had no confidence in Christian's steadfastness. They knew that if Christian rebelled against his new life he might order the return of the Queen and that she would exact immediate and heavy vengeance. So he was gradually withdrawn from public life and, day by day, treated less as a monarch and a figurehead, more as a patient and a prisoner. Soon he was being kept under a military guard while Guldberg and Schack-Ratlou, just as Struensee had done, signed orders and wrote letters in his name.

In the days that followed, Juliane Marie and her supporters pressed on with demolishing Struensee's administration and replacing it with their own. The prisoners were sifted. Those considered the least dangerous were allowed either to leave the capital or to quit the country. Some were kept under house arrest. The principal suspects, Struensee, Brandt, Struensee's brother, Falkenskjold, von Gëhler and Berger the physician, were still kept in harsh conditions although only the first two were shackled and bound day and night. A cabinet council was set up and in February it was reconstituted as a council of state with six members who headed the different branches of the new executive. Osten remained Foreign Minister, Rantzau answered for the army, Schack-Ratlou headed the Treasury, Thott the Chancellery and an Admiral Rømeling was put in charge of the navy. Most importantly for the prisoners, on 20 January, a commission of inquiry, the *Inkvisitsionskommissionen*, was established to examine their conduct and to decide how to proceed against them all, including the Queen. Rumour soon had it that no aspect of her behaviour would be neglected, and by 25 January Gunning's anonymous correspondent wrote that 'Mademoiselle d'Eyben, *dame d'honneur* to the Queen, it is said, will be obliged to come to town to give an account of several little circumstances relative to the Queen and Struensee'.

As the new government was stabilised, Guldberg came to understand that the fulcrum of his difficulties was neither Struensee, chained to the wall in the Kastellet, nor Christian, under guard in Christiansborg, but Caroline Mathilde herself. Outraged as Juliane Marie and her supporters had been at Caroline Mathilde's conduct and her evident enjoyment of both political power and the chance to shape her life according to her own desire, it had been the government of Johann Struensee that they had focused their hatred upon; its tone and tendency as much as the chaos it had produced. But now it was obvious that merely destroying Struensee, his followers and his reforms would not guarantee the existence of their own government. It was Caroline Mathilde, much more than Struensee and Brandt, who was the threat that hung over them. It was she and not they who had been able to sway the King. Struensee they now realised, had been very careful in his treatment of Christian, as he had always maintained. It was Caroline Mathilde who had established what Schack-Ratlou admitted was 'un très grand empire sur son esprit': a great measure of control over his mind.

Privately, Schack-Ratlou and Guldberg now saw that the idea that Caroline Mathilde and Struensee wanted to imprison the King or force him to abdicate was ludicrous. Christian was the lovers' symbol of legitimacy just as much as he was for the present government. But they now realised, too, that he had connived in their plans with a willingness that was perhaps something more than indifference. Christian was fearful of many things, and Caroline Mathilde, especially at her most commanding in her riding habit and spurs, was probably one of them. But his fear was mixed with pleasure and perhaps an anticipation of chastisement, and Guldberg quickly saw that if Caroline Mathilde were ever reunited with the King, she would promptly be able to induce him to do anything that she wanted. The very first thing she would do would be to annihilate those who had destroyed her happiness and removed her from her son. It was for this reason that Caroline Mathilde was guarded so carefully at Kronborg and for this reason that she would have to stay there.

Caroline Mathilde, living under constant surveillance in the cold of Kronborg, unable to go out, knew it perfectly well herself. It made her not despairing but angry. Reiche reported that the Queen was in good health but 'sich sehr ungedulgig und erzürnt bezeigen': she was very impatient and extremely irate. Commandant Hauch reported to Copenhagen with some astonishment that she was reading books from his military library, Polybius, and the *Histoire de Vicomte de Turenne*, a life of a famous French general, as if she were arming herself mentally for some struggle to come. Robert Murray Keith was repeatedly denied permission to visit her, and the only concession the government made to her comfort was to increase her staff. On 19 January three members of her former household were sent to join her, and perhaps to report on her moods and conversations. Observers noted that all were women whom Caroline Mathilde cordially disliked.

Acting to remove Caroline Mathilde permanently either by death or exile would have been relatively simple without the brooding presence of George III and the power of the British Empire and armed forces. Osten and Guldberg decided that their best course lay in trying to keep the matter a family one. They may have been forgetting that George III had the right to declare war without going to Parliament for approval, or they may have reasoned that he would not want any family embarrassment to come out into the open in England and expose him to the ridicule of the press and of his enemies in Parliament. Either way, the Danish government demanded private negotiations with the British Crown, choosing to see no difficulty in keeping the matter secret and within the ambit of the family.

For George III, however, family matters were anything but simple. Although he certainly had a sort of private existence, a skilful and inquisitive press, backed by an eager reading public and abetted by the flamboyant activities of his own family, was eroding it all the time. As sovereign he had certain prerogatives that lay outside the ambit of Parliament's scrutiny. More and more, however, Parliament was criticising and asking questions about the King's role and conduct. All legislation and Civil List settlements had to go through Parliament. Together these three pressures on the Crown, from the press, the public and the House of Commons, contrived to push the King's private affairs inexorably into the public, the parliamentary and eventually the constitutional domain. Events the King wanted to keep private rarely stayed off the newspaper pages for long, and the opposition in Parliament was constantly on the prowl looking for abuses of royal prerogative which would allow them to try to curb further the powers of the Crown.

News-gathering in London was already more efficient than the sovereign's channels of information. As Charles Ernst, Keith's secretary, struggled overland down Jutland, through Holland and across to Helvoetsluys, the news he was carrying was days ahead of him, probably getting out of Denmark from the port of Esbjerg and quickly making it over to Newcastle. By 23 January, just six days after the arrests, reliable accounts reached London, and the next day the *General Evening Post* reported, 'It is affirmed by letters from the Continent that a Royal Princess is certainly detained in a tower inaccessible to every creature except such as are appointed to attend her, but that an absolute silence is imposed throughout the kingdom on this subject.' Other newspapers were soon picking up on the news and any idea that such a sensational story was going to remain a private one was already fanciful.

The London newspaper reports were for the most part strikingly accurate, and although they were lurid enough, the details of the case were too resonant for many writers to ignore. To the image of Caroline Mathilde imprisoned like Rapunzel in a tower were added the evil stepmother of innumerable fairy-tales and Hamlet's castle at Elsinore, with its images of a dead king, a walking ghost and a nation in need of deliverance. The news that Caroline Mathilde was imprisoned at Elsinore had particular force for playgoers, because Shakespeare had recently been enshrined as the national bard and because Britain's most famous actor, David Garrick, had made Hamlet his most famous role. If Christian VII was obviously no Hamlet, the British imagination nonetheless slipped easily into the idea that Juliane Marie was a perfidious Gertrude. Night, treachery and madness all seemed to a grateful Grub Street to have seeped from the pages of Shakespeare into the life of an English princess and Danish queen. To this fantastic, half-true story was added another memory, kept alive in flickers of Jacobite longing and in scores of verses and romances, that of Mary Stuart, another queen imprisoned in a castle. Fotheringay, Elsinore, royalty and deceit: Caroline Mathilde's story was irresistible to the press and to readers precisely because it combined mythic entertainment and a genuine political crisis.

Thus it was into a city already excited by speculation that an exhausted Charles Ernst finally made his way on the morning of 29 January, nearly two weeks after he had left Copenhagen. It was hardly a propitious moment to arrive. The Duke of Cumberland's antics were still exciting attention, Princess Augusta, visiting from Brunswick, was vociferously unhappy and bitter about her marriage, and worst of all, the Princess Dowager was dying. Nonetheless, for the King, business went on as usual; it was a Wednesday morning and he was dressing in the Queen's House for the mid-week levee. When the Secretary of State for the Southern Department, Lord Suffolk, was announced, the King's valets stopped their brushing and powdering and were hurriedly ordered from the room. Suffolk, with Ernst in tow, came ponderously in. Keith's dispatch confirmed the newspaper reports. Ernst supplied some extra detail, 'in person' to the King, and then repeated everything to the ailing Princess Dowager who insisted on a first-hand report. At the same time the Danish ambassador von Diede arrived with Christian VII's letter to his mother-in-law.

The King cancelled the morning's levee, and sent messengers galloping to his aunt Princess Amelia and his brother the Duke of Cumberland with the news. Then he closeted himself with Lord Suffolk in his study. Shocked, angry, worried for his mother and still smarting from the Duke of Cumberland's announcement of his marriage six weeks before, he was not in the best frame of mind to draft a measured response. It was his nature, and, he felt, his duty to react with the feeling not only of a brother but also of a father figure. Whatever happened. An affront to one of his siblings was an affront to him in both capacities, while any reprehensible behaviour on their part showed, he believed, an intolerable neglect of the love and respect they always owed him.

The news from Denmark pulled the King powerfully in opposite directions. On the one hand, the treatment that Caroline Mathilde had received called forth his proudest resentment as her brother and as King of England. On the other, if rumours of her adultery or meddling in politics contained any truth at all, he would not be sparing with his moral condemnation. The news, moreover, touched his rawest nerve, the memory of his own abandoned love. For the moment he refused to believe that his sister could have neglected her royal and marital duty and acted upon her passion, and he refused to contemplate its rumoured object, a man who was not only a commoner but a court servant as well. So Keith, as he himself recorded in his notes, was 'left very much at large in Lord Suffolk's m[anuscript] letter', which was sent off with Ernst at the end of the day. But the Queen's innocence was to be presumed, the official press was to be kept silent and all negotiations were to be secret.

Although George made it clear to Caroline Mathilde herself that he saw her as the victim of malign forces within the Danish court, he typically stirred a bitter pinch of condemnation into his expressions of support. 'Dear Sister', his letter ran, 'I cannot omit taking the first opportunity of expressing the sorrow I feel that your enemies have so incited the King of Denmark as to remove you from his presence. You can never doubt of having a warm advocate in me whose advice if followed might have preserved you from misfortune ... Dear sister, place your dependence on the Almighty Being that forsakes not the depressed. The more you call on him the more he will give you fortitude. I shall be anxious to hear from you.' George knew that his crisp and sealed letter was unlikely to reach Caroline Mathilde and if it did would certainly have been carefully scrutinised on the way. So even this was much more than a domestic correspondence, with ministers in London hovering over one king's shoulder, Juliane Marie and Guldberg in Copenhagen over another's. A more heartfelt note was sent by the ailing Princess Dowager, probably the last letter she ever wrote. 'You are able to judge what the heart of a tender mother feels knowing of your present situation', she wrote, adding, 'Heaven preserve you', and signing herself, 'Your very affectionate and afflicted mother, Augusta'.

Though the Princess Dowager wrote straightforwardly to Caroline Mathilde as a mother to her daughter, the King's letter was necessarily a more complicated document. The diplomatic atmosphere was fetid, and the Danish and British Crowns, while professing sincerity and openness, were already playing a double game. George III responded sincerely to the Danish offer of direct negotiations in order to keep the affair on a family footing. There was at one level nothing he would have liked more, because the last thing he wanted was for his sister's conduct to become a matter of public clamour. He insisted that nothing should go into the *London Gazette*, which printed all official and royal announcements, and he wanted all transactions between London and Copenhagen kept secret. But he must have known that though he corresponded with King Christian's hand, the head he was really dealing with was somebody else's. Certainly he had no intention of trusting the contents of the letters he received from the Danish King.

At the same time as he opened negotiations with the Danish government – sending secret copies of his letters to Robert Murray Keith – George III was preparing for the worst. Very early on, if not on 29 January itself, he discussed with Lord Suffolk and probably the Prime Minister Lord North and the Secretary to the Navy the Earl of Sandwich, the possibility of mobilising a fleet in order to respond to any threat against Caroline Mathilde's life. Knowing that that would bring the affair into the open and make it a matter of state, Suffolk told Keith that a demand would be made 'not . . . in favour of an unhappy Queen but as a claim of right on the part of His Majesty in behalf of a Daughter of England'. Fleet Street was soon buzzing with rumour, and the *Public Advertiser* reported on 1 February that 'a squadron of men of war is to sail immediately for Copenhagen to support the honour of and dignity of England – Denmark must do justice or see its capital reduced to ashes'.

Nonetheless, because they were behaving in a way that went far beyond what would be deemed an acceptable exercise of prerogative by most Members of Parliament, the King and Suffolk were determined to act as quietly and independently as possible. 'The part H.M. takes upon the occasion must be a secret', Lord Suffolk wrote to the ambassador in The Hague. To that end, as he explained, little was written down and 'none of the common clerks of the office could be employed'. Dispatches would not be sent by the usual channels either, but would be given to special messengers who would be sailed to and from The Hague by what Suffolk called 'an extraordinary boat'.

So it was that only three days after receiving news of his sister's arrest, George III had already thought better of a private negotiation between crowned heads. All the letters dispatched to Christian VII after that were merely charades designed to convince the Danish government that he did indeed consider the affair a small-scale and familial one. In fact the opposite was true. George III was already preparing to go to war on his sister's behalf and ready to resort to subterfuge and secrecy in order to do it. If his prompt was his injured pride, his justification, once the nosy British press found out what was happening, was that Caroline Mathilde was not only Queen of Denmark but also, and more importantly, a citizen of Great Britain.

The King's righteous indignation was increased by his anxiety about his mother. In his overwrought emotional condition, he believed that the Princess Dowager had been made worse by the news from Copenhagen. Augusta finally and bravely died during the night of 7 February. The next day George wrote in a draft of a letter to Caroline Mathilde, 'it is with a heavy heart I take up my pen to acquaint you that my mother, after a long and painful illness of near eleven months, died this morning at a little before six. She was perfectly sensible to the last and either from fortitude would not pretend to know her danger, or from natural spirits was ignorant of it.' 'To the last hours', he went on less coherently, 'was anxious to hear from you whose misfortunes certainly have some days shortened her life.' Then he wrote, before deciding against it and scratching out the words, 'I am grieved thinking this will be directed to you at Cronenburg instead of –' Princess Augusta, who had nursed the Princess Dowager through her last three months, implied in her own letter to Caroline Mathilde an even closer connection between the arrests in Copenhagen and their mother's death, writing, 'The last word of our incomparable mother was about you, and after that she neither ate nor slept again.'

Caroline Mathilde, isolated and guarded in Kronborg, could only have felt worse if these letters had reached her. But, although she may have been harbouring a hope that her brother would do something to save her, her devotion to her family had faded, dissolved gradually in the bitterness of being sent away and forgotten in the warmth of her love for Struensee. If her brother thought of her as 'a daughter of England', she did not. From her rooms at Kronborg she looked south to Copenhagen where her lover, her court, her son and her identity lay. She was Queen of Denmark and her brother's only use would be to restore her to her throne.

The new government, though, had other ideas. Rumours that Christian VII intended to divorce his wife on the grounds of adultery were running through Copenhagen, and, by 11 February, Robert Murray Keith's spies told him that orders had gone out of Christiansborg for the fitting up of the 'old palace' at Aalborg in the far north of Jutland. It was to this remote town that Caroline Mathilde was to be exiled after her divorce, apparently, far away from Copenhagen and vulnerable to adventurers and assassins alike.

The evidence that Guldberg's government needed to divorce and exile the Queen was at once all around and unusable. Even in London the newspapers were full of stories about Copenhagen. Some openly asserted, as the *London Magazine* put it on 11 February, 'the Queen's fidelity to the King's bed was long ago suspected'. Others declared that she had followed the Princess Dowager's example of 'meddling too much in political and party disputes'. Horace Walpole wrote gleefully that bets were being taken in London coffee houses on the chance of war with Denmark. Sir Edward Hawke was named by several newspapers as the man already chosen to command the fleet and both Kensington Palace and Somerset House in the Strand were picked out as probable retreats for the rescued Queen.

For Guldberg report was not enough. He wanted something written down. The divorce of a reigning queen was not unprecedented but it would be extremely daring, and a divorce without evidence would almost certainly lead to war. Guldberg had to rid himself of Caroline Mathilde, but he had to do it with aplomb, and by mid-February with not a sheet of evidence found, the case was looking shaky.

George III, grieving for his mother and angry that his family's affairs were, as the London Chronicle put it, 'a general topic of conversation', reacted with exaggerated feeling to the news that Guldberg was planning to disgrace his sister. It was time, he decided, to 'proceed to the next step'. 'You are therefore authorised', Suffolk wrote formally to Keith on 28 February, 'to declare to the Danish Ministers, or to any of the Royal Family of Denmark, that if they proceed to a divorce you have His Majesty's orders – and I hereby convey to you His Majesty's orders – to depart from Denmark without taking leave. The consequences of such a mark of His Majesty's resentment must be left to their own surmises. In the present moment I cannot ascertain them. This threat may be conveyed in a variety of shapes more or less offensive as occasions may suggest.' Suffolk added that Keith must 'do everything possible to prevent a divorce', and offered him unlimited secret service credit to help him do it. But failure meant departing without leave, and, in the language of diplomacy, that meant war. George III, initially so cautious and worried about secrecy, now veered the other way, convinced that the Danish government was playing a duplicitous game and furious that what he saw as his own unimpeachable honour had been violated. He was determined, if his sister were to be divorced by Christian VII, to batter the Danish government into submission with the full might of the British navy, and he would leave it to Lord Suffolk, Lord Sandwich and the Prime Minister Lord North to justify the matter as an affair of state and worthy of the enormous cost to the public purse.

Baron von Diede, the Danish envoy in London, must have described to his masters in Copenhagen both the rumours of war and the scornful way he was now being treated at St James's. Guldberg, getting almost daily reports of Keith's visits to Osten and his increasingly bellicose demands, had to act to diffuse the tension and threat hanging over his government. But he had failed to get anything out of Caroline Mathilde and had found no evidence of a conspiracy against King Christian. So he changed course and decided to concentrate on Struensee and Brandt, still imprisoned in the Kastellet without news, visitors, comfort or hope.

Everything that had been or would be said about Struensee's state of mind and behaviour since the moment of his arrest was filtered through the new regime's machine of news and rumour. Once in the Kastellet, Struensee was bound with misrepresentation and misunderstanding as much with chains and shackles. Even those things that he himself demonstrably wrote were designed to serve a purpose that is and was not always obvious. After his arrest the mystery that surrounded Struensee's motives grew thicker and soon became impenetrable. The one person who commented upon his behaviour, and perhaps the person who knew him best, was the Queen, but she was far away in Kronborg and had no idea how he was being treated or what was passing through his mind.

Possibly Struensee quickly became unclear what he wanted himself. After a month in solitary confinement his mind may have descended to a place of fear where little light filtered in from above. Early on, perhaps, he had allowed himself to believe that Caroline Mathilde would be able to come and save him or that the King would assert himself and demand his release. But as the weeks passed, dreary, cold and without any news or change, hope must have been extinguished, and death more and more present, stalking his cell, daring him to run or fling himself at it. It was widely reported that he wept at night. Perhaps he did, and then in the day recovered his self-possession.

Alone in his cell Struensee would not have known that just three days after his arrest the government had set up an Inkvisitsionskommissionen, a commission of enquiry. The Inkvisitsionskommissionen's members, eminent, grave men from Denmark's most important institutions, especially the judiciary, had spent weeks sifting through the prisoners' papers. Struensee's associates stood accused as much of living out their beliefs as of any specific crimes, though charges were found to bring against them. As for the doctor himself, his crime of sleeping with the Queen was nowhere written. To be sure, searches had turned up Caroline Mathilde's silk-embroidered garters, the 'ties of feeling' she wore under her gowns, wrapped around her solid thighs. They had found the sketches commissioned from Peder Als and the pearl-heavy insignia of the Order of Matilda that Struensee had worn in public. But ribbons could not divorce a queen or jewels convict her lover. Now the Inkvisitsionskommissionen wanted evidence and needed to trap Struensee into giving it. On 28 January a sub-commission, the Forhørskommissionen, was established for that single purpose.

On the morning of 20 February, Struensee was unshackled from the wall of his cell. A fur coat was thrown over his shoulders. Flanked by guards, he was led across the beaten-earth compound of the fortress, unshaven and unsteady now that the weights had been lifted from his limbs. His accusers, five men he knew, sat ranked in front of him in the commandant's house. They had a long list of questions, and went down it remorselessly. Two days, 238 questions; 238 well-weighed answers. Struensee was a match for them, careful, level, yielding nothing.

Then everything changed. Did the Forhørskommissionen, frustrated by failure, bring torture, which Struensee himself had abolished, or the threat of torture, to bear? Did Struensee's mind suddenly give way and fall into hopelessness? Did he, after so many days alone, flare up in defiance and dare them to do their worst, convinced somehow that he could tell the world what he had done and get away with it? No one was saying, no one writing. But to the 239th question, Struensee said enough about his relationship with the Queen to make it clear to the men who faced him that he was at the point of confession or explanation. Relations between him and Caroline Mathilde, he agreed, 'had gone as far as they could between people of two sexes'. Triumphant, the commissioners stopped there, sending Struensee back to his cell to face his statement for three days and nights.

On 25 February they brought him back. The mood was brisk, final and uncompromising. The commissioners, Guldberg among them, made it clear that 'they now expected more detailed information from him'. The questions came remorselessly on, and the doctor answered carefully still, but humbly and truthfully. 'When did he have this first intercourse, where and on what occasion?' As far as he remembered, Struensee replied, it was in February during a trip to Holstein in 1770, when he had been in the Queen's cabinet, sitting with her, talking or reading. 'Did this close intimacy between him and the Queen continue?' 'Yes,' Struensee answered with bald simplicity. Did he use a dark staircase in Christiansborg to get to her room by a roundabout way?' Yes, he did. Guldberg was interrogating Struensee in the name of God and for the good of his country; he wanted more. To put Struensee to death was not enough; if Louise Augusta could be proved to be his child she might be declared illegitimate and the stain of Struensee's upstart blood be removed for ever from Denmark's royal family. So, did he know whether during the trip to Holstein in 1770 the King had ever spent a whole night with the Queen? Knowing that the Holstein trip chimed with the moment of Louise Augusta's conception, Struensee was disingenuous, his daughter spared. The King and Queen, he said, thinking of the testimonies of servants, had never spent a whole night together, but Caroline Mathilde had gone to King Christian each morning, 'when he was still in bed, and lain half an hour or a whole hour with him'.

After nine questions, nine answers and a signature. It was not so much a confession as a signed interrogation, not so much an abject admittance of a crime as an agreed statement of the facts. Struensee testified to his intimacy with Caroline Mathilde but did not declare on paper any contrition; he did not sign a confession of a crime and nowhere on 25 February put his name to any word of the Queen's adultery or his own crime of lèse-majesté. They would be added later as the obvious implications of what he had agreed had happened.

The commissioners were triumphant. Struensee's signature would send him to the executioner's block and they quickly let it be known in Copenhagen that he had willingly answered their questions. Outsiders were aghast. 'They would have it believed at present that Struensee himself confessed the whole', a sceptical Ralph Woodford wrote to Robert Gunning on 6 March. 'His courage, I am assured, forsook him upon hearing from the Commission that the queen was no longer at Copenhagen which he did not know before. Yet I cannot believe him wretch enough to have done a thing infamously aggravating his own guilt.' Many already believed, especially since Brandt had also admitted that he had hit the King, that torture had been threatened or used. As for Struensee, if threats had made him confess, the clarity and detail of his confession were still unaccountable. Did he want, perhaps, to leave a record of his love, carefully copied into the archives of the state? There in his own words and in the lurid statements of the Queen's maids was the story of his ascent to power, and a testimony of his care of the King and passion for the Queen, how they left the sheets of her bed rumpled, how he carried in his pocket a handkerchief stained with his semen and her blood, how the sofas in her apartments had to be re-covered when they were past cleaning, and how, unlike most men and women, they made love naked and he left her, as she hinted, like Eve, in a state of nature on the bed.

Locked in Kronborg, bounded by water, Caroline Mathilde was ignorant of the sensational news in Copenhagen. There, rumours of war flowed through the streets. To staunch them, Guldberg wrote to London in King Christian's name a letter so suffused with religiosity that Lord Suffolk must have known that the King was not its author. Not even brotherly feeling, Guldberg wrote triumphantly when he came back home from the citadel on 22 February, would stand in the way of honour, of truth and of religion, when George III received the explanations that were being prepared. George would realise that it was 'la Reine seule', the Queen alone, who had brought this mortification upon him.

But in London, quite separate difficulties were brewing. Both Parliament and the press were beginning to lean on the Prime Minister, Lord North, asking that his government act over the affair and lift the secrecy surrounding it. By mid-March the fairy-tale of Caroline Mathilde's arrest and imprisonment in a faraway castle by an evil stepmother had been replaced in some newspapers by calls for clarity and decisions. Junius attacked Lord North in the *Gentleman's Magazine* with the strident claim that the House of Hanover was not a private family at all, but in fact a kind of public property in which the people had an interest, and it was therefore 'highly criminal' to proceed with what he called 'this cautious secrecy'. 'You must be conscious', he wrote, addressing the Prime Minister, 'that the people have a right to be informed of every transaction which concerns the welfare of the state. They are part of a mighty empire, which flourishes only as their happiness is promoted; they have a kind of claim in every person belonging to the Royal Lineage. How can they possibly remain neuter and see their Princess imprisoned by a Banditti of Northern Vandals?' Responding to new rumours that Caroline Mathilde might be killed in exile, Junius concluded wildly, 'The blood of our Sovereign's sister shall not be suffered to cry in vain for vengeance; it shall be heard; it shall be revenged.' There was, he was saying, no such thing as a private life of the royal family; everything the King did was potentially an affair of state in which the public had an interest and which it had therefore the right to know about and scrutinise.

No other newspaper made so explicit a defence of the public interest. But few accepted the King's belief that his family business was outside the ambit of parliamentary and even public interest. George III might forbid any news about Caroline Mathilde in the official *London Gazette*, but no other newspapers shared his scruples. Although editors were careful not to print Caroline Mathilde's Christian names, referring to her simply as the Queen of Denmark, they openly assumed the veracity of Struensee's confession and wrote candidly of the chances of Caroline Mathilde's divorce, death or exile. The story had old resonance: a princess having an affair with a royal favourite and a government that was behaving secretively and without the scrutiny of Parliament. Jibes linking Struensee to Lord Bute threatened to reopen the wounds left by the years of Wilkesite tumult.

Paradoxically, however, it was perhaps the very veracity of these allegations that stayed the critics' hands. Wilkesite opposition and demands had tried to demonstrate that the King was abusing his prerogative by allowing the 'secret influence' of his mother and Lord Bute to determine policy. But this charge was based on the assumption that Lord Bute was the lover of the Princess Dowager, an allegation which had hints of smoke, but no fire. Lacking substance themselves, the insinuations about Augusta and Bute could be used as a platform upon which to carry other demands. Caroline Mathilde's story was different for the simple reason that it was true: the Queen had indeed been sleeping with the favourite. She had had his child and endorsed his power in the country. Caroline Mathilde's affair was beyond manipulation, its truth greater and more shocking than any satirist could make it.

It remained for critics to turn their attention to St James's and to Lord North's administration. A story worth pursuing was brewing there, the very story in fact that opposition figures had been chasing for a decade: the King's secret assertion of his prerogative and the implications that it held for the power and reach of Parliament. More than any scandal it was this sort of enquiry that Lord North and Lord Suffolk feared. In Plymouth and Portsmouth the wharves were stacked with provisions and sailors were gathering. But secrecy was the watchword, and questioned in Parliament, Lord North declared that unless expressly ordered to do so by the House, he would not reveal so delicate an affair. Everything would become clear in time, he added, and the ministry would be justified.

With Struensee's signed statement in his pocket, Guldberg was full of righteous confidence. He now had the means to silence George III, break the doctor and try the Queen, and was prepared to use it. At Kronborg, Guldberg knew, Caroline Mathilde was still angry and steadfast. She knew that Struensee had been arrested and was confined in the Kastellet. She asked her maid if he was in chains, and if he knew that she was at Kronborg, and then said nothing more.

On 6 March the commandant at Kronborg gave Caroline Mathilde George III's official notice of her mother's death. Though she had lost her affection for her mother the news must have shocked her, but she kept her composure. Her chamberlain Holstein reported to Copenhagen that she angrily refused to sign the drafted reply that was immediately laid in front of her, saying that as she was not allowed to write her own letters, she would not put her name to anyone else's. Eventually she did agree, but only on the condition that Osten was told that she had not wanted to. Similarly, when she was told that the Danish court had proclaimed mourning for the Princess Dowager, she declared haughtily, as the Queen and as Struensee's partner, that deep mourning had been abolished, and that if any alteration was to be made to this decree she demanded to be informed.

Two days after this blow, the new regime sent Caroline Mathilde a request from the commission which was investigating her conduct, for what was formally called an audience. It was, she knew, no request, but an order, and she must have been aware that its purpose was threatening and that an interrogation was likely. Four men arrived: Otto Thott, a Privy Counsellor in the new government, Schack-Ratlou, who was assuming more and more prominence within it, and two judges, Kragh-Juell-Wind and Henrik Stampe. They carried a document which supposedly contained the King's instructions, as well as the evidence gathered by the Inkvisitsionskommissionen and Struensee's signed questions – enough, they hoped, to make her terrified and ready to sign a confession of her own.

Caroline Mathilde had had no lawyer or adviser with her during her long imprisonment. She had been unable to send any letters and had received only those that the government had decided to send on. On the morning of 9 March she faced her four visitors alone in her chambers, defiant and angry still, but completely unprepared for and ignorant of what they would say or try to do. First one of the interrogators handed her a letter from the King in which Christian's desire for 'silence in order not to create passions among the people', was stated. Then she was read the power of attorney given by the King to the commissioners and only then did the long process of depressing her spirits really begin. Forty-six pages of what the protocol called the 'species facti' were read aloud to her, evidence about her behaviour and her love, about her relationship with the King and with Struensee taken from the interrogations of her maids, her lover and her friends which had been conducted in the last six weeks. Reading them page by page must have taken well over an hour, and this evidence was followed by a sheet even more devastating, the questions posed to Struensee in the citadel on 25 February and answered by him. A copy of this paper, now described by everyone simply as Struensee's confession, was given to her to look at while one of the commissioners – usually identified later as Schack-Ratlou – read aloud from the original. Then the commissioners told the Queen, as they had planned, that her confession wasn't necessary, but that it was needed to allow the King to be lenient. After that, three questions, framed as if they had been written by the King, were read out to her, written up in the commissioners' report as: '1. If on her side she will confess the same.'; '2. If she does not thus confess to having broken the marital vow to me.'; and, '3. If she does not likewise confess to having broken the act of marriage to me.'

What happened then, and in what order, is not clear and not recorded in any official documents. It was claimed that Caroline Mathilde stood firm, denied the right of the commission to question her, admitted nothing and answered every question with a brusque and angry negative. She roundly declared Struensee's confession a forgery, and maintained an irate composure. But then, it was said, Schack-Ratlou, seeing the need for a dramatic gesture that would shake Caroline Mathilde to her heart, turned the original version of Struensee's confession round in his hand, showing her for the first time her lover's signature. Many insisted that when she saw it, Caroline Mathilde's self-possession fled and her resolve was broken. Ralph Woodford was in no doubt that the government had proceeded against her with sleight of hand and even cruelty. Writing to Robert Gunning a few days after the news of the Kronborg meeting seeped out he said, adding his customary swipe at the British envoy, 'Their proceedings with regard to the Queen seem to be continued with a good deal of harshness – in spite of Sir Robert Keith's preeminent ability – if not to be unfair, by not allowing her counsel, or even *la prévenir d'avance*, and upon so delicate a point it is not surprising the sight of a certain handwriting should bring on a fainting fit.'

Even if Caroline Mathilde did not crumble when she saw Struensee's signature and name, some time during the readings or the questioning, she was trapped and was briefly convinced, by her own hope and love and by the wording of the protocol, that if she acted as the government wanted she could win leniency both for herself and her lover. Caught off her guard, she answered the three reiterated questions – yes, yes and yes – and she signed them, joining her name to Struensee's in poignant and final fatality.

Falkenskjold later wrote that Caroline Mathilde had only written the first syllable of her name before she saw that her signature would have precisely the opposite effect from the one she imagined. She stopped, and it was Schack-Ratlou who seized her hand and guided it while she wrote on. But Falkenskjold languished in exile and in gaol. He was Struensee's friend and wanted to believe anything of those who condemned him. Caroline

Mathilde's signature shows no appreciable break after the first syllable. She wrote and only afterwards realised what she had done. Angrily she withdrew her confession and protested her innocence.

It was too late. The commissioners were triumphant. They told Caroline Mathilde that her case, with confession and evidence already prepared, was going to trial and that she was to be allowed to choose a lawyer. That evening they left Kronborg carrying everything Guldberg needed to forward to London and to proceed against the prisoners. He had in fact already sent off a copy of Struensee's confession. On 13 March he dispatched a messenger with details of the commissioners' visit to Kronborg and a letter from Christian VII to his cousin which, for the first time, admitted that the government intended that the Queen should be divorced. In Christian's letter, Guldberg abandoned the religious language that he had used earlier and now adopted a tone of high-minded and jubilant restraint. 'Your Majesty will see', he wrote, 'that the Queen, far from discrediting Struensee, has confirmed his confession by her own admission and by her signature. After having replied in the affirmative to the questions, she has agreed to a divorce and to a dissolution of our marriage.' After saying that Caroline Mathilde's trial would be held behind closed doors and that the sentence against her would never be published, Guldberg, carried away by his creation of a personality and voice for the hapless Christian, continued with obvious pleasure, 'Occupied utterly by her unhappy passion, the Queen seems to have closed her heart to any other feeling.'

Had he read what he was signing, Christian might have noticed that his new minister had little understanding of his character. The King himself would never have written such a sentence. He had harboured no jealousy of Struensee, and although his feelings for Caroline Mathilde may have been compounded of admiration, fear and a desire for excitement, they had never included either passion or love. Sympathetic understanding was something the King had never experienced, except perhaps towards his dog.

When the commissioners left, Caroline Mathilde's calm and fortitude went as well. Count Holstein reported that on the night of 10 March she barely slept, and in the morning he was concerned enough to call a physician from Elsinore to look at her. The doctor bled her for the colic, but she still was unable to sleep, tormented by the memories of her capitulation to the commissioners and by visions of the future. 'She sleeps very little', Holstein wrote, 'and becomes greatly upset by the slightest thing she hears.'

On 13 March, a divorce commission, the Skilsmissekommissionen, was

Caroline Matilda, fifteen years old, and an English princess, sad and downcast before her marriage to Christian VII of Denmark, by James Watson after a pastel by Francis Cotes of 1766.

CHRISTIANSBOURG, PALAIS DE COPENHAGUE
Dédié au Roy.

Christiansborg Palace from the front, much as it would first have appeared to Caroline Mathilde. The royal stables were housed in the wing to the right, the royal theatre on the opposite side.

Caroline Mathilde, Queen of Denmark, renamed, and, four years later, mannish, confident and transformed, dressed in the uniform of the Danish Life Guards by Peder Als in 1770.

King Christian VII in the first of three companion ovals painted by Jens Juel in 1771; haunted by his imaginings and often gripped by mania.

Johann Friedrich Struensee; thirty-four years old, a German doctor, the King's friend, the Queen's lover, the country's ruler.

Queen Caroline Mathilde, head high, twenty years old and every inch a mature woman.

Voltaire's essay on the freedom of the press, addressed to
King Christian, commissioned by Johann Struensee in 1770.

Caroline Mathilde with her son, Prince Frederik, watercolour sketch by Peder Als, 1771.
The little Crown Prince clutches his watering-can, his mother reclines with deliberate
femininity on the sofa.

Kronborg Castle, where the ghost of Hamlet's father walked the ramparts and Caroline Mathilde was imprisoned.

Caroline Mathilde's garters, her 'ties of feeling', bought for her by Struensee and constantly worn to remind her of him.

The executions of Struensee and Brandt outside Copenhagen on 28 April 1772. The carriage that brought them stands in front of the platform, the cart that bore their dismembered bodies away waits to the side.

Caroline Mathilde's and Struensee's daughter, Princess Louise Augusta, painted by Jens Juel in 1785, with her mother's ample bosom and her father's prominent acquiline nose.

George III by an unknown artist in 1775. After years of trouble with his siblings, his American subjects were about to rise up and cause him even more misery.

established. Its purpose was not to reach a decision either about Caroline Mathilde's guilt or her fate; that had already been taken. It was to show, to the Danish people and the British government alike, that justice was taking its course, with all appropriate ceremony and gravity, weighted with evidence and endorsed by the most illustrious men in Denmark. They were wigged, gowned and surpliced, in black and gold and red, and their judgment would bear no appeal. Five high-ranking clergymen, four state councillors, several judges of the supreme court, two officers from the army, two from the navy and a representative of the civic government of Copenhagen: thirty-five men sat in a line to try a single absent woman.

So, in contrast to the jostle and noise of an English trial, the commission that sealed Caroline Mathilde's fate was a scholarly affair that proceeded behind closed doors. With Christian VII kept firmly inside the palace next door, Struensee locked in his cell half an hour's walk away, and Caroline Mathilde immured on Zealand's northern tip, none of the principals was present. The King, indeed, had never been interviewed; he was too volatile a witness to risk. One day he might have ordered the release of Struensee or demanded to see his wife, the next turned idly away; either way revenge and justice were ideas that he had no interest in. Guldberg, hiding behind the notion that to call the head of state to account for himself would be either legally impossible or beneath the dignity of a king, had simply left Christian out of everything, and presented him, in his own name, with a fait accompli.

Once the commission had appointed a prosecutor, Bang, and a lawyer for the Queen, Peter Uldall, papers were drawn up to be presented to Caroline Mathilde informing her of proceedings against her. On 18 March Peter Uldall set off for Kronborg to serve them on his client. He arrived as the sun was going down, a humane, steady, conventional man, impressed but not over-awed by his task. He brought with him in the carriage a conviction that the Queen was a young woman corrupted by the people around her and by a licentious court. Caroline Mathilde had his considerable sympathy, but he could never think of her as a woman who played her own role in the drama she had helped to create. Struensee, he was convinced, had earned her friendship by reconciling the King to her. 'What good wife would not be grateful for that?' he asked in the memoirs he wrote a few years later. Gratitude, though, decomposed into vice and sensuality. 'With success, Struensee, Brandt and all she surrounded herself with did everything to exterminate the voice of religion in her.' Having lost her active faith, Uldall believed, Caroline Mathilde must have fallen into misery. But her lover and companions told her that the way to rediscover her happiness was to 'fulfil sensuous desires', as Uldall put it, and by 'vigorous riding, dancing, frank speech and manners'. Bit by bit she fell into the 'limitless lust' that was her downfall and must inevitably end in her exile.

At four in the afternoon Uldall began his long conference with Caroline Mathilde. He was immediately shocked by her demeanour, taken aback by the stubbornness and anger he found mixed with her despair. Although Uldall made some attempt to explain and discuss the way he had planned her defence, Caroline Mathilde – and with very good reason – was only intermittently interested in the proceedings. Having had several days to ponder what she had done, she was careful to retract her confession and declare her innocence. But throughout the long evening's discussion she also returned again and again to Struensee, convinced that he had been tricked into signing his confession. 'They also caught me unawares,' she told Uldall, admitting, 'then I signed everything they wanted.' She was sure, though, that Struensee would not have fallen into such a trap, and insisted that he must have been tortured. 'I assured her that Struensee had confessed willingly', Uldall wrote. 'I tried to raise her pride by telling her how much he had done wrong against her. It seemed to have some effect, and would have had more if she had known to the full his cowardice, but she always returned to this; he must have been forced.'

Caroline Mathilde had refused to think that Struensee might be put to death. Uldall was determined that she should understand that she would see neither the King nor her lover again. About Christian she said little and seemed to care less. 'All her care was directed towards the wretched Struensee. When we talked about his fate she cried and trembled.' But she was angry too. She had found out that Rantzau was part of the conspiracy and her hatred of him flared up. 'From her looks and on a couple of occasions I noticed that she thought he should pay for everything', Uldall wrote. Despite her indifference towards him, Caroline Mathilde was eager to see her husband, certain that she could persuade him to revoke the arrest warrants and stop all legal action. Uldall maintained in his memoir that the King had suddenly discovered the Queen's adultery 'on the seventeenth of January', and that the affront to his honour had made him determined to arrest her. But Caroline Mathilde understood her husband better. 'I always feared that he would sacrifice me if somebody put evil in him against me,' she said, and after toying with the idea of writing to him, she gave it up, declaring simply, 'It is no use.' With open eyes she saw too that her confession would be sent to London and that her brother would believe it. 'Now they can tell him everything against me,' she said bitterly.

As for Struensee's political reforms and his commitment to a new way of life, Caroline Mathilde saw herself as a part of the enterprise. If she had not been a murdering, controlling Messalina or Agrippina, as Rantzau asserted, she had understood and sometimes disagreed with her lover's decisions and changes. His taking control of the executive in July the year before had been a mistake, Caroline Mathilde told Uldall. 'Had Struensee followed my advice in not becoming cabinet minister, everything would have been better.' Uldall did not hear her, and saw only innocence corrupted. 'She spoke Danish as well as I did, as well as English, French and German', he wrote in admiration, adding that 'had her heart been formed with a good upbringing, I think she could have made her husband and the country happy'.

By the time Uldall went up to Kronborg, news of the Skilsmissekommissionen had leaked out, and on 21 March Reiche wrote to his superiors in Hanover that 'the large secret commission . . . is now said to have discussed the divorce of the King and Queen', and that the plans for Caroline Mathilde to be sent to Aalborg, which he had mentioned a fortnight earlier, 'were still in place'. On 23 March, Keith angrily told Osten, face to face, that if a divorce was declared, he had orders to depart without leave, the diplomatic prelude to war. But on 20 March, Christian's letter enclosing Struensee's confession had been handed to George III in the Queen's House. Its effect was tumultuous. Neither Lord Suffolk nor the King questioned its veracity. Immediately, the fiction of Caroline Mathilde's innocence was torn away. George III was disgusted at having finally to confront the truth of the rumours about his sister and personally affronted that she had so far scorned her duty and station as to stoop to an affair. After a hurried conference with him, Lord Suffolk wrote to Sir Robert Keith the same day, saying, 'I must frankly tell you that His Majesty's justice cannot be so warped, even by his fraternal affection, as to deny that, supposing this to be a true state of the case, the King of Denmark has a right to sue for the dissolution of the marriage.' Keith was ordered to withdraw his threat of leaving Copenhagen, and Suffolk added that, 'it is not His Majesty's wish that his sister should reside in Denmark'.

In London the mood was bleak. George III had protested strongly and without result about his cousin's refusal to let him have any personal correspondence with his sister, and now he was forced to recognise that his strategy had failed. The private correspondence between monarchs had never, in fact, been private, the family affair had quickly escalated into an affair of state, and Caroline Mathilde was still a prisoner. George felt a stinging sense of personal failure both as the head of his family and in the eyes of the world. Had he known of a letter Caroline Mathilde wrote to him from Kronborg on 3 April, in which she demanded help from him, saying his honour was too tied up in the affair for him to stay a spectator and calling on him as her brother to free her, he would have felt worse still.

At first these contending angers combined, as his troubles had so often done in his youth, to produce inertia. But then reports arrived that Caroline Mathilde was shortly to be moved from Kronborg to Aalborg. Once out of sight she could easily be violently silenced for ever. On the morning of 4 April Suffolk and the King met the Prime Minister Lord North and perhaps Lord Sandwich, Secretary to the Navy. They decided then that the time for negotiation had finished and the time for force had arrived. 'All His Majesty's confidential servants', Suffolk told Keith on 7 April, 'have unanimously resolved, and their resolution is approved of by His Majesty, that a fleet should be sent to Copenhagen to demand the Queen of Denmark, and in case of refusal to the demand so made, to proceed to hostilities. . . . In consequence of this resolution, which was formally taken three days ago, orders have already been dispatched for preparing a fleet of ten ships of the line with a proportionable number of frigates, and two bomb ketches, which will be ready to sail under the command of an Admiral in a fortnight.' Admiral Sir Charles Hardy was called up to command.

At first, the King and his advisers seem to have thought of sailing round into the Baltic and blockading and bombarding Copenhagen alone, forcing Guldberg's government to submit simply by an attack on the capital city. But by 7 April they were thinking of a much wider war. Now Suffolk asked Keith about 'the situation and strength of Copenhagen, Elsinore and the neighbouring fortresses, the means of attacking them from the sea, either by bombardment or cannonade, the degree of security to the shipping in those two parts, and the state of the channels, the coasts and of whatever else may affect the approaches or operations of a fleet'. But he added that separate naval deployments were now being planned to 'annoy the trade or other dominions of Denmark', if war were declared. The aim, he concluded, was not just to bring 'justice', but also to deal out a world-wide and humiliating punishment to the Danish government and nation, and to make the court of Copenhagen 'sensible that outrageous indignities to the Crown of England cannot pass with impunity'.

For all the agitation in London, a sense of things ending was settling over the Danish capital. On 2 April the Skilsmissekommissionen reconvened, and Bang's indictment and then Uldall's defence were laid before it. Despite the commission's foregone conclusion, Uldall wanted to make his defence as credible as possible. Posterity, and his conscience, demanded it.

Uldall began his defence of the Queen by pointing out that under Danish law the confession of an accused person could not be used as evidence against them, and that, besides, Caroline Mathilde had withdrawn her signature that confirmed Struensee's confession and had declared herself innocent. Beyond that he threw doubt on the statements of Caroline Mathilde's household servants, and those of Brandt and Professor Berger, saying that none of them had conclusive proof of any intimacy of the Queen and Struensee carried beyond the bounds of propriety. In mitigation of any proofs of unusual behaviour, Uldall quoted what he called, 'Her Majesty's words exactly as she uttered them': 'If I have possibly acted incautiously, my age, my sex and my rank must excuse me. I never believed myself exposed to suspicion, and, even though my confession appears to confirm my guilt, I know myself to be perfectly innocent. I understand that the law requires me to be tried: my consort has granted me this and I hope he will, through the mouths of his judges, acknowledge that I have not made myself unworthy of him.'

It was no use, of course. Caroline Mathilde's words may have been recorded for her son and the future to read, but on 6 April the commission formally announced that the King had repudiated the Queen, both for the public welfare and to preserve the honour of his royal house. The judgement was taken to Christian and he signed the formal sentence. With that, Caroline Mathilde was no longer Queen of Denmark, though her two children were declared legitimate. A relieved Osten told Keith on 7 April that he could now visit Caroline Mathilde at Kronborg and that she could write to her brother. The next day Guldberg sent off to George III a copy of the verdict and details of the retreat Caroline Mathilde would have at Aalborg. At the same time, Peter Uldall and a senior lawyer, State Councillor Horn, went up to Kronborg themselves to read out the verdict to Caroline Mathilde and to announce where she would be imprisoned if no agreement could be made with George III about her future.

Caroline Mathilde asked first to talk to Uldall, and at one-thirty in the afternoon, with Andreas von Hauch and Councillor Horn waiting in the ante-room, he was led into the Queen's apartment. Their meeting was emotional and, for Uldall at least, profoundly uncomfortable. He had no good tidings to bring and no comfort to offer and Caroline Mathilde burst into tears several times. Struensee and her children were still constantly with her in her thoughts. After Uldall told her that her marriage had been annulled she said simply, 'I imagined so,' and passed straight on to her lover. 'How are things with Struensee?' she asked. Uldall told her that he had been appointed to defend Struensee as well and she pressed him about the sentence for what she called 'the crime he is accused of'. Uldall told her he was sure it would be death and added, 'Political reasons strengthen my belief.' Caroline Mathilde broke down, crying and shaking. 'If I asked the King for him?' she said when she had got control of herself again. 'It will be of no use,' Uldall told her baldly, 'if nothing else the safety of the regime demands his death.' 'Should I not be able to talk to the King?', Caroline Mathilde demanded again. Uldall, who knew perfectly well that Caroline Mathilde was being held in Kronborg precisely so that she could not reach Christian, and so that he could not find her, replied simply that he doubted it.

When the commissioners had assured her that her trial and fate would be kept a secret Caroline Mathilde had believed them and she was shocked when Uldall told her that Councillor Horn would read out her sentence to her. She seemed to have no idea that her story had run right round Europe; that the most intimate details of her life had been printed in the London press; that, as the *General Evening Post* bluntly put it, 'the worst prostitute that ever Covent Garden produced could not have had more gross abuse bestowed on her'. 'Could I not declare the sentence had been announced to me?' Caroline Mathilde asked Uldall, adding that that way, 'It need not be as well known as I sense it will be.' Then she turned to thinking about her exile, and mentioned going back to London. But Uldall, knowing that George III had never suggested it, said gently, 'I fear that in your situation England and London would be much too unpleasant.' Caroline Mathilde thought a little and then agreed, passing straight on to her children, bursting into tears again when Uldall told her that she could not expect to keep either of them with her.

Prince Frederik, Caroline Mathilde sensed, was lost. But Princess Louise

Augusta, whom she was still breast-feeding, was the living reminder of her happiness, the part of Struensee that she still had with her. All Caroline Mathilde's physical and emotional comfort was now concentrated in her daughter, and her hopes for the future too. Struggling to control her tears again she turned away from Uldall and walked to the window, looking out on to the fading afternoon. 'I must have her with me,' she burst out to Uldall, 'I will declare that she does not have anything to do with that family. Can I not then keep her?' As gently as he could Uldall pointed out that if Caroline Mathilde made a public declaration that Louise Augusta was Struensee's child she would be admitting her own adultery. Perhaps realising that her rehabilitation in Denmark would depend on continuing to declare her innocence, Caroline Mathilde acquiesced, only to start crying again when she thought first of Struensee and Brandt and then of her son. His life, she feared, was in danger from her enemies, and particularly from Juliane Marie. But after Uldall reassured her about the Prince, she returned again to her main concern, her lover. She was still convinced that Struensee had been forced to confess under duress, and that coercion exonerated him from any responsibility for her own misery. 'Tell him,' she said to Uldall, 'that I am not angry at him for what he has done to me.' Uldall was uncomfortable again, and seeking to end the conversation he suggested that he call Councillor Horn and General von Hauch so that the sentence could be read out.

When the two men came in, Caroline Mathilde listened in silence and then, with what Uldall called 'the greatest composure', signed the sheet of paper Horn held out to her. Finally she demanded twice to speak to the King, still thinking of him as her lifeline and her hope of salvation. Horn told her he would pass on her demand, but made no promise to tell the King himself, and the two men went away, breaking the mood and leaving Uldall calmer and able to proceed to his own task, reading out his now obsolete defence. Then with Caroline Mathilde reiterating yet again her desire for Louise Augusta, he said goodbye, leaving her still a prisoner and lonelier than ever.

There was nothing secret about the verdict against Caroline Mathilde. The Danish government was pressing ahead with plans to move Caroline Mathilde to Aalborg as soon as possible. Her future chamberlain was already on his way there, it was rumoured that her apartments were being fitted out with damask wallpaper and French carpets, and sailors were loading the twenty-four-gun frigate *Tranquebar* with stores for the journey. Robert Murray

Keith, arriving back in Copenhagen from his first visit to Caroline Mathilde in her captivity and hearing the same stories, asked Osten to delay her departure, claiming that Princess Louise had chickenpox and could not be separated from her mother.

The little Princess was indeed ill, but Keith was also stalling for another reason. Since Uldall's visit four days earlier, Caroline Mathilde had thought better of leaving the country and taking up her brother's offer of a retreat in his Hanoverian territory at Celle. 'The Queen, it is asserted in many letters, prefers Aalborg to Celle, fully persuaded that the K[ing] will soon take her from thence', Ralph Woodford reported to Robert Gunning. King Christian, for months absent from the drama, had suddenly begun to play a part in conjecture. 'It is said', Woodford went on, 'that since the sentence the King of Denmark, assisting at a tragedy, became moved, returned home melancholy, [and] the next morning ordered his equipage early. He was weak enough to tell where he had a mind to go, which was to Kron[borg]. He was dissuaded, or more properly forced from it. But sometime after he rushed into the Q[ueen] Dow[ager's] apartments tenant l'épée à la main, sword in hand.' Woodford went on confidentially in French to explain that the King was reported to have slashed the Queen Dowager's tapestries and smashed up the porcelain and glass with his sword before retreating quietly to his rooms.

If Christian really wanted to reach his wife, Caroline Mathilde was an immediate threat to Guldberg's government. A single meeting between them would be enough to reverse the revolution and bring a vengeful queen back to Copenhagen. Woodford sensed that Caroline Mathilde knew how close she was to a return and believed that she was determined to stay in Denmark for that very reason. 'But surely', he wrote, 'liberty and safety ought to prevail in her mind.' The time had come to get rid of Caroline Mathilde one way or another. To his surprise, Keith found Osten smoothly amenable when he arrived with his threat of war on 15 April. Subject to certain terms, the Foreign Minister conceded, the British could come and take Caroline Mathilde away. The first was a guarantee from the British Crown that she would never return to Denmark, the second a demand that the British navy would not enter Danish waters to remove her. Keith angrily brushed these requests aside. British ships, he replied, would sail right up to the walls of Kronborg and take Caroline Mathilde away.

They had avoided war and got rid of the Queen. Despite his fears that over the border in Germany she would still be a potent force, and that

George III would support her burning desire for her children and her throne, Guldberg's government agreed. The same day the hapless Danish King wrote, 'apprové, Christian', in his spidery hand on a formal declaration allowing Caroline Mathilde to leave the country. A few hours later Keith drove up to the gates of Kronborg Castle with the declaration in his hands and a chivalrous glow that he was Caroline Mathilde's deliverer in his heart, carrying, 'to an afflicted and injured Princess the welcome proofs of fraternal affection and liberty restored'.

But Guldberg and his ministers were still jumpy, anticipating British duplicity and nervous about the future. They saw danger in George III's refusal to acknowledge his sister's divorce publicly and in the obvious slight contained in every letter from London that still referred to Caroline Mathilde as Queen of Denmark. They wanted a formal guarantee that Caroline Mathilde would never again step onto Danish soil and were anxious at their failure to get it. Three things held London back: the possibility that Caroline Mathilde might one day be recalled either by Christian VII or by her son; her own angry determination to seize back what had been snatched away from her; and Lord Suffolk's desire to remind Osten that although the immediate victory was his, Britain was Europe's strongest nation and the British government resented being outwitted even by seasoned diplomats from a minor power. Suffolk wrote to Keith accordingly. 'At the same time, therefore, that you disdain submission to any condition of a guarantee from His Majesty against the return of the Queen into Denmark, you may frankly avow His Majesty's wish that she may never again see that country. . . . After such a declaration of his intentions, made by you, His Majesty will think himself bound in honour to abide by them. But he cannot agree to an express condition which the court of Copenhagen has no right to require.'

Although they had not yet been handed Christian VII's signed statement saying that Caroline Mathilde might leave the country, by 20 April Lord Suffolk was confident that the Danish government had given up the tussle over her place of exile. She was to be escorted from Kronborg by the British navy, sailed down to the southern bank of the Elbe above Hamburg and, once it was ready, installed in the castle at Celle in George III's Hanoverian dominions, no queen but an angry and miserable exile, dependent on her brother and unable to leave without his permission.

On 24 April the Earl of Sandwich sent messengers down to the dock-yards in Plymouth and Portsmouth to scale down the plans for the departure of the fleet. No war machine would sail now, but a flotilla of ships small enough to bring reassurance, large enough to demonstrate British naval might. It was a race against time because the ships in Plymouth were watered, stocked and ready to sail, as Suffolk put it to Sir Robert Keith, and 'would have been sailed if the countermand had been a few hours later than it was'. As it was, when the fleet was stood down, Suffolk and Sandwich congratulated themselves that they had turned away a crisis. An 'abundance of speculation and stock-jobbing will be prevented by this means', wrote a relieved Lord North, who knew from his experience of the last war that hostilities always produced dangerous instability on the London exchange, with large amounts of currency and stock speculated against different outcomes.

Peace settled on the shipyards at Portsmouth and Plymouth. But in Copenhagen, a few days later, the city's gulls, wheeling above the docks, attracted by the movement of barrels and ropes, the bustling sailors and officials, the loading of biscuit and water and the ships' cats strutting the decks, would have seen eight ships of the line slip out of Nyholm into the spring waters of the Baltic, shaking out their heavy cream sails after a winter's inactivity, heading quietly north. Admiral Rømeling was taking no chances; his warships would sit over the horizon, guns ready, until the British had come and gone.

Others in the government were even more anxious. Prince Frederik and several others argued strongly that Caroline Mathilde should be packed off to Aalborg, and picked up from there, because she posed a continued threat so close to Copenhagen. But Schack-Ratlou wrote to the Prince, characteristically whispering caution. Even though he agreed that the menacing appearance of a British squadron in the sound off Elsinore might make the Danish government seem weak and vulnerable, the Queen, he said, had no supporters to seize the moment and rise up to free her. Pointedly now referring to Caroline Mathilde as princess rather than queen, Schack-Ratlou explained to Prince Frederik, 'It is without doubt disagreeable to keep for much longer in the vicinity of the King a Princess who has such a great dominion over his mind, who has abused him in a most disgusting way in the eyes of the world, and who without doubt is occupied solely in finding a way to re-establish herself so as to loose her hatred and vengeance against those whom God has used as instruments for the salvation of Denmark and against the King himself.' Besides, he added with satisfaction, Caroline

Mathilde was so well guarded that it was impossible for her to escape and get to the King, or even to write to him. All the Prince had to do, Schack-Ratlou intimated, was to hold his nerve and wait.

Caution was the watchword. Quietly the government moved swiftly to judge and disperse those members of Struensee's government and Caroline Mathilde's court still under arrest. A simple rule was to be applied: leniency for those who shared and helped in the experiment, and for those who led it the harshest punishment and strictest application of the law. By the end of April Struensee's brother, Professor Berger, General Gëhler and his wife and Falkenskjold all knew that exile or temporary imprisonment would be the worst that they would have to endure. Falkenskjold was dealt with harshly because of his fidelity to the beliefs that Struensee propounded rather than any particular transgression. He endured four years in the remote snow-blasted fortress of Monkholm in Norway before he was released into exile. Most of the others though were sent back to their estates or made their way to Hamburg. Brandt and Struensee Guldberg intended to dispatch far beyond all human reach.

In the three months since the coup d'état, prisoners and witnesses had talked and talked. But none had offered any real evidence of a conspiracy to dethrone King Christian, and the Inkvisitsionskommissionen soon abandoned any idea of netting either Johann Struensee or Enevold Brandt on that charge. Brandt was finally charged with appropriating royal funds, abetting Struensee in his affair with the Queen and, most importantly, with assaulting and biting the King, a crime punishable by death. Struensee's crimes, nine in all, were laid before the commission on 21 April by the Attorney-General, Frederik Wivet, who announced without mincing his words, 'Count Johann Friedrich Struensee has committed a crime of high treason, in that he has undertaken to seduce, in a most daring and audacious manner, the first lady in the kingdom, whose confidence he has obtained by the basest means.' He called Struensee's seduction of the Queen the 'most daring and unparalleled crime, of which history scarce furnishes us with an example', and claimed that from it all his other crimes flowed. As Osten and Christian VII had promised George III, Caroline Mathilde was never mentioned by name in Wivet's indictment, but her spirit and presence were everywhere. The prosecutors needed them to be because having an affair with the Queen was the only charge that Struensee had put his name to and the only one for which the evidence, if admissible, was overwhelming.

Wivet cited as evidence of Struensee's 'audacious behaviour', not only the signed confessions, but the testimonies of Brandt, Berger and Caroline Mathilde's maids. He wrote that, 'not content with seducing the royal virtue, his conduct seemed to declare that he wished to make her infamy known before the whole world', and declared that Struensee might, even before he submitted any defence, 'read his well-merited punishment in the Danish code of laws'. Struensee was also charged with being aware of Enevold Brandt's treatment of the King; with endangering the life of Crown Prince Frederik by his barbaric system of education; with hiding information from the King and signing Cabinet orders in his own hand; with defrauding the Treasury; and finally with selling a piece from the crown jewels. That he would be found guilty was beyond doubt.

For Guldberg, trial, conviction and execution were not enough. He wanted a spiritual victory too. Piety had come back to Denmark and Struensee must welcome it, and confess the error of his ways. The doctor's recantation, published to the nation, would cement the legitimacy of the new government and break any lingering strands of the godless enchantment he had woven over the country. Guldberg's aim was nothing less than Struensee's conversion, his instrument a man of God, Balthasar Münter, the pastor who had delivered a sermon of thanks for Struensee's overthrow after 17 January.

Later, Münter wrote that he approached Struensee on his first visit at the beginning of March with a simple desire, 'to look to the welfare' of his soul and to get him ready to meet his death. Yet he knew his mission had a wider purpose, to set back the Enlightenment experiment that Struensee had begun, an experiment that might end with the death of religion itself. All sensible people could see, he wrote, that during Struensee's administration, 'religion had everything to fear, and that the morals of the people, at least in the metropolis, were in danger of becoming wild and ungovernable'. On 17 January, 'the rights of virtue and piety had been secured from the danger that seemed to threaten them', and he now was charged with making sure that the way of life that Struensee represented and promoted was, in Denmark at least, killed off at the root.

Münter brought with him a method of conversational interrogation perfected over the last two centuries by Lutheran pastors who had been trained to extract confessions from women accused of witchcraft. Gaining the confidence of their hapless charges, pastors had learned how to use their beliefs against them, demolishing them one by one with arguments from scripture until the battered victim capitulated, declared herself guilty and went to her death a penitent and poignant example to others. In Münter's own account of what he called Struensee's conversion this strategy was obvious and transparent. He talked with generous sympathy; he brought books that attempted to use the instrument of reason to prove the existence of God, of the afterlife and finally of the divinity of Christ. Day after day, he came back, like a friend, picking up the thread of the argument where he had left it, and leaving books he knew Struensee would read to while away solitary hours of unwanted thought. At the end he claimed a complete success. Struensee was forthright about his lack of belief, laying out for Münter a simple set of conclusions from the great debates about the nature of the body and soul, and saying that he regarded man as an organised machine. It was a conclusion to which his own meditations had led him. God it may be who first set this machine in motion; but when it stops, that is to say, when man dies, he was convinced that everything died with him. He was not denying that man had free will, but believed that his actions are determined by his sensations. 'You will hardly make me believe that there is a future life,' he told Münter, adding, 'I have made so many observations from anatomy and physic which confirm it, that I think it will be impossible for me to renounce my principles.' But Münter apparently made him do just that, bringing Struensee slowly to his knees, renouncing first Helvétius and then Voltaire and declaring after six weeks that he was 'reconciled to God through Christ'.

Very soon after Münter began his visits to Struensee's chilly cell, the government was hinting that the prisoner was crumbling. By the time Uldall went to Kronborg on 8 April news of his conversion was circulating throughout Copenhagen. Caroline Mathilde, however, was not convinced by the news that her lover was 'now quite changed and religious'. 'She smiled at that', Uldall wrote, 'and did not believe it, or at least not the seriousness of the change in his thoughts.' Caroline Mathilde may have thought that Struensee was either toying with Münter or was clothing himself in religiosity to save his skin. But Münter had already implied to Struensee that he was going to his death, saying that he was 'preparing his soul for eternity', and the doctor himself must have realised that his chances of emerging from the citadel a free man were very slender. Parts of Münter's narrative, especially the letters between Struensee and his parents, had all the stagy overcharged emotionalism of an epistolary novel and much was surely invented to serve the needs of the government. Many at the time were as sceptical as Caroline Mathilde that six weeks, even with a man skilled at turning sinners, would be enough to shatter the bedrock of Struensee's life.

Certainly, Struensee's prison writings bore no mark of a mind in ruins or a personality destroyed and remade. He was terrified of course, and he bit his fingers nervously when Uldall came to him on 13 April and told him how he was to die. But when Uldall mentioned the defence he proposed to put forward, Struensee was equable and indifferent, not seeming to expect clemency or freedom. He admitted his failure to foresee the conspiracy against him and knew that nothing could be done to change his fate. Of his defence he said wearily, 'I regard it as a pure formality.' Death was inevitable, but the future might tell his story in another way. Struensee meant that it should, and in his cell he wrote several documents, including a statement describing the illness of the King and a refutation of the charges against him.

Struensee's apologia for his beliefs and practice of government was finished and dated on the day after Uldall had told him he was likely to be executed. It was a dry, incisive and orderly statement that gave no hint that its author, as he wrote it, was still manacled and had to drag his heavily chained hand along each line and down each page as he wrote and lift it ponderously to dip his pen in ink. His account of his career was careful and partial, the rise to power not of an ideologue but of a servant of the King and Queen and the common good. 'An ardent desire of rendering myself useful, by actions that could be of real and extensive benefit to the society I lived in, was the only object of my wishes', he declared. Offering an analysis of Count Holk's weak and extravagant government, he presented himself as a man of common sense, a doctor, after all, who could see the ill and prescribe the simple remedies: frugality, self-reliance and efficiency. No dangerous radicalism peeked out from his wide-ranging 'general plan for the management of state affairs', just a careful bureaucrat, who grouped resolutions and reforms with academic precision under seven different headings: foreign affairs, finance, justice, the army, the navy, the court and the King's own affairs. As for his motives, his disinterested sincerity was obvious in his indifference to all the threats made against him while he was in power, and clearly he had never amassed any fortune from government funds. He had, he wrote, no 'dangerous designs against His Majesty', adding, 'I never expected that I should be accused of having employed unlawful means to maintain myself in power.' Christian himself should be allowed to judge his guilt or innocence. Finally, he gave an account of Prince Frederik's education, burying in it a ringing defence of both his own medical practice and his belief in the commonality of all people. 'If it be advantageous', he wrote, 'that a Prince should have his first education common with all men, that he should receive the strength of body which is never derived from a delicate education . . . that he should not too soon be apprised of the dignity he was born to, in order that it might not become a burden or inspire him with pride which must be checked with moral principles; if, finally, that early education is deemed the best, which is the most natural, I believe that no one will find that adopted with the Prince in any degree to be censured.'

The court, reconvening on 22 April, had no use for any of this. Its judgment, signed by nine of the commissioners, including Guldberg himself, simply declared that Struensee had confessed to 'a certain atrocious crime, at the bare recital of which human nature shudders, and which the faltering tongue seems unwilling to repeat', and that he was also guilty of all the other crimes he had been charged with. When Uldall, hastening straight to the citadel, read the sentence out to Struensee, he was surprised at what he called the doctor's 'fortitude' and 'calmness of mind'. Interrupted in the final paragraph of his apologia, Struensee picked up his pen when Uldall had finished, doggedly wrote out the last five or six lines, and added the document to the letter he had already written to Christian appealing for his life.

Like Caroline Mathilde, Struensee must have known that such an appeal was hopeless. On 27 April Christian VII signed the statement, 'We hereby approve, in every respect, of the sentence pronounced by the Commission of Inquisition.' What he thought or felt, the King could not say. In ringing tones, which sounded out from another, more barbaric age, the sentence declared that Struensee 'has forfeited his honour, his life and his estates; that he shall be degraded from his dignity as Count, and all other dignities conferred upon him; that his Coat of Arms which he has as Count, shall be broken by the executioner; that his right hand, and afterward his head shall be cut off while alive; and that his body shall be quartered and laid upon the wheel, but his head and hand shall be stuck upon a pole.'

Struensee tried to keep a calm appropriate to a philosopher, though nothing in the Enlightenment imagination could prepare him for so medieval a scene. He understood the end was near, telling Uldall when he visited him that day, 'I have thought through everything that might happen in order not to be too surprised.' As he spoke, carpenters were building a huge scaffold at Østerfælled, an open space between the north and east gates of the city. It sat twenty-four feet square and rose twenty-seven feet above the ground. Round the city perimeter, beyond the western gate, two poles and four wheels lashed to posts were also hauled upright and anchored into the soft spring ground, waiting like sentinels for their grisly burdens.

All through the night of 27 April, crowds moved through the silent city, massing at the eastern gate, drawn to the place of ending. At eight in the morning the next day, under a cold overcast sky with wreaths of mist hanging down to a grey sea, the gate was opened and the crowd moved like a flood to surround the scaffold, leaving a narrow channel for the carriages of the victims to pass through. Up on the scaffold, silhouetted against the sky, stood the executioner and his assistants, masked, gloved and animal-like.

In the hush that followed the arrival of the coaches, Enevold Brandt was first up the steep wooden steps to the platform. He climbed slowly, hampered by the shackles that still bound him hand to foot. Behind him came a pastor, Dean Hee, who would recite prayers as the axe came down. At the top, in a bold gesture, Brandt threw back the warm fur cloak that had guarded him against the cold. The executioner raised his axe and struck off his iron fetters which fell clattering down on the wooden boards. Then the King's bailiff stood forward and read out Brandt's sentence for the waiting crowd to hear, the words ringing through the still air. At the end, Brandt declared his innocence in a firm voice and nodded when the bailiff asked him if the coat of arms he held up were his. Seeing his acknowledgement, the bailiff swung the shield in the air and broke it into pieces, destroying, in one ancient gesture, Brandt's honour and his nobility.

After a series of exhortations and prayers, Hee took Brandt's hand, and led him forward, delivering him to the executioner with the last touch of humanity he would ever feel. Brandt refused help in undressing, taking off his hat and his green velvet coat and waistcoat. As he rolled his white shirt-sleeve slowly up his arm, the executioner stepped impatiently forward, roughly pulling the shirt up above the elbow and opening it out at the neck.

No call came to stop, no pardon from the King. Brandt knelt down and put his bare right arm on one wooden block, his head on another. As Hee moved back reciting a prayer, the executioner stepped forward and in two heavy swipes hacked off first Brandt's outstretched hand and then his brown-haired head. Swiftly again the executioner's assistants came forward in the hush that followed, stripped the body of its breeches, stockings and shoes, and cut it into four quarters, drawing out Brandt's entrails, his warm heart, stomach and intestines. Each quarter, dripping blood, was dangled over the scaffold and lowered into a waiting cart. Brandt's head was held up, turned to every corner of the field, and then, with the single hand, roped down to lie with the body-parts. The executioner threw sand over the execution blocks. In dumb expectation the crowd waited, its humanity as stained as the boards from which the puddled blood dripped slowly down.

While his friend died, Struensee waited in the closed carriage. Prayers, thuds, exclamations came through the window to join the beating of his frightened heart. Now that his turn had come he climbed the scaffold, ashen-faced but steady. The closeness of death made his hands shake and he needed help from the executioner to take off his favourite blue velvet coat. Seeing the blood of his friend seeping up through the sand on the blocks he took several seconds to force his hand and his head down on the wood. When the first blow of the axe came down and took off his hand, Struensee's body rebelled and began to tremble. The second blow missed his head and the desire for life made him start up. The executioner's assistant pulled his head down again and the third blow came down, slicing obliquely. When the head rolled off, part of the chin was left behind.

Struensee's body, cut and quartered, his guilty genitalia roughly hacked off, was added to the abattoir bits of Brandt piled up below. The waggoner with his steaming cargo drove across the city to where the wheels and stakes waited. There the two heads were roped up to the pole-tops and the severed right hands nailed to the wood below. Struensee's genitals and the quartered bodies were laid on the wheels and weighted down with criss-crossing iron chains. In the weeks to come Copenhagen's gulls picked the marrow from inside the bones that the rats left.

Thinking of her dismembered love, Caroline Mathilde must finally have known it was time to go. Two British frigates and a sloop were working across the North Sea, and the Queen waited, watching the days grow longer and the sudden spring arrive. 'Obstinate easterly winds', as Keith called them, made the going slow. But by 15 May the convoy was beating north past the mouth of the River Elbe. In the sound the patrolling Danish warships were on alert for treachery. High aloft the foretopmen watched the easterly horizon for the faint outline of rigging against the sky, but, as London had promised, only three sails were sighted, the frigates *Southampton* and *Seaford* and a sloop, the *Cruiser*.

Waiting at Kronborg, still breast-feeding her infant daughter, Caroline Mathilde wrote to London a note of farewell in a gossamer language to disguise her mood. 'Dear Brother,' it ran, 'I suppose that this will be the last letter that you will receive from me in Denmark. I have the consolation in leaving this country to know that my children are in good health. Louisa has had the measles and I have not been well, but we are now both recovered. I do not think it impossible that I may sometime or other see them again. I am afraid they will spoil my son, as it is their interest that he should be as easy to govern as his father is.' This letter sent, with his books packed and his furniture gone, Keith had one final duty to perform. Sheet by sheet he fed into the sumptuous stove every paper that referred to the events of 17 January and the months afterwards. Into the flames went all his letter books, his copies of the diplomatic correspondence between the court of St James's and the Danish royal family, every dispatch sent or received and all his own notes. Lord Suffolk and the King wanted it that way. Months later, Ralph Woodford, arriving to take over, was astonished that diplomatic etiquette had been so flouted. 'I find there is no correspondence left for me to examine and look over', he wrote to Robert Gunning, adding, 'I expect therefore to walk like a blind man and tumble often in the dirt.'

The same incendiary caution took hold in London. In the offices of Lord North and the Earl of Suffolk, in the Admiralty and Lord Sandwich's private lodgings, flames were licking relentlessly at every paper about Caroline Mathilde's adulterous love for Struensee and George III's secret decision to launch a fleet to save her. White dust and ashy fragments, as the King intended, would soon be all that was left of her passion and his secret use of royal prerogative. Both would soon be forgotten.

George III had reckoned without his sister. Captain Macbride's convoy rounded the point at Kronborg and dropped anchor in the shallow waters off Elsinore on 27 April. Three days later Caroline Mathilde said goodbye to her daughter, following behind her as she lay in another's arms, watching the carriage disappear across the drawbridge with tears running down her face. With the summer sun still riding the sky beyond the castle she was handed up to the deck of the *Southampton* from a Danish royal cutter, looking with shaky composure at the place where her daughter had been. As she stepped aboard, the royal standard of the kings of Great Britain rose fluttering to the masthead. But Caroline Mathilde was not a Briton any more. She was to herself the Queen of Denmark, and determined to remain so. When the small convoy sailed two days later the great guns at Kronborg sounded in farewell a twenty-seven-gun salute, echoed back by the watching Danish men-of-war. Caroline Mathilde, though, was not saying goodbye. She went into exile with anger in her arms and only hatred for company. Her heart was in Denmark and she meant to return.

6

An Honest Man

Queasy and uncomfortable guests, Caroline Mathilde's suite watched the low green land of Denmark recede as the *Southampton* slid through the Sound and beat languidly up the eastern side of Jutland. Captain Macbride reported that the morning after his small convoy left Kronborg it was overhauled by two Danish men-of-war, shadowing them through Danish waters, just out of sight over the horizon. Summer lulls made the going slow, but after six days at sea the three ships dropped anchor in the Elbe estuary beyond the port of Stade. Stade was in George III's own territories and on his orders Hanoverian officials greeted Caroline Mathilde like a reigning queen not a disgraced divorcee. Cannon sounded, bells rang, and from the tower of St Wihadi's Church trumpets and drums sounded across the rooftops and over the lapping waters of the river. Caroline Mathilde's new household officials assembled, and her Danish companions and servants packed their trunks. The very next day, in fact, a sad and relieved Count Holstein left for Copenhagen, taking with him Caroline Mathilde's lady-in-waiting, von Mösting, five maids, twenty other servants, a page and a diamond ring from Caroline Mathilde to look on and remember the anxious care he had given to her.

After two days the rest of the party travelled across land to Göhrde, a hunting lodge buried in forested country three miles from Lüneburg. Göhrde was safe and remote in Hanoverian land and no visitors could reach Caroline Mathilde there unannounced. Then the last of Caroline Mathilde's ties with

Denmark was cut; Robert Murray Keith left her, heading back to London, and to laudatory articles in the British press. When he arrived he found that the *Town and Country Magazine* was calling him 'the heroic Minister'. Adopting a tone quite different from its usual bantering censure, the magazine declared of his relationship with his Parisian companion, 'Miss P—lle', whom, it said, he had found in a milliner's shop in the Haymarket, that it was 'a connexion of so agreeable, so rational a nature, that it is almost beyond the reach of censure'. Keith did not linger long in London. He soon left for something he had longed for more than his mistress's embrace or his sisters' Edinburgh conversation: Vienna, with its agreeable court and empress, its music, sunshine and cards. Vienna was, as the Earl of Suffolk wrote to him, 'a more eligible situation' than Copenhagen had ever been, and Keith was to stay as ambassador there until his retirement in 1792.

Writing to Caroline Mathilde on 1 May, George III described Göhrde as 'an agreeable summer residence', where she would find 'the quiet that you must wish for at first'. The King, who always referred to Caroline Mathilde pointedly as the Queen of Denmark in all his correspondence, was determined that the Danish government should see that she was regally received and treated. 'I have ordered', he continued, that 'every sort of Honour should be showed to you.' Even so he could not resist reminding his sister that the loss of her children was a tragedy she had brought upon herself. 'The parting with your children', he wrote, 'is a distress in which all who have any feeling must greatly sympathise with you, but, dear sister, this would have equally attended your remaining prisoner in Denmark, and must be looked upon as the natural consequence of the whole transaction.' Caroline Mathilde was in no mood to bow to her brother's chiding. But she knew he held the keys to her freedom. Adopting the tone of breathless sweetness, she replied as if she were enjoying a summer jaunt rather than beginning a permanent exile, 'I am vastly pleased with the Göhrde, the forest is really delightful. I am sure if you ever see it (as I hope you will) you will be astonished at the beauty of it. The Ladies that are here seem to be very good sort of people, at least they do everything in their power to be agreeable to me. I know it is owing to your orders and that all the happiness that I can have comes from you.'

Behind the saccharine, Caroline Mathilde was already planning, trying to think how she could get information from Copenhagen and write to her exiled and scattered supporters. She knew that she was really her brother's prisoner, and must have suspected that he would plant in her household officials who would read her letters and report on her visitors. She needed at least one person close to her whom she could trust and who might open the path to the exiles in Hamburg, Altona and southern Denmark. Straightaway she thought of Louise von Plessen who had been living in Celle since her dismissal in 1768. Surprisingly, George III agreed to his sister's request, though his acquiescence may have owed a good deal to Madame von Plessen's reputation as a puritanical woman who would frown on any sort of romantic intrigue. He was putting in that night's post, the King wrote on 23 June, 'my directions that M. de Plessen be invited to attend you. She is certainly a woman of good principles and I can never have any objections to her in my dominions. When formerly about you it arose from her known attachment to those given up to French politics.' The King did not want Madame von Plessen to be granted her old post as head of Caroline Mathilde's household, but she was given permission to attend the Queen and, in Celle, to invite her to her house.

After this small victory Caroline Mathilde lay low, content to soften up her brother with flattery and knowing that her comfort and the extent of her freedom lay in his hands. The King sent musicians from Hanover to play for her, a library of books in English, German and French to be assembled for her at Celle, and the sort of advice that he believed it was his duty, as the head of the family, to give. 'Dear sister', he wrote, 'continue that circumspection in your behaviour that has gained great credit during your misfortunes. It is the most effectual means of showing what a blessing you might have been if those that had surrounded you had possessed any principle of honour and integrity.' Caroline Mathilde responded carefully, reacting to news of her family in England but dropping into it titbits she had picked up from Denmark which concerned her much more closely. In July she told him that she had not heard from her children; in September she reported that she had had a letter from the Duke of Cumberland, who, she said, 'had certainly not wrote to me for two years'. As if she herself had not been a flagrant adulteress disdainful of etiquette she added submissively, in deference to her brother's hostility to his new sister-in-law, 'I hope you will not disapprove of my having answered him. I have taken particular care not to mention his Duchess.' With George lulled into satisfaction she added guilelessly, 'a report runs here as if the K[ing] of D[enmark] was to go to Italy. I own I fear if it is true that they will make away with him. It is likewise said that P[rince] Frederik is going to be married to the P[rincess] of Schwerein, but she is so young that I suppose it will not be this year.' Things in Denmark, she was trying to hint, were going against her, the King's life was in danger, and if the Hereditary Prince married he might produce an heir who could usurp her son's place.

George III reacted angrily to his sister's proddings and to her failure to live the retired and virtuous life he had chosen for her. 'Your letters seem to point out how much Denmark still employs your mind', he wrote severely in October. 'As far as relates to the health, education and welfare of your children, I shall undoubtedly take every method of satisfying your curiosity, but any further than that can only serve to keep your mind in a state of disquietude that can never be of any advantage and must be detrimental to your health. Whenever the present horrid people that manage that kingdom are either removed by death or the intrigues of some new party, it cannot avail anything in your favour. But your leading an exemplary life will by degrees turn the cry in your favour and will hereafter make your son step forward in defence of his mother; I doubt but that many dissatisfied people will try to make up to you but I trust you will not give ear to their proposals. Others will be encouraged by the Danish court to sound you with no other view than to pry into your thoughts. Believe me dear sister, the only dignified as well as safe part for you is to give up all thoughts of that country, at least till your children can be in a situation to come to your assistance.'

Caroline Mathilde had no intention of waiting in cloistered seclusion while everyone forgot about her. That autumn, while Hanoverian officials were filling the offices in her household, she made one more attempt to employ one of her old friends. In her last letter from Göhrde on 10 October she wrote to her brother, 'As I wish to have somebody about me that can settle all my affairs, I have thought of Struensee, who was in the Chamber of Finances at Cop[enhagen], and whose conduct was approved of by most people. Sir R. Keith can certainly give you his character.' Carl August Struensee, Johann's older brother, would not only be a link with the exiles, but would be an ever present reminder of her past and her daughter. George III naturally refused her request, but Caroline Mathilde was undaunted. She wrote to Struensee in his banishment at Lübeck north of Hamburg and sent him money as well.

At Göhrde, Caroline Mathilde lived regally, dining off gold plate as she had at Hirschholm, attended by a dozen pages from local aristocratic families. She walked off her anger in the woods, as she had walked in Copenhagen, exhausting her new Hanoverian waiting women. But gradually, and perhaps at the insistence of George III, ties with her old family were renewed. Her sister Augusta came over twice from Brunswick and Queen Charlotte's brother, Prince Carl of Mecklenburg-Strelitz, visited Göhrde at the end of August. The Hanoverian court physician and philosopher, Johann Georg Zimmerman, attending the Queen as a doctor but observing her as a man of letters, wrote that she was 'very lively, very vivacious in society'. She was very witty, he added, 'reads a lot, the whole morning, and every night till 2; she is very beautiful and very pitiable'.

On 20 October 1772, at the end of a fine hot autumn afternoon, Caroline Mathilde and her entourage finally arrived in Celle. Her new home was a moated castle, stuccoed-white. It rose three storeys above its central courtyard and at its corners grew domed towers like sweet cakes new risen in the oven. Less steepling than the Renaissance castles of Denmark and more baroquely feminine with its plaster and curves than the formidable bulk of Christiansborg, it was nonetheless hard to leave and impossible to hide strangers in. Beyond the moat and all round the castle were green formal gardens and to the south of it was the small trading town of Celle itself, sitting on the confluence of two rivers, a tight grid of half-timbered town houses, snug above the floodplain.

For fifty years the castle had been empty, forlornly leaning on the little town in its lee, staffed by caretakers. Now it would fill up. George III had squeezed Caroline Mathilde's dowry back from a reluctant Danish government and provided her with an ample new income from discrete Hanoverian and Irish funds. Her court, he decreed, was going to be magnificent enough both to satisfy his own family honour and to flaunt her royal status to any passing Danes. It was true that the informality that Caroline Mathilde loved was to be abandoned; she could henceforth only admit the nobility on court days. The wives of officials she might allow in at other times but not when the nobility were with her. But despite these restrictions, there was bound to be music and grandeur, and Celle's traders and innkeepers, dressmakers and craftsmen looked forward to fattened times, welcoming her in crowds, wearing red and white ribbons in their bonnets and buttonholes.

On his way to Vienna at the beginning of November Sir Robert Murray

Keith called on the Queen in her new home. George III, sending a letter to his sister with his trusted envoy, wrote that he hoped that the visit would be 'agreeable' to her. But Keith, as Caroline Mathilde knew very well, had come not to bring pleasure but to send back a report. As Lord Suffolk wrote to him before he left London, 'You cannot be too minute and ample on all points of your mission to Zell. A thousand little circumstances, which would, of course, be passed over on other occasions, will be interesting on this. And I think I may venture to assure you that the more comfortable your accounts are to this hint, the better they will please.' Keith, in other words, would be writing for the King.

Keith had two long talks with Caroline Mathilde; she was carefully ingratiating, spinning him a sticky web of pleasantries. Keith stuck fast. 'Nothing', he wrote, 'could be more frank and explicit than her answers to a great number of questions, which she permitted me to ask upon any subject that arose.' 'Her Majesty appears very desirous to communicate to her royal brother, all her views and wishes in the most confidential manner; hoping to obtain in return His Majesty's advice and directions, which she intends implicitly to follow.' Caroline Mathilde, he added, received her brother's letter and the 'repeated proofs of his Majesty's fraternal affection and friendship ... with the warmest expressions of gratitude and sympathy'.

For a start, Caroline Mathilde was insistent that her Copenhagen thoughts were light and domestic. 'Her Majesty talked to me of several late incidents at the Court of Denmark', Keith reported, 'but without appearing to take much concern in them.' 'In regard to Denmark', he added, 'the Queen declares that, in the present situation of that court, she does not wish for any correspondence or connection there, beyond what immediately concerns the welfare and education of her children. That she has never written a single letter to Denmark since she left it, or received one from thence. That the only person belonging to that Kingdom from whom she hears, lives in Holstein, and is not connected with the court.'

Only when she began to talk about her children did Caroline Mathilde's composure falter. She 'expressed great anxiety', Keith wrote, about 'the false impressions which may be instilled into the minds of her children, particularly regarding her self'. Keith reassured the Queen that Prince Frederik and Princess Louise would grow in time to make up their own minds, and, as he put it, she 'seemed willing to lay hold on that hope, yet could not help bursting into tears when she mentioned the danger of losing . . . [their] affections'. All in all Keith was delighted with the Queen's 'perfect health' and 'very good spirits', and left for Dresden with an easy heart.

Her liberator dispatched, Caroline Mathilde was quick to write to her sister in an altogether different spirit. Enveloping Augusta in a cloud of pique, she thanked her for proposing an itinerary for the next summer, complained that their brother had refused her permission to stay at Herrenhausen and said that now was not the time to put the whole plan to him because 'il est dans l'humeur de me refuser tout': he was in a mood to refuse everything. She had asked him to furnish an apartment in the castle at Celle for Augusta, she went on, but he had turned her down. 'Encore un mot de notre bon frère', she ended up sarcastically: one more word about our good brother. He had sent her musicians back to Hanover, saying that they cost too much to maintain at Celle.

Caroline Mathilde was unwise to try and catch her sister in her own annoyance. Augusta was unhappy and untrustworthy, pulled by conflicting loyalties and too inconsistent to be dependable. Besides, someone in the castle was intercepting and copying parts of the Queen's correspondence, and this letter went straight to London and onto her brother's desk. Written only three days after Keith had dispatched his own favourable account, it must have made the King aware that one of his sister's qualities was a mercurial ability to present to others only the facets of herself that she wanted them to see.

As her confidence grew, Caroline Mathilde showed herself to visitors, townspeople and most of all her brother, as every inch the Queen she had been in the last two years in Denmark. Knowing that spies from Copenhagen would report all the details of her life at Celle, she provocatively used the arms of the Danish royal family and made her servants in the castle wear the red and gold royal Danish livery. Accompanied into the town by a uniformed footman, she presented herself everywhere as Queen of Denmark and not as a princess of England, letting her servants speak her mind while keeping silent herself. Only to her visiting sister did she reveal her wishes. After one of her visits, on 22 December 1772, Augusta wrote to her sister, referring to one of their conversations and urging caution, saying that her return to Copenhagen must be a return to King Christian as well, and that if she conducted herself with 'prudence', her past would be forgotten in time. 'But for the love of God', she concluded, 'behave wisely and evenly to every one who comes to you.' This letter, too, was soon in London, confirming to the King his sister's duplicity.

As the year went on, Caroline Mathilde became less guarded and more cheerful, living as informally as the rules of her small German-style court allowed, venting her pent-up feelings by talking of those things that were regarded as legitimate objects of interest, especially her children. Madame d'Ompteda, the controller of her household, was soon telling visitors that not a single day passed in which the Queen did not talk about her young children and show her tenderness for them. Once, Madame d'Ompteda would say, she heard Caroline Mathilde talking to herself in her bedroom, crying bitterly. Going in to console her, she found her addressing the miniature of her son that hung by her bed. In February 1773 visitors from Copenhagen brought a medallion of Louise Augusta to add to the picture of Prince Frederik. Louise Augusta was a toddler now; the change in her was a call to action. At the same time, one correspondent whose letter was intercepted by George III's spies, said that the Queen was asking for news of Reverdil and obviously thinking about the past. Another visitor reported her unguarded assertion that her son would one day revenge her and restore her to the throne. To try to make up for the loss of her children and to still some of her sadness, Caroline Mathilde adopted a little girl, Sophie von Bennigsen, in March 1773. Sophie's mother had just died and her father had enlisted with the Russian Imperial Army. She was just a few months younger than Crown Prince Frederik, and in caring for her, Caroline Mathilde must have hoped that she might catch echoes of her own lost children's thoughts and feelings as they grew.

Despite her melancholy and her anger, Caroline Mathilde began to sing again, telling her sister at the end of 1772 that she had sung with an accompanist for the first time 'depuis Copenhagen', since her arrest. By the next year the twenty-piece orchestra from Hanover was visiting regularly. There were concerts and comedies in the castle theatre and Caroline Mathilde accompanied herself on the harpsichord while she sang in the evenings. Her days were regular and sociable, especially in the spring and summer when she was often outside in the town, or in the castle gardens, and, if her brother allowed, could make visits to the surrounding countryside or to Hanover itself. In May 1773 a young professor from Göttingen, Georg Christoph Lichtenberg, passed through Celle; he saw the Queen and asked the towns-people about her habits. 'She has had two tents put up on bastions in the town', he recorded, probably meaning on the grassy mounds that overlooked the moat at each corner of the castle, 'under which she has breakfast every morning, and takes tea in the afternoon. Weather permitting, I am told, she walks through the streets, greets people in a friendly manner, and allows children to kiss her hand. When she eats everyone is allowed to see her as long as she is seated. For a lady her age she is uncommonly plump, and has a pair of piercing, if not lively, eyes.'

Such visitors came more and more to see a woman whose story was now being circulated throughout Europe, in prints, in poems and in legends. Parts of Struensee's interrogation, including the infamous questions about his relationship with her, had been copied, perhaps with the connivance of the government in Copenhagen, and printed in the press in several countries. Angry exchanges between the British and the Danish governments finished with the protestations of von Osten that all copies of what Ralph Woodford called 'the most detestable part of Struensee's deposition', would be suppressed and destroyed. Nonetheless bits of gossip still got out of Denmark, and the publication of Münter's *Narrative of the Conversion and Death of Count Struensee*, in the summer of 1772, which was rapidly translated throughout Europe and was said to have sold half a million copies, added to the aura of legend and scandal surrounding the Queen. When Lichtenberg came back to Celle in August, he noted, as many visitors did, that something was hidden behind Caroline Mathilde's easy manner. 'Her countenance is not entirely free', he wrote, 'and in her eyes, especially as soon as she stops smiling, glares something defiant and very fiery. Her complexion is healthy, though more pale than red, and her face is certainly not what one could describe as beautiful. One can see there, in my opinion, the courage and resolution which she certainly displayed at her arrest.' The same summer, Dr John Moore, travelling through Europe as tutor and companion to the young Duke of Hamilton, spent several days at Celle, and wrote in the book he published of their travels, 'The youth, the agreeable countenance and obliging manners of the Queen have conciliated the minds of everyone in this country. Though she was in perfect health and appeared cheerful, yet, convinced that her gaiety was assumed and the effect of a strong effort, I felt an apprehension of melancholy which it was not in my power to overcome all the time we remained at Zell.'

Alone, Caroline Mathilde played music, embroidered and read. Parcel by parcel her library grew, in English, French, German, Danish and Italian.

Books arrived from her brother in London and from his agents in Hanover. Others must have been sent by well-wishers, passed on by visitors or ordered directly from booksellers: King George, for instance, would surely not have sanctioned his sister's reading of *The Ambitious Step-Mother, A Tragedy*, or *The Letters of Lady Rachel Russell*, the famous correspondence, published in 1774, of a woman whose husband had been executed for the crime of high treason nearly a century before. Caroline Mathilde's library reflected her talent for languages, her broad tastes from devotional works to bawdy verse novels like Christopher Anstey's *The New Bath Guide* of 1766, and her continued interest in Denmark and in the ideas that had shaped her life there. Among the obvious volumes of Swift, Pope, Goldsmith, Johnson, Beattie, Hume and Molière, and the Bibles and prayer books in several languages, were complete sets of Rousseau and Voltaire and Helvétius's *De l'Homme* in an edition of 1773. Numerous histories of Denmark were accompanied by atlases, Danish court calendars for each year, and books about the countries round the Baltic, including Finland and Russia and, in 1773, *Visconti sur la Revolution arrivée en Suède, il 19 d'Août 1772*. Caroline Mathilde described her books to her brother as 'a great amusement', but they were also ways of remembering the past and of planning the future. For whatever she did, and despite the distractions of music, of gardening, of her little foster child and her jaunts to Herrenhausen and the environs of Hanover, Caroline Mathilde had Denmark in her mind. To her correspondent Mrs Moore she wrote on the last day of 1773, 'I do everything in my power to appear cheerful and I believe impose on most of those that are not particularly acquainted with me.'

From time to time rumours and stories of half-baked plots reached Celle, fuelled by the waning popularity of the new regime in Copenhagen. As early as the end of 1772 Caroline Mathilde heard of an attempt to stir up sentiment in her favour, and by the beginning of 1773 a concerted attempt was made by her supporters to reach her and to try to gather support for her return. On 19 February a civil servant in the employment of the King of Poland, von Krohne, wrote to Caroline Mathilde's chamberlain, von dem Busche, from Lübeck, where Carl August Struensee and other Danish exiles lived. Recently returned from Celle where he had met von dem Busche and perhaps the Queen too, he told Busche that at Lübeck he picked up the news from Denmark first hand, and he wanted to be able to pass it on to the Queen himself. 'People believe', he wrote excitedly, 'and it is certainly true, that the party of Her Majesty the Queen in Copenhagen will soon get the upper hand and that Her Royal Highness will return with the greatest satisfaction. These are not dreams, but the truth.' Struensee's confidant Henrik Gude, who had been the commandant of Copenhagen, was poised on the brink of power, he went on: 'Gude, a friend of Struensee, got a regiment, and the Queen's enemies are so terrified that they are on the verge of leaving the country. Count Rantzau certainly asked permission to leave the country, out of sheer terror that the Queen would return, and I have seen the letter in which this was granted. Now I think the Queen ought to strike while the iron is hot.' To further the Queen's cause Krohne had himself written a defence of Caroline Mathilde, which he asked von dem Busche to give to her. If she approved, Krohne went on, he would have it printed outside Germany, where it could not be censured, and then diffused, 'throughout Europe'.

Writing back a week later, Busche politely dampened Krohne's rebellious fire. Grateful though he was to Krohne for his good intentions towards the Queen, he said, he could not possibly show her the essay written in her defence. It would give her pain, which it was his duty to prevent, and, besides, he thought it dangerous to meddle in the affairs of the great. As far as Caroline Mathilde was concerned, he concluded, it would be best to leave her in her brother's hands, because he certainly 'will know the right time to get the justice that is due to this great princess'.

Krohne slipped away and out of sight. Caroline Mathilde, however, was less circumspect than her chamberlain. A month or so earlier, perhaps responding to the same rumours that Krohne had picked up in Lübeck, and knowing that the new government in Copenhagen was now riven with internal disagreement, Caroline Mathilde wrote to Carl August Struensee, replying to his New Year good wishes and covertly calling on him for support. 'You already know, perhaps, that many of those who suffered with us are now in Oldenbourg', she said. 'They say that they are all very discontented, that they have always hoped to return to Cop—.' Struensee replied on 12 February, thanking her for the money she had sent him, and picking up her train of thought about the exiles in Oldenbourg. 'I know that those who are at the moment in Oldenbourg may well be unhappy there, but without a great revolution, without a revolution that every good Dane wishes for – without a revolution that can't be brought about unless – I would rather for the moment be in Oldenbourg than in Cop—.' Struensee was telling Caroline Mathilde that there could be no revolution unless she was part of it, and his energetic dashes and omissions expressed his wishes without his having to spell them out at danger to himself.

Caroline Mathilde was made less guarded and more impatient by the news, but her impolitic outbursts were soon reported; Krohne's letter found its way to Hanover, Struensee's to London. Whatever Caroline Mathilde knew, her brother and his closest advisers knew too. Reaching a queen who was a prisoner in all but name and encircled with moats and spies seemed an insurmountable difficulty for scattered Copenhagen exiles. But in June 1774, a new chamberlain, Adolf Franz von Seckendorf, arrived at Celle. He came as a Hanoverian court servant, but before the year was out he had become less of a jailer and more of an ally to Caroline Mathilde than von dem Busche had ever been. Then, towards the end of that year, chance threw into the path of the exiles an unmarked adventurer, a lover of risk already fascinated by Caroline Mathilde's story.

Pitching up in Hamburg on 30 September 1774, Nathaniel William Wraxall was a young man on the lookout for excitement and subterfuge. He had come to Hamburg not with the intention of finding a boat to ship him out of Germany to Hull, as he said, but to seek out men who still harboured hopes of revenge against Guldberg's government and were determined to get back to Denmark, to their estates, fortunes and lives at court.

Wraxall was born in 1751 into a successful but unspectacular merchant family in Bristol. In a lifetime of writing and rewriting his own history and the history of his times, he smudged even this beginning, claiming that he came from an ancient family that had given its name to Wraxall in Somerset. He grew into a good-looking young man, with sculpted lips and heavy hooded eyes. Attracted by his beauty, people were repelled by his presence. He seemed hidden and inscrutable and went through life inspiring fear and scepticism. Many believed that he was a consistent fantasist or liar. But Wraxall seemed to enjoy the discomfort he caused, and was determined to live as an adventurer and die a rich man.

Coming back from India at the age of twenty-one with money in his pocket but a name still to make, Wraxall determined on literary success. His was an age of exploration in ink as well as across land and sea, and all across the globe young men were returning from their travels with profitable narratives tucked in the pockets of their great-coats. South of the Bay of Biscay there was hardly a scrap of land left for an ambitious traveller to write his name on. Wraxall contemplated his atlas, perhaps with the story of Caroline Mathilde's exile already in his mind, and decided to head in the opposite direction. He would go north, lasso the Baltic littoral and claim it for himself in a series of letters that would make him famous.

Unlike most travellers, who went as sailors in a large company, as members of diplomatic missions or as young men cotton-woolled on the Grand Tour, Wraxall travelled by himself with a single servant, wrapped in his own sinister mystery. Arriving from Norway on the island of Zealand, in the middle of April 1774, he made his way straight to the house of Nicholas Fenwick in Elsinore, eager for an introduction to the castle commandant at Kronborg. Fenwick declined to take him there but he sent his servant, and the two made their way into the huge fortress and up to the royal apartments on the first floor where he thought Caroline Mathilde must have been confined, later describing them as 'vast, unfurnished, hideous bare walls, never warm in July I should suppose'. Back in the town, people told him that the Queen was never in fact confined there, but Wraxall kept his description anyway: it served as a metaphor for the conditions she endured, and for the cruelty of her jailers.

Fascinated by the bleak romance of Caroline Mathilde's imprisonment, Wraxall sought out Struensee's gaol in Copenhagen's Kastellet too. 'It is not above ten feet square, with a little bed in it and a miserable iron stove', he wrote. To complete the melancholy tour, he stood beneath the skulls and bones of Brandt and Struensee, picked bare under the chains on the wheels where they had been strapped exactly two years before, looking up 'with mingled commiseration and horror'. Caroline Mathilde, he had already decided, would be his heroine, Struensee his wronged hero. 'It was', he concluded, 'the minister and not the man who had become obnoxious.' Like the Earl of Clarendon or Sir Thomas More, Wraxall insisted, Struensee was battling against a monarchical tyranny for the greater good, and like them he would be a hero to future ages.

By the time that he wrote it up for publication a few months later, Wraxall's narrative was more than an engaging traveller's tale. It had become a weapon in a plot. After circling the Baltic, Wraxall's written text, A *Tour through some of the Northern Parts of Europe*, ended in Hamburg in September 1774 with its author homeward bound. In fact, his real adventure was only just beginning. In the memoirs he wrote to be published after his death, based apparently on what he called his 'Private Journal', his journey included detours and meetings that the version published in the spring of 1775 left out altogether. From Strelitz on the bulging Pomeranian plain, Wraxall did not go straight to Hamburg as his written account had it, but looped down to Celle, 'impelled by a desire to pay my respects to the young Queen of Denmark'.

Wraxall saw Celle in double vision, as an adventurer sniffing danger and subterfuge and as a romantic who had sucked up the spirit of Horace Walpole's Gothic novel, *The Castle of Otranto*, with its apparitions, curses, lowering citadel and young noblewoman called Matilda. 'There was in the aspect of the castle of Zell,' he wrote, 'its towers, moat, drawbridge, long galleries, and gothic features, all the scenery realising the descriptions of fortresses where imprisoned princesses were detained in bondage.' But fantastic imaginings overlapped with life itself. At Stettin Wraxall had seen the Princess Royal of Prussia, 'who was there confined for her gallantries'; at Württemberg, he had heard, the Princess of Tour and Taxis was immured for the same reason; and at Celle the ghost of Sophia Dorothea, the adulterous wife of George I, who was born and buried there, looked down on her great-granddaughter.

Wraxall spotted spies everywhere, and at Celle he believed that Princess Augusta was George III's agent, planted there to watch the Queen and report to London. 'I know the fact from the Queen's own mouth', he wrote in his *Posthumous Memoirs*. On his very first day in Celle, Wraxall had dinner with the Queen, who asked him innumerable questions about Denmark, about King Christian and the Queen Dowager, and about her children, asking if the Crown Prince was still dressed in his Rousseauian clothing. Wraxall told her he was not, noting carefully as he talked the rusty red of the Queen's gown, her stoutness and prettiness. With the greedy eye of a man living a fairy-story, he scanned her face. Caroline Mathilde's lower lip was too large, he decided, but her fine eyes were eloquent, her nose well shaped and her small white teeth even and perfect. 'Her face is very handsome: they are His Majesty's features, but all softened and harmonised.' 'She was very gay', he concluded, 'and seemed in no way a prey to melancholy.' Knowing that he was bound for Hamburg, Caroline Mathilde asked Wraxall to carry a letter to Mr Matthias, the British minister to the Hanse towns, asking when he expected the French comedians who came down from Hamburg each year to entertain her at Celle.

At the house of Ralph Woodford's successor in Hamburg, Mr Hanbury, Wraxall soon met a group of Danish exiles. Among them were Baron von

Schimmelman, Struensee's former Minister of Taxes and his wife, and Baroness von Bülow who had been one of Caroline Mathilde's ladies-in-waiting. The Baroness's brother Baron von Bülow, who was in exile at Altona and had been arrested on 17 January, had been the Queen's Master of Horse. In Altona too were Enevold Brandt's former mistress the Countess of Holstein, whom Wraxall observed with detachment through his opera glass at the theatre one night, and Bernard le Texier, a French Huguenot who had served Christian VII as treasurer on his ruinously expensive European tour, and who had left Copenhagen as soon as Struensee's government fell.

Soon Wraxall was invited to the house of Jerome Matthiesen, a Hamburg merchant who was le Texier's brother-in-law. Matthiesen's grand house on a main street by the harbour in Hamburg was for thirty years a refuge and meeting place for exiled and disgruntled radicals from all over Europe and North America. The most advanced politics held sway there, encouraged by Matthiesen himself and then by his son Conrad, who married Susanne de Cercy, daughter of the writer Madame de Genlis who supported the French Revolution and then left France in the Terror. Exiled Danes, rebellious Americans, agents of revolutionary France and conspiring United Irishmen all met at the Matthiesens', plotting the rebellions and revolutions that convulsed the two continents in the last three decades of the century.

The Danish exiles watched Wraxall for several days, and then Bernard le Texier approached him at his lodgings. Would he be ready 'to serve the Queen of Denmark'? Wraxall recorded the minute he met his destiny in his 'Private Journal'. 'A momentary astonishment covered me, but it neither altered my cheek nor faltered my tongue. I felt in the most unbounded degree where it might lead. I was conscious where it must lead. I felt myself born for the achievement and I ardently embraced it. "Yes", I said in reply, "I am the man you seek; give me the commission; I am ready in a day, an hour, a minute."

So Wraxall's adventure began. He stayed on in Hamburg letting boat after boat leave for England, and waited. After a few days le Texier sought him out again, this time accompanied by Ernst von Schimmelman, the eldest son of the Danish nobleman Wraxall had already met. Schimmelman was well known to Guldberg's agents both in Copenhagen and in Hamburg and his family was extremely wealthy and influential in Denmark. He had been a close friend of Otto von Falkenskjold and of the court physician Christian Berger, and was incensed by the harsh treatment of the prisoners and the treatment of the Queen. Soon after Caroline Mathilde's arrest, he and a friend, August Hennings, had tried to establish a secret communication with her in Kronborg by sending anonymous letters to Robert Murray Keith. When they failed, Schimmelman had prudently left Copenhagen and joined the rest of his family in exile in Altona. Now he was ready to try again, and, 'with great agitation and apprehension', as Wraxall put it, he laid out to him a plan for a new coup for the restoration of the Queen. Anything that the Schimmelmans had a hand in was taken seriously in Denmark, and the plan, it turned out, already had influential backers.

Having reeled Wraxall in, Schimmelman handed him on to Baron von Bülow, telling him in explanation, 'My affairs call me to Copenhagen, where my presence may be eminently useful to the cause.' Bülow was a man, Wraxall wrote, 'who joined to great caution, calmness as well as ability', qualities he put down to his Hanoverian extraction and training. He had supervised Caroline Mathilde's riding, and no man, Wraxall thought, 'could be better acquainted with her character, virtues and defects'. Sensing that danger was Wraxall's opiate, Bülow stressed the risks of the enterprise ahead. The first task, he said, was to sound Caroline Mathilde out, to make sure 'that she is disposed to return to Copenhagen; where, during the King's incapacity, and the minority of her son, she must be vested with supreme authority'. The Queen would only confide in Wraxall if she was certain both of his good intentions and his credentials. Von Bülow flattered Wraxall by saying that, since it was too dangerous to give him a letter signed by any of the conspirators, he must write it himself and put it in the Queen's hand. To back it up he could only give him an impression of his own seal, but, he told Wraxall, 'The instant Her Majesty sees it, she will know that you are come from *me*, and she will lend implicit confidence to all you lay before her.' Once he had the Queen's confidence, Bülow concluded, Wraxall had to stress the importance of George III's involvement, because, as he put it, 'without his approbation, if not his aid, we cannot long maintain, though we may effect, a revolution'.

Wraxall arrived at Celle incognito on 9 October, and sent a note to von Seckendorf saying that he had executed a commission for the Queen at Hamburg and was back with an answer for her. Invited to dinner, Wraxall spent the morning writing, 'briefly but accurately' setting out for Caroline Mathilde the points von Bülow had put to him but reserving, as he put it, 'the *names* of the two principal persons by whom I was deputed to wait on her, and the *credential* entrusted to me'.

At half past one, on tenterhooks, Wraxall went to the castle. He knew not only that the Princess of Brunswick was there – and von Bülow had warned him to beware of her – but that he had to present his letter when the household assembled in the drawing room, 'forming a small circle, till dinner was announced'. He was afraid that the letter 'might agitate the Queen; perhaps so powerfully as to excite an emotion in her manner or countenance, capable of betraying the nature of my errand'. So he double-wrapped it, warning Caroline Mathilde on the first sheet not to open the letter until she was alone and to make sure that her sister Augusta did not see it.

Seeing Wraxall when she came into the drawing room, Caroline Mathilde 'advanced with a quick step' towards him, holding out her hand and saying, 'I am glad to see you again. I understand you have a letter from Mr Matthias.' 'I have,' Wraxall answered, and put his letter into her hand. Caroline Mathilde walked to a window to read it and returned quickly, flushed in the face and so flustered that Wraxall himself began to lose his composure. But then dinner was announced and the whole company filed after the Queen and Princess Augusta into the dining room. There Wraxall was alarmed to see that as the dessert was passed round, Caroline Mathilde pushed back her chair, pulled out his letter and read it hidden on her lap, 'raising her head from time to time, uttering a few words, and then resuming her occupation'. Alarmed by this imprudence, Wraxall left the castle after the coffee had gone round and went back to his lodgings.

The next day, having sent Caroline Mathilde von Bülow's seal and been given hers in exchange, Wraxall left Celle. He struck out across aqueous wooded country making for Hamburg by back routes. Once there he gave von Bülow the Queen's seal; the plot was set fair, and the exiles were confident. Count von Laurvig, the governor of Norway, promised to secure Christiana, the capital city, for the Queen, and in Holstein, the governor of Glückstadt would hold that fortress for her. The plotters were amassing formidable allies; Christiana stood guard over Denmark's northern borders, Glückstadt over its southern lands. More than that, Bülow went on, 'their friends were numerous and powerful in the army, the navy, the guards, in the metropolis, and even about the person of the King himself'. Now they wanted to fix the third element of their plan, the involvement, tacit or otherwise, of George III, his envoy in Copenhagen, and, behind them both, the British navy. Sending Wraxall back to Celle, they charged him with asking Caroline Mathilde to appoint him her agent and with sending him to London to confront the King.

Tracking down to Celle for the third time, this time in the persona of a French merchant, Wraxall met Caroline Mathilde on 24 October in a small pavilion in the Jardin Français. Talking in English so that her lady-in-waiting could not understand, they walked round the garden in the autumn sunshine. Although Wraxall recorded in his 'Private Journal' that they 'conversed most closely, most familiarly, almost unreservedly', Caroline Mathilde was careful and calculating in their hour-long discussion. She assured him that she approved of every aspect of the plan put to her, and said she would write to her brother immediately, pressing him 'to send a minister to Copenhagen without delay . . . and urge the necessity of advancing to the party engaged in her restoration a sum of money'. But she declined to pay for anything herself, saying her finances would not allow it, and adding that she could not give Wraxall a copy of her letter as there was no time to write it before he had to leave again. She would, however, write not only to her brother, but also to Lord Suffolk, whose conduct towards her after her arrest 'merited her utmost regard', announcing Wraxall's arrival in London. As a second safe-guard she would also write to Baron von Lichtenstein, the marshal to the court of Hanover who was then in England. One way or another, then, if the King refused to meet Wraxall face to face, his message would still get through.

The next morning as Wraxall set his course for London, Caroline Mathilde sat down to write to her brother, Lichtenstein and Lord Suffolk. If to the last two she wrote in explicit terms about her Danish supporters, she appealed to her brother as her protector and friend. 'Since the last letter I wrote you', she began, 'I have heard so many frightful accounts from Cop[enhagen], that I can no longer help imparting them to you, who are the only friend I have to who[m] I can complain without fearing that my frequent repetitions on so dismal a subject should alter your friendship for me. The weak constitu-tion of the King, and P[rince] Frederik's marriage makes my anxiety for my son's life grow every day stronger. How easily they could make an end of him without its being known, particularly as there is nobody to keep them in fear. A tender father as you are cannot be surprised at the grief that I must feel for the child's situation. For God's sake order your resident to have a constant eye upon those that are about him.' Knowing that her brother responded emotionally to appeals to his position as head of the family, Caroline Mathilde painted herself as desperate and alone. Although she had been assured by Wraxall only the day before that she had many supporters in all walks of life in Denmark, she finished her letter by appealing again for her brother's protection. 'I have no other hope, I repeat it again, but in your friendship for me, and am persuaded that with the principles you have you will never abandon so near a relation, and one who is so sincerely attached to you, as is your most affectionate sister, Caroline M.' Dating her letter 25 October, she gave it to the Hanoverian courier who regularly stopped at Celle on his way up to Hamburg.

To avoid being tailed, Wraxall cut across country to Osnabrück and took a boat from Helvoetsluys to Harwich, clattering into London through Whitechapel on 15 November. He had been travelling, as he proudly recorded, seven months and four days by the time he reached British soil at Harwich, and he was, to the watching world, an author in the making, with his tour of the Baltic and its 'barbarous nations and Polar regions', already partly written in his trunk. The next morning he hurried round to Lord Suffolk's house in Downing Street. Told that Suffolk was laid up with gout and unable to do any business, he made his way to Baron von Lichtenstein's apartments in Pall Mall. Lichtenstein had him shown up straight away and immediately produced for him Caroline Mathilde's letter. Then, 'in a long and confidential conversation', as Wraxall put it, they went over the project together and Lichtenstein promised to put the case before the King.

Two days later, after Lichtenstein had talked to George III, not at St James's but in the greater privacy of the Queen's House, the two men met again. The King, Lichtenstein reported, was sympathetic to the Danish nobles' plan of restoring his sister to the throne. But he insisted on doing business entirely through Lichtenstein, saying that, 'though all cordiality has ceased between him and the Danish court and government since his sister's arrest, yet, as relations of peace and amity still subsist between the two crowns, he wishes to retain the power of denying, in case of any unforeseen accident, that he has seen or received an agent for the purposes of effecting her restoration'. His Majesty, Wraxall wrote, expressed, 'an insuperable reluctance to commit himself to any act which, if it became known, could be construed as an infraction of the treaties subsisting between the courts of London and Copenhagen'. Finally, though, on 3 February 1775, the King came to a compromise which on the one hand meant that his signature would not be found on any incriminating documents, but on the other would give the Danish conspirators and Caroline Mathilde herself confidence to proceed.

Lichtenstein would write the King's declaration, signing and sealing it himself. Wraxall would take it to Celle, show it to Caroline Mathilde and take it, if she approved, to the Danish exiles in Hamburg.

While he had been waiting for the King's reply, Wraxall had made his debut as a writer, bringing out his *Northern Tour* on 1 February 1775. So it was as a man of letters that he set off again, the King's declaration in his pocket. In Celle again, he gave the paper to von Seckendorf and the next day was spirited into the castle and along its gloomy servants' corridors, then left alone in a large room that overlooked the damp gardens. Caroline Mathilde came in by herself almost immediately, dressed in a brown silk polonaise gown, with a sleek green trim, her hair powdered and a locket in her bosom. They stood together in one of the window embrasures and as Caroline Mathilde talked Wraxall noticed that, like her brother George, she often ran over her words in the hurry of her speech, and that these vocal trips 'rather augmented, than diminished, her attractions', as he put it. Although he realised that, 'towards me . . . it was natural that she should express much good-will and condescension', and he was impressed by her regal bearing, he nonetheless sensed in her a degree of calculation, a determination to win over to her cause those whom she met.

Nothing could make up for the fact that Wraxall, despite his best efforts and his long wait in London, had failed, and come away with nothing more than a promise from George III to support any coup that was successful rather than to help a revolution in progress. Von Bülow, running through the King's declaration when Wraxall finally reached Hamburg at the end of February, saw the difficulty straight away. So did the Queen's supporters in Copenhagen. They know they are powerful enough to accomplish the Queen's recall, von Bülow explained to Wraxall, but maintaining it would be their difficulty. It was vital that they change the King's mind on this point, and they were 'therefore determined to draw up a letter to the above effect, addressed to the King of England in their joint names, and to limit their request to this single point. That granted, they are ready, without delay, to proceed to action.' The conspirators in Copenhagen wanted an assurance both from Caroline Mathilde that as soon as the blow was struck she would set out for Copenhagen, and from George III that he would let her go. Time, though, was of the essence, and though the conspirators would wait for the King's reply to their request, 'they neither could nor would long defer the blow'.

Back went Wraxall to Celle, where he was taken to Caroline Mathilde's private library. Two candles were burning, the bookcases were thrown open, and Wraxall was left to wait in the silence for the Queen. Leaving her sister alone after dinner she came to him, dressed in a crimson satin gown, her hair powdered once again, but without jewels. Wraxall pulled forward a chair for her but she refused it, and the two stood together, as they had done before. The Queen, Wraxall wrote in his *Posthumous Memoirs*, 'either had, or impressed me as having, an air of majesty, mingled with condescension altogether unlike an ordinary woman of condition'. They talked for two hours, Caroline Mathilde lively and smiling, 'her countenance animated with the prospect of her approaching emancipation from Zell'.

When Wraxall left, Caroline Mathilde wrote to George III again, saying, 'The D. nobility having through a letter which was delivered to me yesterday by the same person who carried their first demand to England, desired me most humbly to back this request to you, I could not refuse the doing it, though I fear I go rather farther than it may be you approve of. The justice that appears in their whole plan and behaviour will I hope be sufficient excuse for me. If that which they desire with so much warmth is not entirely against the promises you have made, I join in their request to entreat and by this means forward this scheme for my son's happiness.' The Danish nobility, she went on, 'will most likely not have the courage to desire you to write a few lines yourself to your resident at Copenhagen to stand by them when the blow has been struck, as that is one of their greatest wishes, so I take the liberty to name it particularly, as it is not to go through the hands of your Secretary of State, and therefore cannot pass for a ministerial act.'

Arriving with this letter in London on 5 April, Wraxall found another, from von Lichtenstein, waiting for him. Lichtenstein was going back to Hanover, but he warned Wraxall not to expect either a meeting with the King or any documents signed and written by him. George, wrote Lichtenstein, 'ne donnera rien d'écrit de sa main touchant cette affaire, ne permittant d'agir autrement': he will neither give anything written in his hand that touches this affair, nor permit himself to act in any other way. Any letter the King wrote to his sister would bypass Wraxall and go either to von Lichtenstein in Hanover or to the Queen directly.

Unbeknownst to Wraxall, who was left disconsolately waiting, George III was writing to Caroline Mathilde himself. He dated his letter 23 April and sent it by hand with his brother-in-law Prince Ernst of Mecklenberg-Strelitz, who lived in Celle and commanded the garrison there. 'Dear Sister', he wrote, 'It is very natural to imagine that you are anxious to know what has happened on the arrival of Mr Wraxall, but I thought it would be highly imprudent to trust to the common post a single line which might in the smallest degree seem to look towards that affair; but as this letter will be delivered to you by Prince Ernst, I just mention the affair on which you shall hear further from [me] on the return of the messenger and by Monsieur de Lichtenstein who will by that conveyance receive as full instructions as I can think myself at liberty to give.' The King explained that he could not meet Wraxall himself, because 'I should not acquaint any other person with what had past in this affair and did not choose to see the gentleman and still less to commit anything on paper'.

George III's letter struck a familiar tone of high-minded probity, while it clearly signalled his support for the plot. 'My dearest sister', George wrote, 'it is not by calling myself an honest or an honourable man that I can deserve either of these epithets, but by a correct conduct; for to get you safely out of Denmark I certainly said I would not assist in getting you back to that Kingdom. What I said I will scrupulously fulfil.' Fulfilling the letter of his undertaking to the Guldberg government was one thing, though, and longing for revenge was another. So he ended his letter by writing, 'Indeed, I cannot, dear sister, say more than if the D[anish] nobility shall at any time bring the King to recall you with that eclat and dignity that alone can make it advisable for you to return to his kingdom, I shall not only not prevent your going but support I hope [those] who have been accessory to it. But from what I have declared I cannot either enter further into the affair or be entrusted with the plans on which they mean to act. No consideration shall get me to go a step further. I sent my ultimatum when the young man went back to Hamburgh and shall therefore say nothing more.' More endorsement than refusal, George III was telling his sister that he would do nothing to stand in her way and that he would stand by a successful coup.

Whether the King's statement went far enough for the Danish nobility and for Caroline Mathilde herself was never put to the test. George's letter was returned to him unopened, along with the one he had sent to von Lichtenstein. Prince Ernst of Mecklenberg-Strelitz never reached Caroline Mathilde in Celle either. Scarlet fever was raging there and on 11 May 1775 the Queen of Denmark became one of its victims.

Wraxall, arriving back at his Jermyn Street lodgings from a visit to his father in Bristol on the morning of 19 May, was met by his servant who gave him the news. Hurrying to the St James's Coffee House round the corner, he ran into Lord Hertford, who told him that a courier had arrived the night before with confirmation from Celle. Wraxall took refuge in his pen, writing to his father, 'Imagine my dear father the shock I received on hearing this moment, on my arrival here, that the Queen of Denmark is dead. I am wrapt in horror, sorrow and consternation.'

Caroline Mathilde's death was not so much sudden as unexpected. She was still such a young woman – only twenty-three when she died – and appeared so robust and, latterly, so full of excited hope, that some people refused to believe that she had died from an infectious disease. Many of her supporters, particularly in Hamburg and Copenhagen, insisted that she had been poisoned by an agent of Guldberg's government or even of Juliane Marie. As proof they pointed at the lack of an autopsy and the swiftness with which her funeral was held and her body interred in the vault of the dukes of Celle underneath the nave of the old church in the centre of the town. Much later, others suggested, after looking at the doctors' records of her illness, that her wildly racing pulse before she died hinted not so much at infection but at the porphyria that drove her brother mad thirteen years later, and that her having apparently been fully conscious and articulate until the very end also made fever an unlikely cause of her death. Still others convinced themselves that she was not dead at all, that the body wrapped in white silk and buried in a double-skinned pine and oak coffin belonged to a servant, and that she herself had been smuggled to America, a queen over the water, waiting for her call.

Caroline Mathilde's illness, in fact, followed scarlet fever's inexorable path: tiredness and lassitude, a loss of appetite, temperature rising. On 6 May, her physician Friedrich von Leyser, realising the gravity of the case, sent for the help of the court physician at Hanover, the same Johann Georg Zimmermann who had attended Caroline Mathilde at Göhrde in 1772. Zimmermann confirmed von Leyser's professional opinion: for Caroline Mathilde nothing could be done. As the ugly red rash spread across her whole body and her fever rose, her chaplain Pastor Lehzen knelt and prayed at the bedside, murmuring her favourite hymns and passages of the Bible. At the end, he recorded, death came easily in the late evening of 10 May. After a turbulent journey through life, Caroline Mathilde 'fell asleep like a tired wayfarer', worn out and weakened by the fever.

The shock Wraxall felt at Caroline Mathilde's death, and the immediate mourning announced by George III in London, were matched by the horror of Caroline Mathilde's supporters in Copenhagen and the relief of the government there. Henrik Stampe, one of the members of the Inkvisitsionskommissionen who had sat at the trials of both Struensee and Caroline Mathilde, expressed the feelings of many of those involved in the coup of 17 January 1772 when he said, 'Alas, it is not until now that I feel that my head is safe.' It was left to Daniel Delaval, the British Resident in Copenhagen who had replaced Woodford the year before, to record the reaction of the Danish royal family and relay it to London. 'Orders were given yesterday, as I am positively assured', he wrote, 'to put the Prince and Princess Royal into the deepest mourning worn here for a mother.' Count Andreas Bernstorff, he added, was responsible, 'but as consistency is not to be expected here, he could not prevent the Royal Family's appearing at the play on Wednesday and yesterday evenings, and what was worse, their assistance on Thursday night at a ball in dominoes at the theatre, where they made the King of Denmark dance, though they had ordered young Schack to inform him on Wednesday night with the circumstance he was in, with which he was most affected. And yesterday at Court (where I was not) his countenance and manner were such as startled the Foreign Ministers who approached him.' Resident Reiche reported likewise that Christian asked repeatedly on hearing the news, 'Is it true that she is really dead?', and seemed agitated and moved. On the Friday, he added, no court was held, and that night Crown Prince Frederik was kept away from the theatre.

When a member of a ruling family died it was customary for its head to inform his relations in other European courts officially. No longer considering Caroline Mathilde as one of them, the Danish royal family were making it clear to Delaval and to George III that they would not go into mourning until the envoy gave them an official announcement of her death. Swallowing the implication that doing this meant accepting that his sister was no longer a member of the Danish royal family, George III nevertheless described her in all the letters to his brother and sister monarchs in Europe as Queen of Denmark. In Copenhagen, officials were anxious about accepting a notice from Delaval which implied that the divorce had been illegal. But Schack-Ratlou, advising the Hereditary Prince Frederik, was inclined to let it go. 'The pleasure of giving the title of Queen of Denmark for the last time to a sister who by his own admission neither could nor should have used it any more, is so petty and deluded, that it seems to me that we can let it be, and simply give thanks to God that despite the harm done by this, the King cannot throw any more obstacles in our way', he wrote. When the letter was accepted from Delaval, though, the Danish government had the last word. As Schack-Ratlou advised, George III's 'mistake' was noted and the court went into mourning not for a Danish queen but for an English princess.

As soon as Caroline Mathilde died the incendiary obliteration of her memory began again. Either by her own request or for fear of what they might contain, all her papers in the castle at Celle were put to the flames. Back from officiating at her funeral in his capacity of Grand Marshal of the Electorate of Hanover, von Lichtenstein reported to Wraxall that he too had destroyed everything that could refer to the plot in which he had acted as intermediary between George III and his sister. What remained of Caroline Mathilde at the Queen's House and Windsor survived only accidentally. Despite his dislike of the Danish royal family, George had no wish that his own dealings come under any scrutiny or to remember the shameful side of his sister's life, and the determined effort she had made to create a life for herself from the ruins of a dynastic marriage.

In Celle the castle kitchens closed, mice left and dust began to gather. Hanoverian officials catalogued and dispersed Caroline Mathilde's library, distributed tokens to members of her household and sent back her small fortune to the Hanoverian treasury. Princess Louise Augusta and Crown Prince Frederik were left by their mother's will books, jewellery, her portraits, numerous objects and a thick pile of sheet music that she had played and sung in the long evenings at the castle. By 8 August 1775, the officials were working through Caroline Mathilde's wardrobe, reducing her to entries in their notebooks. Her letters were burned to weightless ash, her clothes lay formless in their trunks, and the beautiful satin gown that Wraxall had seen her wearing only five months before no longer rustled and sighed as Caroline Mathilde moved in it. 'Robe ronde, of couleur de rosé satin, embroidered with silk, and decorated with chenille', wrote the cataloguers simply, and passed efficiently on to 'a robe of soft velvet, with silver and silk, with silver lace'.

Two people, though, refused to forget Caroline Mathilde as easily as the

Danish and British governments might have hoped: her children. In Copenhagen Crown Prince Frederik kept his mother vividly alive in his heart, and helped his sister, as she grew, to love her too. In 1784, when he was sixteen, the Crown Prince was given a seat on the Council of State. Seizing the opportunity of his father's presence on the occasion, he drew out of his pocket a document that, when signed by King Christian, would dissolve the government and put in its place another more favourable to himself. As he had long done, Christian obediently signed his name, writing his customary 'apprové', across the paper. Despite fumbled attempts to induce the King to revoke his decision, Guldberg's administration was abruptly ended and the Crown Prince was proclaimed regent immediately. He remained regent through the long twilight of his father's reign, becoming King Frederik VI in 1808.

Frederick married his cousin Maria Sophia of Hesse. Seven of their eight children died soon after birth leaving him with only one daughter, and no male heir. The throne of Denmark passed on his death to the family of the woman who had helped imprison his mother, Juliane Marie. By the time King Frederick died in 1839, his half-brother's son had married his half-sister's daughter. Thus it was that Princess Louisa's daughter, Johann Struensee's granddaughter, became, for seven years, Queen of Denmark, an ending her doctor grandfather could never have foreseen.

Some time after he came to power in Copenhagen Prince Frederik began patiently to assemble a paper monument to Caroline Mathilde. Eventually catalogued in the Royal Archive as *Papirer vedrørende kongens moder*, 'Papers concerning the king's mother', Prince Frederik's collection included all the documents of the divorce commission, the documents that related to Caroline Mathilde's trial, all the diplomatic correspondence between the Danish and British royal houses after the arrests, Commandant Hauch's reports from Kronborg, and collections made by several other people, including Uldall, about Caroline Mathilde's arrest and trial. Some of the items, like the much-loved red-embroidered garters Caroline Mathilde called her 'ties of affection', were poignantly personal; others clearly inauthentic, like the copy of a letter purportedly written by her to Christian VII from Kronborg, which somehow found its way into the archive from the successful epistolary novel of her story published in 1776, the *Memoirs of an Unfortunate Queen*. In wanting to know his mother, Frederik saved her in Copenhagen for posterity. Nowhere else, certainly not at the Queen's

House or at Windsor, where much of the material that concerned her disappeared, does Caroline Mathilde's intelligent, demanding, tragic voice, speak out so powerfully.

7

'Oh God! It is all over!'

On 18 May 1772, while Caroline Mathilde scanned the horizon beyond Kronborg for the sails of the *Southampton*, she might have seen, if her telescope had been able to look far enough, a grandly beautiful woman in a sumptuous house beyond Windsor. Caroline Mathilde knew that full chin and bosom and that tipped-up, proud nose. They belonged to the Duchess of Gloucester, a sister-in-law she had often seen before she left London, but had never been able to acknowledge. The Duchess would have had a triumphant air that day. For her too a new life was beginning, not one of exile like Caroline Mathilde's, but one of exposure, success, esteem and fortune. Her husband, Prince William, had landed back in Britain, gaunt from sickness and travel, and the Royal Marriage Act meant that he would have to officially announce their marriage. The Duchess's days of hiding and subterfuge were ended. Prince William, however, had none of his wife's bravado. He wanted to stand by her, and knew that honour demanded it. But he was worried that the King's reaction would be hostile, that he would be forbidden to go to court and held back in his profession.

The Duke had been a gauche, sulky boy, never his mother's favourite, shaded out by Prince George's standing and Prince Edward's quick wit. He peered short-sightedly at the foggy world, letting much of it pass him by. When the Princess Dowager mocked him one day he shrank into himself and went quiet. 'Now you are sullen,' his mother burst out. No, he said, he was just thinking. 'And pray what are you thinking of?' 'I was thinking', he said, 'what I should feel if I had a son as unhappy as you make me.' He grew into a reserved young man, fair and taller than his brothers Edward and Henry, but with the curvaceous lips, lapping chin and straight lashes of all the Hanoverians. Like King George he had a dogged intelligence, but by the time he came back from his travels at the age of twenty-eight, youthful uncertainty was hardening into an insistent concern for form and etiquette. Respect and standing were what he wanted. Despite asthma and stomach troubles, he had already risen in the army to the rank of major-general and had hopes of one day standing at its head as his uncle had done.

Released from the sequestered misery of Leicester House and given the title of Duke of Gloucester and an income of £12,000 a year when he turned twenty-one, Prince William emerged tentatively into the world keeping carefully away from women and gambling. Closer in temperament to the King than his other two brothers, he became his confidant and favourite sibling in the turbulent years after Lord Bute's resignation in 1762. For the next decade George leant on Prince William for sympathy and support, so the news of the Prince's serious illness on the Continent at the end of 1771 was devastating to him. When the Prince's doctor John Hunter finally arrived from Italy with news of his recovery, the King wrote to his brother with a rare and open happiness. 'It is impossible to express the joy I have felt ever since the arrival of Hunter on Thursday', he said, adding, 'for I own the letters of the 18th ultimo which I received on Tuesday had possessed my mind with the greatest grief. I expected no other account than that Heaven had taken you from me, though thanks to God my mind is now at ease. I can scarcely relate what I have suffered without tears, but this has only taught me how much I love you.'

Prince William had already made two journeys across the Channel before his trip of 1771. In 1769 he was sent by the King to check up on his unhappy sisters Augusta and Caroline Mathilde. Knowing that George shared his opinion of Princess Augusta, he reported from Brunswick, 'I . . . saw my sister who is very tolerably well and as questionable and gossiping as ever. She pretended to be very glad to meet again.' Caroline Mathilde was taller and fatter, he said, though he wrote nothing about her misery. The following year he was back, chaperoning his mother on her return to Germany and the ill-fated meeting with her youngest daughter at Lüneburg.

Despite these voyages though, many in London noticed as early as 1764 that Prince William was a man of fixed habits who trod a ponderous orbit round one shining star, Maria, Dowager Countess Waldegrave. At twenty-eight, Lady Waldegrave was eight years the Prince's senior, mother to three young girls and the widow of the King's unloved tutor James, the 2nd Earl Waldegrave. Her experience of the world was incomparably greater than Prince William's, her family very different.

Caution and passion fought for supremacy in the minds and hearts of the Hanoverians. In some of Frederick's children, especially Caroline Mathilde and the Dukes of York and Cumberland, feeling came to the surface, stirred in, according to each individual temperament, with indiscretion, folly or high spirits. In others, particularly the King and the Duke of Gloucester, passion was dampened by caution and a reserve that made quarrelling torture and life a battle between duty and desire. George and William were skilled nurturers of grudges, unlikely to flare out and clear the air. The Walpoles, on the other hand, made resentment an art and a pastime. Angry dispute and demonstrative reconciliation were a way of life for them, tenaciously fuelled in eloquent letters that were passed round, drawing in brothers, sisters, children and friends, lasting so long that their original causes often seemed lost, flashing out down the years like the dying embers of a fire. Beauty and youth dissolved Maria's disputatiousness, and Prince William, in awe and love, had made no study of her family.

Sir Robert Walpole had three sons: his heir Robert, Edward and Horace. None followed his footsteps far and his long domination of English politics remained the high point of the family's fortunes. Robert died young, leaving a son who sold off the great picture collection his grandfather had amassed at Houghton Hall in Norfolk, and suffered several periods of madness. Sir Robert's second son Edward was a handsome young man, who held several lucrative offices that his father had picked up for him, but who had no political ambitions and little intellectual success. After a relatively gregarious early manhood playing music with friends and writing competent doggerel verse, Edward retreated, throwing round himself an ostentatious cloak of failure. As his younger brother Horace garnered fame for his literary productions, antiquarian pursuits, broad and fashionable knowledge and circle of famous friends, Edward determined to become distinguished by his inaccessibility. By the 1760s he had cut away his friendships and rarely saw his brother, even though Edward's house in Pall Mall was only a few minutes' walk from Horace's in Arlington Street.

Edward was made a baronet after his father died, but never sought to profit from the title. In 1733, when he was twenty-seven, back from the Grand Tour and installed as a young man of leisure in good lodgings above a milliner's shop in Pall Mall, he fell in love with the shop's beautiful assistant, a fifteen-year-old girl called Dorothy Clement. Moved upstairs and installed as both mistress and head of the household, Dorothy produced four children in four years, and when she died in 1739, a miserable and still devoted Edward brought her sister Jane to run his house and act as a surrogate mother to his three girls and two-year-old son.

Dorothy's beautiful little girls were and remained devoted to Jane Clement, but she endured a torrid time with her employer which culminated in an explosive quarrel in 1766. Four surviving letters which Sir Edward wrote her over the three months of the altercation began, in order: 'Madam, the many indignities I have suffered through your pride and insolence, have at last brought me to the following resolutions . . . to remove you from my house'; 'Madam, I have once more for your sake taken our quarrel into consideration, and . . . I will once more permit you to stay if you choose it'; 'Madam, As you leave me tomorrow and go to my house in town in order to take your things away, I require you to leave that house likewise by next Sunday at noon'; 'Madam, You are permitted to return to my house . . . When you arrive, I shall take no notice of what has passed nor exchange a word with you concerning the quarrel but let everything appear as if you had only been out and was come in again.' Jane came back and stayed for many years, managing Sir Edward and mothering his children.

To those children, though, especially his three daughters Laura, Maria and Charlotte, Sir Edward was a loving, distracted, father. He called the girls his 'frogs', and delighted in sending them charmingly fey letters, lavishing particular attention on his favourite, Laura, whom he called 'the celebrated Lady Laura of the silver locks'. Despite the village seclusion of Egham on the edge of Windsor Great Park, where the children grew up, and his own reclusive habits, Sir Edward always planned to bring his children into the daylight. The Walpoles were not merely illegitimate. Their mother, whether milliner's assistant or a worker in a second-hand clothes shop as another account had it, was little more than a street girl, and stories ran round that she was discovered sitting on top of a rag-and-bone cart like an enthroned goddess. The girls' beauty partly washed away the stain of their birth, but Sir Edward was determined to redeem them, and perhaps his own worldly failure too. Generous settlements would ease their way to good matches. Edward had a harder road. He could not inherit his father's title and unless his talents shone bright enough to eclipse his origins, public life would be closed to him. Like many an illegitimate aristocratic son, he was sent to an academy at Homerton east of London, and was then apprenticed to a merchant. But he hated City life and petitioned to join the army. Once in the Dragoons gamblers and debts discovered him. A quarrel inevitably followed, with his father ending a vituperative letter of 1754: 'I am determined to make my life easy and happy with your sisters, who are good children to me and that you shall suffer for your own wickedness, for I will not', signing off, 'I am your affectionate father, though less so than I was'.

Laura, Sir Edward's oldest girl, marrried first, in 1758. Her husband, Frederick Keppel, was a cleric, a younger son of the 2nd Earl Albemarle. The marriage linked Laura into the powerful extended family that had the dukes of Richmond at its centre, and Foxes, Hillsboroughs and Wentworths clustered round them. It was a famously radical family and Laura soon caught its political temper, quarrelling vigorously with her siblings over the American War, the tone of successive British governments and, inevitably, the French Revolution.

It was Maria, though, whose beauty landed the biggest prize. She had abundant straight auburn hair which she often wore unpowdered, a fine oval face, large wide brown eyes and a small, fashionable mouth. Her figure was statuesque and she made no scruples about displaying its charms. She was, one observer concluded when she was in her twenties, 'the handsomest woman in England', and her uncle Horace wrote, as if his niece were a painting, 'she has not a fault in her face and person, and the detail is charming'. Her marriage, in 1759, to Lord Waldegrave, was considered a triumph for the family. Waldegrave was forty-four, an even-tempered courtier and politician who needed an heir more than he wanted a wife. He was happy to marry into the Walpole family and pleased that Maria was twenty years his junior and a beauty as well. Tagged onto his ungainly person were a country house, Navestock in Essex, the prospect of royal favour, and a becoming title. Maria brought youth, beauty, several thousand pounds and her burning ambition.

The young Countess Waldegrave had three children in the next three years, and though all were girls, the future for herself and the Waldegrave title looked assured. Pregnancy did not stop her launching herself in London society. She was painted in profile by Joshua Reynolds, loosely draped in white silk, lost in thought, chin on hand. At court she encountered the famous beauty, Lady Coventry, and cleverly befriended her. Together they strolled through Hyde Park, mobbed by crowds, delighted to be celebrated, two young women happy that their youth and beauty had struck such a good bargain with wealth and power.

Disaster struck early in 1763, when Lord Waldegrave died suddenly of smallpox, leaving Maria pregnant and impecunious. The lucrative offices that had sustained her society life died with her husband and she was left with a modest jointure, three children, and, if her baby was another girl, the prospect of losing Navestock and her London house to the incoming earl, her husband's younger brother. Perhaps the strain was too much for her body, perhaps, as cruel gossip had it, Maria's pregnancy was just an attempt to keep her riches for a bit longer. Either way there was no baby at the end of it. Crossly taking the title of Dowager Countess, Maria found lodgings at Windsor Castle, and tried to accustom herself to one thousand a year. Though her income a year later had grown to £2,130, her outgoings on housekeeping, servants, coach and chair ate up half that sum and she was left, she complained to Jane Clement, with only a thousand pounds to pay for her children, her footmen and her clothes.

At Windsor, the dean soon noticed a marked increase in attendance at chapel services; boys from Eton school, which lay below the castle, had a new pastime, gazing at Maria as she prayed. Less than a year after her husband's death the Dowager Countess had an admirer grander, richer and more insistent than any love-struck schoolboy: Prince William Henry, then nearly twenty-one and just emerging from the tightly bound chrysalis of the Princess Dowager's household. Maria was immediately caught up with the idea of a man whose ermine would cover her mother's rags for ever and who would maintain her so splendidly that she would never feel the windy fragility of her position again.

Prince William began to send amorous notes to the beautiful widow, and at the beginning of May 1764, in his gauche and formal way, he asked her for some sort of commitment to him, an arrangement that would give her a household and a life that he paid for. At this point, Maria's family stepped in. Although Sir Edward Walpole fervently wished for his daughters' advancement, and his brother Horace was watching with interest to see how far Maria's beauty could take her, neither of them could approve of her liaison with Prince William, not least because they could not imagine any way in which it might be legitimised.

As the family writer, Horace Walpole was called upon to draft a letter from Maria to the Prince which would allow her to slide away from the entanglement with her honour intact. Whether the Prince had asked her to be his wife or his mistress was left unclear in Horace Walpole's decidedly vague reply: if it were the former it was better left both unwritten and unsaid. 'Your Royal Highness', Horace Walpole wrote on his niece's behalf, 'commanded me not to give you a direct answer till you should be of age, but my duty, my character, and every reason of honour and prudence oblige me to put an immediate end to a correspondence which would bring disgrace either on your Royal Highness or on me. . . . My vanity was not blind enough to make me aspire to a situation for which I am not proper, and which, if I could attain, nothing but ruin could happen to me and my children, and misery to your Royal Highness. Let me therefore with all humility intreat your Royal Highness never to think of me more.'

Eloquent though it may have been, this letter was never Maria's. Its fervent entreaty was Horace's, its sincerity his as well. Within two weeks of signing it, Maria was accepting the Prince's visits again. Her confidence in her own beauty and allure was unbounded; if she could ensnare Prince William she could surely bring the King around too. Besides, she had no interest in being merely a royal mistress. She was determined to become a royal duchess and certain that she could hold off the Prince's advances for long enough to get her way.

For Horace Walpole, the prospect of his own family's story suddenly having to incorporate a member of the royal family was double-edged. If on the one hand it was an opportunity to gossip and speculate about the highest echelons of society – and Walpole fell upon gossip with the anticipation and relish of a confirmed gourmand – on the other he nursed tenderly a complicated hatred of the King that made him dislike the rest of the Hanoverians too. His proud hostility was based partly on a perceived or imaginary personal antipathy and partly on his whiggish sympathies and suspicions about the King's use of the royal prerogative. Unfortunately, at the moment of Prince William's approaches to Maria Waldegrave, this dislike was reaching the highest pitch. Its cause, in 1764, was the King's vendetta against Walpole's cousin and lifelong love, Henry Seymour Conway.

Conway was a military man with the manners and habits of a society gentleman with artistic leanings. He had a fine figure, the face, it was often said, of an angel, and his cousin's unswerving devotion. After half a lifetime of military service, Conway arrived back in England after the Peace of Paris in 1763 and fell headlong into the Wilkes affair. He voted repeatedly with the opposition over Wilkes's banishment from Parliament, and spoke out forcibly against the legality of general warrants. The King was enraged and at the end of the parliamentary session in 1764 Conway was stripped of his offices and of his regiment. He was soon prepared to forgive the King, and even, later, to serve in other administrations. But Walpole, who had fought the fight on his cousin's behalf with his only weapon, the pen, took defeat every bit as personally as George III was wont to do. He was determined that he would get even, and get even on his own terms. Not content with taking every opportunity to savage him, Walpole accumulated page by page, letter by letter and volume by volume a portrait of the age in which the King was cast in the worst possible light. Walpole chose his correspondents carefully and was equally astute about the disposition of his manuscripts after his death. Like the rest of his family, he was tenacious in dispute and he was determined that his picture of the King would survive both their deaths and come to stand, irrefutably, for the man himself.

Walpole's circle of Conways, Richmonds, Foxes, Townshends and men about town prided itself on its worldly informality. He dreaded and resented the need to observe the courtly protocols – the kneeling, kissing hands, and formal dress – that any incorporation of the Duke of Gloucester would involve. After the Duke's attentions were redoubled and Maria felt sure of him again, she brought him to see Walpole's Gothic cottage at Strawberry Hill. Her uncle was not at home. Despite the gossip that drifted through St James's, Walpole decided to ignore the liaison, though he was unable to stop a contradictory wisp of pride curling out from under his disapproval. His correspondent Gilly Williams, writing to their mutual friend George Selwyn, reported that Prince William's attachment to Maria 'flatters Horry not a little, though he pretends to dislike it'.

While his younger brother Prince Henry was beginning to taste the delights of drawing rooms and Vauxhall walks, Prince William's conduct became more and more husbandly. Lady Mary Coke noted censoriously that he was almost always late for Sunday prayers at the Chapel Royal because he spent Saturday nights out of town with Lady Waldegrave and that he 'dined or supped' with her four or five nights a week. On 9 November 1766 she recorded with shock and disbelief in her running journal that at court that day, 'Lady Bridget Lane sat over against me. When the two Dukes came in to the King's closet she bent forward and said to me, "Married", meaning the Duke of Gloucester who I think must have heard her. I replied very softly, I don't believe it, upon which she repeated, "Married; I can assure you its true." Thinking it not a proper subject so near the King I made no answer.'

In London and the country Maria had her young daughters with her for some of the time. Often, though, they were parcelled off to her sister at Windsor or sent to stay with their great-uncle. Oddly, because she had had three children in three successive years after her marriage to Lord Waldegrave, no children now appeared to confirm her liaison with Prince William. Nonetheless, the permanence of their relationship was built into the increasing grandeur of their homes. In 1767 the Prince commissioned a new country house outside Windsor. Called St Leonard's Hill when it was finished in 1768, its suburban name belied the magnificence of the building, which Horace Walpole called 'a palace'. In London Maria took a splendid new town house in Portman Square on the new development north of Oxford Street. In 1769 she swapped it for another, 'not yet built'. Altering the plans at the drawing stage, she ordered rooms as big as her ambitions: one grand salon forty-two feet long, another of thirty-six, two other public rooms and a snug closet all on the first floor.

Matters continued in this way, with rumours and sniping but no definite confirmation of the state of the relationship, until the Duke returned from his continental journey on 18 May 1772. In the grip of his illness at Livorno a few months before, he had confessed his marriage to his Gentlemen of the Bedchamber Colonels Rainsford and Heywood, but he was still reluctant to make any official announcement. The fact was, though Maria may not have known it, that the King already knew Prince William was married, and so did at least one of his siblings, Caroline Mathilde. George had almost certainly not asked his brother face to face to confirm or deny the fact, not wanting to give Prince William the choice of having to tell him or having to lie. They had carried on, both knowing what the other knew, saying nothing.

George III, in both his public and his private capacities, hated to be flouted and had no wish to acknowledge publicly that his favourite brother had gone behind his back. British princes, in his view, would marry foreign, probably German, princesses, and he himself would make the selection. Still less did he wish to pay for the new large royal household that a declaration of the marriage would necessitate. He loved and needed the Duke of Gloucester and the cloak of ignorance allowed him to see him without having to receive Maria or give her the title of Duchess. But Prince Henry's determined stand when he married Anne Horton made it impossible for Prince William to carry on in the old way. Maria demanded that he declare the marriage as Prince Henry had done. Her pride forbade her being upstaged by the Duchess of Cumberland, whose vulgarity she was determined to look down upon, and Prince William was trapped. At first he tried to play for time, giving Maria permission to write to her family but staying silent himself, going to St James's Palace and riding with his brother as usual.

Maria's letter to her father was histrionic and wooden, but contained enough phrases that would make the situation absolutely clear when they were planted in the newspapers. With a humility that her tone utterly belied, and a side-swipe at her rival the Duchess of Cumberland, she said her only wish was to tell her family her long-held secret. 'To secure *my* character, without injuring him, is the utmost of my wishes; and I dare say that you and all my relations will agree with me that I shall be much happier to be called Lady Waldegrave and respected as Duchess of Gloucester, than to feel myself the cause of his leading such a life as his brother does, in order for me to be called your Royal Highness.'

Sir Edward Walpole was delighted by his daughter's letter, calling it 'one of the sweetest examples of sense, language and goodness of heart that I ever saw'. Though he wrote Maria a letter of scrupulous politeness, Horace detected behind her theatrical modesty the bright flame of worldly pride. In his *Last Journals*, a long account of his middle and later age that he left for posterity, he added that, 'she wrote to her sister . . . a letter which did not breathe total self-denial. That she recounted with pleasure the magnificent presents the Duke had bought her was natural . . . [But] she desired her sister to make confidences of her marriage to persons not likely to keep the secret . . . these symptoms convinced me that the natural ambition of her temper would not long be smothered.'

Whoever leaked it – and Maria roundly blamed her father – the contents of her letter to Sir Edward Walpole were laid out in the press less than a fortnight later. The *Morning Chronicle* of 28 May reported more or less accurately, 'the Dow—r Lady W—ve has declared her marriage to his R. H. the duke of G—r, in a letter to her father, with the *consent* of her *royal husband*.

This report (which has been current in the *bon ton*, and since it was first whispered, remains *uncontradicted*) adds that they were married in the year 1766, and that her Ladyship declares, in the epistle to Sir E—d W—e, that there is no issue by this marriage.'

Sir Edward Walpole deftly solved the problem of having to wait on his son-in-law, kneel before him and kiss his hand by citing his reclusive nature. If his daughter 'were Queen of England', he announced, 'I do not believe, near as St James's is, that I should ever go there'. Horace, backing him up, claimed that his brother had not set foot outside his house in Pall Mall for six months. The Duke of Gloucester, though, who had made no public statement himself, was unwilling to receive his Walpole relations, and the Duchess made no attempt to force him to do so, saying, with some justification, 'I do not like to lay the Duke open to any more refusals.' More important to Maria than the public obeisance of her family was the approbation of the King. Despite casting George as the villain of her story, she hoped he would soon soften towards her. For that to happen, she needed a more public declaration of her marriage than her leaked letter had offered.

One thing might soften the King's heart, or at least force him to increase the annual subsidy paid to the Duke: the arrival of a new prince or princess. Sentiment would demand that he make provision for any Gloucester children, and honour would require that he acknowledge them. Resourcefully, Maria found in August 1772 that she was expecting a baby. On 13 September Prince William sent a letter to his brother which counted as a public declaration of his marriage.

It was an odd letter, formal in tone but appealing under its stiff surface to the intimate relationship he had always enjoyed with the King. Admitting that his brother was 'supposed', or believed, to be in ignorance of his marriage, Prince William tacitly conveyed his knowledge that George was in possession of that important fact. Assuring him that he would never have made the marriage public if he had not been forced, he attempted both to mollify the King and to mitigate any sentence that he might have to serve. 'Sir', the letter ran, 'I am grieved much at finding myself obliged to acquaint your Majesty with a thing which must be so disagreeable to you; but I think the world being so much acquainted with my marriage, whilst your Majesty is still supposed to be ignorant of it, is neither decent nor right. I will not pretend to justify the action. It is now six years since, being in September sixty-six; and I hope you will believe, Sir, it would never have been made public, had it not been for a variety of accidents which have made it necessary for me now to declare it to you.'

George III was horrified. Prince William was the only sibling he felt at ease with and able to confide in. Although he was fond of Queen Charlotte, passed his nights by her side and was a faithful husband, he never broached his rule, early learned writing his essays about French monarchs and their mistresses, of keeping politics firmly out of his home. With his brother he could at least gallop away his cares and lean on the security of a life together. If no one knew the King's inner thoughts – though trusted ministers like Lord North occasionally saw glimpses of them, like the smoke wafting from the top of a volcano – Prince William at least could make some of them quiet by his presence and companionship. Now all that was threatened. George would never swallow his pride and give up his strictures about foreign brides and the duties of his brothers under the Marriage Act, the more so because he feared that leniency to one generation might lead to rebellion in the next. If William were welcomed back, what might the future Prince of Wales not do, what liberties his subjects demand? A public declaration by Prince William would have to be followed by a public proscription by the King, instructions that those who visited him would not be received at St James's and notices sent to foreign courts to that effect.

Horace Walpole, getting the order of events wrong, believed that the King had called Prince William's treasurer Legrand begging him to stop any letter. In fact the King seems to have got Prince William's letter and then asked him to retract it. Reluctantly, the Prince refused. Though he cited Prince Henry's declaration as the reason, he probably knew that his wife was pregnant and his hand was forced by that knowledge. 'As yr Majesty was so good to send me word if it still remained secret I might come to you as usual, I thought it my duty to give it twenty-four hours fair consideration', the Prince wrote, concluding with less dignity than his brother Henry in the same situation, 'It is most distressful to me to find myself obliged still to offend you more by not being able to come into your Majesty's proposals. I very heavily feel the misfortune I labour under, and always meant to keep my marriage secret until my death, or the birth of children, but this unhappy declaration of my brother's I fear calls upon me as a man of honour not to conceal it any longer. I have then but two things to chuse; either to abandon *her*, which your Majesty would not approve of, or to declare it, and submit to a proscription from your presence, which I will flatter myself may end after a certain time.'

Less a ringing declaration of love than an expression of regret that boded ill for the future of his relationship with Maria, Prince William's letter nonetheless stood by the public declaration of his marriage. Maria herself chose to see in the King's reluctance to accept Prince William's letter a chink of hope for their future rehabilitation and acceptance at court. 'His behaviour has been such on this occasion, that we have all the reason in the world to be grateful to him,' she told her uncle the next day. Others were simply surprised that a long-held secret, about which the King would not ask and would not be told, had come out. 'I had always hoped that Brother William would not make known his marriage, and I think him very much to be pitied', Caroline Mathilde wrote from the hunting lodge at Göhrde when the news reached her on 10 October.

Some sign of what the future held for the Duke and Duchess was gained in the next few weeks as they waited in his lodgings at Hampton Court and in the grandeur of Gloucester House in Upper Grosvenor Street for visitors prepared to defy the King's proscription. Sir Edward Walpole did not stir from Pall Mall but Horace managed the short journey from Strawberry Hill to Hampton Court. Stiff and gouty, he stood throughout the visit, advertising his niece's exalted public status. But privately he warned his friend Henry Seymour Conway, who was angling for the vacant governorship of Guernsey, not to go, telling him it would be 'madness' to stake his fortune, 'against a romantic visit of ceremony'.

Maria was hurt and angry, the Walpole choler heating her up inside. Enemies massed before her eyes. One was Seymour Conway's brother, Lord Hertford, whom she believed was implicated in her social ostracism. Another was her father, whom she began to blame for her own isolation and the failure of the Duke's army career. Sir Edward had been leaking the details of her marriage to the press, she told Jane Clement. 'That letter has been I may almost say my ruin, for I am certain but for that the Duke would have been at the head of the army – now he never will – but my father has ever been my greatest enemy.' Determined to foist her own thwarted ambition onto her hapless parent she went on, 'Was he as indifferent to the world as I am he would not be so fond of worldly honours – would he consider if this world will soon, very soon, pass away, he would be less elated with a feather in his cap, for my being a Princess is no more than that to him.' Maria could not actually write a whole letter without grasping meatily at the insubstantial world. She had been reading the Princess Dowager's will, which had just been made public, and calculating Prince William's winnings. 'I am quite disappointed about the Princess of Wales's riches. They fall very, very short indeed, and we are so much distressed for money that it is uncomfortable.'

Most galling of all, people persisted in making comparisons between the Duchesses of Cumberland and Gloucester. Maria, who declared herself proud to be 'more respected than Mrs Horton', was incensed by the connection. She was angered by the Duchess of Cumberland's cheerful acceptance of her shady status, and she felt that any transactions between them would bring her down imperceptibly to the Cumberlands' level. Furious that she had felt compelled to receive them at St Leonard's Lodge, she told Jane Clement on 21 September that Prince Henry, 'does not repent what he has done, and she is fully convinced that no one ever became royalty better – and is as much at her ease with the Duke of Gloucester as if she was a Princess born . . . You see at once that she never kept good company. She will be disappointed, for she told a friend of mine, before I saw her, that she and I should have a box at the opera together and have a great many jolly parties; as to him, poor young man, he has been so long shut up in his own house that I do assure you he was much prouder and happier coming here than any Windsor miss could be. She looks like an actress and is very flaunting in her dress.'

In her fertility at least, Maria had the better of her rival, who never produced any children. Her pregnancy, she told Jane Clement, was seen by many of her acquaintances as a 'happy event', because 'now Parliament must think of me, for let me be what I will, my children must be princes'. Her hopes of rehabilitation advanced with her pregnancy. She began to plan grand futures for her Waldegrave girls, who were now twelve, eleven and ten years old, thinking to bring them into the light of her splendour once she was accepted at court. By October 1772 she had secured Jane Clement a suite of prime lodgings at Windsor Castle, in the fat round bulk of Winchester Tower which dominated the complex and looked out over the smooth meadows along the Thames and to the delicate Gothic pinnacles of the chapel at Eton school. Maria wanted her three girls to live there too, close enough to visit her for the day. A month later, making incremental advances in grandeur, she and the Duke retitled St Leonard's Hill Gloucester Lodge in honour of their union.

By the end of the year this optimism had faded away. The King remained implacable, determined to heap upon Maria's hope of advancement all the responsibility and blame for his brother's downfall. The Duke seemed to be courting opposition politicians, a risky strategy to adopt towards a brother whom he knew placed huge importance upon family loyalty. 'Our cards will some time or other turn up trumps – notwithstanding the King's false and trumpery heart', wrote Maria defiantly a few days before Christmas. But she still gathered and hoarded enemies, prompting Horace Walpole to write and warn her to lie low. 'In this country nobody escapes', he wrote, adding, 'You will say it is very fine in me to preach, who am warm and imprudent like you and your father – but ... I have felt the inconvenience of incautious anger, and wish my experience may all turn to your service.'

At the beginning of May 1773 the Duke of Gloucester wrote to his brother asking for members of the Privy Council to attend the Duchess's lying-in, which her doctors anticipated would be soon. The King, seeing in this request another attempt to force him to accept his brother's marriage, declined, replying frostily, according to Horace Walpole, that 'at a proper time after the delivery of the Duchess, your marriage, as well as the birth of her child, shall be enquired into'. The way Walpole interpreted the King's reply, though, may have owed more to family hastiness than royal anger. George III never doubted the legality of his brother's marriage; what upset him was not its manner but its having happened at all, and particularly its having been made public. Maria, for her part, was desperate to have a public enquiry into the marriage heard before she gave birth, so that no hint of illegitimacy could taint her child, and the Duke backed her up. The King gave way, but Princess Amelia reported to Lady Mary Coke that he had said to her, 'After this I shall draw a curtain over the whole affair, for it can never have my approbation.'

The archbishop of Canterbury, the Lord Chancellor and the bishop of London convened to enquire into the validity of the marriages of both the Duke of Gloucester and his younger brother Prince Henry on 23 May. The Cumberlands had the easier task, because the chaplain who married them was still alive and their witnesses could also be called forward. For his part the Duke of Gloucester assembled a legal team led by John Dunning, who three years before had acted for his brother at the King's Bench. Frederick Keppel, Maria's brother-in-law, came forward and explained that she had confessed everything when the Royal Marriage Act was passed the previous year. Prince William's lawyers produced depositions from Colonels Rainsford and Heywood declaring that he had said the same in the heights of his fever at Livorno in 1771. On 26 May the King's team reported that both marriages were evidently legal, and the depositions of all the witnesses were written into the minute book of the Privy Council. When Princess Sophia entered the world three days later her mother had the satisfaction of knowing that her new daughter was the product of a legal marriage. Surely now, she reasoned, she was entitled to a royal household and an allowance from the Civil List.

Try as she might, Maria did not seem to be able to avoid the Duchess of Cumberland. On 26 June, when her daughter was christened Sophia Matilda, after the Queen of Denmark and the old Hanoverian Electress, the Duchess of Cumberland was there in 'a full dressed sack of rose coloured lutestring trimmed with point, a diamond stomacher, sleeve knots, necklace and earrings and a vast number of diamonds in her hair'. The Duke of Cumberland's Gentleman of the Bedchamber, talking the christening over with the Duchess of Northumberland, agreed, though, that Maria outshone her, and 'never in the highest bloom of her youth', had she looked more beautiful. The Duke was delighted with his daughter, declaring, despite the fact that his wife was now thirty-seven, that 'he hoped to have a dozen children'. One among the crowd was bound to be a son, especially since three months later the Duchess was pregnant again.

In their need for cash, at least, the Cumberland and Gloucester households stood together and equal. One way of saving money was to go abroad, particularly to Rome, where grand palaces could be rented cheaply and a stream of loafing Grand Tourists brought constant company. Travelling as private persons was imperative since the King had notified foreign courts and British ambassadors not to receive his brothers officially, but it saved money too. In August 1773 Maria announced to Jane Clement: 'the Cumberlands are going to Italy – *he* does not *feel himself*, therefore will mind no slights – she cares for nothing so [long as] she is stared at, therefore they will both be happy.' For the moment at least, the Duke of Gloucester preferred to stay at home and campaign for an increase in his allowance. Such a measure could only be proposed in Parliament by the opposition, and the Duke and Duchess of Gloucester chose the Duke of Richmond for the task. They could not have chosen a man more unlikely to bring them success. Richmond was an implacable opponent of Lord North's government and a strong supporter of the angry and restless American colonists. As if this was not enough, memories of the King's passion for his sister Sarah Lennox made

Richmond altogether unsuitable. 'The Duke of Richmond is particularly unwelcome to his Majesty', Horace Walpole warned at the beginning of 1774, 'and the measure will be thought the more hostile, if proposed by his Grace . . . Thus every door to a reconciliation in the R[oyal] Family would be shut.'

Less than a year later, when their second child Carolina Augusta Maria was a few months old, the Gloucesters tried for forgiveness and cash again. Horace Walpole tried to dissuade them once more, suggesting the Duke could only appeal to the King from the House of Lords, begging the peers to intercede with the King on his behalf. The Duke, though, preferred to write to his brother directly, 'flattering myself, as I cannot help, that this letter may strike your Majesty in the dutiful light it is intended, your Majesty will have a satisfaction in knowing that you have been the means of quieting the mind of a brother who never meant to offend you'. The King quickly moved to make sure that any interventions on his brothers' behalf in Parliament would be frustrated by Lord North. 'I cannot deny', George wrote to his trusted Prime Minister, 'that on the subject of the Duke of Gloucester my heart is wounded. I have ever loved him with the fondness one bears [more] to a child than a brother. His whole conduct from the time of his publishing what I must ever think a highly disgraceful step had tended to make the breach wider. I cannot therefore bring on myself a repetition of this application to give him hopes for a future establishment for his children, which would only bring on a fresh altercation about his wife whom I can never think of placing in a situation to answer her extreme pride and vanity.' The King insisted that any public announcement he might be forced to make would 'totally avoid mentioning the lady'. Though he told Lord North that he would take care of his brother's children if the Duke died, he was implacable where Maria was concerned and determined that, even at the cost of his brother's peace of mind, she should have neither royal household nor royal recognition. When later the Duke of Gloucester went to see Lord North about the possibility of his poverty being raised in Parliament, the Prime Minister gave him short shrift. 'My abhorrence of Lord North is beyond expression,' Maria told Jane Clement later, adding, 'his treatment of the Duke that morning he was with him was such as I *never, never* can forget or forgive.'

The Duchess knew that the King stood behind Lord North and her hatred of him reached new heights after this second refusal. Soon she began to tie all her misfortunes together and lay them at his door. When her second daughter died in March 1775 at the age of nine months she turned her anger and grief into the whisper that the King had refused to allow the child to be buried in the royal vault in Westminster Abbey. When their debts mounted she explained them as the result of the King's mistreatment and not her own extravagance. Going abroad in the summer of 1775 she saw herself as banished from her country and her rightful place in it rather than heading to healthy sunshine for the Duke's health and a cheaper way of life. In Rome in the autumn, installed in the damask-draped spaces of the Teodoli Palace overlooking the Piazza Colonna, her thoughts turned inevitably to home, her grievances and her children there.

Maria had left her three young girls, now aged fifteen, fourteen and thirteen, in the care of Jane Clement at Windsor and under the eye of her sister Laura Keppel, whose husband was Dean of Windsor as well as Bishop of Exeter. Occasionally they visited Horace Walpole at Strawberry Hill or their aunt Lady Dysart at Ham. But Laura Keppel, who had two daughters of the same age, felt herself most responsible for them. Even before her sister had left for Italy, Mrs Keppel was grumbling to Jane Clement. 'I'm sure my sister has great obligation to us', she wrote, 'for we devote ourselves to 'em, and really five girls sometimes bother one. But I believe she will never reckon herself obliged to one, as they do not live with me. For 'tis the oddest way of thinking she has, that everybody is to sacrifice all their own comfort for her, and she never gave up her own way for anybody.' Once the Duke and Duchess had left for Italy, Mrs Keppel confessed to Jane Clement that her daughters and the Waldegrave girls no longer got on. The Duchess's oldest girl Laura was 'pert' with her daughter Anna, and all three were too grand to take on her visits to her husband's parishioners. 'I own I dread this winter on their account', she confessed to Jane Clement, 'for I know I shall be much blamed. They are taught to be vastly above the Windsor people and to treat them with great contempt. Therefore this winter will be very dull for Miss Keppel will go out with me and I cannot presume to take Lady Laura to plebeians.' 'I wish most sincerely never to have anything more to do with them', she burst out on 9 September, and a month later told Jane Clement, 'I have received a letter from the Duchess this morning of so extraordinary a sort that I believe she is distracted. She uses me so ill I cannot bear it.'

Jane Clement needed all the discretion she could find. Maria, too, scribbled and shared her troubles. 'I can open my heart to you without disguise', she wrote from Rome, and Jane was indeed bombarded with her fears and hopes. Early in 1776 Maria at last joyfully reported the birth of a son, Prince William Frederick, born at the Teodoli Palace on 15 January. He was not a beautiful baby, she admitted, less robust than Princess Sophia who was a fair, fat, cheerful angel, and 'like the King'. But he represented dynastic success, and the Duchess was determined to celebrate. 'Last Monday the month was up', she wrote to Jane Clement on 16 February. 'My boy was christened; all the English – 32 – present; we are overrun with English. ... As to Sophia she thrives nobly, such a face for breadth you never beheld! William too comes on very much, but he is small boned so that he does not yet cut a great figure; I think him like his father, excepting his mouth which is like mine.'

Only a few months later anxiety had returned. Her torments were her old friends and she could not give them up, relentlessly treading the well-worn path to her unhappiness. Though she told Jane Clement on 26 May, 'I am grateful to the good God for giving me a son', the malevolent figure of the King tarnished even that joy. 'Every time I look at my two infants', she wrote, 'my heart is full, for I see in them objects of real distress, if any accident should happen to their father.' Fear of penury had her adding and re-adding incomings and outgoings and sending Jane Clement the resulting sums. Magnificence in Rome cost them £10,000 pounds a year, but Gloucester Lodge was an expensive folly, draining away thousands in annual interest, and they could only chip away slowly at their debt of £40,000. Maria was convinced that the Duke and Duchess of Cumberland criticised her extravagance, and she wanted Jane to silence them by making public the wealth she brought to her marriage, 'to silence the wicked impertinence of the Duchess of Cumberland who could not say *then* that I ruined the Duke'.

Her girls, left at home, were another site of worry. 'My poor girls would never have had any vexations could they have lived with me', she sighed, as if she had never agreed to leave them behind in England. 'Mrs Keppel has lost every feeling for me', she announced soon afterwards. 'All her letters are in a style I do not like for she treats me not only with an air of superiority but as if my character was such a great respect for rank that I can think no person of quality can behave ill. ... The Duke says she writes like an older sister. ... I own I cannot help being very much concerned at her ways.'

For all the splendour, Maria was often lonely. 'You must know how much relief it gives me and how much easier I feel after opening my heart to you', she confessed to Jane. In Rome, the days passed in opulent boredom. Neither Maria nor her husband had got what they wanted. She was unable to admit that being married to Prince William was not enough. She had wanted to be seen, visited and envied in her success, and the King had thwarted her. Even if they returned to England she would never be able have a royal household with herself as its magnificent centre because the King would make sure that no one came to see her, and as she put it, 'every lady is too poor and too mean, not to be bribed by something to keep away'. 'It is not debt which makes us live out of England,' she explained to Jane again on 4 April 1777, 'it is the Duke's health first, and then the constant persecution we meet with from the King, who will never be at rest whilst one person of quality comes to Gloucester House.' Maria had aimed higher than her rival the Duchess of Cumberland and could never be content with the rackety sidelined life that the Duchess cheerfully enjoyed. Without the admiration of society Maria's sense of self-worth withered and bitterness wrapped itself around her.

The Duke too faced a tedious future. He was only thirty-two when his son was born, but his career in the army was over and he could have no other official role while his brother kept him so firmly in the shade. His little family was a thin one to pad out long dull days and a small one to chance against childhood illness and future disaster. Ceremony, routine, and a sense of duty fulfilled were the things that made him feel himself and being cut off from them amongst free-wheeling exiles and excited Grand Tourists in the decaying capital of imperial greatness was no recipe for a happy future. Early in 1777 he decided to try again to bring himself to his brother's notice and to pave the way for a return to England. Provision for the King's children and a proposal to pay his debts from the Civil List were to come before Parliament in the spring, and, unknown to the Duke, his father-in-law wrote on his behalf to Lord George Germain who led the War Office. Sir Edward Walpole was characteristically effusive, hinting that the King was letting his brother sink beyond hope by doing nothing about his situation, and asking, 'Is it fit that the brother (and such a brother) of so great a Prince as is the King of England, should live sequestered and proscribed for want of a help that would be trifling in the general burthen?' Maria told Jane Clement on 4 April, just before the family set off for the north of Italy, 'You cannot imagine how much the Duke fretted at my father's writing to Lord George Germain about his debts.' But the Duke himself seemed to bear Sir Edward little ill-will, writing excitedly to him from Venice about Lord George

Germain, 'If you could find by him that it would be pleasing to the King that I should come over now, I will set out immediately, to show how desirous I am to give the King every mark in my power of duty and attachment ... If coming over now should be approved of I will leave my family at Verona and return to them, as I feel it necessary to pass another winter at Rome.' War had taken hold in America and the Duke must have felt that in the crisis rehabilitation both with his brother and in the army was possible.

But from the Queen's House no word came. The King remained implacable and the Duke, in Venice, sank like the city in the torpid heat, going down with asthma and stomach trouble. Advised to leave the city for higher ground and convinced that travel would do him good, he moved with his family to Padua, Verona and then up to Trento at the foot of the crumbly steepling Dolomites. There, emaciated and exhausted he lay in the house of two local nobles. In the heat of summer he was swung a navy-style cot so that he could sleep and his attendants could turn him over. Maria became convinced as the weeks passed that William would die and that she and her children would be left ostracised and destitute. Not trusting the local doctors, she dispatched a courier to London, who arrived there on 5 July with a request for society doctor Robert Adair and his colleague Dr Jebbe to set out immediately for Italy.

When Jebbe and Adair arrived in Trento after a non-stop overland journey of ten days, they found the Duke still lying on his back, weak, but apparently recovering. A few weeks later, though, his condition worsened suddenly and reports reached the English press and George III that he had only days to live. Duty demanded that the King respond, and Maria was able to report delightedly to Horace Walpole on 4 September that not only was her husband out of danger but that 'his mind is quite at ease *now*, which is one consolation, for he received a letter from the King by yesterday's post, a very kind one indeed, assuring him that his brotherly affection has *never has abated* and *never* will, and to promise him that if he dies he will be a protector to his family'. Maria did not want her uncle to advertise the contents of the letter, particularly as her happiness or calculation glossed over the fact that nowhere was she mentioned in it, but she did want him to let her enemies and the press know that the King had written because, as she put it, 'that will make *various* people look about them, and that pleaseth me much'. Triumphant, she felt that both the Duke's recovery and his rehabilitation were close at hand.

When the party finally arrived back in England towards the end of October, though, they found no royal welcome and no acceptance into society. The rebel colonists in America seemed to be sweeping all before them, and, as Horace Walpole put it, there was 'not a word of any other sort of news'. Prince William's safe return prompted the King to make good his promise to provide for his children, but the proposal he put to his brother was partly designed to prevent any application on the Duchess's behalf. 'I should have thought', the King wrote tetchily to Lord North on 29 November, 'that the very handsome proposal delivered by you in my name to the Duke of Gloucester, would have deserved in turn at least the civility of not applying for public provision for a person who must always be odious to me.' The settlement, voted by Parliament in spring of the following year, duly provided annuities for the Duke's children if their father died, but made no provision for their mother.

Back in the purgatory of Gloucester House Prince William became increasingly dissatisfied. When the French came into the war the next year he asked the King's permission to join the army of the King of Prussia, but George III, never for a moment forgetting how his brother had flouted his authority, peremptorily refused to allow him any public role, even one in the service of an ally. Given a position, sent abroad or to America with the army, the Duke would be publicly received and so too, necessarily, would his wife. A royal household, reception at court and Maria's triumph would follow, and George would never allow disloyalty such a reward. Better the Duke's frustration than the Duchess's victory.

As the idle months passed, Prince William came more and more to see his own life not as a romantic adventure or as a worthwhile sacrifice of his career for love and family, but as the King did, the story of a young man manipulated by a scheming, ambitious woman. Trapped by a mistake from which he could never recover he turned against his wife, no longer defending her against attack and no longer seeing her conduct as a response to an intolerable vendetta by the King. Maria was in her forties now. She had come back from Italy still handsome, but too thin for her years and too old to have any more children. In his heart, to his brother and before the world the Duke began to betray her, stripping her little by little of her pride and self-respect.

In the warm early days of June 1780 anti-Catholic hatred spread over London, fanned by an unlikely aristocratic agitator, Lord George Gordon.

Pale and long-haired, dressed like a Methodist and speaking like a feverish demagogue, Gordon harangued huge crowds assembled under the aegis of the virulent Protestant Association in St George's Fields on 3 June. Over the next few days mobs attacked the houses of prominent Catholics, released the inmates of several prisons including the King's Bench and Newgate, and burned the buildings to the ground. The homes of hated individuals, including Lord Mansfield, Lord North and the Earl of Bute, were surrounded or ransacked. On 7 June, the King, acting on the advice of the Attorney-General, Lord Wedderburn, ordered out the army. Troops closed the bridges and surrounded the Bank of England, shooting dead scores of rioters, dispersing the rest, gradually bringing the City of London and Westminster under their control.

Seizing the opportunity, Prince William wrote to his brother assuring him of his support. By 9 June shops were reopening in the charred and sullen city and the King had no need of it. But something prompted him to relent. Perhaps he had longed for his brother in the hot days of the riots; more likely he already knew that Prince William was prepared to come to him on his terms, tacitly acknowledging the King's version of the story. 'I wish to be on the best terms with my brother', George wrote to William on 9 June, 'and that we may not disagree, therefore, when we meet I hope it will be understood that nothing is to be mentioned in the conversation between us about the Dss. of Gloucester. I shall be happy at any time to see the Duke of Gloucester's children.'

Loyally, Horace Walpole declared that when he received this letter the Duke of Gloucester threw it into the fire, saying, 'It is not fit that this letter should ever be seen.' The Duke of Cumberland had already been to see the King on similar terms, but his wife had no particular wish to endure levees or the Chapel Royal, and absorbed the insult cheerfully. Maria, on the other hand, had staked everything on the King's acceptance. When a few days later, Prince William went to his brother, agreeing not even to refer to her, she must have known that the compact that had formed the basis of their life was broken. But she may have known something else as well. Her husband had a mistress, who was two months' pregnant with his child.

In the end, Maria's insistence that she have a royal household had made it easy for her husband to desert her. While some aristocratic wives and widows had companions to help them while away dull days and long firelit evenings, only the royal family had official ladies- and gentlemen-in-waiting who were paid a salary and expected to act as maids, confidants and dressers. Unable to attend St James's, Maria was determined to have her own small court, with liveried servants, ladies-in-waiting and levees at which visitors were expected to kiss her hand. The Duke too, 'stood upon form', as she put it, and ponderously insisted on deference and ceremony. Amongst the Duchess's ladies was an ambitious and impecunious Irish aristocrat, Lady Almeria Carpenter, seventeen years her junior, beautiful and without scruple. Some time in the winter of 1779 she had become the Duke of Gloucester's lover; by the following June she was pregnant, spirited out of the way when the time came to give birth in January 1781 and back in Gloucester House before rumour reached the press. Her daughter by the Duke was baptised with the name of Louisa La Coast, brought up on a farm near Hampton Court, and never acknowledged by either of her parents. 'I cannot say that the year 1780 was a happy one', Maria confessed to her cousin Anne Clement in the New Year. She may not have known who her husband loved, but she knew that his affections were waning and she knew that their earlier solidarity in the face of the King's recalcitrance was gone.

In 1783 Maria, the Duke and their household left the country again, travelling first to Strasbourg, then to Switzerland, before going back to Italy and to Nice. Once out of Britain Prince William took no trouble to hide his new love. From then on Lady Almeria ruled his heart. Maria simply ran his household, a disappointed, thwarted woman burying herself in her children's love, trying not to feel her husband's desertion. As she always had, she confided in her Clement relations. After what Maria would later describe as 'five miserable years abroad', her aunt Jane wrote to her daughter Anne Clement, 'I wish she would make up her mind not to regard their goings on, and that would hurt him more than she is aware of, as it now gives them pleasure to see her fret and lose her beauty. But if she could bring herself to take [no] notice of them, it's five to one he might return to her again.' But Jane loved Maria, and had had a lifetime with the volatile Walpole temperament. Prince William showed no such compassion. 'I am indeed severely punished for my juvenile indiscretion', he told the King two years later. Henceforth he, Lady Almeria and Maria would live an unhappy and uneasy three-cornered life. Prince William and Princess Sophia were mostly in their mother's care but after their return to England in 1787 even they were frequently denied to her. It was left to Horace Walpole to write the inevitable moral of his niece's story. There was nothing so transitory as the happiness of red liveries, he said, hinting that he had studied closely the miseries of courts.

In the first years of his quarrels with his brothers, George III's domestic and political miseries threatened to pull him down into anger and sadness. By 1775, although he was still only thirty-four years old, five of his eight siblings were dead. Caroline Mathilde had died in May, Elizabeth, Frederick, Louisa and Edward years before. George was estranged from Prince William and Prince Henry, neither seeing nor speaking to them. Only with Augusta was he on any sort of terms, but she was in Brunswick and they had little to say to one another. He adored his children, especially when they were small and yielding, and he was fond of his wife, but he could never share with her his manifold troubles. Nonetheless, in the newspapers, the King's domestic life was usually presented as one of unalloyed happiness. 'A Sketch of their Majesties' domestic life at Kew during the Summer Season', which was published in the Annual Register for that year, painted their comfortable summertime life. 'Their Majesties rise at six in the morning', it ran, 'and enjoy the two succeeding hours in a manner which they call their own. At eight, the . . . [older children] are brought from their respective apartments to breakfast with their illustrious parents. At nine the younger children attend, to lisp or smile their good morrows. . . . and once a week [the King and Queen], attended by the whole offspring in pairs, make the little delightful tour of Richmond Gardens. . . . The sovereign is the father to his family. Not a grievance reaches his knowledge that remains unredressed, nor a character of merit or ingenuity disregarded, so that his private conduct must be allowed to be no less exemplary than it is truly amiable.'

If his offspring, in 1775, accepted their father's firm hand with dutiful obedience, George III's other children, his subjects, were proving less manageable. His American subjects, in particular, had been causing him daily distress. After the end of the Seven Years War in 1763 a belief had developed in the administration that the American colonists should be made to contribute towards their own defence – that they should be taxed, that is, to reduce the burden of a national debt hugely swelled by the costs of war. Accordingly, a Stamp Act was passed in 1765 which taxed paper transactions such as contracts and bills of sale in America by means of a printed stamp bought and fixed to each document. The Act was greeted with fury by many

Americans, who responded by boycotting British goods and refusing to pay bills owed to British merchants. But the reaction was political as well. The popular orator Patrick Henry, speaking in the House of Burgesses at Williamsburg, Virginia, hinted that America would be the downfall of the King and that the revolt against taxation would turn into a political rebellion too. 'Caesar had his Brutus,' he declared, 'Charles 1st his Cromwell, and George the Third . . .' There he was stopped by the Speaker calling 'Treason,' but his words lay hanging in the air to drift round the colonies and pick up meaning.

The Stamp Act was repealed in March 1766. But when, a year later, the Chancellor of the Exchequer, Charles Townshend, introduced and carried a Bill for imposing duties on goods to be imported into America, the French statesman the Duc de Choiseul wrote gleefully to the French minister in London, 'Let England but attempt to establish taxes in her colonies, and these countries, greater than England in extent, and perhaps becoming more populous – having fisheries, forest, shipping, corn, iron and the like – will easily and fearlessly separate themselves from the mother country.'

The King had always been a viscerally emotional man when he was personally tangled up in an issue. In time his first, hot reactions would harden, like cooling lava, into an immovable solidity. 'No man can gain the King', wrote his inveterate adversary Charles James Fox, and on issues that mattered to him, no man did. George was unshakeable in his insistence upon the immutability of the constitution, which he had sworn in his Coronation Oath to uphold. He almost never changed his opinion of individuals and he stood by his own decisions with unswerving perseverance. When, late in his reign, he was pressed to consent to emancipation for his Roman Catholic subjects he replied with typically extreme resolution, 'I can give up my crown, and retire from power. I can quit my palace and live in a cottage. I can lay my head on a block and lose my life; but I can *not* break my Coronation Oath.'

It was just in this spirit that George III approached the complex, looming and vital problems in America. The great political and economic changes in America, and the colonists' gradual move towards rebellion, war and independence, were far beyond the influence, or even the responsibility, of the King. But as far as George was concerned he was the father of his subjects, and the colonists, both rebellious and loyal, were his children. He had pledged to uphold the constitution as it was embodied in his Coronation Oath for all his subjects and was responsible for their welfare. They, in turn, owed him their duty, love and obedience.

In thinking of his country in this way George was by no means alone. The notion of the nation as a family with the King as its father and its citizens as his children was commonplace and widely used both as a figure of speech and a more deeply held belief about the way in which the various parts of the nation were organically connected to one another. Moreover, if the King was his subjects' father, and the head of the national family, the nation itself, from which he was inseparable, was often seen as the mother of its citizens and of the dependent territories which it had adopted or brought into being. Britain, or England, was thus America's 'Mother Country', and was frequently and habitually referred to in this way by both British and American writers and politicians.

For George III, though, these formulations were real as well as allegorical and symbolic. A loving and tender father to young children and to his siblings as long as they remained dutiful and loyal, George had never been taught and never developed any means of negotiating and compromising with those in his family, from his brothers to his sons and daughters, who wanted to live in different ways than the ones he thought best for them. Towards his American subjects he behaved in exactly the same way. As his children, and like his children, they must be brought to acknowledge their duty to their father and their king. If honour would not bring them back to their motherland, then force must do so instead.

In 1775, obedient to his father's strictures, raw and angry after the death of Caroline Mathilde and the quarrels with his brothers Henry and William, George made the colonists' struggle his struggle and their defection his own loss. Family and nation were inseparable for him, and when the American men and women who were a part of his family repudiated his fatherly love and protection, it almost broke him. Controlling his own family was one battle he fought with limited success. But trying to deal with the Americans in the same way was a battle in which he was bound to be defeated. To the rebellious Americans the King himself, as a person, was a marginal, symbolic figure. He was never the political centre of their quarrel with Britain, even though, as head of state, he was necessarily the focus of the emotive and brilliant Declaration of Independence signed at the second Philadelphia Congress in July 1776. The rebel colonists were fighting two entwined battles, one against their mother country and one with their loyal fellow Americans;

in both George III was a distant element. Politically and as an idea, finding a way to cast off the monarchy and become a republic was of more consuming interest to the thinkers, politicians and inhabitants of America than the man far away who wore the crown. To the Americans, in the end, framing a new constitution and choosing a president were to be far more important than casting off their last king. To George, for a time, it seemed the end of his world.

The grievances of the colonists exploded in the spectacle of the Boston Tea Party in December 1773, when a group of Bostonians, dressed as Mohawk Indians, boarded tea ships in the port of Boston and tipped their cargoes into the harbour in protest against British imposition of duty. From the beginning George was determined to be firm, never considering either negotiation or conciliation, regretting the repeal of the Stamp Acts and reaching immediately towards the use of the army. Less than three months after the Boston Tea Party the King eagerly accepted the stringent assessment of the situation in Massachusetts given to him by General Gage, who had led the British army in North America in the Seven Years War, and who had recently come back from Massachusetts. 'Since you left me this day', the King reported to Lord North of 4 February 1774, 'I have seen Lieutenant General Gage, who came to express his readiness, though so lately come from America, to return at a day's notice, if the conduct of the Colonists should induce directing coercive measures. . . . He says they will be lions whilst we are lambs, but if we take the resolute part they will undoubtedly prove very meek. . . . I wish you would see him and hear his ideas as to the mode of compelling Boston to submit to whatever may be thought necessary. Indeed all men now seem to feel that the fatal compliance in 1766 has encouraged the Americans annually to increase their pretensions to that thorough independency which one state has of another, but which is quite subversive of the obedience which a colony owes to its mother country.'

Since the Americans had harnessed political and economic grievances together and had invoked the spirit of the Act of Settlement by asserting that it was unconstitutional and tyrannical to tax them without giving them representation, the mood in the Westminster Parliament had hardened against them. Haunted by the mocking spectre of John Wilkes and by the popular opposition he had stirred up at home, government MPs balked at the idea of conceding any ground to the colonists. There were, after all, millions of Britons who paid taxes without having the right to vote, and any move towards the American position might result in renewed pressure for reform of Parliament and the franchise. A series of measures passed in the spring of 1774 designed to assert British authority in Boston and Massachusetts were accordingly anything but conciliatory. George III was delighted with the government and convinced that a resolute firmness would bring the Americans round. After reading a pamphlet from the Quakers of Pennsylvania that was more robust than he had expected from such a pacific source, he wrote to North in pained surprise, 'they seem to wish for England giving ... way to the opinions of North America. The die is now cast, the colonies must now either submit or triumph. I do not wish to come to severer measures, but we must not retreat; by coolness and an unremitted pursuit of measures that have been adopted I trust they will come to submit.'

When the time for severer measures came, in 1775, the King was in no doubt that force was the only way to bring the colonists to do their duty. His mind ran along the same lines continually, never straying towards abstract issues or the wider political significance of any events, never thinking of negotiation or even discussion, always within the confines of the family model he insisted upon. After the battle of Lexington in April 1775, when it seemed clear that the army in America would have to be strengthened with new recruits from Britain and a muster in Hanover, he stiffened himself for the fight, writing to North on 5 July, 'I have no doubt but the nation at large sees the conduct of America in its true light, and, I am certain, any other conduct but compelling obedience would be ruinous and culpable; therefore no consideration would bring me to swerve from the present path, which I think myself in duty bound to follow.'

Despite his aggressive certainty, George III could have been in no doubt about the colonists' own resolve when he read the Declaration of Independence approved by Congress in Philadelphia exactly a year later. The clarion call of the Declaration, beautiful in its assertion that all men were created equal and granted liberty by God, ugly and disastrous in its refusal of those rights to the many thousands of slaves confined on the plantations of Georgia, Virginia and South Carolina, made almost no mention of Parliament. Instead all its gathered fury was necessarily directed at the King himself. 'The history of the present King of Great Britain', its writer Thomas Jefferson declared, 'is a history of repeated injuries and usurpations, all having in direct object the establishment of an absolute Tyranny over these states.' To prove this assertion, he went on, 'let these facts be submitted to a candid world'. Thus, in clause after clause which followed the famous preamble, Jefferson laid at George's door a damning catalogue of ill-treatment and concluded defiantly, 'In every stage of these Oppressions We have petitioned for Redress in the most humble terms: our repeated Petitions have been answered only by repeated injury. A Prince whose character is thus marked by every act which may define a Tyrant is unfit to be the ruler of a free people.'

It was not surprising that in the face of such sustained hostility the King began to see faint hearts and disloyalty all around him. The war ebbed and flowed, and even before the disastrous surrender of General Burgoyne's army at Saratoga in October 1777, George had to rally the spirits of his Prime Minister, who was fast falling into gloom. After Saratoga, and again when the French came into the war the next year, Lord North threatened to resign. The King was having none of it. He had taken to getting at North not only directly but also through John Robinson, an official at the Treasury who had the Prime Minister's ear. 'I know our situation is not pleasant', George told Robinson soon after the French navy began to threaten British supply lines in the Atlantic, 'but it behoves everyone the more to exert every nerve, to bravely stand forth at this hour of danger. Britain had better be totally destroyed than crouch.' America, George believed, was the link that tied all the colonies to their mother country, and if America was lost, the whole necklace of colonies that encircled, enriched and gave might to the mother country, would break, its jewels dropping one by one. Should the Americans succeed in winning their independence, he told Lord North just before the Spanish came into the war in June 1779, 'the West Indies must follow them, not independence, but must for their own interest be dependent on North America. Ireland would soon follow the same plan and be a separate state; then this island would be reduced to itself, and soon would be a poor island indeed.' It was as if the loneliness and isolation that George had felt during the crisis over Caroline Mathilde and the quarrels with his brothers was being repeated again with his colonists, and at such moments, and especially when Lord North threatened to resign, his resolve must have been shaken. Significantly, though, the King never stopped seeing the events in North America in personal terms. Criticised as a young man for not attending to his studies, George had solemnly promised Lord Bute, to throw off his indolence and work for his own salvation. Now, as if from the outside, he saw in his country a version of the young man he had once been, idle and inattentive. The solution, he saw, as early as 1778, was to 'rouse' the nation, 'from a lethargy that may prove very fatal', in just the same way as Bute had long ago roused him.

In the first few years of the American War the King's enthusiasm and robustness were shared by most of the government and the country. But as the years passed and the Americans learned how to fight an effective guerrilla war without ever committing their main army to a pitched battle, as they harried British forces by land and cut British supply lines at sea, as casualties mounted and young men never came home, support for the government and the King ebbed away. The pool of goodwill was drained, leaving the government husky and dry, led by a broken man who no longer believed in his task. Ferociously attacked in Parliament and petitioned from outside by reformers who were beginning to demand for themselves some of the rights they saw being won by the Americans, North knew the end was inevitable. When in the autumn of the next year news arrived that General Cornwallis had surrendered the British army at Yorktown, his extravagant cry of 'Oh God! It is all over, it is all over!' had in it a pinch of relief that took the edge off his despair and failure.

But it was not, by any means. From the nadir of Yorktown the British fought on, partly to secure the huge landmass they still held in Canada and the empty north-west, partly because the King refused to give up. It was in these months, from the end of 1781 until all hostilities stopped in 1783, that George was later found to have been so culpable; the war was lost, but soldiers and sailors still died. America seemed a graveyard of British youth; the statesman and orator Edmund Burke claimed at the end of 1781 that a hundred thousand men had died there. The Mediterranean was still an inferno and in the West Indies the French and Spanish were encroaching on British territories. Minorca was lost in January 1782, St Kitts and Nevis a month later. Neither was won back, although Admiral Rodney restored morale by crushing the French fleet off Les Saintes a few months later. North was finally allowed to resign in March, and a new government was returned to negotiate both American independence and a general peace. When, on 19 November a draft peace treaty was put to Parliament, the King, writing to Lord North's old ally, Thomas Townshend, was one of the very few who refused to accept the inevitable, 'Parliament having to my astonishment come into the idea of granting a separation to North America has disabled me from longer defending the just rights of this Kingdom. But

I certainly disclaim thinking myself answerable for any evils that may arise from the adoption of this measure, as necessity, not conviction, has made me subscribe to it.' The King's letter was untidily eloquent of his state of mind: 'independence', which he had written first, was heavily written over with a term he characteristically picked from family life: 'a separation'.

Constitutionally the King certainly had no responsibility for the cutting of the bonds between Britain and the American colonies. The failure nagged at him nonetheless; despite what he wrote and said, he took it personally. The Americans had deserted him. Like a doting mother who spoiled her children, Britain had been too kind to the colonists. 'The too great lenity of this country increased their pride and encouraged them to rebel', George wrote, and his ministers, even Lord North, had successively failed to bring the colonists back to their duty. Like his brothers, the Americans ought to have paid the price, but like his defiant eldest son who was now beyond his control, they had got away with their insolence and seized their independence. In the turmoil after the resignation of Lord North, in which two administrations came and went in as many years and the King was finally forced to accept a government in which his ally Lord North had teamed up with his detested nemesis Charles James Fox, he thought seriously about abandoning his throne altogether. He had contemplated abdication before, partly to bring North back to his side, but this time, in the spring of 1783, he sat in his study in the Queen's House and wrote out a statement that he planned to read before Parliament. In his mind he had arrived at a point of utter failure. The government above party that he had promised to restore to the country was further away than ever; the arrival of his louche enemy Fox as joint head of the administration demonstrated with stark clarity the lack of virtue in the governing class; America was lost, Ireland restless and the light of empire dimming. The flat lands of Hanover seemed to beckon him to a home he had never seen except through the shimmer of the painter's varnish. In Hanover, perhaps, he could be again the father of his people, beloved, serene, above the fray. Although on his first appearance in Parliament he had declared in ringing tones that he gloried in the name of Briton, George wanted now to repudiate that messy identity and to go back to his German roots, to the Leineschloss and the peace of Grosse Garten at Herrenhausen where the noisiest intruders would be the paunchy ducks who pecked at the buckles on his shoes.

'When first I appeared as your sovereign in this place now above twenty-two years [ago]', he began, 'I had the pleasing hope that being born among you I might have proved the happy instrument of conciliating all parties.' His failure, slow at first with Bute and Wilkes, had gathered through the long war years and culminated in the turmoil of the last two years and this moment. 'That hour has now come', he wrote, when he was, 'no longer of utility to this Empire'. 'I am therefore resolved', he concluded, 'to resign my crown and all the dominions appertaining to it to the Prince of Wales, my eldest son and lawful successor, and to retire to the care of my Electoral dominions, the original patrimony of my ancestors. For which purpose I shall draw up and sign an instrument to which I shall affix my private seal. I trust this personal sacrifice will awaken the various parties to a sense of their duty, and that they will join in the support and assistance of the young successor.'

Perhaps it was the thought of his son, dealing cards at Cumberland House, flirting with actresses in Fox's untidy lodgings, that stayed the King's hand. The feckless Prince showed no capacity to take up any office, and George would retire to Hanover leaving the hated Fox in charge. Other voices urged him to reconsider too. Thomas Pitt, Chatham's nephew, convinced him that the unholy alliance between Fox and North would tear itself to pieces long before the King had settled himself in Hanover. Most important, though, George was king, born to shoulder his kingdom, and like Atlas, he could not set it down.

George never delivered his abdication speech, but he kept it amongst his papers, to remind him of how close he had come. The desolation that had brought him to write it returned every now and again in years to come and pricked him painfully. Nothing brought him up against his disasters more than having to receive the new American minister to the court of St James's in 1785. George had always placed great importance on the protocols at court and what they meant. That was the reason why he signalled his fury at his brothers' marriages by refusing to receive them or their wives at court, and why he ruthlessly insisted on the duchesses' continued exclusion. Receiving an ambassador was fraught with symbolism, since the ambassador was the surrogate of the head of the state he served, and everywhere except the Vatican, that was a monarch or a prince. It was for this reason that ambassadors met monarchs behind closed doors, standing to show their equality with the King, and in complete privacy. The first visit of the American ambassador forced King George to acknowledge, as they stood face to face, that his colonists had grown up; they had got away from him, and the nation they had formed was one with no king. Both the King and John Adams, the man appointed for the task, felt how personal and difficult the occasion was bound to be. Adams, a short-legged, baggy-eyed, garrulous lawyer from Massachusetts who would be elected second President of the United States in 1797, knew that he would be nervous and had taken the precaution of learning his short introductory speech by heart. The King, too, had planned what he would say, both in welcome and in personal exculpation.

Smartly dressed, Adams arrived at the arched gatehouse of St James's Palace on I June 1785 as the King's chamberlain had instructed him. The drawing room was already crowded for the day's levee, but Adams was given special treatment, led through the crowd to the door of the King's closet, which he described as a bedchamber (he took time to assure his American correspondents that George did not actually sleep there). The doors were opened and Adams was left alone to approach the King, bowing, as he had been told to do, three times on the way. When he got close enough to speak, Adams began, 'The United States of America have appointed me their minister plenipotentiary to Your Majesty.' Usually fluent and gabby, he was now halting and nearly overcome with emotion, standing for his new nation in front of the man it had cast off. 'I felt more than I did or could express', he wrote home afterwards, still tongue-tied. Feeling welled up in the King as well. He listened with 'dignity but with apparent emotion', as Adams went through his speech, which expressed hope for a complete reconciliation between 'people who, though separated by an ocean and under different governments, have the same language, a similar religion, and kindred blood'. Though his words sank deep into British memory they were uttered more rhetorically than sincerely; privately Adams declared that he had not a drop of blood in his veins that was not American, and, despite his emotion, held his head high in front of the British King.

Years of courtly habit came to George's aid as he replied, although his stutter and his habit of pausing in sentences where grammar least demanded it were both amplified by his choking emotion. 'He was indeed much affected', Adams wrote sympathetically. Nonetheless, the King still wanted both the ambassador and the Americans to understand exactly why he had stood so firm in the war, ending his remarks by saying, 'I wish you, Sir, to believe and that it be understood in America that I have done nothing in the late contest but what I thought myself indispensably bound to do by the duty which I owed to my people. I will be very frank with you, I was the last to consent to separation; but the separation having been made, and having become inevitable, I have always said, and I say now, that I would be the first to meet the friendship of the United States as an independent power.'

The contest was indeed over and the King had acknowledged America as a nation on equal terms with his own. The charged atmosphere, heavy with unspoken feeling, needed a few words of small talk, and George rose well, even slyly, to the occasion. Was it true, he asked Adams, as he had heard, that he was 'the most attached of all his countryman to the manners of France'? Adams, remembering his legal training, replied smoothly that his attachment was all to his own country. The King, a polished courtier again, said, 'An honest man will never have any other,' and with a bow, signalled the end of the interview.

Conclusion

After the Treaty of Versailles ended the long conflict in Europe and America in 1783, after the end of the Fox/North coalition which collapsed as Thomas Pitt predicted, and after the arrival in government of William Pitt, who managed George III with skilful deference, an unlooked-for peace began to spread over the King's mind. Though he may have been loath to admit it, and though he was still as punctilious as ever in transacting government business, George began to step back from his intense emotional involvement in the nation's politics. He was weary of the fray, and he saw, besides, that Pitt without him would do everything necessary that could make the monarchy secure and his person respected.

Gradually, too, the temper of the times came to match the King's habits, his fidelity and gruffness, his economy and piety. After his first bout of illness and delirium in the winter of 1788, George III, in his frailty and dignity, endeared himself to his subjects. The French Revolution and in particular the national revulsion at the execution of Louis XVI sealed his popularity, The King's dull ordinariness, his lack of extravagance or cosmopolitan style, his insularity and his honesty were hailed as mirroring the character of the nation and acting, as the nation did, as a bulwark against the chaos and excess that ruled in France. The culture of sensation and celebrity, the intense scrutiny of private life by the press and public that had bounded and tarnished his brothers' lives, was pushed underground, condemned by patriots and evangelicals alike as febrile, vicious and inappropriate in a time of war. As the

1790s wore on, as the nation embarked on a long and gruelling conflict that was fought to protect the monarchies of Europe against the principles and practice of first republican and then imperial France, George III inspired the loyalty and the love of his subjects in a manner unthinkable at the height of the American War. The spectres of tyranny and bad government, of secrecy and double-dealing, that had hovered around his head for the first twenty years of his reign fled across the Channel. Lodging first in the Jacobin regime and then in the pugnacious figure of Napoleon, they left the King to gather to himself all the good qualities of Britishness that many of his subjects had signally failed to find in him before.

For a little while, the fragile truce between George and his brothers endured as well. Although he could never be close to his brothers while he refused to acknowledge their marriages and although they were proscribed the court, both Prince Henry and Prince William were allowed to visit their brother privately after their reconciliations of 1780. As the breach between the Duke and Maria Gloucester grew wider and the Duke more publicly endorsed the story about his early life which gave him an innocent's role and made her an ambitious schemer, so the King quietly slipped back into his earlier affection. Lady Almeria Carpenter, however, stood between the Duke and a full restitution. As the Duke's mistress, she, no more than Maria, could be received at court, so Prince William continued in uneasy limbo, accepted once again but officially still outside the tight circle of court society.

The Duke of Cumberland, however, never repudiated his wife, and he soon soured his relationship with the King once more by befriending the errant Prince of Wales. Never losing his love of nicknames and disguises and harking back to his own pseudonyms of Jones and Griffith, the Duke insisted on calling the Prince of Wales Taffy, much to the King's disgust. Believing that his brother could offer his son only a bad example of domestic arrangements and a disorderly way of life, George became even more angry when the Duke invited the Prince and the most important members of his new household to dine at Cumberland House at the end of 1780. The ensuing quarrel threw their relationship back a decade. The Duke of Cumberland knew that the King's prohibition was a judgement on the way he and the Duchess lived, reacting with predictable pique. 'As I supposed that every mark of attention on my part to the Prince could not but be agreeable to Your Majesty, it was with the utmost astonishment and mortification I learnt Your Majesty had forbidden the Prince's establishment to accept my invitation to dine at Cumberland House. After this public proof of Your Majesty's intention to exclude me from the benefits of society enjoyed by the rest of mankind, it is impossible to receive with satisfaction those attentions (however flattering) all Your Majesty's subjects wish to pay me when I am conscious they thereby incur Your Majesty's displeasure. Thus condemned by Your Majesty to a situation so repugnant to my own feelings, all that remains for me is to request permission to withdraw from Your Majesty's dominions and as a Citizen of the world seek an asylum in some other part of the globe.'

Trapped in the country by the war with France and Spain, Prince Harry had to wait until the peace of 1783 before he could carry out his threat. In the meantime he pointedly annoyed his brother by coming out against the war in America, throwing his hand in with an opposition which by then included his old lawyer John Dunning. By 1780 Dunning had so far forgotten his service to the royal family as to be the framer and tabler of the famous motion that summed up two decades of opposition suspicion about secret government: 'The influence of the Crown has increased, is increasing and ought to be diminished.' His rancour extended to his former client too. When the Duke of Cumberland, running into Dunning in the lobby of the House, exclaimed that he had sat up all night and nearly put his eyes out reading Richard Price's famous defence of the colonists, Dunning's sardonic reply that the pamphlet had opened rather than closed the eyes of most who read it was a long-delayed revenge for the professional humiliation he had suffered at the court of King's Bench ten years before.

It was really debt and not the King which drove the Duke and Duchess of Cumberland abroad in the years after the peace. For three years they wandered the Continent, travelling the highways of France, from Calais to Paris, from Paris to the Loire, to Dijon along the Saône and up the Rhine to Strasbourg in the Holy Roman Empire. South again, and across the Alps, they spent months bumping up and down the prickly spine of Italy. Spending what he hoped to save, playing cards with soldiers, Prince Harry was less and less robust, his wife admirably and blowsily cheerful. In the summer of 1786 they turned up at Spa in the Low Countries, where the Duke summoned Robert Adair to take care of his failing eyes and lungs. Once back in London that November they stayed, shored up in Cumberland House, still friendly with the Prince of Wales and his mistress-wife Mrs Fitzherbert, two childless couples unwelcome at court, making their own society.

Conclusion

On 12 September 1790 the Duke wrote his last letter to the Prince of Wales. Six days later, at forty-five, with his lungs gone, he died, leaving his widow to the mercy of the King. George III gave Anne a pension of £4,000 a year, but she had the Duke's debts to pay and it would never be enough. Cumberland House, already heavily mortgaged, had to be sold, and the Duchess decided to go abroad again. In May 1792 she sent a last letter to her brother-in-law from Cumberland House, reproaching him for his lack of generosity and kindness. 'I have, Sir,' she wrote, 'reconciled myself to the melancholy necessity of quitting your Majesty's dominions for ever, and shall depart with the consolation of having rendered the Duke of Cumberland's life happy, his death easy and his memory respected, and in the hope that the unoffending and unfortunate may find friends in every part of the Christian world.'

The King was deaf to this rebuke and Anne unequal to sustaining it. France was no place for an English duchess in the most turbulent years of the revolution, and soon after the execution of Louis XVI, she was back. London was too expensive and the Duchess was unwilling to live out her last years in uneasy proximity to the royal family at her last piece of property, Cumberland Lodge in Windsor Great Park. She opted instead for the cut-price gentility of Tunbridge Wells, hanging on there until she died discreetly and without complaint in 1803.

With the Duchess of Gloucester the end was longer and more anguished. After 1781, when she was forty-five and he thirty-eight, she and the Duke were husband and wife only in name, living in separate suites at Gloucester House, keeping up appearances abroad. Prince William tried to ingratiate himself with the King by complaining about Maria, writing about her as if he had never been captivated by her beauty and pride. In their quarrel their children were the unhappy weapons, ricocheted between their warring parents. In 1787, when the whole family was in Geneva, and the children were fourteen and eleven, the Duke threatened to remove them altogether from his wife. He wanted to send Prince William to university despite his extreme youth, and to give Princess Sophia into the care of a governess who would, as he put it to the King, 'keep her clear of the Duchess but at meals and in the evening society'. 'I now avoid all conversation', he went on, 'as she heats herself so indecently. I have told her that if she lets the children from this time alone, and behaves more respectfully to me before the World, she may remain in my house . . . I hope Your Majesty will forgive my troubling you with all this detail, but my heart is very full.'

From the winter of 1787 the Duke and Duchess stayed in England. While he regretted the loss of his army career and consoled himself with Lady Almeria Carpenter, she went into old age dreaming of the life she might have had, still angry at the one she was forced to put up with. She could not understand her husband's love for Lady Almeria, writing to Anne Clement in June 1790, 'His mistress is grown fat and red faced – yet he prefers her to me. What then avails my good looks?' But she had come to accept by the end of that year that Prince Willliam had 'no remains of liking' for her, despite the fact that, as etiquette demanded, they still dined together every day. By the early 1790s as her sixties approached, she had come to fear Lady Almeria not so much as a rival wife but as a rival mother who might, with her husband, steal her children's love. 'I once feared that *they* and *their* friends had hurt his affection to me', she wrote to Anne Clement about her son Prince William in 1793, 'but I have no reason to think so at present, he is only affection to me, and as he is now old enough to judge for himself I hope he will never be shook.' William, seventeen by then, had grown into a stolid young man without any of the Walpole friction and sparkle. Commissioned into the army at thirteen, he joined for long enough to see active service in Flanders in 1794 and in the Lowlands five years later. When he came back unharmed from Holland his mother, as usual, curdled her own happiness, exclaiming, 'I suppose when people are blessed in their children a good husband would be too much felicity.' Eventually, in 1816, William was allowed to marry his childhood love, George III's fourth daughter Princess Mary; too late for any children but in time for almost twenty years of an open and proud married happiness his parents never knew.

Princess Sophia was left to be her mother's more constant companion. 'My Sophia and I pass many evenings tête-à-tête', Maria reported to Anne Clement in November 1794, when her plump and passive daughter was twenty-one, 'and although we acknowledge they might be gayer we feel that we have no obnoxious people with us.' Sophia, often in the company of the worthy works or the formidable person of the moralist and religious writer Hanah More, was her mother's solace. Never underestimating her own good qualities, Maria wrote in 1797, 'My poor dear maid Vernon used to say years ago that Sophia was the only child I had that was like me in everything – and so it proves.' After the Duke of Gloucester died in 1805, Sophia gave her mother her whole attention. They moved together to the village of Brompton south of Kensington, where new developments were pushing out the last green spaces between the older suburban villas. Although she renamed her house Gloucester Lodge, and the road than ran beside it became Gloucester Road, Maria was too weary now to live in state. Her last two years were spent in her daughter's company with increased piety and lessening bitterness. She died, 'perfectly resigned', as her daughter put it, in 1807. By then, at the age of seventy-two, she had abandoned her lifelong pursuit of earthly glory, and consoled herself with the more certain reward of the world to come.

In her older age the Duchess of Gloucester, finding common cause with other wronged royal wives, had befriended first the miserable Princess of Wales and then, by letter, the Duchess of Brunswick, the Princess's mother. Princess Augusta's life had been a miserable one and she had spent much of it longing to return to England. When her daughter Princess Caroline married the Prince of Wales in 1795 some of her dynastic hopes were finally fulfilled. But from the moment they met, Princess Caroline and the Prince of Wales disliked one another, she reportedly claiming that he was fat and not nearly as good-looking as his portrait had made out, he simply turning away at the sight of her and calling out to his equerry, 'Harris, a brandy.' Alcohol and other women thereafter consoled the Prince, and anger consumed the Princess. Princess Augusta, in Brunswick, might have been thankful that an heir to the throne, Princess Charlotte, was born from their very brief cohabitation. But after her birth the Prince of Wales refused to live with his wife and the young Princess of Wales was left to her boredom and humiliation, another royal daughter married abroad and into unhappiness to serve dynastic ends.

Far away, the Duchess of Brunswick could do little about her daughter's misery. In 1806, when Prussia declared war on France and the seventy-one-year-old Duke of Brunswick was appointed commander-in-chief of the Prussian army, the Duchess was caught in a maelstrom that swept happiness aside in a fight for survival. At Jena on 14 October of that year, Napoleon defeated the bulk of the Prussian army. At the battle of Auerstädt the same day, the Duke of Brunswick, at the head of the remainder, was seriously wounded. The French killed twenty-five thousand men from the Prussian forces. The rest scattered and fled, leaving the French to overrun and occupy first Brunswick and then Berlin. The Duchess, with her two long-incapacitated sons and a widowed daughter-in-law in tow, struck out from her devastated palace for the safety of Altona, where her husband lay mortally wounded. When Karl Wilhelm died a few days later, the homeless Duchess fled up north to her sister's old kingdom with only her jewels and a little cash to fund her exile. Her destination was Augustenborg, a small town perched over the water on a peninsula curling east from Jutland, well beyond the border with Schleswig Holstein and the reach of Napoleon's marauding armies.

At Augustenborg the years were peeled away. In the modest castle there, Princess Louise Augusta, whose striking aquiline nose and thick golden-brown hair came unmistakably from her father Johann Struensee and whose fine, ample bosom was her mother's, came out to greet her aunt and offer her sanctuary. In the Duchess's closet Princess Louise had hung a portrait of Caroline Mathilde, as a comfort and a reminder of what they both had lost. The picture may have survived the great fire that had ravaged Christiansborg Palace twelve years before, but it might have been one that Princess Augusta already knew, the crayon portrait in a gold frame that Caroline Mathilde had hung in the castle at Celle and bequeathed with her other pictures to her children in 1775. Princess Louise was almost four when her mother died, and thirty-five now, though Caroline Mathilde had been dead for thirty-one years. Despite her sheltered and cautious upbringing, Princess Louise's behaviour and beliefs seemed still to owe more to her mother and father than to her years in the court of Juliane Marie. She was impetuous and romantic, a confirmed supporter of the French Revolution and an outspoken Napoleonist. She knew, too, as her mother had done, the value of gesture, wore the latest French Empire-line gowns and made sure that her children were educated in thoroughgoing Rousseauian manner.

The Duchess of Brunswick, broken in spirit and left without funds, was too weary now to indulge her niece's radical temper. She threw herself on her brother's mercy, begging him to allow her to come to England to live with her daughter. In handwriting that had become tiny and shaky after his second bout of illness in 1804, George replied, giving her permission to return to her original home. With her two younger sons, Augusta finally arrived in London in September 1807, putting up in Montague House in Blackheath near Greenwich with her daughter the Princess of Wales. It was hardly the homecoming she had spent so long wishing for in the cold years of her estrangement from Duke Karl Wilhelm. She was old, 'very deaf, and looking much older than she ought', as her daughter put it. Her memory was shaky and the trauma of war and loss had ravaged her. Unable to live easily with her daughter the Duchess soon moved next door, buying Lord Chesterfield's villa and renaming it Brunswick House. Germany, that she had so hated when she moved there, was much on her mind. Her Hanoverian roots, sitting below the surface and kept alive in a lifetime at Brunswick, proved stronger than her childhood memories. She talked to her sons in German and she loved to invite her brother to dinner, asking him to let her know which German dishes were his favourites. Too old at sixty-nine to find her way back into the English society she had left forty-five years before, she stayed on in Blackheath after her daughter left to live in Kensington Palace in 1808, and died in 1813, 'a melancholy specimen of decayed splendour', as one visitor put it, and a relic of an earlier age.

Death came slowly for the King, strolling through the empty spaces in his mind like a hiker sure of his destination, unhurried and taking his time. By 1810 George III was blind, infirm at seventy-two, and muffled by gathering deafness from the world. At the end of that year, during celebrations for the fiftieth anniversary of his accession, he appeared in public for the last time, leaning on the Queen's arm, guided round a wide circle of courtiers, friends and his own middle-aged children. Even for a deaf man he spoke too loudly. His countenance was flushed, his fever and madness coming on again. Without his knowledge, a few weeks later, the Lord Chancellor signed a Regency Bill and George III, recovered from his delirium but weak and wandering, was henceforth king only in name. For nine more years he lingered on, visited less and less by his family, abandoned to the corridors and spartan rooms of his apartments at Windsor Castle, no king but a patient and an old man. The plainest of clothes hung on his gaunt frame and his long white hair lay in tatters down his back. Sometimes he sat at his harpsichord and banged out tunes he had once played with care and delicacy. Sometimes he wept and mumbled to himself or sang in a quavering voice. Often his mind retreated to earlier times. In empty rooms dead ministers and kings arrived; they sat and talked about far-off events, imagined duties and long-lost love. In the end the King had gone even from himself, a dying man mourning the dead. 'I must have a new suit of clothes,' he announced one day, 'and I will have them in black in memory of George the Third.' 'He was a good man,' he said, pronouncing with unclouded reason his own short epitaph.

Notes

Introduction

p.1 'I have no other hope'] Caroline Mathilde to George III, Royal Archives, Windsor, RA GEO/52347.

p.4 'The original patrimony'] George III's abdication document drawn up in the spring of 1783, in Bonomy Dobrée, ed., *The Letters of King George III*, London 1935, rptd 1968, p. 171.

p.4 'The first morning . . .'] George I quoted in Ruby Arkell, *Caroline of Ansbach. George the Second's Queen*, London 1939, p. 41.

p.7 L. von Schrader's reports to George II on the princesses of Holstein-Glücksburg, Wolfenbüttel, Ploeniz, and Saxe-Gotha, Niedersächsisches Hauptstaatsarchiv Hannover, Königliches Hausarchiv, Dep 84 B 1557, ff.1–37.

1: Fritz ist Dode

p.9 'Someone whispered that the King'] Hannover, Dep 103 XXIV Nr 3270, B1181, contains about one hundred pages of material about Frederick's last illness including a note that Augusta personally instructed Lord North to tell the King.

p.10 'Accounts had it'] for George II's remarks, see Michael De-la-Noy, *The King Who Never Was: The Story of Frederick, Prince of Wales*, London 1996, p. 290.

p.10 'be put in a box'] *The Political Journal of George Bubb Dodington*, ed. John Carswell and Louis Arnold Dralle, Oxford 1965, p. 107.

p.10 'turned short'] Dodington, *Journal* p. 112.

p.11 'When Prince Frederick's eldest son'] Prince George, quoted in De-La-Noy, *The King Who Never Was*, p. 285.

p.12 'Friedrich was left alone in Hanover'] Hannover, Dep 84 B1139, the education of Prince Friedrich Ludwig 1713–21, includes George I's instructions to his chamberlain J. F. von Grote, and detailed reports from Frederick's tutors on his studies and progress.

p.14 'The first of these was the Prince of Wales'] George II quoted in *Lord Hervey's Memoirs*, ed. Romney Sedgwick, London 1963, rev. 1970, p. 18.

p.15 'the most agreeable young man'] Lady Bristol quoted in Sir George Young, *Poor Fred, the People's Prince*, London 1937, p. 43.

p.15 'The character of the Prince'] R.A. Roberts ed., *Diary of Viscount Percival, afterwards First Earl of Egmont*, 3 vols, London 1920–3, vol. 2, p. 207.

p.15 'With nothing to keep him at court'] Queen Caroline's relationship with Lord Hervey, her hatred of her son and her final illness are all well described in Lucy Moore, *Amphibious Thing. The Life of Lord Hervey*, London 2004.

p.16 'Sitting in his castle in Weimar'] Hannover Dep 84 B1157, 1169, 1557, include details of von Schrader's missions to German courts and the marriage negotiations and contract. The wedding is described in Egmont, *Diary*, vol. 2, p. 264.

p.17 'All this time'] the Queen described the incident in a long letter to her daughter Anne, Princess of Orange, reproduced in Arkell, *Caroline of Ansbach*, pp. 297–9.

p.18 'The Earl of Bolingbroke'] quoted in Walter Sichel, *Bolingbroke and his Times*, 2 vols, London 1901, vol. 2, p. 357. The politics of the Prince's circle are discussed in Linda Colley, *In Defiance of Oligarchy. The Tory Party 1714–60*, Cambridge 1982.

p.19 'As soon as the public'] Lord Essex's letter to the prince, and 'Georgius Rex', London, 1737, single sheet broadsides.

p.20 'The first proved supremely easy'] Prince George's birth is described in Egmont, *Diary*, vol. 3, p. 207.

p.22 'He played the father and husband well'] quoted in Captain Henry Curteis, *A Forgotten Prince of Wales*, London 1912, p. 291.

p.24 'Early in January 1749'] the whole document is quoted in Young, *Poor Fred*, pp. 172–5.

p.26 'Unbeknownst to him'] Lord Bute's introduction is described in Morris Marples, *Poor Fred and the Butcher. Sons of George II*, London 1970,

p. 85: Prince Frederick's assessment of him in J. Heneage Jesse, *Memoirs of the Life and Reign of King George the Third*, in 3 vols, London 1867, vol. 1, p. 56.

p.27 'It was Frederick who was dead'] Hannover, Dep 103 XXIV Nr 3270, B1181, fol 31, a *post mortem* which describes his lungs as enlarged, full of fluid and having several lumps and small tumours; it concluded that he died of suffocation after one of these tumours suddenly burst. A doctor's report on the moments of his death, fols 4–5, describes him as having a bout of coughing, turning on his side, gasping for breath and dying nine minutes later.

2: A Sayer of Things

p.30 'established a character,'] *The Political Journal of George Bubb Dodington*, ed. John Carswell and Lewis Arnold Dralle, Oxford 1965, p. 180.

p.31 'She admitted to Dodington . . .'] Dodington, Journal, pp. 174 and 178.

p.31 'Years later, Prince William . . .'] J. Heneage Jesse, *Memoirs of the Life and Reign of King George the Third*, 3 vols, London 1867, vol. 1, p. 21.

p.33 'I got home between ten . . .'] Dodington, *Journal*, p. 180.

p.33 'She really did not well know . . .'] Dodington, *Journal*, p. 178.

p.34 'The Princess sent to me . . .'] Dodington, *Journal*, pp. 240–1.

p.34 James, Earl Waldegrave, *Memoirs from 1754 to 1758*, London 1821, p. 3.

p.35 Waldegrave, *Memoirs*, p. 55.

p.36 'My dear Lord . . .'] George, Prince of Wales to Lord Bute, 31 June 1756, from *Letters from George III to Lord Bute 1756–1766*, ed. Romney Sedgwick, London 1939, pp. 2–3.

p.37 'I beg you . . .'] *Letters from George III to Lord Bute*, p. 5.

p.37 'It will sooner or later . . .'] Bute to the Prince of Wales. *Letters from George III to Lord Bute*, p. liii.

p.38 'My friend is . . . attacked . . .'] *Letters from George III to Lord Bute*, p. 3.

p.40 'If the government . . .'; 'I begin now to think . . .'] *Letters from George III to Lord Bute*, pp. 6–7.

p.40 'Again famous for being . . .'] *Letters from George III to Lord Bute*, pp. 6 and 14.

p.41 'If you should resolve to remain a little longer . . .'] *Letters from George III to Lord Bute*, pp. 6 and 14.

p.43 'nothing but Dutchmen . . .'] Prince Edward to George, Prince of Wales, 13 October 1759, RA GEO/5426; 'A good many . . .'] Prince Edward to

George, Prince of Wales, 10 October 1759, RA GEO/54260; 'The prodigious rolling . . .' Prince Edward to George, Prince of Wales, 9 September 1759, RA GEO/54260.

p.44 'In the extensive running letters . . .'] published as *The Letters and Journals of Lady Mary Coke*, ed. J. A. Home, 4 vols, Edinburgh 1889–96, rptd 1970.

p.45 'he can never omit an opportunity . . .'] Prince Edward to Lady Mary Coke] letters from the Duke of York to Lady Mary Coke with some copies and drafts of replies, 1758–66; most letters, many undated, 1758–62. Private Collection, catalogued but unpaginated, on temporary loan to National Register of Archives for Scotland, NRAS 859.

p.47 'You must come'] Horace Bleakley, *Ladies Fair and Frail: Sketches of the Demi-Monde During the Eighteenth Century*, London 1909, p. 53.

p.48 'Miss Fisher is forced'] Bleakley, *Ladies Fair and Frail*, p. 61.

p.49 'daily increasing admiration of the fair sex . . .'; 'everything I can form to myself . . .'; 'as to what he has hinted at . . .'; 'I mean to lay my whole breast . . .'; 'If I must either lose'] Prince George to Lord Bute, 1759, *Letters of George III to Lord Bute*, pp. 35–40.

p.50 'the case admits . . .'; 'think, Sir . . .'] Lord Bute to Prince George, *Letters from George III to Lord Bute*, fn. p. 39.

p.50 'I am born . . .'] George III to Lord Bute, winter 1759–60, *Letters from George III to Lord Bute*, p. 39.

p.50 'I thought the just . . .'; 'Our evening has been spent . . .'] *Letters from George III to Lord Bute*, pp. 39, 40.

p.51 'melancholy thoughts . . .'; 'not in every particular . . .'] George III to Lord Bute, 20 May 1761, *Letters from George III to Lord Bute*, p. 55.

p.52 'There are an amazing number . . .'] the Duchess of Northumberland to her son, 26 July 1761, from *The Diaries of a Duchess: Extracts from the Diaries of the First Duchess of Northumberland (1761–1776)*, ed. James Greig, with a foreword by the Duke of Northumberland, London 1926, pp. 28–9.

p.53 'The fault of his constitution . . .'] Fanny Burney's diary, quoted in John Brooke, *King George III*, London 1972, p. 291.

p.54 'a large joint of meat . . .'] the Duchess of Northumberland to her son, 4 April 1762, from *Diaries of a Duchess*, p. 43.

p.56 'Tho' in the bosom . . .'; 'My health is every day impairing . . .'] The Earl of Bute to Dr Campbell, 30 January 1763, in *Letters from George III to Lord Bute*, p. lxii.

p.59 'our hero'] Duchess of Brunswick to the royal treasurer Mr Le Grand, 30 April 1765, Royal Archives, Garth Papers, RA GEO/Add 21/8.

p.60 'All we have heard'; 'that she hoped'] Richard Rigby in Jesse, *Memoirs of the Life & Reign of George the Third*, vol. 1, p. 316.

p.62 'We that live to please . . .'] William Cooke, *Memoirs of Samuel Foote Esq.*, 3 vols, London 1805, vol. 1, p. 150.

p.63 'He is a man . . .'] Boswell's journal, 27 November 1762, *Boswell's London Journal 1762–63*, ed. Frederick A. Pottle, New York and London 1970, p. 53.

p.64 'I, without the least restraint . . .'; 'come Boswell'] both from an unpublished poem of 1760, quoted in Frederick A. Pottle, *James Boswell, the Earlier Years 1740–1769*, London 1966, p. 49.

p.65 'Sir, Permit me'] James Boswell, *The Cub, at Newmarket*, London 1760, rptd 1762, dedication.

p.65 'He imagined me'] *Boswell's London Journal*, pp. 52–3.

p.67 'men of letters'; 'joint exhibition of wonders'; 'Feats were performed . . .'] Richard Lovell Edgeworth, *Memoirs, written by himself and concluded by his daughter Maria Edgeworth*, 2 vols, London 1820, vol. 1, pp. 122–3.

p.67 'although he generally preferred . . .'; 'a royal hand'] Cooke, *Memoirs of Samuel Foote*, vol. 1, p. 140.

p.67 'Admitting that the best can happen . . .'] Foote to Garrick, 26 February 1766, in Philip A. Highfil, Jnr, Kalman A. Bunin and Edward Langhans, *A Biographical Dictionary of the English Stage*, Carbondale, IL 1978, vol. 5, p. 343.

p.68 'I am better rather . . .'; 'singular humanity . . .'; 'I took the liberty . . .'] Foote to Sir John Delaval, mid-March 1766, quoted in Francis Askham, *The Gay Delavals*, London 1955, p. 111.

p.68 Samuel Foote, *The Lame Lover*, London 1770, p. 6.

p.69 'to fit up a theatre . . .'] Edgeworth, *Memoirs*, vol. 1, pp. 124–5.

p.69 'Never having heard . . .'] *Letters and Journals of Lady Mary Coke*, vol. 1, p. 101.

p.69 'chiefly with his Royal Highness . . .'] Earl of March to George Selwyn, *Selwyn Correspondence*, vol. 2, p. 117.

p.70 'I shall not have the pleasure . . .'] George III to Lord Bute, 2 November 1764, *Letters from George III to Lord Bute*, p. 239.

p.70 Henry St. John to George Selwyn, *Selwyn Correspondence*, vol. 2, p. 103.

p.70 'The Duke's habits . . .'; 'Mr and Mrs Garrick . . .'] from *The Life of General*

Sir Robert Wilson, ed. Rev. Herbert Randolf, 2 vols. London 1862 vol. 1, p. 20.

p.71 'went together to the place . . .'] *Letters and Journals of Lady Mary Coke*, vol. 1, pp. 205–6.

p.71 'less than eighty-six in a minute . . .'] Randolf, *Life of General Sir Robert Wilson*, vol. 1, p. 21.

p.71 'Brother. A report is very prevalent . . .'] George III to Duke of York, 14 July 1767, Royal Archives, RA GEO/15823.

p.72 'spoke French vastly well'] Maria Waldegrave to Jane Clement, 28 July 1766, Clement Mss., Lewis Walpole Library, Yale University. Unpaginated.

p.72 'I can assure you I go through . . .'] Henry St. John to George Selwyn, 25 August 1767, *Selwyn Correspondence*, vol. 2, p. 184.

p.73 'My Dear Brother'] Duke of York to Prince William, Duke of Gloucester, 9 September 1767, Royal Archives, RA GEO/54288.

p.73 'after a long illness'] Henry St. John to the Duke of Gloucester, 7 September 1767, Royal Archives, RA GEO/54289.

p.74 'constantly under my eyes'] Henry St. John to George Selwyn, 10 November 1767, *Selwyn Correspondence*, vol. 2, pp. 192–3.

p.74 'by the death'] *Edgeworth Memoirs*, vol. 1, p. 154.

p.74 'He burst into tears'] quoted in Highfill *et al.*, *Biographical Dictionary of the English Stage*, vol. 5, p. 355.

p.75 'The sad and unexpected news'] *Letters and Journals of Lady Mary Coke*, vol. 2, p. 136.

p.75 'They have neither of them'; 'I made no answer'; 'I prayed to God'] *Letters and Journals of Lady Mary Coke*, vol. 2, pp. 138, 140, 145.

p.76 'I have passed a sleepless night'; 'That he should not think of me'] *Letters and Journals of Lady Mary Coke*, vol. 2, pp. 147, 151.

p.76 'explaining that after dictating'] *Letters and Journals of Lady Mary Coke*, vol. 2, p. 152.

p.77 'I dreamed a good deal'] *Letters and Journals of Lady Mary Coke*, vol. 2, p. 152.

3: A Dangerous Prescription

p.78 For negotiations about the marriage of Caroline Mathilde and Prince Frederick, her dowry and settlement, see Hauptstaatsarchiv Hannover, Königliches Hausarchiv Hannover, Dep. 84 A, 20; Dep. 84 B 1024.

p.79 Details of Christian's fears taken from Reverdil's memoir, *Struensee et la Cour de Copenhagen 1760–1772. Mémoires de Reverdil, Conseiller d'état du Roi Chrétian VII*, Paris 1858, pp. 4–24.

p.80 'To an amiable and manly countenance'] William Cosby, dispatch to London, 27 March 1764, quoted in W. H. Wilkins, *A Queen of Tears. Caroline Matilda, Queen of Denmark and Norway and Princess of Great Britain and Ireland*, 2 vols, London 1904, vol. 1, p. 63.

p.82 George III to Lord Bute] *Letters from George III to Lord Bute*, 3 May 1766 p. 249.

p.82 'the common cause'] Henry Seymour-Conway, letter to Robert Gunning, envoy to the court of Copenhagen, 13 June 1766, The National Archives: Public Record Office SP 75/119. Dispatches were often numbered by their senders and almost always dated. Dispatches in cipher – that is, code made up of numbers – were numbered alphabetically and transcribed by officials in London with the transcriptions running above the lines of numbers. They are bound in runs of volumes, in which letters like Seymour-Conway's are sometimes interpolated.

p.83 'His fine house'] Fenwick's house is clearly marked on the beautiful scale model of the town in its museum.
'In 1766 he recorded'] Robert Gunning, dispatch of early 1767, TNA:PRO SP 75 /120.

p.84 'her dowry'] In Hannover Mss, Dep. 84 A 53, the sum is described as £40,000 and 40,000 'RThal Leibrente', in the dispatches as £40,000 and 40,000 ecus routed through the electorate of Brunswick-Lüneburg. The Leibrente was Caroline Mathilde's widow's jointure if Christian died.
'place some hopes'] Titley dispatch, 4 June 1765, TNA:PRO SP 75 /120.

p.85 'before she set out'] Duchess of Northumberland, *Diaries of a Duchess*, p. 63.

p.85 'very pretty in the midst'] Lady Mary Coke, 1 October 1766, *Letters and Journals*, vol. 1, p. 65.

p.86 Elizabeth Carter quoted in J. Heneage Jesse, *Memoirs of the Life and Reign of George III*, 3 vols, London 1867, vol. 2, p. 13.

p.86 'the malice, deceit'] George III to Caroline Matilda, 2 October 1766, Royal Archives, RA GEO/1581–43.

p.87 'Dear sister, I think I can no way'] George III to Augusta, Duchess of Brunswick, end of September 1766, Royal Archives, RA GEO/15810–11.

p.88 'We are now'] Caroline Mathilde to George III, 8 October 1766, Royal Archives, RA GEO/52289.

'anxious Hanoverian officials'] for details of her journey, Königliches Hausarchiv Hannover, Dep. 84 B 1573, fols 64–106, Dep. 84 B 866, Dep. 84 B 867, Dep. 103, XXIV 2656.

p.88 'I think I am'] Caroline Mathilde to George III, 20 October 1766, Royal Archives, RA GEO/52290.

p.90 'another, probably more accurate'] population tables drawn up by order of Johann Struensee, sent by Robert Gunning in his dispatch to London of 15 August 1769, and bound in with SP 75/122. This was, presumably, a secret pamphlet that Gunning had acquired with his discretionary funds.

p.92 Frederiksborg and Frederiksberg are two different castles, the former out in the countryside, the latter on the edge of the capital. Information about Copenhagen and Christiansborg in the eighteenth century taken from Christian Elling, *Christiansborg Interiører. Studier over residensslottet i det 18. århundrede*, Copenhagen 1944; Ole Feldbæk, *Den Lange Fred. 1700–1800*, Copenhagen 1990; Ole Feldbæk, *Gyldendal og Politikens Danmarkshistorie*, Copenhagen 1990; Kristian Hvidt, Svend Ellehøj and Otto Norn (eds), *Christiansborg Slot*, vol. 1, Copenhagen 1975.

p.95 'All access to either'] Robert Gunning, dispatch of 18 November 1766, TNA:PRO SP 75/119.

p.95 'the sweetness of her disposition'] Robert Gunning, dispatch of 6 December 1966, TNA:PRO SP 75/119; 'I fear I shall not go'] Caroline Mathilde to George III, 9 December 1766, Royal Archives, RA GEO/52293.

p.95 'You remember what I said'] Caroline Mathilde to George III, 11 November 1766, Royal Archives, RA GEO/52292; ditto, 13 January 1767, Royal Archives, RA GEO/52294.

p.97 'she took great pains'] [Otto von Falkenskjold], *Authentic Elucidation of the History of the Courts of Counts Struensee and Brandt, and of the Revolution in Denmark in the Year 1772. Printed privately but not published by a personage principally interested, translated from the German by B. H. Latrobe*. London 1789, p. 11. This edition is a pirated version of the 1788 German translation of the French original.

p.98 'dispatched with reluctant haste'] Falkenskjold, *Authentic Elucidation*, p. 9.

p.99 'I fear that my letters'] Caroline Mathilde to George III, 14 March 1767, Royal Archives, RA GEO/52295.

p.100 'Reverdil reported . . .'] Reverdil, *Struensee*, pp. 77–8, p. 132.

p.100 'His Danish Majesty'] Robert Gunning, dispatch of 26 January 1768, TNA:PRO SP 75/120.

p.103 'Her mind is too good'] quoted in Svend Cedergren Bech, *Struensee og hans tid*, Copenhagen 1972, p. 97.

p.103 'The Queen, God be praised'] Titley dispatch, 29 January 1768, TNA:PRO SP 75/120.

p.104 'could easily conceive'; 'as the foundation'; 'this great event'] George III to Caroline Mathilde, drafts and final copy, Royal Archives, RA GEO/15870, 15871, 15872.

p.105 'I am so to acquaint you'] Lord Weymouth to Robert Gunning, 8 April 1768, TNA:PRO SP 75/121; 'you know very well', George III to Lord Weymouth, 8 June 1768, quoted in Jesse, *Memoirs*, vol 1, p. 450.

p.105 'audacious criminal'; 'I fear anarchy'] George III to Lord Weymouth, 30 April 1768, quoted in Jesse, *Memoirs*, vol. 1, p. 432.

p.108 'I find they have just'] George III to Lord Weymouth, 7 May 1768, quoted in Jesse, *Memoirs*, 4 vol. 1, p. 434.

p.108 'The King of Denmark'] George Whately to George Grenville, W. J. Smith ed., *Grenville Papers*, 4 vols, London 1852, p. 372.

p.109 'very seriously to run away'] Johann Struensee, 'memoire om Kongens Tilstand', 'Mémoire du Comte Struensee sur la situation du Roi', in Holger Hansen (ed.), *Inkvisitsionskommissionen af 20 januar 1772, uddrag af dens papirer og brevsamlinger til oplysning om Struensee og hans Medarebjdere*, 3 vols, Copenhagen 1927–32, vol. 2, p. 163.

p.110 'Mrs Cornelys had put'] *Annual Register*, August 1768, quoted in Williams, *Queen of Tears*, vol. 1, p. 160.

p.110 expressed 'astonishment and pleasure'] *Gentleman's Magazine*, vol. XXXVIII, 1768, p. 442.

p.111 'dead, apparent at your sight'] see Marius Kwint, 'The Legitimization of the Circus in Late Georgian England', *Past and Present*, no. 174, p. 76, and pp. 72–82, *passim*.

p.111 'I have to talk'] Warnstedt quoted in Bech, *Struensee*, p. 115.

p.112 'We had a great deal'] the Earl of March to George Selwyn, undated [October], 1768, *Selwyn Correspondence*, vol. II, p. 328.

p.112 'in a private box', and following] the *Gentleman's Magazine*, vol. XXXVIII, November 1768, p. 448.

p.116 On doctors, medicine, the Enlightenment and the *Encyclopédie*, see Laurence Brockliss and Colin Jones, *The Medical World of Early*

Modern France, Oxford 1997; Peter Gay, *The Enlightenment, an Interpretation*, 2 vols, New York 1973; Christopher Fox, Roy Porter and Robert Wokler, *Inventing Human Science: Eighteenth-Century Domains*, Berkeley, CA 1996; Martin S. Stamm, *Cabanis. Enlightenment and Medical Philosophy in the French Revolution*, Princeton, NJ 1980; Arthur M. Wilson, *Diderot*, Oxford 1972.

p.119   Frederick the Great's *Eulogy on Julian Offray de La Mettrie*; de La Mettrie, *L'Homme machine*, Leiden 1748, critical edition with an introductory monograph and notes by Aram Vartanian, Princeton, NJ 1960; Claude-Adrien Helvétius, *De l'Esprit or, Essays on the Mind and Several Faculties* (trans.), London 1759.

p.120   Helvétius, *De l'Esprit*, pp. 161, 149.

p.120   Helvétius, *De l'Esprit*, p. 170.

p.123   'Those amusements'] Gunning's dispatch, 18 February 1769, TNA:PRO SP 75/122.

p.124   'carousel', and following] Gunning's dispatch, 25 July 1769, TNA:PRO SP 75/122.

p.125   'I ran to the door'] Elisabeth von Eyben quoted in Bech, *Struensee*, p. 154.

p.126   'Your long silence'] George III to Caroline Mathilde, 12 November 1769, Royal Archives, RA GEO/15886.

p.126   'I am extremely sorry'] Gunning's dispatch, 21 November 1769, TNA:PRO SP 75/122.

p.128   'not only clever'] Peder Uldall, in Julius Lausen and P. Fr. Rist (eds), *Efterladte optegnelser af generalfiskal Peter Uldall – Dronning Caroline Mathildes Defensor, i Memoirerer og breve*, Copenhagen 1914, rptd 1969, p. 13.

p.129   'all avenues'] Gunning's dispatch, 25 November 1769, TNA:PRO SP 75/122.

p.129   'never came that way'] Horn's and Brunn's testimony, Statens Arkiver, Copenhagen, Rigsarkivet, Kongehusets Arkiv. Frederik VI, 111. Papirer vedrørende kongens moder. 38, 7, pp. 20–8. See also Kongehusets Arkiv. Frederik VI, 111. 38, 6, question 5, for Struensee's confirmation of the maids' account.

p.130   'the politics of Denmark'] Gunning's dispatch, 2 January 1770, TNA:PRO SP 75/123.

p.131   'was performed on his Royal Highness'] Gunning's dispatch, 19 May 1770, TNA:PRO SP 75/123.

Notes

p.131 Struensee, 'memoire om kongens Tilstand', in Hansen (ed.), *Inkvisitsions-kommissionen*, pp. 162–70.

p.134 'The Queen's birthday'] Christian VII to Juliane Marie, 30 July 1770, quoted in Bech, *Struensee*, p. 186.

p.135 'I confess it grieved me'] Prince Charles of Hesse, *Memoirs de Mon Temps*, quoted in Wilkins, *A Queen of Tears*, vol. 1, p. 232.

p.136 'Mr Bernstorff and the officials'; 'With regard to the court's movements'] Ralph Woodford to the Earl of Rochford, dispatches of 17 and 13 July 1770, quoted in Wilkins, *Queen of Tears*, vol. 1, p. 234.

p.136 'an extraordinarily excessive taste'] Bernstorff, quoted in Bech, *Struensee*, p. 186.

p.137 'beautiful and cheerful'] Bernstorff, quoted in Bech, *Struensee*, p. 190.

p.137 'Their intimacy showed'] Enevold Brandt, to the Inkvisitsionskom-missionen, quoted in Mattias Hattendorf, *Hoefische Reglements und Lustbarkeiten. Die Besuche von Caroline Mathilde und Christian VII in Hamburg und Holsten, 1766–1772*, Berlin 1999, p. 80.

p.138 'exceedingly amusing'] Bernstorff, quoted in Bech, *Struensee*, p. 191.

p.139 'their Danish Majesties'] Ralph Woodford to Robert Gunning, Gunning MSS, British Library, BL Egerton MSS 2699, f. 141.

'Albrecht reported'] Details of the complicated and hasty organisation of the meeting, instructions from Hanover, and Johann Frederick Albrecht's reports of it to the Privy Council in Hanover are in Hauptstaatsarchiv Hannover, Königliches Hausarchiv Hanover, Dep. 84 B1209, fols 4–23.

p.141 'their Majesties'] Robert Gunning's dispatch, 8 September 1770, TNA:PRO SP 75/123.

p.141 For Bernstorff's pension see *Correspondance Ministérielle du Comte J. H. E. Bernstorff*, Copenhagen 1882, p. 487.

p.143 'We have had a great many changes'] Caroline Mathilde to George III, 1 October 1770, Royal Archives, RA GEO/52303.

'without scruple to the Queen of Denmark'] Gunning's dispatch, 6 October 1770, TNA:PRO SP 75/123.

'l'esclave de la Russie'] Caroline Mathilde to George III, Royal Archives, RA GEO/52304–5.

p.145 'Le Roi vient d'abolir'] Caroline Mathilde to George III, 10 December 1770, Royal Archives, RA GEO/52304–5.

p.146 'King of Denmark'] Christian VII's decree of 27 December 1770 quoted in Sir C. F. Lascelles Wraxall, bart, *Life and Times of Her Majesty Caroline*

Matilda, Queen of Denmark and Norway and sister of H. M. George III of England, 3 vols, London 1864, vol. 1, p. 305.

4: A Lewd and Adulterous Conversation

p.147 Gunning's dispatch] 6 October 1770, TNA:PRO SP 75/123.

p.148 'an assignation at the White Hart'] *Gentleman's Magazine*, December 1769, vol. 39, p. 607.

p.149 Augusta, Duchess of Brunswick to her treasurer, Mr Le Grand, 1764, Garth Papers, Royal Archives, RA GEO/Add 21/8.

p.150 'I now made frequent visits'] *Authentic and Interesting Memoirs of Miss Ann Sheldon (now Mrs Archer), written by herself*, London 1787, p. 169.

p.150 'the proper officers'] Polly (Mary) Jones, letter to the *Town and Country Magazine*, vol. 1, 20 August 1769, p. 408.

p.151 'who had long entertained'] Polly (Mary) Jones, letter to the *Town and Country Magazine*, vol. 1, 20 August 1769, p. 408.

p.151 'by his merit'] *Town and Country Magazine*, vol. 1, September 1769, pp. 449–51.

p.152 'a snug retreat'] *Town and Country Magazine*, vol. 1, September 1769, pp. 449–51.

p.153 'Lady Grosvenor was in the most joyous spirits] Lady Mary Coke, 24 August 1766, *Letters and Journals*, vol. 1, p. 27.
'A story was generally propagated'] *An Apology for the Conduct of Lady Grosvenor, Addressed to the Ladies*, Dublin 1770, p. 8.

p.154 'certainly was not in the habit'; 'We entered'] *Authentic and Interesting Memoirs*, vol. 2, pp. 68, 210.

p.154 'tied to such a mate'] *An Apology for the Conduct of Lady Grosvenor*, p. 31.
'used her extremely ill'] deposition of Henry Vernon, 1 December 1770, in *Copies of the Depositions of the Witnesses examined in the course of the Divorce now pending in the Consistory Court of the Lord Bishop of London, at Doctor's Commons. Between the Right Honourable Richard, Lord Grosvenor and the Right Honourable Henrietta, Lady Grosvenor, his wife*, London 1771, p. 217.

p.155 'a man of sober, chaste and virtuous life'; 'unmindful of her conjugal vow'] Lord Grosvenor's Libel, 1 March 1770, rptd in *Copies of the Depositions*, p. 251.

p.156 'The great importance of the cause'] *Copies of the Depositions*, p. 2.

p.156 'that has universally agitated'] [A Civilian], *Free thoughts on seduction, adultery and divorce. With reflections on the gallantry of princes, particularly those of the blood-royal of England*, London 1771, p. 6.

p.157 'the boy has my orders'; 'I thank you'] Lady Grosvenor to Prince Henry, in *The Genuine Copies of Letters which passed between His Royal Highness the Duke of Cumberland and Lady Grosvenor*, 5th edition, London 1770, letter 1, p. 1.

p.158 'she supposed it was for *something bad*'] *Copies of the Depositions*, p. 76.

p.158 'cried very much'] *Copies of the Depositions*, p. 76.

p.158 'The wind was not so contrary'] *Genuine Copies*, letter 111, p. 4.

p.159 'seemingly very cool'] deposition of Caroline Vernon, *Copies of the Depositions*, p. 157.

p.160 'that she must go out of the house'] deposition of Hannah Birch, *Copies of the Depositions*, p. 121.
'My dearest friend'; 'Yesterday he shook hands with me'] Lady Grosvenor to Prince Henry, *Genuine Copies*, letter IV, pp. 6–7.

p.161 'I think I've laid'] *Genuine Copies*, letter IV, p. 8.

p.161 'If you have a mind'] 'Jack Sprat' to Lord Grosvenor: *Genuine Copies*, letter VIII, p. 20. The *Town and Country Magazine* suggested that 'Jack Sprat' was in fact an alias of the Countess D'Onhoff. See *Town and Country*, vol. 2, July 1770, p. 377.

p.163 'in a claret coloured great coat'] and following, deposition of Mary Spencer, *Copies of the Depositions*, p. 41.

p.164 'Staffordshire graziers'] deposition of William Roberts, *Copies of the Depositions*, p. 126.

p.164 'He will sit for half an hour'] Lady Grosvenor to Prince Henry, *Genuine Copies*, letter VII, p. 17. 'Once more and no more'] 'Jack Sprat' to Lord Grosvenor, *Genuine Copies*, letter XI, p. 23.

p.165 'My maid tells me'] Lady Grosvenor to Prince Henry, *Genuine Copies*, letter XII, p. 23.
'What a vast deal'] Lady Grosvenor to Caroline Vernon, *Genuine Copies*, letter X, pp. 21–22.

p.165 'Never mind what any of them says'] Lady Grosvenor to Caroline Vernon, *Genuine Copies*, letter XIII, p. 30.
'the best thing we can do'] Lady Grosvenor to Prince Henry, *Genuine Copies*, letter XIV, p. 35.

p.166 'and forcing open the front room'; 'I am wretched to find'] Caroline Vernon to Lady Grosvenor, *Genuine Copies*, letter XVIII, pp. 49, 45.

p.167 'they were in or upon'] deposition of Matthew Stephens, *Copies of the Depositions*, p. 174.

p.167 'Do you know', 'Much tumbled from top to bottom'] deposition of Robert Betton in *Trials for Adultery, or the History of Divorces, being select Trials at Doctors' Commons, for adultery, cruelty, fornication, impotence etc. from the year 1760 to the present time, including the whole of the evidence on each cause*, London 1779, 12 vols, vol. V, p. 23.

'he was not in her Ladyship's bedchamber'] deposition of Matthew Stephens, *Copies of the Depositions*, p. 185.

'go, go along'] deposition of Robert Giddings, *Copies of the Depositions*, p. 111.

p.168 For procedures in the courts] see Lawrence Stone, *The Road to Divorce: England 1530–1987*, Oxford 1995, pp. 196ff.

'paid a visit'] *An Apology*, p. 35.

p.169 On the King's Bench see John Beattie, *Crime and the Courts in England 1660–1800*, Oxford 1986, p. 18.

p.170 On Westminster Hall see J. H. Baker, *The Common Law Tradition, Lawyers, Books and the Law*, London 2000; Dorian Gerhold, *Westminster Hall, 900 years of history*, London 1999.

p.170 5 July] the date is given in some accounts as 1 July, but that was a Sunday. Newspapers reported the trial from 6 July onwards.

'took his younger brother', 'The Court was never known', 'Muslin curtains'] *General Evening Post*, 6 July 1770.

p.171 'high quality', 'No sum could be a recompense'] Alexander Wedderburn reported in the *Gentleman's Magazine*, vol. 40, July 1770, p. 315.

p.171 For Mansfield's judgments in crim. con. cases see Edmund Heward, *Lord Mansfield: A Biography of William Murray, 1st Earl of Mansfield 1705–1793, Lord Chief Justice for 32 years*, 2 vols, Chichester and London 1979, vol. 1, p. 54.

p.171 'aimons toujours', 'all delusion'] Prince Henry to Lady Grosvenor, *Genuine Copies*, letter III, pp. 5, 3.

'occasioned much merriment'] *General Evening Post*, 7 July 1770.

p.172 'from setting a bad example'] Alexander Wedderburn quoted in the *General Evening Post*, 7 July 1770.

p.172 'My learned friend'] John Dunning quoted in *An Apology*, p. 28.

'in love with Lady Grosvenor'] deposition of John Giddings, *Copies of the Depositions*, p. 103.

p.173 'that she knew Mr Giddings'] Abigail Mary Boisgermain, quoted in *The*

Trial of His R—— H—— the D—— of C—— July 5th 1770 for Criminal Conversation with Lady Harriet G——r, London 1770, p. 58.

p.174 'a question between A and B'] quoted in Heward, *Lord Mansfield*, p. 137.

p.174 'Upon the arrival of the jury'] *The Trial of His R—— H—— the D—— of C——*, p. 60.

p.174 'be a charge upon the public'] *Free Thoughts on Seduction*, p. 74.

'the little remorse he seem'd to have'] *Letters and Journals of Lady Mary Coke* vol. III, p. 261.

p.175 'to the most useful and beneficial public charities'] *The Trial of His R—— H—— the D—— of C——*, p. viii.

p.175 'A subject of a most private and delicate kind'] George III to Lord North, 5 November 1770, in W. Bodham Donne (ed.), *The Correspondence of King George the Third with Lord North, from 1768–1783*, 2 vols, London 1867, vol. 1, pp. 33–4.

'This takes a heavy load off me'] *Correspondence*, p. 34.

p.175 'the cost of [the] suit'] Duke of Cumberland to Mr Le Grand, Royal Archives, Garth Papers, RA GEO/Add 21/8.

p.176 'I flatter myself'] George III to Lord North, 5 November 1770, *Correspondence*, vol. 1, p. 34.

p.176 'my way of thinking'] George III to Lord North, *Correspondence*, p. 34.

p.176 'the most important and remarkable trial'] *The Trial of his R—— H—— the D—— of C——*, p. iv.

p.177 'A king of Great Britain'] *Free Thoughts on Seduction*, p. 3.

'See, how dishonouring'] *The Adulterer, A Poem*, London 1769, unpaginated.

p.177 'saluted with twenty-one guns'] *Diaries of a Duchess*, ed. Greig, p. 142.

'was convinced of the intrigue'] 'Miss W——tts, The Cheshire Cornuto', *Tête-à-Tête, Town and Country Magazine*, vol. 2, pp. 401–2.

'As I have now got rid of my wife'] *An Apology*, p. 37.

p.179 'strange women'] *Copies of the Depositions*, p. 299.

p.179 'accidentally'; 'sitting at her work'] depositions of Elizabeth Roberts, Elizabeth Newton, Elizabeth Elwes, Mary Muilment, Mary How, all in *Copies of the Depositions*, pp. 209–40.

p.179 'to advertise for a maid servant'] deposition of Alice Tipping, formerly Alice Williams, otherwise Charlotte Gwynne and Charlotte Williams, *Copies of the Depositions*, p. 229.

p.180 'covered in vermin'] *Authentic and Interesting Memoirs of Miss Ann Sheldon*, vol. 2, p. 209.

'hath led, and doth continue to lead'] Allegation of Henrietta, Lady Grosvenor, 1 December 1770, *Copies of the Depositions*, p. 299.

p.181 'it is impossible for me'] Duke of Cumberland to George III, 3 November 1771, Royal Archives, RA GEO 54427/8.

p.182 'After walking for some time'] George III's memorandum on his brother's marriage, RA GEO/15948–9, quoted in John Brooke, *King George III*, London 1972, p. 273.

'the more I reflect'] George III to the Princess Dowager, 3 November 1771, RA GEO 15934, quoted in Brooke, *George III*, p. 275.

'Dear Brother'] George III to the Duke of Gloucester, 19 November 1771, Royal Archives, RA GEO/15938–40.

p.183 'it is impossible'] George III to Duke of Gloucester, 19 Nov 1771, Royal Archives, RA GEO/15942.

p.183 'No person whatsoever'] Duke of Cumberland to George III, 3 November 1771, Royal Archives, RA GEO 54429–30.

p.183 'Since my note of this morning'] Junius to John Wilkes, 6 November 1771, quoted in John Cannon (ed.), *The Letters of Junius*, Oxford 1978, p. 435.

p.184 'Intelligence Extraordinary'] *Public Advertiser*, 8 November 1771, quoted in Cannon, *Letters of Junius*, p. 435n.1.

p.184 'ready to do anything'] Duke of Cumberland to George III, 10 November 1771, Royal Archives, GEO 54431.

'The king does not desire'] Duke of Cumberland to Colonel Deaken, 25 November 1771, Royal Archives, GEO 54432.

p.185 'a stain the D of C has put on me'] George III to the Duke of Gloucester, 19 Nov 1771, Royal Archives, GEO/15942.

'I now wash my hands'] George III to the Princess Dowager, 28 November 1771, Royal Archives, RA GEO/15944, quoted in Brooke, *George III*, p. 275.

p.186 'I expected no other account'] George III to the Duke of Gloucester, Royal Archives, GEO/15939–40.

'behaviour in this last instance'] Duke of Gloucester to George III, 22 November 1771, quoted in Brooke, *George III*, p. 277.

p.186 'I do expect every nerve'] George III to Lord North, 26 February 1772, quoted in Brooke, *George III*, p. 276.

p.187 'It was dangerous'; 'natural right'; 'I must now say a few words'] *The*

Parliamentary History of England (Hansard), vol. XVII, Ad 1771–1774, pp. 390–410. The Act is often referred to as the Royal Marriages Act.

5: A Daughter of England

p.190 'I appoint this man'] Christian VII, quoted in W. H. Wilkins, *A Queen of Tears: Caroline Mathilde, Queen of Denmark and Norway and Princess of Britain and Ireland*, 2 vols, London 1904, vol. 1, p. 317.

p.192 'Nothing could be more licentious'] John Brown, *The Northern Courts; Containing original memoirs of the Sovereigns of Sweden & Denmark since 1766, including the extraordinary vicissitudes in the lives of the grandchildren of George the Second*, London n.d., p. 113.

p.192 'As no declaration has yet been made'] Robert Gunning, dispatch to London, 12 February 1771, TNA:PRO SP 75/124.

p.194 'As no step taken in the education of a prince'] Gunning's dispatch, 6 October 1770, TNA:PRO SP 75/123.

p.195 'not subject to any restrictions'] A. P. Bernstorff, quoted in Svend Cedergreen Bech, *Struensee og hans tid*, Copenhagen, Forlaget Cicero 1989, p. 231.

p.196 'by planting a bean'] Jean Jacques Rousseau, *Emile, ou De l'education*, 2 books, Paris 1760: this edition, trans. Alan Bloom, London 1991, Book II, pp. 98–99.

p.197 'Rashness and revenge'] Gunning dispatch, 4 April 1771, TNA:PRO SP 75/124.

p.197 'of great acquired abilities'] the same Gunning dispatch of 4 April 1771: 'as His Majesty did not wish'] Gunning dispatch, 23 March 1771, TNA:PRO SP 75/124.

p.198 'a smooth, designing, self-interested man'] Gunning, the same dispatch of 23 March 1771.

p.198 'It is better to let'; 'Immoral conduct'] Johann Struensee, in Holger Hansen (ed.), *Kabinetsstyrelsen I Danmark 1768–1772*, 3 vols, Copenhagen 1916–1923, vol. I, pp. 191–5, vol. 2, p. 620.

p.200 'His conversation discovers nothing'; 'It is universal matter of wonder'] Gunning dispatch, 4 April 1771, TNA:PRO SP 75/124.

p.200 'an obstacle'] Caroline Mathilde's 'opinion', given in George's reply of 22 March, Royal Archives, RA GEO/15912.

p.201 'those talents and that vivacity'; 'the new ministry'] Gunning dispatch, 12 February 1771, TNA:PRO SP 75/124.

p.202 'You are Brandt'; 'der kleine Man'] Elie Salomon François Reverdil, in 'Struensee et la Cour du Copenhagne 1760–1772', from *Mémoires de Reverdil*, Paris 1858, pp. 255–7.

p202 'no tone of indecency'] Reverdil, *Mémoires*, p. 259.

p.204 'all orders'; 'and no longer effected'] decree of 15 July 1771, quoted in Sir C. F. Lascelles Wraxall, Bart, *Life and Times of Her Majesty Caroline Matilda*, 3 vols, London 1864, vol. 1, p. 348.

p.205 'the whole attention'] Robert Murray Keith dispatch, 21 July 1771, TNA:PRO SP 75/125.

p.205 'I am sorry, my dear G;' 'Your wines, coach houses'] Keith to Gunning, 9 April 1771, BL Egerton Mss 2700, ff. 166–70.
'I have hired'] Keith to his father, June 1771, quoted in Mrs Gillespie Smyth, *The Romance of Diplomacy: Correspondence and Memoirs of Sir Robert Murray Keith*, 2 vols, London 1861, vol. 1, p. 146.

p.206 'I certainly am'] Keith to his sister from Dresden, 27 December 1769, quoted in Smyth, *Romance*, vol. 1, p. 124.
'I am very willing'] Keith to Henry Drummond, 7 April 1771, quoted in Smyth, *Romance*, vol. 1, p. 143.

p.206 'going grey in the service'] Ralph Woodford to Robert Gunning, 8 November 1771, BL Egerton Mss 2700, f. 294.
'I do not find Keith'; 'I have never had'] Ralph Woodford to Robert Gunning, 4 October 1771, BL Egerton Mss 2700, f. 291.

p.207 'My situation'] Keith to his father, August 1771, quoted in Smyth, *Romance*, p. 217.
'A man may smile'] Keith to his father, 7 November 1771, in Smyth, *Romance*, p. 229.

p.208 'malignant leveller'; 'His morals are founded'] Keith dispatch, 18 November 1771, TNA:PRO SP 75/125.

p.208 'the happiness of a human'] Struensee quoted in Asser Amdisen, *Til Nytte øg Fornøjelse, Johann Friedrich Struensee (1737–1772)*, Copenhagen 2002, p. 126.
'partiality for Count Struensee'] Keith dispatch, 18 November 1771, TNA:PRO SP 75/125.

p.208 'bloody fighting'] Bolle Luxdorph, quoted in Bech, *Struensee*, p. 271.
'It would seem as if'] Keith dispatch, 20 September 1771, PRO SP 75/125.

p.210 I am indebted to Dan Andersen for this account of the war with Algiers and to Jacob Seerup for showing me the models of Struensee's bomb ketches in Copenhagen's Orlogsmuseet. See Dan Andersen, *The Danish Flag in the Mediterranean. Shipping and Trade, 1747–1807*, 2 vols, unpublished PhD thesis, Univ. of Copenhagen, 2001, vol. 2, pp. 184–196.

p.210 'It has been whispered about'] Keith dispatch, 21 September 1771, TNA:PRO SP 75/125.

p.211 'I will give up nothing'] Von Falkenskjold, *Memoirs*, quoted in Wilkins, *Queen of Tears*, vol. 2, p. 16.

p.212 'the apprehensions of the Prime Minister'] Keith dispatch, 7 January 1772, TNA:PRO SP 75/125.

p.214 'The Almighty has chosen'] Queen Juliane Marie to Hereditary Prince Frederik, 7 October 1771, Danish Royal Archive, quoted in Claus Mechlenborg, '"Une Créature subalterne", En borgersøu vej til indflydelse under den danske enevaele: Ove Høegh Guldberg 1731–1772', *Fortid og Nutid*, June 2003, p. 122. This letter, although it is housed in the Royal Archive in Copenhagen and assumed to be authentic, may be corrupted, though its sentiments are echoed in other letters written by the conspirators.

p.215 'You've arrived very late'] Caroline Mathilde, quoted in Wilkins, *Queen of Tears*, vol. 2, p. 56.

p.217 'My son, Your Majesty'] Juliane Marie as written up by Köller, quoted in Wraxall, *Life and Times of Caroline Matilda*, vol. 2, p. 103.

p.218 'Do you know who I am?'; 'I am a minister of state'] Struensee and Brandt quoted in Wraxall, *Life and Times of Caroline Matilda*, vol. 2, pp. 103, 108.

p.219 'Madam, I have found it necessary'] Christian VII to Caroline Mathilde, (original letter in French), quoted in Wilkins, *Queen of Tears*, vol. 2, p. 66.

p.221 For the vegetation north of Copenhagen see William Coxe, AMFRS, *Travels into Poland, Russia, Sweden and Denmark*, 4 vols, London 1787, vol. 4, p. 318. The writer Mary Wollstonecraft, travelling the same route in 1795, described the countryside as 'diversified with wood, mostly beech'. At Copenhagen, haunted by Caroline Mathilde's story, she saw King Christian, whose sorry appearance seemed to her to tell a sad tale of the futility of kings: sitting 'with vacant eye, erect, receiving the homage of courtiers, who mock him with a show of respect'. He was 'in fact, merely a machine of state, to subscribe the name of king to the acts of the government ... for he is allowed to be absolutely an idiot, excepting that now and again an observation, or trick, escapes him, which looks more like madness than imbecility.' See Mary Wollstonecraft, *Letters written during a short residence in Sweden, Norway, and Denmark*, London 1796, letter 18.

p.223 'forced his way'] Smyth, *Romance*, vol. 1, p. 250.

p.223 'by order of the King'] summary of Keith's dispatches to Lord Suffolk, presumably written for George III or his secretary, Royal Archive, RA GEO/15960.

p224 'The conduct of the Queen'] Christian VII to the Princess Dowager, 17 January 1772, Copenhagen, Kongehusarkivet, Frederik VI, 44, pk. 3 (original in French).

p.224 'pale as a corpse'] Dorothea Biehl, quoted in Bech, *Struensee*, p. 332.

p.225 'Taking part in these events'] 'Une Créature subalterne', ibid., p. 125.

'*Dieu, la virtue*'; '*ceux donc dieu s'est servi*'] Kongehusarkivet Frederik VI, 44, pk. 3.

p.225 'As to the intimacy'] Woodford to Gunning, 6 March 1772, BL Egerton Mss 2701, fol. 206.

p.225 'As is known unofficially'] Residenten Reiche to Hannoverian officials, 21 January 1772, Königlisches Hausarchiv Hannover. Hauptstaatsarchiv Hannover, Dep. 84 B 869, fols 4–5 (original in German).

'An Act for Abdication'] anonymous paper probably from a spy, 25 Jan 1772, BL Egerton Mss 2701.

p.226 'Mademoiselle d'Eyben'] BL Egerton Mss 2701, fol. 14b.

Three commissions were eventually formed. On 20 January an inquisition commission (Inkvisitionskommissionen), proposed on 18 January was created to gather evidence from all the prisoners except Caroline Mathilde. On 28 January another commission, the Forhørskommissionen (the 'interrogation commission') was created to investigate Caroline Mathilde's behaviour. On 13 March the Skilsmissekommissionen (the 'divorce commission') was set up at the suggestion of the interrogation commission. Although the way these commissions were set up seems to indicate a desire to separate out Caroline Mathilde herself from the rest of the prisoners, in practice much of the evidence against her was gathered by the first commission, and so their functions overlapped, as did their personnel.

p.227 'un très grand empire'] Schack-Ratlou to Hereditary Prince Frederik, 17 April 1772, Breve fra A. S. v.d. Osten til Dronning Juliane Marie ang. det britiske kongehus, Kongehusarkivet, Frederik VI, 44. pk. 3.

p.227 'sich sehr ungedulgig'] Reiche to Hanover, 1 February 1772, Haupt-staatsarchiv Hannover, Dep. 84 B 869, fols. 8–9.

p.229 'It is affirmed'] *General Evening Post*, 23 January 1772, quoted in Wraxall, *Life and Times*, vol. 2, p. 159.

p.230 'in person'] Charles Ernst, letter probably written to Robert Murray Keith's father, 29 January 1772, British Library, BL Add. Mss 35,503, fols 208–9.

p.230 'left very much at large'] British Library, BL Add. Mss 35,503, fols 211–2. This is the only writing on the affair that survived, in the form of scribbled notes, presumably written by Keith at the time and then forgotten in his archive.

p.230 'Dear Sister, I cannot omit'] George III to Caroline Mathilde, 29 January 1772, Kongehusarkivet, Frederik VI, 41, pk. 2.

p.231 'You are able to judge'] the Princess Dowager to Caroline Mathilde, 29 January 1772, Kongehusarkivet, Frederik VI, 41, pk. 2.

p.231 'not in favour'] Lord Suffolk to Robert Murray Keith, 1 February 1772, Royal Archives, RA GEO/Add 27/20.

p.232 'The part H.M. takes'] Lord Suffolk to Joseph Yorke, Ambassador to The Hague, 4 and 11 February 1772, Royal Archives, RA GEO/Add 29/32, 33.

'it is with a heavy heart'] George III to Caroline Mathilde, 8 February 1772, Royal Archives, RA GEO/15956.

p.233 'The last word'] Princess Augusta to Caroline Mathilde, 11 February 1772, Kongehusarkivet, Frederik VI, 41, pk. 2.

p.233 'the queen's fidelity'] *London Magazine or Gentleman's Monthly Intelligencer*, vol. XLI, 11 February 1772, p. 96.

p.234 'a general topic of conversation'] *London Chronicle*, 6 Feb 1772, vol. xxxi, p. 122.

'You are therefore authorised'] Lord Suffolk to Robert Murray Keith, 28 February 1772, Royal Archives, RA GEO/Add 27/42.

p.236 'had gone as far as they could' and the following statements] from the interrogation of Struensee on 25 February 1772, Kongehusarkivet, Frederik VI, 38, pk. 6, and the interrogations of Caroline Mathilde's maids, pk. 10.

p.237 'They would have it believed'] Woodford to Gunning, 6 March 1772, BL Egerton Mss 2701, fol. 20b.

'Many already believed'] this was the opinion of Peter Uldall, Caroline Mathilde's lawyer, given to the divorce commissioners on 2 April.

Korrespondence med det britiskhe kongehus, 17/1–17/5 1772, Kongehusarkivet, Frederik VI, 41, pk. 1.

p.238 'la Reine seule'] Christian VII to George III, 22 February 1772, Kongehusarkivet, Frederik VI, 41, pk. 1 (original in French, presumably by Guldberg).

p.238 'Junius']*Gentleman's Magazine*, March 1772, pp. 130–3. Junius's modern editor, John Cannon, does not include this letter in his edition of Junius, perhaps because it was published in the *Gentleman's Magazine* rather than the *Public Advertiser* (and therefore might be claimed not to be by Junius himself), perhaps because it was written a few months after the last of Junius's letters in the *Public Advertiser*, perhaps because the content of the letter (although not the characteristic link between private life and politics and attacks on the Prime Minister and the king) is feminine and domestic.

p.240 Christian's desire for 'silence'] Instructions for the Interrogation of Caroline Mathilde, Kongehusarkivet, Frederik VI, 38, pk. 7.

p.241 'three questions'] from the same Instructions for the Interrogation of Caroline Mathilde.

p.241 'Their proceedings with regard'] Woodford to Gunning, 24 Mar 1772, BL Egerton Mss 2701, fol. 24.

p.242 'Your Majesty will see'] Christian VII to George III, 13 March 1772, Kongehusarkivet, Frederik VI, 41, pk. 1 (original in French).

p.242 'She sleeps very little'] Count Holstein, 12 March 1772, quoted in Harald Jørgensen, *The Unfortunate Queen Caroline Mathilde's Last Years 1772–1775*, Copenhagen 1989, p. 31.

p.243 'What good wife'; 'With success'; 'fulfil sensuous desires'] Peter Uldall, *Memoirer og Breve*, pp. 4, 16.

p.244 'They also caught me'; 'I assured her'] Uldall, *Memoirer og Breve*, p. 6.

p.244 'All her care'; 'from her looks'; 'I always feared'; 'Now they can tell'] Uldall, *Memoirer og Breve*, pp. 4, 8, 10, 12.

p.245 'Had Struensee followed my advice'] Uldall, *Memoirer og Breve*, p. 12.

p.245 'the large secret commission'] Reiche to Hanover, Hauptstaatsarchiv Hanover, Dep. 84 B 869, fol. 26 (original in German).

'On 23 March'] Keith to Osten in 'Précis de ce qui e passé avec le Cour d'Angleterre', paper describing diplomatic events and meetings, perhaps by Osten, Kongehusarkivet, Frederik VI, 41, pk. 3. (original in French). 'I must frankly tell you'] Suffolk to Keith, 20 March 1772, Royal Archives, RA GEO/Add 27/60.

p.246 'a letter'] Caroline Mathilde to George III, 3 April 1772, 'de ma prison à Cronberg', intercepted, Kongehusarkivet, Frederik VI, 44, pk. 4.

p.246 'All His Majesty's'] Suffolk to Keith, 7 April 1772, Royal Archives, RA GEO/Add 27/88.

p.246 'the situation and strength'] Suffolk to Keith, Royal Archive, RA GEO/Add 27/91.

p.247 'Her Majesty's words'] Peter Uldall, quoted in Wilkins, *Queen of Tears*, vol. 2, p. 161.

p.247 'A relieved Osten'] Kongehusarkivet, Frederik VI, 41, pk. 3.

p.248 'I imagined so'] Uldall, *Memoirer og Breve*, pp. 21–2.

p.248 'Could I not declare', and following] Uldall, *Memoirer og Breve*, p. 22.

p.249 'I must have her with me', and following] Uldall, *Memoirer og Breve*, pp. 23–4.

p.249 'the greatest composure'] Uldall, *Memoirer og Breve*, p. 24.

p.250 'The Queen, it is asserted'; 'that since the sentence'] Woodford to Gunning, 21 April 1772, BL Egerton Mss 2701, ff. 29, 27.

p.250 'But surely'] Woodford to Gunning, 21 April 1772 BL Egerton Mss 2701, f. 29.

'Keith found Osten'] Kongehusarkivet, Frederik VI, 41, pk. 3.

p.250 'to an afflicted princess'] Keith to his sister Anne, 4 May 1772, quoted in Smyth, *Romance*, vol. 1, p. 288.

p.251 'At the same time, therefore'] Suffolk to Keith, 15 April 1772, Royal Archives, RA GEO/Add 27/96.

p252 'would have sailed'] Suffolk to Keith, 24 April 1772, Royal Archives, RA GEO/Add 27/111.

'abundance of speculation'] Lord North, 28 April 1772, in Hon. Sir John Fortescue (ed.), *The Correspondence of King George III*, 6 vols, London 1972, vol. 2, p. 337.

p.252 'It is without doubt disagreeable'] Schack-Ratlou to Hereditary Prince Frederik, 17 April 1772, Kongehusarkivet, Frederik VI, 44, pk. 3. (original in French).

p.253 'Count Johann Friedrich', and following] from Wivet's indictment, quoted in Wraxall, *Life and Times*, vol. 2, pp. 256–95.

p.254 'to look to the welfare'; 'religion had everything to fear'; 'the rights of virtue'] from the English edition of Münter's book, *A Narrative of the Conversion and Death of Count Struensee formerly Prime Minister of Denmark, by Dr. Munter, translated from the German by the Rev. Mr Wendelborn*, London 1773, p. 1. Münter obviously talked to Struensee and listened carefully to what he had to say. But Struensee's capitulation and conversion – and especially the letters he was supposed to have written to his family and friends – are far too close in style and tone to the contemporary epistolary novel to be anything but a deliberate forgery.

p.255 'he regarded man'; 'You will hardly make me believe'] Münter, *Narrative of the Conversion and Death of Count Struensee*, pp. 10–11, 8.

p.255 'She smiled at that'] Uldall, *Memoirer og Breve*, p. 23.

p.256 'I regard it as'] Uldall, *Memoirer og Breve*, p. 26.

p.256 'An ardent desire', and following] Struensee's apologia, in Wraxall, *Life and Times*, vol. 2, p. 328–366.

p.257 'a certain atrocious crime'], in Wraxall, *ibid.*, vol. 2, p. 276.

p.257 'We hereby approve'], in Wraxall, *ibid.*, vol. 3, p. 67.

p.257 'I have thought'] Uldall, *Memoirer og Breve*, p. 27.

p.260 'Dear Brother, I suppose'] Caroline Mathilde to George III, 24 May 1772, Royal Archive, RA GEO/52315.
'I find there is'] Woodford to Gunning from Hamburg, 31 July 1772, BL Egerton Mss 2701, f. 89.

p.260 'With the summer sun'] Reiche, reporting to Hanover, has a different version of events, saying that Princess Louise Augusta was sent to Copenhagen on the evening of 29 May, and Caroline Mathilde went on board a British sloop, not a Danish one.

6: An Honest Man

p.262 'Captain Macbride reported'] report to the Admiralty, 18 June 1772, in Fortescue, *Correspondence of King George III*, vol. 2, p. 362.

p.263 'the heroic Minister', and following] *Town and Country Magazine*, July 1772, pp. 345–8.
'a more eligible situation'] Lord Suffolk to Robert Murray Keith, 1 May 1772, Lord Suffolk's letters to British Ambassadors, 1772, Royal Archives, RA GEO Add 27/108.

p.263 'an agreeable summer residence', and following] George III to Caroline Mathilde, 1 May 1772, Royal Archives, RA GEO/15971.
'I am vastly pleased'] Caroline Mathilde to George III, 9 June 1772, Royal Archives, RA GEO/52318.

p.264 'my directions'] George III to Caroline Mathilde, 23 June 1772, Royal Archives, RA GEO/15980.

p.264 'Dear sister, continue that circumspection'] George III to Caroline Mathilde, 23 June 1772, Royal Archives, RA GEO/15920.

'had certainly not wrote to me'; 'a report runs here'] Caroline Mathilde to George III, 2 September 1772, Royal Archives, RA GEO/52328.

p.265 'Your letters seem to point out'] George III to Caroline Mathilde, late October 1772, Royal Archives, RA GEO/15992.

p.265 'As I wish'] Caroline Mathilde to George III, 10 October 1772, Royal Archives, RA GEO/52333.

p.266 'very lively, very vivacious'] Johann Georg Zimmerman, quoted in Norbert Steinau, 'Caroline Mathilde im Kurfürstentum Hannover 1772–1775', in Juliane Stiglitz-Otten and Norbert Steinau (eds), *Von Kopenhagen nach Celle. Das kurze leben einer Königin. Caroline Mathilde 1751–1775*. Begleitpublikation zum Anlaß einer Ausstellung des Bomann-Museums Celle zum 250 geburstag der dänischen Königin Caroline Mathilde. Celle 2001, p. 132.

p.267 'You cannot be too minute'] Suffolk to Keith, quoted in Mrs Gillespie Smyth, *The Romance of Diplomacy: Correspondence and Memoirs of Sir Robert Murray Keith*, 2 vols, London 1861, vol. 1, p. 300.

p.267 'Nothing could be more frank'] Keith to Suffolk, from Celle, 2 November 1772, quoted in Smyth, *Romance*, vol. 1, pp. 301–4.

p.268 'il est dans l'humeur'] Caroline Mathilde to Augusta, Duchess of Brunswick, 5 November 1772, Royal Archives, RA GEO/52356.

p.268 'But for the love of God'] Duchess of Brunswick to Caroline Mathilde, 22 December 1772, Royal Archives, RA GEO/52367. (original in French).

p.269 'Madame d'Ompteda'] Madame Catharine Charlotte von Ompteda, breve til Johann Bülow og Kongerensraad Georg Nielsen, September 1787, Kongehusarkivet, Frederik VI, 44, pk. 8. The letter to her asking for information calls Caroline Mathilde a person 'very dear to the heart' of the Crown Prince.

p.269 'She has had two tents'] Georg Christoph Lichtenberg quoted in Otten and Steinall (eds), *Von Kopenhagen nach Celle*, p. 133.

p.270 'the most detestable parts'] Ralph Woodford's dispatch, 2 December 1772, TNA:PRO SP 75/126.

'Her countenance is not entirely free'] Lichtenberg, quoted in Otten and Steinau (eds), *Von Kopenhagen nach Celle*, p. 134.

'The youth, the agreeable countenance'] Dr John Moore, *A View of Society and Manners in France, Switzerland and Germany*, London 1779, quoted in W. H. Wilkins, *A Queen of Tears: Caroline Mathilde, Queen of Denmark and Norway and Princess of Britain and Ireland*, 2 vols, London 1904, vol. 2, p. 262.

p.271 Details of Caroline Mathilde's library from Königlisches Hausarchiv Hannover. Hauptstaatsarchiv Hannover, Dep. 84 B 919.

'I do everything in my power'] Caroline Mathilde to Mrs Moore, 31 December 1772 (perhaps the wife of her recent visitor Dr Moore, someone unconnected to the British court in whom she felt she could confide, although her letter went straight to London), Royal Archives, RA GEO/52393.

p.271 'People believe', and following] von Krohne, Conseilleur princ. du Roi du Pologne at Lübeck, to Kammerherr von dem Busche at Celle, and his reply, Königlisches Hausarchiv Hannover. Hauptstaatsarchiv Hannover, Dep. 103 IV 236, unpaginated.

p272 'You already know', and following] Caroline Mathilde to Carl August Struensee, 15 January 1774, Royal Archive, RA GEO/52396, and his reply, 12 February 1774, Royal Archive, RA GEO/52408–9. (originals in French.)

p.274 'vast, unfinished'; 'with mingled commiseration'; 'it was the minister'] Nathaniel William Wraxall, *A Tour through some of the Northern Parts of Europe, particularly Copenhagen, Stockholm and Petersberg, in a series of letters by N. Wraxall, Jun.*, London 1775, pp. 8, 52, 42. Wraxall's publication history is complicated. He published several books and long pamphlets in his lifetime as well as *Historical Memoirs of My Own Time*, 2 vols, in 1815. He also wrote the *Posthumous Memoirs of His Own Time*, in three volumes, which were published in 1836, five years after his death. In the latter he refers frequently to, and quotes from, his 'Private Journal', and to letters that he wrote or received, all of which now appear to be lost or destroyed and are not in the collection of his papers now at Yale University. To complicate matters further, Wraxall's grandson, Sir C. F. Lascelles Wraxall, wrote his own three-volume life of Caroline Mathilde, *Life and Times of Her Majesty Queen Caroline Mathilde*, in 1864, writing in the introduction that he had 'ransacked' these lost letters, the 'Private Journal' and another account, a 'Historical Narrative of the Attempt to Restore the Queen', for his own work. Consequently, passages appear in the *Life and Times* that are nowhere in Nathaniel Wraxall's published work and cannot thus be corroborated, though they are often rewritten by Wraxall himself in his *Posthumous Memoirs*.

When Nathaniel Wraxall published the *Historical Memoirs*, after a long career that bafflingly combined honours and obscurity, many critics declared that he was untrustworthy if not actually a liar. But in his account of Caroline Mathilde, a narrative that seems initially incredible turns out, where it can be corroborated, to be very substantially correct. Wraxall may have embroidered to make himself appear more heroic than he actually was, but on the crucial point of the role of George III, he told no more than he knew, and what he knew was perhaps the basis of much of his subsequent career. Why and how he was knighted and became an MP are not clear, but letters in the National Archives make it obvious that he wanted preferment in return for withholding knowledge that intimately concerned the King. (See PRO 30/8/192, letters to William Pitt of 1787, 'My request is, to be created a Baronet', etc., and PRO 30/70/4, letters to Pitt from 1796, 'I take the liberty of requesting you to inform me whether you have presented to the King the letter and narrative which I drew up'; 'in consequence of your refusal of my request, I shall hold myself completely at liberty to make whatever use I think proper of the papers in my possession'.)

p.274 'It is not above'; 'with mingled commiseration'; 'It was the minister and not the man'] Wraxall, *A Tour through some of the Northern Parts*, pp. 46, 49, 41.

p.275 'impelled by a desire'] Nathaniel William Wraxall, *Posthumous Memoirs of His Own Time*, 3 vols, London 1836, vol. 3, p. 374.

p.275 'There was in the aspect of the castle of Zell'; 'who was there confined'] Wraxall, *Posthumous Memoirs*, pp. 375–6.

p.275 'I know the fact'] Wraxall, *Posthumous Memoirs*, vol. 2, pp. 375–6. 'innumerable questions; 'Her face is very handsome'] 'Private Journal', quoted in Wraxall, *Life and Times*, vol. 3, pp. 173–4.

p.277 'with great agitation'] Wraxall, *Life and Times*, vol. 3, p. 180.

p.277 'My affairs call me', and following] Wraxall, *Posthumous Memoirs*, vol. 2, pp. 380–1.

p.277 'briefly but accurately', and following] Wraxall, *Posthumous Memoirs*, vol. 2, pp. 382–5.

p.279 'conversed most closely'] Wraxall, *Life and Times*, vol. 3, pp. 194, 196.

p.279 'Since the last letter'] Caroline Mathilde to George III, 25 October 1774, Royal Archive, RA GEO/52347.

p.280 'in a long and confidential conversation'] Wraxall, *Life and Times*, vol. 3, p. 203.

p.280 'as relations of peace' and following] Wraxall, *Posthumous Memoirs*, vol. 2, pp. 394–5.

p.281 'brown silk polonaise'] 'Private Journal', quoted in Wraxall, *Life and Times*, vol. 3, p. 222.

'rather augmented, than diminished'] Wraxall, *Posthumous Memoirs*, vol. 2, p. 400.

p.281 'therefore determined to draw up'] Wraxall, *Life and Times*, vol. 3, p. 226.

p.282 'either had, or impressed me as having', and following] Wraxall, *Posthumous Memoirs*, vol. 2, pp. 406–8.

p.282 'The nobility having through a letter'] Caroline Mathilde to George III, 25 March 1775, Royal Archive, RA GEO/52348.

p.282 'Arriving with this letter'] Wraxall, this time, was carrying Caroline Mathilde's letter to her brother. See Wraxall, *Posthumous Memoirs*, vol. 1, p. 409.

'ne donnera rien d'écrit'] Lichtenstein to Wraxall, 24 March 1775, quoted in Wraxall, *Life and Times*, vol. 3, p. 235.

p.282 'Dear Sister', and following] George III to Caroline Mathilde, 23 April 1775, Royal Archive, RA GEO/16030.

p.284 'Imagine my dear father'], Wraxall, *Life and Times*, vol 3, p. 302.

p.284 'fell asleep like a tired wayfarer'] von Leyzen, quoted in Wilkins, *Queen of Tears*, vol. 2, p. 299.

For details of Caroline Mathilde's illness and death, see Hauptstaatsarchiv Hannover, Dep. 84 b 881, ff. 67–72; Dep. 84 B 882 ff. 47–60. A strong case has been made out, also, that Caroline Mathilde died of porphyria, the genetic disorder inherited and carried by the Hannoverians that was almost certainly the root cause of George III's illnesses. See Ida Macalpine and Richard Hunter, *George III and the Mad Business*, London 1969, pp. 223–8.

p.285 'Alas, it is not until now'] Stampe, quoted in Svend Cedergren Bech, *Struensee og hans Tid*, Copenhagen 1989, p. 393.

'Orders were given yesterday'] Daniel Delaval, dispatch, 20 May 1775, PRO SP 75/131.

'Is it true'] Reiche to George III, 20 May 1775, copy in Hannover, Hauptstaatsarchiv Hannover, Dep. 84 B 881, f. 67.

p.285 'The pleasure of giving the title'] Schack-Ratlou, probably to Hereditary Prince Frederik, May 1775, Kongehusarkivet, Frederik VI, 44, pk. 8.

p.286 'Hannoverian officials'] Details of Caroline Mathilde's bequests are in Hauptstaatsarchiv Hannover, Dep. 84 B 883 and B 919.

'robe ronde, of couleur de rosé'] and following, Hauptstaatsarchiv Hannover, Dep. 84 B 891.

p287 *Memoirs of an Unfortunate Queen*, London 1776. This epistolary novel, regarded as inauthentic at the time, made its way into the hands of Frederik or his officials, who seem to have copied out this famous letter to look like an original document. It has usually been regarded as genuine in Denmark, but its style has so much in common with that of contemporary epistolary novels and the content of the book is so clearly an attempt to make Caroline Mathilde into an unwavering Voltaireian that there can be no doubt that it is the work of an efficient Fleet Street hack.

7: 'Oh God! It is all over!'

p.289 'Now you are sullen', and following] Prince William in J. Heneage Jesse, *Memoirs of the Life and Reign of King George the Third*, 3 vols, London 1867, vol. 2, p. 7.

p.290 'It is impossible to express'] George III to Duke of Gloucester, 9 November 1771, Royal Archive, RA GEO/15940.

p.290 'I . . . saw my sister'] Duke of Gloucester to George III, Royal Archive, RA GEO/54305.

p.292 'Madam, the many indignities', and following] Sir Edward Walpole to Jane Clement, 28 October 1766, 6 November 1766, 12 November 1766, 31 December 1766, from *The Yale Edition of Horace Walpole's Correspondence*, vol. 36, *Horace Walpole's Correspondence with the Walpole Family*, ed. W. S Lewis and Joseph W. Reed, Jnr, New Haven, CT and London 1973, Appendix 4, pp. 317–21.

p.292 'the celebrated Lady Laura'] Sir Edward Walpole to Laura Walpole, n.d., Clement Mss, Lewis Walpole Library, Yale University, Farmington, CT. This collection is unpaginated and has no call numbers, although it is dated where possible, and sorted into folders according to the recipient.

p.293 'I am determined to make my life easy'] Sir Edward Walpole to Edward Walpole, September 1754, Clement Mss, Lewis Walpole Library.

p.293 'she has not a fault'] Horace Walpole to Horace Mann, quoted in Violet Biddulph, *The Three Ladies Waldegrave (and their mother)*, London 1938, p. 32.

p.294 'her income a year later'] Maria Waldegrave to Jane Clement, 1766, Clement Mss, Lewis Walpole Library.

p.295 'Your Royal Highness'] Maria Waldegrave to the Duke of Gloucester, 3 May 1764, in Biddulph, *The Three Ladies Waldegrave*, p. 56.

p.296 'flatters Horry'] Gilly Williams to George Selwyn, in John Heneage Jesse, *George Selwyn and his Contemporaries, with Memoirs and Notes*, 2 vols, London 1843, vol. 1, December 1764, p. 334.

p.297 'Lady Bridget Lane'] Lady Mary Coke, 9 November 1766, in J. A. Home (ed.), *The Letters and Journals of Lady Mary Coke*, 4 vols, Edinburgh 1889–96, vol. 1, p. 94.

p.298 'To secure my character'] Duchess of Gloucester to Sir Edward Walpole, 19 May 1772, in *Horace Walpole's Correspondence*, vol. 36, pp. 66–7.

p.298 'one of the sweetest examples'] Sir Edward Walpole to Horace Walpole, 20 May 1772, in *Horace Walpole's Correspondence*, vol. 36, p. 65.
'she wrote to her sister . . . a letter'] Horace Walpole, *Last Journals*, quoted in his *Correspondence*, vol. 36, p. 69, n. 3.

p.298 'The Dow—r Lady W—v'] *Morning Chronicle*, 28 May 1772, quoted in *Horace Walpole's Correspondence*, vol. 36, p. 67, n.10.

p.299 'I do not believe'] Sir Edward Walpole, to Horace Walpole, 20 May 1772, *Horace Walpole's Correspondence*, vol. 36, p. 65.
'I do not like'] Duchess of Gloucester to Jane Clement, 24 August 1772, Clement Mss, Lewis Walpole Library.

p.299 'I am much grieved'] Duke of Gloucester to George III, 13 September 1772, Royal Archives, RA GEO/54333.

p.300 'As yr M[ajesty] was so good'] Duke of Gloucester to George III, 15 September 1772, Royal Archives, RA GEO/54334.

p.301 'His behaviour has been such'] Duchess of Gloucester to Horace Walpole, 16 September 1772, in *Horace Walpole's Correspondence*, vol. 36, p. 73.
'I had always hoped'] Caroline Mathilde to George III, 10 October 1772, Royal Archive, RA GEO/52333.

p.301 'against a romantic visit'] Horace Walpole, *Last Journals*, quoted in *Horace Walpole's Correspondence*, vol. 36, p. 76, n. 2.

p.301 'That letter has been', and following] Duchess of Gloucester to Jane Clement, 24 August 1772, Clement Mss, Lewis Walpole Library.

p.302 'more respected than Mrs Horton'] Duchess of Gloucester to Jane Clement, October 1772, Clement Mss, Lewis Walpole Library.
'does not repent', and following] Duchess of Gloucester to Jane Clement, 21 September 1772, Clement Mss, Lewis Walpole Library.

p.302 'happy event', and following] Duchess of Gloucester to Jane Clement, 19 November 1772, Clement Mss, Lewis Walpole Library.

p.303 'Our cards will sometime or other'] Duchess of Gloucester to Jane Clement, 20 December 1772, Clement Mss, Lewis Walpole Library.

'In this country nobody escapes'] Horace Walpole to the Duchess of Gloucester, 15 November 1772, in *Horace Walpole's Correspondence*, vol. 36, p. 86.

p.303 'at a proper time'] Horace Walpole, *Last Journals*, quoted in *Horace Walpole's Correspondence*, vol. 36, p. 92.

'After this I shall draw a curtain'] Lady Mary Coke, 1 June 1773, in *The Letters and Journals of Lady Mary Coke*, vol. 4, p. 168.

p.304 'a full dressed sack', and following] the Duchess of Northumberland, 26 June 1773, in James Greig (ed.), *The Diaries of a Duchess*, London 1926, p. 204.

p.304 'the Cumberlands are going to Italy'] Duchess of Gloucester to Jane Clement, 15 August 1773, Clement Mss, Lewis Walpole Library.

p.305 'The Duke of Richmond'] Horace Walpole to the Duchess of Gloucester, 27 January 1774, in *Horace Walpole's Correspondence*, vol. 36, pp. 100–2.

p.305 'flattering myself, as I cannot help'] Duke of Gloucester to George III, 27 January 1775, Royal Archive, RA GEO/54345.

'I cannot deny'] George III to Lord North, 16 January 1775, in *The Correspondence of King George III with Lord North from 1768–1783*, (ed.) W. Bodham Donne, 2 vols, 1867, vol. 1, pp. 221–2.

'My abhorrence of Lord North'] Duchess of Gloucester to Jane Clement, 26 May 1776, Clement Mss, Lewis Walpole Library.

p.306 'I'm sure my sister has great obligation to us', and following] Laura Keppel to Jane Clement, 4 March 1774, 19 August 1775, 9 September 1775, 16 September 1775, Clement Mss, Lewis Walpole Library.

p.306 'I can open my heart to you'; 'like the King'] Duchess of Gloucester to Jane Clement, 26 May 1776, 15 August 1773, Clement Mss, Lewis Walpole Library.

p.307 'Every time I look', and following] Duchess of Gloucester to Jane Clement, 26 May 1776, Clement Mss, Lewis Walpole Library.

p.307 'My poor girls'; 'Mrs Keppel has lost'] Duchess of Gloucester to Jane Clement, 20 July 1776, Clement Mss, Lewis Walpole Library.

p.307 'You must know'; 'every lady is too poor'; 'It is not debt'] Duchess of Gloucester to Jane Clement, 26 May, 20 July 1776, Clement Mss, Lewis Walpole Library.

p.308 'Is it fit that the brother'] Sir Edward Walpole to Lord George Germaine, 4 May 1777, Correspondence of Sir Edward Walpole, Lewis Walpole Library.

'You cannot imagine'] Duchess of Gloucester to Jane Clement, 4 April 1777, Clement Mss, Lewis Walpole Library.

p.309 'If you could find by him'] Duke of Gloucester to Sir Edward Walpole, May 1777, Correspondence of Sir Edward Walpole, Lewis Walpole Library.

p.309 'his mind is quite at ease', and following] Duchess of Gloucester to Horace Walpole, 4 September 1777, in *Horace Walpole's Correspondence*, vol. 36, pp. 135–7.

p.310 'I should have thought'] George III to Lord North, 29 November 1777, in Hon. Sir John Fortescue (ed.), *The Correspondence of King George III*, 6 vols, London 1972, vol. 3, pp. 499–500.

p.311 'I wish to be on the best terms'] George III to the Duke of Gloucester, 9 June 1780, Royal Archive, RA GEO/54354.

p.311 'It is not fit'] Horace Walpole, 4 September 1777, in *Horace Walpole's Correspondence*, vol. 36, pp. 135–7.

p.312 'I cannot say'] Duchess of Gloucester to Anne Clement, 1 January 1781, Clement Mss, Lewis Walpole Library.

p.312 'I wish she would make up her mind'] Jane Clement to Anne Clement, 2 September 1788, Clement Mss, Lewis Walpole Library.

'I am indeed severely punished'] Duke of Gloucester to George III, 22 June 1787, Royal Archive, RA GEO/54382–3.

p.313 'A Sketch of their Majesties' domestic life at Kew during the Summer Season'] *Annual Register*, 1775, quoted in Jesse, *Memoirs of the Life and Reign of King George the Third*, vol. 2, p. 34.

p.314 'Caesar had his Brutus'] Patrick Henry quoted in Jesse, *Memoirs of the Life and Reign of King George the Third*, vol. 1, pp. 319–20.

p.314 'Let England but attempt'] Duc de Choiseul, August 1767, quoted in Jesse, *Memoirs of the Life and Reign of King George the Third*, vol. 1, p. 524.

p.314 'No man can gain'] Charles James Fox in Jesse, *Memoirs of the Life and Reign of King George the Third*, vol. 2, p. 42.

'I can give up my crown'] George III, *ibid.*, p. 43.

p.316 'Since you left me'] George III to Lord North, 4 February 1774, in Bonomy Dobrée, *The Letters of King George III*, London 1935, rptd 1968, p. 49.

p.317 'they seem to wish'] George III to Lord North, 11 September 1774, in Dobrée, *Letters of King George III*, p. 105.

p.317 'I have no doubt'] George III to Lord North, 5 July 1777, in *The Correspondence of King George III with Lord North*, p. 253.

p.318 'I know our situation'] George III to John Robinson, 29 August 1778, in Dobrée, *The Letters of King George III*, p. 125.
'the West Indies'] George III to Lord North, 11 June 1779, in Dobrée, *Letters of King George III*, p. 131.
'to throw off his indolence'] George III to Lord Bute, 1 July 1756, in old Sedgwick, *Letters from George III to Lord Bute*, p. 3.

p.319 'from a lethargy'] George III to Lord North, 14 November 1778, in Dobrée, *Letters of King George III*, p. 128.

p.319 'Parliament having to my astonishment'] George III to Thomas Townshend, 19 November 1782, from *The Huntington Library: Treasures from Two Centuries*, San Marino 2004, p. 36.

p.320 'The too great lenity'] George III to Lord North, 31 May 1777, in Dobrée, *Letters of King George III*, p. 117.

p.321 'When first I appeared'] abdication document written by the King, early 1783, in Dobrée, *Letters of King George III*, p. 170.

p.322 'The United States of America have appointed me'] and following in David McCullough, *John Adams*, New York 2001, pp. 355–7.

Conclusion

p.325 'As I supposed'] Duke of Cumberland to George III, 31 January 1781, Royal Archive, RA GEO/54454.

p.327 'I have, Sir'] Duchess of Cumberland to George III, 3 May 1792, Royal Archive, RA GEO/54502. Some sources suggest the Duchess died in Trieste in 1808.

p.327 'keep her clear of the Duchess'] Duke of Gloucester to George III, 22 June 1787, Royal Archive RA GEO/54382–2.

p.328 'His mistress'; 'I once feared'; 'I suppose when people are blessed'] Duchess of Gloucester to Anne Clement, 15 June 1790, March 1793, 4 November 1799, Clement Mss, Lewis Walpole Library.

p.328 'My Sophia and I'; 'My poor dear maid'] Duchess of Gloucester to Anne Clement, November 1794, 30 November 1797, March 1793, 4 November 1799, Clement Mss, Lewis Walpole Library.

p.330 'very deaf'; 'a melancholy specimen'] in Flora Fraser, *The Unruly Queen, the Life of Queen Caroline*, London 1996, pp. 194, 214.

p.331 'I must have a new suit of clothes'] George III quoted in J. Fitzgerald Malloy, *Court Life Below Stairs or London under the Georges 1760–1830*, London 1885, p. 377.

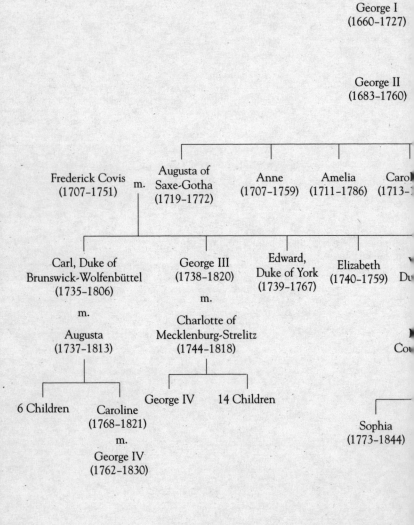

BRITISH ROYAL FAMILY

Dorothea
6–1726)

ne of Ansbach
683–1737)

am, Duke of
mberland
721–1765)

Mary
(1723–1772)

Louisa
(1724–1751)

m.

Frederick V
King of Denmark
(1723–1766)

y,
ster

Henry Frederick,
Duke of Cumberland
(1745–1790)

m.

Louisa Ann
(1749–1768)

Frederick
William
(1750–1765)

Caroline Mathilda,
(1751–1775)

m.

Christian VII,
King of Denmark

e,
rave

Anne Luttrell
(1742–1808)

William
(1776–1834)

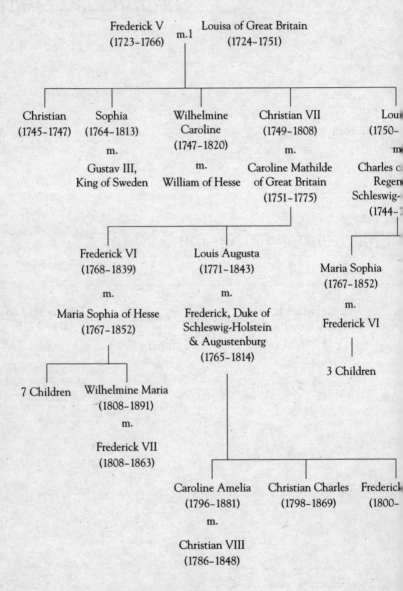

Frederick V
(1723–1766)   m.1   Louisa of Great Britain
(1724–1751)

Christian
(1745–1747)

Sophia
(1764–1813)
m.
Gustav III,
King of Sweden

Wilhelmine
Caroline
(1747–1820)
m.
William of Hesse

Christian VII
(1749–1808)
m.
Caroline Mathilde
of Great Britain
(1751–1775)

Lou
(1750–
m
Charles
Rege
Schleswig-
(1744–

Frederick VI
(1768–1839)
m.
Maria Sophia of Hesse
(1767–1852)

Louis Augusta
(1771–1843)
m.
Frederick, Duke of
Schleswig-Holstein
& Augustenburg
(1765–1814)

Maria Sophia
(1767–1852)
m.
Frederick VI

3 Children

7 Children   Wilhelmine Maria
(1808–1891)
m.
Frederick VII
(1808–1863)

Caroline Amelia
(1796–1881)
m.
Christian VIII
(1786–1848)

Christian Charles
(1798–1869)

Frederick
(1800–

DANISH ROYAL FAMILY

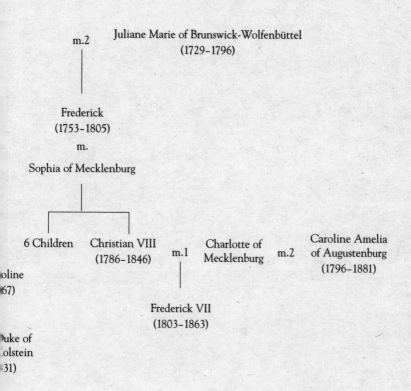

m.2   Juliane Marie of Brunswick-Wolfenbüttel
(1729–1796)

Frederick
(1753–1805)
m.
Sophia of Mecklenburg

6 Children   Christian VIII
(1786–1846)   m.1   Charlotte of
Mecklenburg   m.2   Caroline Amelia
of Augustenburg
(1796–1881)

oline
67)

Frederick VII
(1803–1863)

Duke of
olstein
31)

IX
06)

Index

Index

Index